Advances in Cosmetology

Beauty Therapy Technology, Treatments, Sustainability, and Holistic Wellness

Richard Skiba

AFTER MIDNIGHT
PUBLISHING

Skiba, Richard (author)

Advances in Cosmetology: Beauty Therapy Technology, Treatments, Sustainability, and Holistic Wellness

ISBN 978-1-7638440-9-4 (Paperback) 978-1-7638811-0-5 (eBook) 978-1-7638811-1-2 (Hardcover)

Non-fiction

Contents

Chapter 1

Introduction to Beauty and Cosmetology

The Evolution of Beauty Therapy

Cosmetology encompasses a wide range of practices designed to enhance physical appearance, including skincare, haircare, nail treatments, and makeup application. Within this broad field, there are specialized areas that focus on specific aspects of beauty care. Aesthetics, for example, centres on skincare treatments such as facials, waxing, and other non-invasive therapies aimed at improving skin health and appearance. Trichology involves the study and treatment of hair and scalp conditions, addressing issues like hair loss and scalp disorders. Nail technology focuses on nail care, offering services such as manicures, pedicures, and artificial nail enhancements. Makeup artistry emphasizes the application of cosmetics to enhance and highlight facial features.

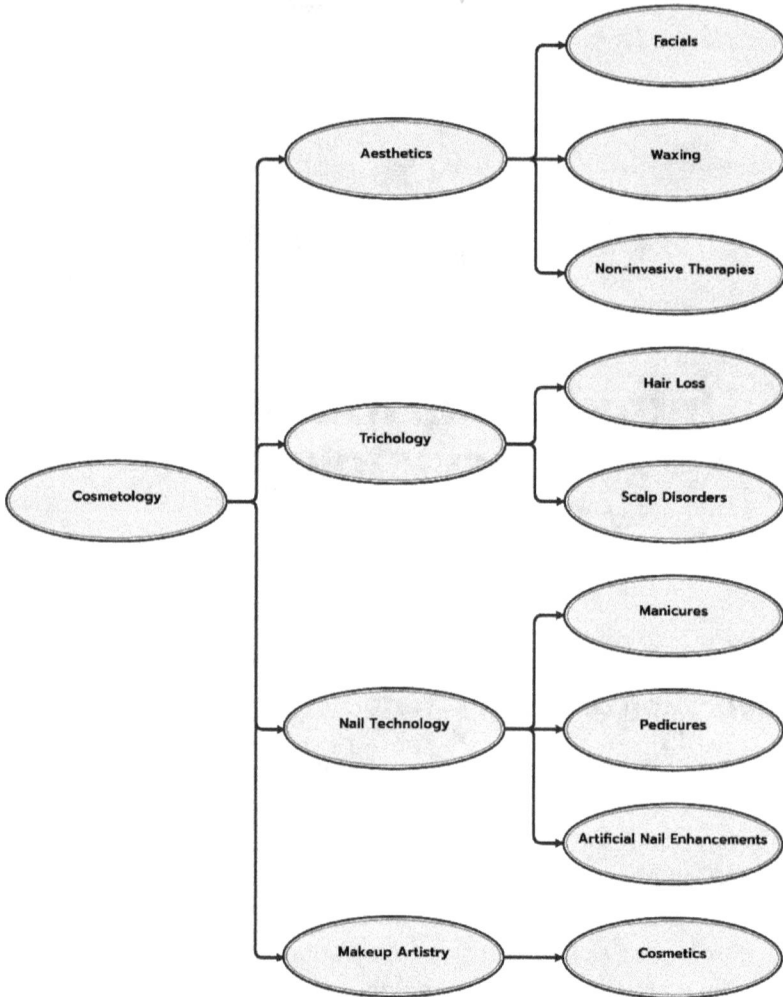

Figure 1: Example of practices within Cosmetology.

Beauty therapy often aligns closely with aesthetic practices, particularly when it comes to skincare and spa treatments. In professional and academic settings, practitioners specializing in these areas are commonly referred to as aestheticians or skincare specialists. These professionals are trained to provide personalized treatments and services that cater to individual beauty and wellness needs, reflecting the technical and diverse nature of cosmetology.

Concept of Physical Beauty

Human physical beauty is a concept that encompasses various attributes perceived as attractive or aesthetically pleasing. This perception is influenced by a combination of biological, cultural, and personal factors.

Symmetry plays a crucial role in the perception of beauty, as it is often associated with health and genetic fitness. Research indicates that symmetrical faces are generally perceived as more attractive, suggesting an evolutionary basis for this preference [1]. The "Golden Ratio," a mathematical proportion, has also been linked to perceptions of beauty, particularly in facial features. Studies have shown that faces aligning with this ratio are often rated as more attractive, reinforcing the idea that certain proportions are universally appealing [2].

Clear and healthy skin is frequently associated with youth and vitality, which are key indicators of physical beauty. Smooth, glowing skin is often perceived as a sign of good health, and individuals with such skin are typically viewed as more attractive [3]. Furthermore, a healthy body, characterized by balanced weight and toned muscles, is generally seen as attractive, as it suggests an active lifestyle and overall well-being [2]. This connection between physical appearance and health is well-documented, emphasizing the importance of skin quality in beauty standards.

Cultural norms significantly shape perceptions of beauty, with different societies emphasizing various traits such as body shape, height, and specific facial features. For instance, beauty standards can vary widely across cultures, influenced by historical, social, and media representations [4]. Trends in beauty, such as preferences for tanned skin or specific hairstyles, are often propagated by the fashion and entertainment industries, further illustrating the dynamic nature of beauty standards [5].

Specific facial features contribute significantly to perceptions of beauty. For example, large, bright eyes are often considered attractive, as are full, symmetrical lips and a straight, white smile [1]. The shape and symmetry of the nose and jawline also play important roles in beauty assessments. Research indicates that these features are consistently admired across various cultures, highlighting their universal appeal [2].

Youthful traits, such as smooth skin and bright eyes, are universally linked to beauty, as they are often associated with fertility and vitality from an evolutionary perspective [3]. The preference for youthful appearances is evident in societal standards, where aging is frequently viewed negatively in terms of beauty [4]. This emphasis on youthfulness underscores the biological underpinnings of beauty perceptions.

Healthy hair is another significant aspect of physical beauty, with shiny and well-maintained hair often symbolizing vitality and health [5]. Personal grooming practices, including nail care and overall hygiene, also contribute to perceptions of attractiveness. Well-groomed individuals are often viewed more favourably, as grooming is associated with effort and self-care, which can enhance one's attractiveness [3].

Confidence significantly influences perceptions of beauty. How individuals carry themselves—through posture and body language—can enhance their attractiveness, often independent of their physical traits [4]. Graceful movement and deliberate gestures can further contribute to the perception of beauty, suggesting that confidence is a key intangible quality that enhances physical attractiveness [5].

Distinctive features, such as freckles or dimples, can enhance beauty by adding character and individuality to a person's appearance [4]. Embracing one's natural features and reflecting authenticity can also enhance perceptions of beauty, as self-acceptance is often viewed positively in social contexts [5]. This appreciation for uniqueness underscores the subjective nature of beauty, where personal perceptions play a critical role.

The desire to look beautiful and the importance placed on beauty are deeply rooted in psychological, social, cultural, and evolutionary contexts. Psychologically, beauty significantly impacts self-confidence and self-esteem, contributing to a more positive self-image. Research indicates that individuals who perceive themselves as beautiful often experience enhanced self-worth and emotional well-being, as beauty can serve as a form of self-expression reflecting one's personality and creativity [6, 7]. Moreover, engaging in grooming and beauty practices is frequently associated with self-care, which is linked to improved mental health outcomes [8].

Socially, beauty plays a pivotal role in shaping interpersonal interactions and societal acceptance. Attractive individuals are often perceived as more likable and successful, which can lead to more favourable social experiences [9]. The media exacerbates these dynamics by promoting specific beauty standards that individuals feel pressured to meet, thereby influencing their self-perception and social interactions [9, 10]. The phenomenon known as the "halo effect" further illustrates how beauty can skew perceptions of competence and intelligence, impacting first impressions and long-term relationships.

Culturally, beauty standards vary significantly across different societies, often reflecting specific ideals that individuals are encouraged to conform to. In many cultures, beauty is intertwined with notions of status and morality, making it a critical factor in social judgment [10]. For instance, in some societies, adhering to particular beauty norms can signify alignment with cultural values and traditions, reinforcing the importance of beauty in social contexts [11].

From an evolutionary perspective, physical beauty is often associated with reproductive fitness. Traits such as clear skin, symmetrical features, and overall health are perceived as indicators of genetic quality, which can subconsciously attract potential mates [12]. Historically, physical attractiveness has been linked to survival traits, suggesting that the preference for beauty may have evolutionary advantages [13].

Professionally, the impact of beauty extends into economic opportunities. In fields that require public interaction, such as media and sales, physical attractiveness can enhance career prospects and networking opportunities [9]. Attractive individuals are often perceived as more persuasive and charismatic, which can facilitate professional success [8].

On a personal level, beauty allows for creative expression through various means such as fashion, makeup, and body art. The pursuit of beauty can provide individuals with a sense of fulfillment and achievement, as they navigate their personal standards of beauty [6]. Ultimately, the desire to look beautiful is multifaceted, influencing social interactions, personal identity, and cultural perceptions, while also playing a significant role in individual psychological well-being.

Beauty Therapy

Beauty rituals throughout history have been deeply intertwined with cultural, spiritual, and societal norms, reflecting the values and beliefs of their respective eras. Ancient civilizations, particularly those in Egypt, India, China, and Greece, have laid the groundwork for modern beauty practices through their unique approaches to aesthetics, health, and spirituality.

In ancient Egypt, beauty was perceived as a divine expression, intimately connected to the spiritual realm. Egyptians utilized kohl, a lead-based mineral, to enhance their eyes, believing it not only served an aesthetic purpose but also protected against eye diseases [14]. The use of vibrant pigments derived from natural minerals like ochre and malachite was prevalent, symbolizing vitality and a reverence for nature [14]. Additionally, scented oils extracted from flowers and herbs were integral to skincare and perfumery, showcasing a holistic approach to beauty that combined art and science [15]. This connection between beauty and spirituality is further evidenced by the elaborate burial rituals that emphasized the importance of beauty in the afterlife, as seen in the mummification practices that often included the application of cosmetics to the deceased [16].

The ancient Ayurvedic traditions of India revolutionized beauty by integrating it with health and wellness. Ayurvedic beauty therapies emphasized the balance of body, mind, and spirit, with herbal concoctions made from turmeric, sandalwood, and neem being used to address various skin conditions while nourishing the skin. Therapeutic oils, such as sesame and coconut, were employed in massages to promote circulation and detoxification, reflecting the belief that true beauty emanates from inner harmony. This holistic perspective on beauty aligns with the Ayurvedic principle that physical appearance is a manifestation of one's overall health and well-being.

In ancient China, the concept of beauty was deeply intertwined with the principles of Traditional Chinese Medicine (TCM), where harmony was

6

paramount. The holistic approach to beauty emphasized the balance of Qi, or vital energy, which was believed to be essential for achieving glowing skin and overall well-being. This perspective aligns with contemporary understandings of wellness that integrate physical, mental, and spiritual dimensions, as highlighted in various studies on holistic health practices [17, 18].

Skincare rituals in ancient China often included the use of natural ingredients revered for their rejuvenating properties. For instance, pearl powder and ginseng were commonly incorporated into masks and creams, reflecting a belief in their ability to enhance skin vitality and health. These ingredients are valued not only for their aesthetic benefits but also for their roles in promoting overall health, which resonates with holistic health models that emphasize the interconnection of physical and spiritual well-being [19, 20]. The use of such ingredients demonstrates a historical understanding of the relationship between beauty and health, where external appearances were seen as a reflection of internal balance.

Moreover, techniques such as jade rolling and gua sha were practiced to stimulate blood flow and lymphatic drainage, further emphasizing the connection between beauty and health. These practices, which have gained popularity in modern beauty routines, originated from ancient Chinese traditions that recognized the importance of physical manipulation in promoting skin health and vitality [19]. The effectiveness of these techniques in enhancing skin appearance is supported by contemporary research, which suggests that they can improve circulation and contribute to a more radiant complexion [19]. This historical context underscores the holistic approach to beauty, where physical treatments are viewed as integral to achieving a harmonious state of being.

The holistic approach to beauty in ancient China reflects a broader understanding of wellness that integrates various aspects of life. This perspective is echoed in modern holistic health frameworks, which advocate for a balance among physical, mental, emotional, and spiritual health [18]. The ancient Chinese view of beauty as a manifestation of inner harmony aligns with contemporary practices that seek to foster overall well-being through a comprehensive understanding of health, emphasizing that true beauty is not merely skin deep but is rooted in a balanced and healthy lifestyle [17, 20].

The Greeks and Romans held a profound belief that beauty was intrinsically linked to moral virtue and intellectual harmony. This perspective is rooted in the philosophical traditions of ancient Greece, where the concept of the "Golden Ratio" emerged as a standard for beauty, emphasizing symmetry and proportion as reflections of moral and aesthetic ideals [21].

The Golden Ratio, often denoted by the Greek letter Phi (φ), is a mathematical concept approximately equal to 1.618, which has been historically associated with aesthetics and beauty across various domains, including nature, art, architecture, and human proportions. This ratio is defined mathematically as the relationship between two quantities where the ratio of the larger quantity to the smaller one is the same as the ratio of their sum to the larger quantity. This unique property has intrigued mathematicians and artists alike, as it provides a framework for understanding balance and harmony in design and aesthetics [22-24].

In the context of beauty, the Golden Ratio is frequently applied to analyse the proportions of the human face. Research indicates that facial features aligning closely with the Golden Ratio are often perceived as more harmonious and aesthetically pleasing. For instance, the ideal length of a face, measured from the hairline to the chin, divided by its width across the cheekbones, approximates 1.618. Additionally, the distances between key facial features—such as the eyes, eyebrows, lips, and chin—often reflect this ratio, contributing to a visually harmonious balance [25, 26]. The Phi mask, developed by Dr. Stephen Marquardt, serves as a geometric overlay to illustrate how closely a face conforms to the Golden Ratio, and it is utilized in cosmetic enhancements and reconstructive surgeries [27, 28].

The application of the Golden Ratio extends into various beauty-related fields, particularly in cosmetic surgery, where it guides procedures such as rhinoplasty, facelifts, and jawline contouring to achieve balanced results. Makeup artists also incorporate its principles to shape eyebrows and contour facial features, enhancing symmetry in their designs [29]. Furthermore, hairstyling and fashion often draw on the Golden Ratio to balance proportions and complement individual features. Photographers and artists utilize this ratio to create visually appealing compositions that highlight natural beauty, demonstrating its pervasive influence across creative disciplines [30, 31].

Advances in Cosmetology

Despite its widespread application, the Golden Ratio has faced criticism. Beauty is inherently subjective and influenced by cultural, personal, and societal factors. While the Golden Ratio provides a fascinating mathematical framework, it cannot fully encapsulate the diversity of beauty standards or the uniqueness of individual features. Modern aesthetics increasingly celebrate diversity and individuality, challenging the notion that a single ratio can define beauty [25, 26, 32]. Thus, while the Golden Ratio offers valuable insights into human perceptions of symmetry and proportion, true beauty transcends mathematical precision, encompassing individuality, personality, and cultural diversity [33, 34].

The Greeks believed that physical beauty was a manifestation of inner goodness, a notion that was later echoed in Roman culture, which adopted and adapted many Greek ideals [35]. The interplay between aesthetics and ethics is evident in the works of philosophers like Plato, who posited that beauty in the physical realm was a reflection of a higher, moral beauty [21].

In terms of skincare practices, ancient Greeks utilized natural ingredients such as honey and olive oil, which were celebrated for their hydrating and nourishing properties. Honey, known for its moisturizing qualities, and olive oil, rich in antioxidants, were staples in Greek beauty rituals [36]. These natural products were not only valued for their physical benefits but also symbolized a connection to the earth and a holistic approach to beauty that encompassed both body and spirit [37]. The Greeks believed that caring for one's appearance was a reflection of one's character and virtue, reinforcing the idea that beauty was not merely superficial but deeply intertwined with ethical living [21].

Roman beauty rituals further evolved from these Greek traditions, incorporating elaborate bathing practices influenced by both Greek and Egyptian customs. The Romans established thermal baths as social and cultural hubs where individuals engaged in extensive skincare routines involving oils and perfumed balms, transforming skincare into a sensory experience [36]. This practice highlighted the Romans' appreciation for luxury and the sensory pleasures associated with beauty, which were integral to their social interactions and cultural identity [38]. The emphasis on beauty in Roman society was not just about aesthetics; it was a reflection of one's status and moral standing within the community [35].

The lasting impact of Greek and Roman ideals of beauty can be seen in contemporary aesthetics, where the principles of symmetry and proportion continue to influence modern perceptions of beauty. The classical ideals established by these ancient cultures have shaped cultural values and standards of beauty throughout history, reinforcing the notion that beauty is a reflection of deeper moral and intellectual virtues [21, 35]. This enduring legacy underscores the belief that beauty transcends mere appearance, serving as a cultural marker that reflects societal values and ideals.

The beauty rituals of ancient civilizations reveal a profound human inclination to enhance and nurture beauty while fostering a connection to nature and culture. This desire is evident in the practices of ancient Egyptians, who utilized cosmetics not only for aesthetic purposes but also for spiritual and ritualistic significance. Egyptian cosmetics, often made from natural minerals and plant extracts, were believed to possess protective qualities, reflecting a deep intertwining of beauty with spirituality and health [39]. The use of kohl, for example, was not merely for eye decoration but was also thought to ward off evil spirits and protect the eyes from the harsh sun [39].

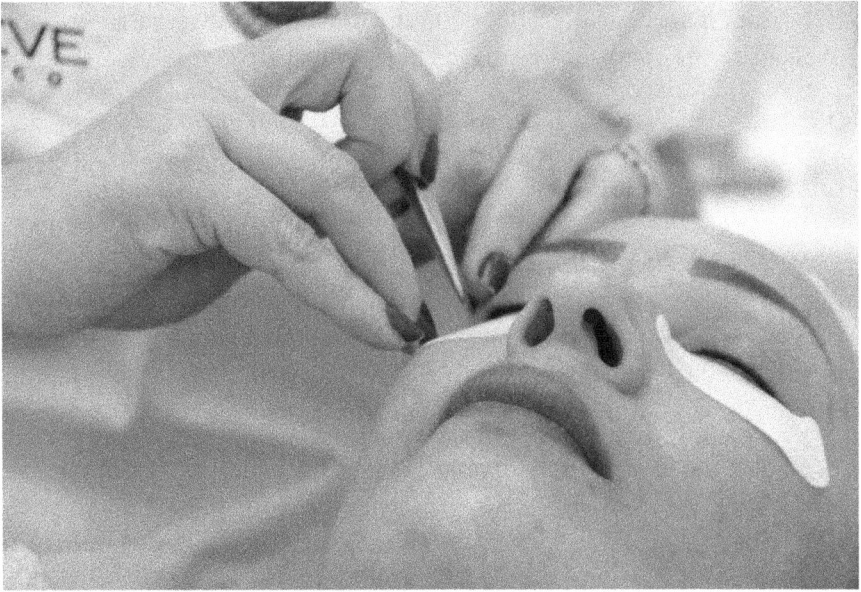

Figure 2: Beauty treatment, a modern day ritual. CC0, via Pixahive.

Similarly, the ancient practices of Ayurveda and Traditional Chinese Medicine (TCM) laid the groundwork for modern beauty therapies by emphasizing holistic approaches to skincare. Ayurveda, with its focus on natural and organic ingredients, promotes the idea that beauty is a reflection of overall health and balance within the body [39, 40]. The Ayurvedic philosophy underscores the importance of nurturing the skin with pure herbal remedies, aligning with contemporary trends that favour natural ingredients over synthetic ones [39, 40]. TCM also shares this holistic view, utilizing herbal formulations and dietary practices to enhance skin health and beauty, which resonates with current preferences for integrative and natural skincare solutions [40].

The echoes of these ancient traditions are increasingly evident in contemporary beauty practices, where there is a marked resurgence in the use of natural ingredients and holistic approaches to skincare. The modern cosmetic industry has seen a significant shift towards formulations that incorporate botanical extracts, clays, and other natural components, reflecting a growing consumer awareness of the benefits of such ingredients [41, 42]. This trend is not merely a passing fad; it signifies a broader cultural movement towards sustainability and wellness, where the lessons of the past inform present-day practices [41, 43].

Understanding the historical context of these beauty rituals provides valuable insights into their cultural significance and enduring influence on modern aesthetics and wellness. The integration of ancient wisdom into contemporary skincare regimens highlights a timeless desire to connect with nature while addressing the complexities of skin health. As modern consumers increasingly seek products that align with their values of sustainability and holistic well-being, the foundational principles established by ancient civilizations continue to resonate [43, 44].

The evolution of beauty treatments has taken a significant leap with the rise of advanced skincare, marking a scientific revolution in the pursuit of radiant and healthy skin. What once consisted of simple cleansers and moisturizers has evolved into an intricate, multi-step routine informed by scientific research and technological advancements. Dermatology, cosmetology, and cutting-edge technology have collectively contributed to the creation of a diverse range of products and treatments targeting specific skin concerns. This progression reflects a growing awareness of the skin's dynamic nature as an organ that requires specialized care. Modern skincare emphasizes prevention, aiming to maintain the skin's health over time, showcasing a holistic approach to beauty that values long-term well-being alongside aesthetic results.

The integration of technology into beauty has redefined the industry, creating a synergy between science and self-care. This intersection has not only elevated the effectiveness of beauty treatments but also transformed how individuals perceive and engage with personal care routines. Technological innovations have introduced a level of precision, efficiency, and personalization that was unimaginable a few decades ago, catering to a broad spectrum of beauty enthusiasts.

One of the most significant advancements is the development of smart skincare devices. These tools, such as facial cleansing brushes and massagers, bring the sophistication of professional skincare into the home. Equipped with advanced sensors, many devices analyse skin conditions in real time and offer tailored advice, ensuring users apply the right techniques and products for their unique needs. This customization empowers individuals to take control of their skincare routines with the guidance of scientific insights.

Laser and light therapies represent another cornerstone of technological advancement in beauty. These non-invasive techniques have become staples in dermatological and cosmetic practices, addressing a range of skin issues such as acne, pigmentation, and signs of aging. By using targeted light waves, these treatments deliver impressive results with minimal downtime, making them accessible and appealing to a wider audience. The precision and efficacy of these therapies have set new standards in beauty treatments, bridging the gap between medical-grade solutions and everyday skincare.

The integration of 3D printing in cosmetics showcases how technology is reshaping the industry's future. This innovation allows for the creation of highly customized makeup and skincare products, tailored to an individual's facial features, preferences, and skin conditions. Consumers can now access formulations designed specifically for them, reflecting a shift towards personalization that has become a hallmark of modern beauty.

Looking to the future, the fusion of artificial intelligence (AI), augmented reality (AR), and biometric skincare analysis promises even greater transformations. AI-driven applications analyse vast amounts of skin data to recommend products and routines with unparalleled accuracy, while AR tools offer virtual makeup try-ons, enhancing the shopping experience by allowing users to visualize results before committing to products. Biometric technologies take personalization to the next level by providing real-time feedback on skin health and recommending immediate adjustments to skincare routines.

The technological advancements in beauty underscore the industry's commitment to innovation, creating opportunities for individuals to embrace more informed and personalized approaches to self-care. This era of beauty tech empowers consumers with knowledge and tools that were once exclusive to professionals, making high-quality beauty solutions accessible to all. As we navigate this evolving landscape, the possibilities for enhancing and redefining our beauty rituals are limitless, paving the way for a future where science and aesthetics coexist harmoniously to meet the needs of every beauty enthusiast.

Psychology of Beauty

Beauty is not merely a superficial trait but a deeply embedded aspect of human cognition and emotion. Our perceptions of beauty are shaped by a complex blend of internal beliefs and external influences, which significantly affect how we view ourselves and interact with our environment. For instance, the internalization of societal beauty standards can lead to feelings of inadequacy, particularly when individuals compare themselves to idealized images presented in media [45, 46]. This psychological exploration highlights the connections between self-perception and societal constructs, offering insights into how beauty shapes our lives and emotional well-being.

Cultural influences are pivotal in defining beauty standards, which are deeply embedded in individual and collective psyches. Across various cultures, norms and traditions dictate what is considered beautiful, influencing personal preferences and self-perception. For example, in some cultures, beauty is associated with symmetry and youth, while in others, attributes like body size or skin tone carry different symbolic meanings [47, 48]. The evolution of these standards often reflects deeper societal values, as seen in the way beauty ideals shift over time in response to cultural changes [49]. Understanding how cultural norms shape beauty ideals provides a lens to examine the diversity and complexity of beauty in a global context, revealing that beauty is not a monolithic concept but rather a multifaceted one influenced by cultural narratives [50, 51].

Media and advertising play a crucial role in amplifying these cultural ideals, exerting a significant influence on individual psychology. The pervasive narrative of perfection propagated through idealized images in advertising, films, and social media can severely impact self-esteem, especially when individuals engage in social comparison [46, 52]. Research indicates that exposure to such idealized representations can lead to dissatisfaction with one's appearance, reinforcing feelings of inadequacy and contributing to mental health issues like anxiety and depression [47, 53]. By critically examining the role of media, we can begin to challenge these harmful narratives and promote healthier representations of beauty, fostering a more inclusive understanding of attractiveness that values diversity [54, 55].

Advances in Cosmetology

From an evolutionary perspective, certain beauty preferences may be hardwired into the human psyche. Evolutionary theories propose that attributes such as symmetry and clear skin are perceived as attractive because they signal health, fertility, or genetic fitness [56, 57]. These traits, rooted in survival and reproduction, may explain the persistence of certain beauty standards across cultures and time. However, this perspective also underscores the subjective nature of beauty, as these evolutionary preferences interact with societal and cultural factors to create a dynamic and ever-changing concept of attractiveness [58, 59]. This interplay highlights the complexity of beauty standards and their implications for individual self-esteem and societal expectations.

Self-esteem and body image are closely intertwined with societal beauty standards, significantly shaping individuals' emotional and psychological well-being. When individuals measure their worth against these standards, they often experience a direct impact on their confidence and mental health [60, 61]. Positive body image and self-esteem are crucial for emotional well-being, yet the pressure to conform to narrow beauty ideals can lead to feelings of inadequacy and self-doubt [52, 57]. Exploring this relationship emphasizes the need for fostering a culture that values diversity and promotes body positivity, which can mitigate the negative psychological impacts of societal beauty standards [55, 62].

Emotional well-being is profoundly affected by personal feelings of attractiveness or unattractiveness. For many, beauty encompasses not only external appearance but also self-perception. Positive self-perception can enhance emotional resilience and life satisfaction, while negative self-perception can contribute to stress, anxiety, and depression [50, 53]. Addressing these emotional dimensions is essential for understanding the psychological impact of beauty on mental health and promoting healthier self-perceptions [46, 58]. Furthermore, social comparison plays a significant role in shaping self-worth, as individuals often evaluate themselves against societal beauty ideals, leading to a cycle of dissatisfaction and striving for unattainable goals [47, 55]. Recognizing the psychological effects of social comparison is crucial in promoting healthier self-perceptions and mitigating its negative impacts.

Richard Skiba

Importance of Innovation in the Beauty Industry

The beauty industry has always been a hub of creativity and innovation, continuously adapting to meet the changing demands and desires of consumers. From groundbreaking product formulations to transformative technologies, innovation drives the industry forward, reshaping how we perceive and interact with beauty. This constant evolution ensures that beauty brands not only meet consumer expectations but also push the boundaries of what is possible, keeping the industry dynamic and relevant [63].

Innovation serves as the foundation for creativity and transformation in the beauty world. It impacts every aspect of the industry, from product development and packaging to marketing strategies and consumer experiences. By adopting innovative approaches, beauty brands can differentiate themselves in an increasingly competitive market, capturing the attention of consumers and creating memorable impressions. This is particularly crucial in an industry where trends evolve rapidly, and standing out is essential for long-term success [63].

Innovation plays a pivotal role in the beauty industry, primarily because it drives growth, meets evolving consumer demands, and addresses pressing societal and environmental challenges. As consumer preferences shift towards personalization, sustainability, and holistic wellness, innovation enables beauty brands to remain relevant and competitive in a rapidly changing market landscape. The beauty and wellness sectors are experiencing significant growth, reflecting a cultural shift where consumers actively pursue products that enhance their overall well-being [64]. This trend underscores the necessity for brands to innovate continuously to align with consumer expectations and market dynamics.

One of the most significant aspects of innovation in the beauty industry is its impact on product development. Advances in technology, particularly in artificial intelligence (AI), biotechnology, and nanotechnology, have revolutionized how beauty products are formulated and marketed. For instance, personalized skincare solutions and AI-powered diagnostic tools allow brands to offer tailored products that meet individual consumer needs, thereby enhancing the effectiveness of beauty routines. Moreover, innovative delivery systems, such as serums with encapsulated active ingredients, exemplify how technology can create more impactful beauty solutions. This focus on personalization is critical as consumers increasingly seek products that cater specifically to their unique requirements.

A key driver of innovation in the beauty industry is the ever-evolving needs of consumers. Today's beauty enthusiasts seek products that align with their values, offer personalized experiences, and deliver effective results. For instance, the demand for cruelty-free, vegan, and eco-friendly products reflects a shift toward conscious consumerism. Brands that can anticipate these preferences and develop solutions that resonate with their target audience gain a significant competitive edge. By responding to these shifting demands, innovation becomes a powerful tool for building consumer loyalty and trust [63].

Technological advancements have revolutionized the beauty industry, transforming how products are developed, marketed, and consumed. Tools like augmented reality (AR) and virtual try-on technologies enable consumers to experiment with makeup and hairstyles without physically applying them, bridging the gap between the physical and digital worlds. Artificial intelligence (AI)-powered skincare analysis and personalized recommendations enhance consumer engagement by offering tailored solutions that cater to individual needs. These advancements not only improve the customer experience but also help brands build stronger connections with their audiences [63].

Sustainability has emerged as another crucial driver of innovation within the beauty industry. Today's consumers are more environmentally conscious, prioritizing eco-friendly and ethical products. This shift has prompted brands to innovate in areas such as sustainable packaging, biodegradable ingredients, and cruelty-free testing methods. By adopting sustainable practices, brands not only reduce their environmental impact but also foster trust and loyalty among eco-conscious consumers, which is essential for long-term success in the market. The integration of sustainable practices into product development reflects a broader trend where consumers expect brands to take responsibility for their environmental footprint.

Furthermore, innovation significantly enhances customer experience and engagement. The rise of augmented reality (AR) and virtual try-on technologies has transformed how consumers interact with beauty products, particularly in online shopping environments. These technologies enable customers to visualize products, such as makeup or hair colour, before making a purchase, thereby creating a more immersive and convenient shopping experience [65, 66]. The ability to virtually "try on" products not only increases consumer confidence in their purchasing decisions but also enhances overall satisfaction with the shopping experience [67]. This technological integration is crucial for brands aiming to capture the attention of tech-savvy consumers who expect seamless and interactive shopping experiences.

In addition to addressing individual needs, innovation in the beauty industry promotes holistic wellness. Modern consumers increasingly view beauty as encompassing mental, emotional, and physical well-being. This perspective has led to the rise of clean beauty products, which are often infused with adaptogens and designed to support self-care rituals that reduce stress and promote relaxation [68, 69]. The demand for products that align with consumers' broader wellness goals reflects a significant shift in the beauty landscape, where brands must innovate to meet these evolving expectations.

Personalized beauty experiences have become a hallmark of modern innovation in the industry. Advanced technologies and data-driven insights enable brands to create tailored solutions, such as customized skincare regimens and product recommendations. Personalized consultations powered by AI and machine learning provide consumers with products that address their unique needs, fostering a deeper sense of connection and loyalty. This approach ensures that consumers feel valued and understood, strengthening their relationship with the brand [63].

Innovation is essential for brands to differentiate themselves in an increasingly saturated market. With thousands of beauty products available, creating unique offerings through groundbreaking formulas, novel applications, or revolutionary packaging is vital for maintaining a competitive edge. This differentiation is not only about product uniqueness but also about aligning with contemporary values such as inclusivity and diversity. Brands that expand shade ranges and cater to underserved demographics can create a more inclusive beauty landscape, thereby broadening their customer base and enhancing brand loyalty.

Advances in Cosmetology

The rise of direct-to-consumer (D2C) brands is another testament to the power of innovation. By leveraging e-commerce platforms, social media, and influencer marketing, D2C brands have disrupted traditional distribution channels. This model allows brands to connect directly with their customers, receive real-time feedback, and cater to niche markets with agility. The ability to bypass intermediaries enables these brands to innovate quickly, respond to trends, and establish a strong online presence, making them key players in the modern beauty landscape [63].

Collaborations and co-creation have further fuelled innovation in the beauty industry. Partnerships with influencers, celebrities, and other brands allow companies to tap into new audiences, combine expertise, and introduce fresh perspectives. These collaborations generate excitement, spark creativity, and foster a sense of community among consumers. By involving customers in the creation process, brands can develop products that truly resonate with their target markets [63].

Investment in research and development (R&D) is the backbone of innovation in the beauty industry. By exploring new ingredients, conducting clinical studies, and pioneering advanced technologies, companies make significant breakthroughs that elevate the entire industry. R&D efforts lead to the creation of innovative formulations, effective skincare solutions, and cutting-edge beauty tools that transform how consumers experience beauty [63].

In a highly competitive landscape, innovation is a strategic necessity for brands aiming to stay ahead. By continuously pushing boundaries, embracing emerging technologies, and anticipating trends, beauty companies can capture consumer attention and establish themselves as industry leaders. Innovation is not just a tool for survival; it is a pathway to growth, differentiation, and long-term success [63].

As we look to the future, the beauty industry is poised for even greater transformation. With rapid advancements in technology, evolving consumer preferences, and an increasing focus on sustainability, innovation will remain the driving force behind the industry's evolution. By fostering a culture of creativity and adaptability, beauty brands can navigate the ever-changing landscape, inspire new ideas, and deliver exceptional experiences that redefine beauty for generations to come [63].

Cosmetologist Licensing Requirements

Licensing requirements to perform cosmetology vary across countries and regions, depending on local laws and regulations. These licenses ensure that cosmetologists meet professional standards, follow safety and hygiene protocols, and are qualified to perform services such as skincare, haircare, nail treatments, and makeup application. Licensing requirements in various parts of the world are outlined below:

United States: In the United States, cosmetology is regulated at the state level. To perform cosmetology services, individuals typically must complete a state-approved cosmetology program, which includes a set number of training hours in areas like hairstyling, skincare, and nail technology. After completing the program, candidates must pass a licensing exam that usually includes written and practical components [70]. Specific licenses may include:

- **Cosmetologist License**: Covers haircare, skincare, and nail services.

- **Esthetician License**: Focuses on skincare treatments, facials, and waxing.

- **Nail Technician License**: Specializes in nail care and enhancements.

- **Makeup Artist License**: Required in some states for professional makeup application. Renewal of licenses often requires continuing education to stay updated on new techniques and safety standards.

Canada: In Canada, cosmetology is regulated provincially or territorially. Requirements vary, but most provinces require the completion of an accredited cosmetology or esthetics program and passing a licensing exam [71]. For example:

- In Ontario, hairstylists must complete a formal apprenticeship and pass a provincial exam.

- In Alberta, practitioners need a Red Seal Certification for hairstyling.

- Licenses for estheticians and nail technicians vary but generally require training and certification.

Advances in Cosmetology

United Kingdom: In the UK, cosmetology is not universally regulated, but many employers and insurance providers require practitioners to hold certifications from accredited training programs [71]. Specific qualifications include:

- NVQ (National Vocational Qualification) Levels 2 and 3 in Beauty Therapy.

- City & Guilds or VTCT (Vocational Training Charitable Trust) certifications in cosmetology fields. While not legally mandatory, obtaining these qualifications helps ensure professional standards and employability.

Australia: In Australia, cosmetology practitioners typically do not require a license to operate, but formal training and certification are necessary for employment and insurance purposes. Practitioners often complete courses through TAFE (Technical and Further Education) or private training providers in fields like beauty therapy, makeup artistry, and nail technology. For specialized treatments, such as cosmetic tattooing or laser procedures, additional certifications and registration with local health authorities may be required [71].

European Union: In the European Union, licensing requirements for cosmetologists differ by country. Some countries, such as Germany and France, require practitioners to complete vocational training and obtain certification or licensure. Others, like Italy, may have fewer formal licensing requirements but still expect practitioners to hold qualifications from accredited beauty schools. Regulations are generally stricter for invasive or advanced procedures, such as laser treatments or chemical peels [71].

Asia: In many Asian countries, cosmetology licensing requirements vary widely. In Japan, cosmetologists must obtain a national license by completing a designated course and passing an exam. In South Korea, beauty practitioners are required to complete approved training programs and pass national licensing exams, particularly for skincare and advanced treatments. In countries like India and Thailand, regulations are less formalized, but obtaining certifications from recognized institutions is essential for credibility and professional practice [71].

Middle East: In the Middle East, cosmetology is regulated in varying degrees. In the UAE, beauty professionals must obtain a license from local authorities, such as the Dubai Health Authority (DHA) or Department of Economic Development (DED), depending on the services offered. Similar regulations apply in Saudi Arabia, where certification and adherence to health and safety standards are required [71].

South Africa: In South Africa, cosmetology practitioners typically require formal training from accredited beauty schools. Certification in specific areas such as hairdressing, skincare, or nail technology is essential for employment and insurance. The Services SETA (Sector Education and Training Authority) oversees qualifications and standards for beauty professionals [71].

Globally, there is an increasing focus on formal training, certification, and adherence to health and safety regulations in cosmetology. While some countries have strict licensing requirements, others emphasize certifications from recognized institutions. Advanced procedures like laser treatments, dermaplaning, or chemical peels often require additional certifications and regulatory approval, regardless of the country.

Before practicing cosmetology in any region, it is essential to research local regulations and obtain the necessary qualifications to ensure compliance and professionalism.

Licensing requirements for innovative new technologies in cosmetology also vary widely depending on the country, the type of technology, and its intended application. Advanced technologies such as laser treatments, microneedling, chemical peels, cosmetic tattooing, and AI-powered diagnostic tools often fall under stricter regulatory frameworks than traditional cosmetology practices. These regulations are primarily designed to ensure client safety and maintain professional standards, reflecting the evolving sophistication of the beauty industry.

Laser and IPL (Intense Pulsed Light) treatments, used for hair removal, skin rejuvenation, and pigmentation correction, require practitioners to complete specialized training courses accredited by recognized organizations. In many countries, practitioners also need regulatory certification from health authorities or licensing boards. For example, in the United States, state cosmetology or medical boards often oversee licensing, while in the United Kingdom, local councils regulate laser treatments. Australian states like

Advances in Cosmetology

Queensland and Western Australia even require radiation safety licenses. Proof of specialized training is frequently necessary to obtain liability insurance for these services.

Microneedling and dermaplaning, which involve skin rejuvenation techniques such as collagen stimulation or exfoliation, also demand additional certifications. Practitioners must complete training programs approved by reputable organizations, covering topics like device usage, hygiene protocols, and client safety. Advanced microneedling, which uses needles that penetrate deeper into the skin, is often classified as a medical procedure in some countries and requires supervision by a licensed physician. Device-specific training provided by manufacturers is also mandatory in many cases.

Cosmetic tattooing and microblading, which involve the semi-permanent application of pigments to enhance features like eyebrows or lips, are typically regulated by public health departments. Practitioners must obtain permits or licenses, complete bloodborne pathogen safety training, and adhere to strict infection control protocols. Some regions require registration with local councils or health authorities, as well as periodic facility inspections. Continuing education is often mandated to maintain these licenses and ensure practitioners stay updated on evolving techniques and safety standards.

AI-powered skin diagnostic tools, such as virtual try-on systems or smart mirrors, generally face less stringent licensing requirements than invasive technologies. While no special licenses are typically required for their operation, practitioners must comply with data protection laws like GDPR in the European Union or CCPA in California if these tools collect or store client information. Many manufacturers also require practitioners to undergo specific training to use these tools effectively and ethically.

Advanced chemical peels, which use innovative formulations to treat conditions like hyperpigmentation and fine lines, require certifications in skin science to ensure practitioners understand the chemistry and application of peeling agents. Licensing often depends on the depth of the peel, with superficial peels generally falling under cosmetology licensing, while medium and deep peels are classified as medical procedures and require dermatologist oversight. Strict adherence to hygiene standards is crucial to minimize risks such as burns or infections.

Richard Skiba

Cryotherapy and CoolSculpting, popular for fat-freezing and body contouring, require device training certification, usually provided by the manufacturers. In some regions, these treatments are classified as medical procedures, necessitating supervision by licensed medical professionals. Liability insurance for these technologies often hinges on proof of adequate training.

Plasma and radiofrequency treatments for skin tightening and wrinkle reduction also demand device-specific certification through approved training courses. The scope of practice is regulated based on the intensity of the procedure, with deeper treatments sometimes requiring medical licensure. Practitioners must comply with regional health and safety standards to offer these services.

Innovative hair regrowth and scalp treatments, such as low-level laser therapy (LLLT), are gaining popularity and require practitioners to complete manufacturer-provided training programs. While non-invasive treatments generally fall under standard cosmetology licensing, advanced or invasive procedures involving prescription medications often require collaboration with licensed medical professionals.

Injectable treatments like Botox, dermal fillers, and platelet-rich plasma (PRP) therapies fall outside traditional cosmetology. These procedures are universally classified as medical treatments and can only be performed by licensed healthcare professionals such as doctors, nurses, or dentists. These professionals must complete advanced certification in administering injectables and adhere to strict regulatory approvals and health standards.

Purpose and Scope of the Book

The purpose of this book is to explore the transformative changes within the cosmetology industry, focusing on the innovative technologies, techniques, and philosophies reshaping the field. It seeks to provide readers with a comprehensive understanding of how cosmetology has evolved from its historical roots into a modern, multidisciplinary practice that integrates cutting-edge technology, sustainability, personalization, and holistic wellness. By addressing both the opportunities and challenges within this dynamic industry, the book aims to educate beauty professionals, enthusiasts, and innovators about the latest trends and developments, equipping them with the knowledge to thrive in this rapidly evolving sector.

The scope of this book encompasses a broad range of topics that define the current and future landscape of cosmetology. Beginning with an introduction to the historical evolution of beauty practices and the importance of innovation, the book delves into emerging technologies, such as AI-driven skin analysis, virtual reality consultations, and diagnostic tools. It highlights revolutionary treatments, including non-invasive procedures, regenerative therapies, and advancements in nanotechnology.

Sustainability is a key theme, with chapters dedicated to the rise of clean beauty, biodegradable formulations, and green salon practices. The book also emphasizes personalization through customized beauty products, DIY innovations, and hybrid approaches that combine wellness with therapy. Holistic beauty practices, such as aromatherapy, acupuncture, and mindfulness, are explored alongside discussions on stress management and its impact on skin health.

Additionally, the book investigates the digital transformation of the beauty industry, examining the role of tech startups, social media influencers, and e-commerce in shaping modern beauty trends. Training and skill development are addressed to prepare future beauty professionals for technological integration and continuous learning. Ethical challenges, such as AI implications, marketing transparency, and cultural inclusivity, are critically analysed to encourage responsible innovation.

Concluding with a vision for the future, the book inspires readers to embrace innovation, sustainability, and ethical practices while reimagining beauty therapy as a blend of science, art, and holistic care. By covering these diverse topics, the book provides a valuable resource for understanding the multifaceted nature of modern beauty therapy and its potential to redefine personal care and wellness.

Chapter 2

Emerging Technologies in Beauty Therapy

AI and Machine Learning in Skin Analysis

The integration of Artificial Intelligence (AI) and Machine Learning (ML) in skin analysis has fundamentally transformed consumer interactions with beauty products and skincare routines. These technologies provide personalized, efficient, and highly accurate solutions tailored to individual skin needs, thus reshaping the beauty and dermatology industries. AI, characterized by its ability to simulate human intelligence, and ML, which involves algorithms that learn from data, are pivotal in processing vast datasets to identify patterns and make predictions relevant to skincare [72].

One of the most significant applications of AI in skin analysis is the development of smart diagnostic tools. These tools utilize high-resolution images captured via cameras or smartphones to analyse various skin features, including texture, pore size, hydration levels, pigmentation, redness, and signs of aging. By leveraging computer vision and image recognition, AI algorithms can detect subtle skin changes that may not be visible to the naked eye, such as early signs of aging or UV damage [72, 73]. This capability enables proactive skincare solutions, allowing consumers to address potential issues before they escalate.

Machine Learning enhances the accuracy and adaptability of these diagnostic tools. By accessing extensive datasets, ML algorithms continuously refine their ability to recognize diverse skin types, tones, and concerns. This learning process is crucial for providing inclusive recommendations that cater to the unique characteristics of different skin profiles, which is particularly important in the beauty industry where diversity is paramount [72, 73]. Moreover, AI-powered platforms analyse individual skin data alongside factors such as age, lifestyle, and environmental influences to suggest personalized skincare products and routines, thereby enhancing consumer trust and satisfaction [73].

Predictive modelling is another critical application of AI in skin analysis. By examining historical data, AI can forecast future skin conditions and recommend preventive measures. For instance, it can predict potential dryness or acne outbreaks based on current skin hydration levels and lifestyle habits, empowering users to take pre-emptive actions [72, 73]. Furthermore, AI tools are revolutionizing the consumer shopping experience by acting as virtual skincare advisors. These advisors analyse uploaded selfies or responses to questionnaires to recommend products tailored to individual skin types and concerns, effectively bridging the gap between online shopping and personalized in-store consultations [72, 73].

In professional dermatology, AI and ML enhance clinical decision-making by allowing dermatologists to analyse patient skin conditions, track treatment progress, and compare results over time. This not only improves diagnostic accuracy but also facilitates more informed consultations and prioritization of treatments [72, 73]. Additionally, skincare brands leverage insights from aggregated skin data to inform product development, ensuring that new formulations meet evolving consumer needs [72].

Despite the advancements brought about by AI and ML in skin analysis, challenges remain. The effectiveness of AI-based skin analysis heavily relies on the quality and diversity of training data. It is essential to ensure that datasets encompass a wide range of skin tones, conditions, and age groups to avoid bias and inaccuracies [72, 74]. Privacy and data security also pose significant

27

concerns, as these tools often collect sensitive personal information from users.

Examples of AI and Machine Learning in Skin Analysis

AI-powered skin diagnostic tools have emerged as innovative solutions in dermatology, leveraging advanced algorithms and image analysis to enhance the accuracy and efficiency of skin condition assessments. One notable example is Neutrogena's SkinID, which utilizes AI to evaluate skin conditions through smartphone camera images. This tool identifies various skin issues, including dryness, uneven tone, and acne, by analysing high-resolution images, demonstrating the potential of mobile technology in dermatological diagnostics [75].

Another significant player in this domain is L'Oreal's Skin Genius platform, which offers a comprehensive analysis of skin texture, tone, and elasticity. This platform not only assesses skin conditions but also recommends personalized skincare routines based on the analysis, highlighting the integration of AI in creating tailored skincare solutions [75, 76]. Similarly, the HiMirror smart mirror employs computer vision technology to evaluate fine lines, dark spots, and pore size, providing users with daily insights into their skin's progress. This continuous monitoring capability exemplifies how AI can facilitate ongoing skin health management [76, 77].

Research indicates that AI tools can significantly improve diagnostic accuracy in dermatology. Studies have shown that AI-assisted evaluations can enhance the diagnostic performance of dermatologists and primary care physicians, particularly in teledermatology settings [75, 78, 79]. A systematic review highlighted that AI tools consistently outperform traditional diagnostic methods, leading to faster and more accurate diagnoses [80, 81]. Furthermore, patient perspectives on AI in skin diagnostics are generally positive, with many expressing enthusiasm for the technology's potential to enhance diagnostic speed and accessibility, although concerns about the loss of human interaction remain [76, 82, 83].

The implementation of AI in dermatology is not without challenges. Issues such as algorithm bias, particularly regarding skin tone and demographic diversity, have been raised, emphasizing the need for comprehensive training datasets to ensure equitable performance across different populations [84, 85]. Additionally, the integration of AI tools into clinical practice necessitates careful consideration of ethical implications, including patient consent and the transparency of AI decision-making processes [86, 87].

The integration of augmented reality (AR) in the beauty industry, particularly by brands like Sephora and MAC Cosmetics, has significantly transformed the consumer shopping experience. These companies have adopted AI-powered AR tools that allow customers to virtually "try on" skincare products and makeup, enhancing interactivity and personalization in the shopping process. For instance, Sephora's Virtual Artist utilizes facial scanning technology to assess skin tone and condition, providing tailored product recommendations that cater to individual needs [88, 89]. This personalized approach not only enriches the shopping experience but also fosters a deeper connection between consumers and brands.

The effectiveness of AR in retail is supported by various studies that highlight its impact on customer satisfaction and purchasing behaviour. Research indicates that AR applications in the beauty sector, such as virtual makeup trials, significantly enhance customer engagement and satisfaction [88, 90]. By allowing consumers to visualize how products will look on them in real-time, AR reduces the uncertainty often associated with online shopping, leading to increased confidence in purchasing decisions [91, 92]. Furthermore, the immersive nature of AR experiences has been shown to positively influence brand perception and consumer loyalty, as customers feel more involved and invested in their shopping journey [93, 94].

The technological advancements in AR have made it increasingly accessible and user-friendly, particularly through mobile applications. The widespread adoption of smartphones has facilitated the integration of AR into everyday shopping experiences, making it easier for consumers to access these innovative tools [95]. As a result, brands that leverage AR technology not only enhance their product offerings but also align themselves with contemporary consumer expectations for interactive and engaging shopping experiences [96, 97]. This trend is further evidenced by the growing number of beauty brands implementing AR solutions, which underscores the technology's potential to reshape the retail landscape [88, 90].

Personalized skincare platforms such as Curology and Proven Skincare leverage artificial intelligence (AI) to deliver tailored skincare solutions. Curology's approach involves users uploading selfies and filling out a comprehensive skin history form, which allows its AI algorithm, in conjunction with dermatologist expertise, to create custom formulations that address individual skin types and concerns. This method exemplifies the growing trend of utilizing AI in dermatology to enhance personalized treatment options and improve patient outcomes [98, 99].

Proven Skincare enhances this model by analysing extensive data, including over 20,000 skincare ingredients and 100,000 consumer reviews, to formulate products that meet specific user needs. This data-driven approach not only personalizes skincare but also aligns with the increasing consumer demand for customized solutions in the beauty industry. The integration of AI technologies in skincare allows for a more nuanced understanding of individual skin characteristics and preferences, which is crucial for effective product recommendations [98, 100].

The effectiveness of these platforms is further supported by advancements in AI that facilitate non-invasive skin assessments, enabling more accurate and personalized cosmetic treatments. These technologies not only improve customer satisfaction but also empower users by providing them with tailored skincare regimens based on their unique skin profiles [98, 101]. Moreover, the ability to analyse vast amounts of data allows these platforms to stay ahead of market trends and consumer preferences, which is vital in the rapidly evolving skincare market [102].

Predictive skin analysis and recommendations are becoming increasingly important in dermatology and skincare, particularly with the advent of AI-driven applications like Troveskin and Skintelli. These applications utilize advanced algorithms to monitor skin conditions and provide personalized recommendations based on various factors, including hydration levels, UV exposure, and sleep patterns.

Advances in Cosmetology

Troveskin's predictive analysis is grounded in the understanding that skin hydration is a critical factor influencing skin health. Research indicates that adequate skin hydration not only enhances the skin's appearance but also serves as a protective barrier against various skin conditions [103, 104]. For instance, studies have shown that lower levels of skin hydration correlate with increased severity of acne vulgaris, highlighting the importance of maintaining optimal hydration levels for skin health [105]. Moreover, hydration plays a pivotal role in the skin's recovery from environmental stressors, such as UV exposure, which can lead to skin damage and accelerate aging [106].

Similarly, Skintelli employs machine learning to analyse how environmental factors, such as pollution and humidity, impact skin health. The relationship between environmental conditions and skin hydration is well-documented. For example, exposure to pollutants can exacerbate skin dehydration and lead to inflammatory responses [107]. Additionally, humidity levels significantly influence skin hydration dynamics, with higher humidity generally promoting better hydration and lower levels contributing to dryness and associated skin issues [108]. This understanding allows Skintelli to provide actionable recommendations tailored to the user's environmental context, thereby enhancing their skincare routine.

Furthermore, both applications consider lifestyle factors, including sleep patterns, which have been shown to affect skin health. Poor sleep quality can lead to reduced skin moisture and compromised barrier function, contributing to accelerated aging and increased susceptibility to skin conditions [109]. By integrating these multifaceted data points, Troveskin and Skintelli can offer comprehensive skincare recommendations that address both preventive measures and treatment strategies.

Artificial Intelligence (AI) has increasingly become a pivotal tool in professional dermatology, particularly in the early detection and monitoring of skin conditions such as melanoma. AI systems like SkinVision and MoleMapper exemplify this trend by utilizing advanced algorithms to analyze skin lesions and track changes over time, thereby enhancing diagnostic accuracy and patient outcomes.

SkinVision employs AI to evaluate skin lesions for early signs of melanoma, providing risk assessments within minutes. This rapid analysis allows dermatologists to prioritize high-risk cases, ultimately improving early diagnosis rates. Research indicates that AI systems can significantly reduce misdiagnosis rates in melanoma detection. For instance, a meta-analysis found that the accuracy of computer-aided diagnosis of melanoma is comparable to that of human experts, emphasizing the potential of AI in enhancing diagnostic performance in dermatology [110, 111]. Moreover, AI's ability to analyse large datasets enables it to recognize patterns that may be overlooked by human practitioners, further supporting its role in clinical decision-making [112, 113].

MoleMapper, on the other hand, focuses on monitoring changes in moles over time. By employing machine learning techniques, it predicts potential risks associated with skin lesions, guiding follow-up care for patients. This continuous monitoring is crucial, as early detection of changes in moles can lead to timely interventions, which are vital for improving patient outcomes in melanoma cases [114]. The integration of AI in such applications not only aids in the identification of malignant lesions but also enhances the overall workflow in dermatology practices, allowing healthcare professionals to allocate their time and resources more effectively [115, 116].

The acceptance of AI tools in dermatology is also noteworthy. Studies have shown that both patients and dermatologists recognize the value of AI in enhancing diagnostic accuracy. For example, a survey indicated that a significant majority of patients support the use of AI as an assistive tool in melanoma screening, reflecting a growing trust in these technologies [117, 118]. Furthermore, clinical studies have highlighted that AI systems can achieve diagnostic performance comparable to that of experienced dermatologists, reinforcing the argument for their integration into routine dermatological practice [119, 120].

The integration of artificial intelligence (AI) in clinical research and product development within the skincare industry is revolutionizing how companies approach product formulation and personalization. Revieve, for instance, collaborates with skincare brands to leverage AI-based insights derived from extensive skin data collected from thousands of users. This data analysis enables companies to identify prevalent skin concerns, such as fine lines and uneven skin tone, facilitating the creation of targeted skincare products tailored to specific needs [74].

AI platforms like Atolla exemplify this trend by collecting individual skin data to formulate custom serums that adapt over time as a user's skin condition evolves. This dynamic approach not only enhances the personalization of skincare but also aligns with the broader movement towards precision medicine in dermatology, where treatments are increasingly tailored to the genetic and phenotypic characteristics of individuals [121, 122]. The use of machine learning algorithms allows for the analysis of large datasets, which can inform product development and improve treatment efficacy [101].

The application of AI in skincare extends beyond product development to include treatment monitoring and patient engagement. For instance, AI tools are being utilized to enhance medication adherence in patients with chronic skin conditions, thereby improving overall treatment outcomes [123]. The incorporation of genetic profiling, such as single nucleotide polymorphism (SNP) analysis, further refines the personalization process, enabling skincare solutions that are not only effective but also minimize adverse reactions [101, 122].

The regulatory landscape is also adapting to these advancements, with guidelines evolving to accommodate the innovative formulations and technologies emerging from AI-driven research [124]. As companies continue to harness the power of AI, the skincare industry is poised for significant transformation, leading to more effective, personalized, and safer products for consumers.

Smart home skincare devices, such as the FOREO Luna Fofo and the Opte Precision Skincare System, represent a significant advancement in personal care technology by integrating artificial intelligence (AI) and skin analysis to provide tailored skincare solutions. The Luna Fofo utilizes sensors to assess skin hydration levels, offering real-time recommendations for cleansing routines tailored to individual skin needs. This functionality aligns with the broader trend of smart home devices that leverage IoT technology to enhance user experience and convenience in daily tasks, including personal care [125, 126].

The Opte Precision Skincare System takes this a step further by employing advanced scanning technology to identify dark spots on the skin. It delivers precise amounts of pigment or serum to both conceal and treat these imperfections simultaneously. This dual functionality not only enhances the efficacy of skincare routines but also exemplifies the convergence of beauty technology and smart home innovations [127, 128]. The integration of such devices into the smart home ecosystem reflects a growing consumer demand for personalized and efficient skincare solutions, which are increasingly facilitated by smart technologies [129, 130].

Further, the development of skincare devices that utilize NFC technology for monitoring skin conditions has been highlighted in recent studies. These devices can measure skin moisture and UV exposure, further enhancing the personalization of skincare regimens. Such innovations underscore the importance of data collection and analysis in the skincare industry, allowing users to make informed decisions about their skincare practices [127, 131]. The ability to collect real-time data and provide actionable insights is a hallmark of smart home devices, reinforcing their role in promoting health and wellness through technology [132, 133].

AI-powered online skin advisors are becoming increasingly prevalent in the skincare industry, leveraging artificial intelligence to provide personalized skincare recommendations. One notable example is Skinsei by Unilever, which utilizes a combination of user questionnaires and AI algorithms to evaluate individual lifestyle factors, environmental conditions, and specific skin concerns. This approach enables the platform to suggest tailored skincare regimens that cater to the unique needs of each user, enhancing the personalization of skincare solutions [99].

Similarly, platforms like Facelytics employ advanced technologies to analyse user selfies, assessing various skin attributes such as age, skin type, and imperfections. This analysis allows for the provision of product suggestions or corrective solutions based on the identified skin conditions. The underlying technology often involves deep learning models, which have shown significant promise in accurately classifying skin conditions and recommending appropriate treatments [134, 135]. For instance, convolutional neural networks

(CNNs) are frequently employed in these applications to enhance the accuracy of skin condition assessments and product recommendations [136].

The efficacy of AI in dermatology is further supported by research indicating that AI algorithms can match or even surpass the diagnostic accuracy of human dermatologists in certain contexts, such as skin cancer detection [137]. This capability is particularly relevant as it underscores the potential for AI-driven platforms to provide reliable skincare advice, thereby improving user outcomes and satisfaction [98]. Moreover, the integration of AI in skincare not only facilitates personalized recommendations but also addresses the growing demand for data-driven solutions in cosmetic dermatology, where traditional methods may fall short [99].

However, it is essential to acknowledge the challenges associated with AI in dermatology, particularly concerning the diversity of training datasets. Studies have highlighted that many AI algorithms may not perform equally well across different skin tones, which can lead to disparities in the effectiveness of recommendations [138]. This concern emphasizes the need for ongoing research and development to ensure that AI-powered tools are inclusive and effective for all users, regardless of their skin type or tone [139].

The integration of artificial intelligence (AI) in retail and e-commerce has transformed customer interactions and enhanced personalized shopping experiences. Retailers like Walmart have adopted AI technologies, such as skin analysis kiosks, which allow customers to scan their skin and receive tailored product recommendations. This application of AI not only improves customer engagement but also facilitates informed purchasing decisions based on individual needs and preferences [140]. Similarly, online retailers like Dermstore utilize AI chatbots to assist customers in navigating personalized skincare purchases. These chatbots leverage natural language processing and machine learning to understand customer concerns and habits, thereby providing customized recommendations that enhance the shopping experience [141, 142].

The effectiveness of AI in retail is further underscored by its ability to analyse vast amounts of consumer data, leading to improved product recommendations and marketing strategies. AI-driven algorithms can predict consumer behaviour and preferences, which is crucial for e-commerce platforms aiming to optimize their offerings [143, 144]. For instance, AI-powered recommendation engines have been shown to significantly influence customer purchase intentions by tailoring suggestions based on previous interactions and preferences [145]. This capability not only enhances customer satisfaction but also drives sales growth for retailers [146, 147].

The role of AI in retail extends beyond mere product recommendations. It encompasses various applications such as inventory management, customer service automation, and personalized marketing campaigns. The synergy of AI with other technologies, such as the Internet of Things (IoT), has enabled retailers to create smart retail environments that enhance customer experiences through personalized interactions and efficient service delivery [148, 149]. For example, AI can facilitate dynamic pricing strategies and real-time inventory tracking, which are essential for maintaining competitiveness in the fast-paced retail landscape [150].

The integration of artificial intelligence (AI) tools in dermatology, particularly for skin health research, has shown significant promise in enhancing product development and efficacy testing. One notable example is ModiFace, which utilizes AI to simulate the effects of skincare products on the skin. This technology allows brands to analyse potential outcomes without extensive human trials, thereby accelerating product development while ensuring safety and effectiveness [151, 152]. The ability of AI to assist in diagnosing skin conditions and evaluating treatment efficacy is increasingly recognized, with studies demonstrating improvements in diagnostic accuracy when AI tools are employed alongside human expertise [75, 85].

AI's role extends beyond diagnostics; it also encompasses the evaluation of skincare products. For instance, the hOSEC (human organotypic skin explant culture) model has been developed as an alternative to traditional animal testing for cosmetic efficacy. This model maintains the structural integrity of human skin, allowing for more accurate assessments of product safety and effectiveness [153, 154]. Furthermore, the use of AI in teledermatology practices has been shown to enhance diagnostic capabilities, enabling primary care physicians and nurse practitioners to make more informed decisions regarding skin conditions [75].

Advances in Cosmetology

The application of AI in dermatology is not limited to diagnostics and product testing; it also plays a crucial role in understanding the underlying mechanisms of skin conditions. Research has highlighted the potential of AI to analyse large datasets, which can lead to the identification of new biomarkers and treatment strategies for chronic inflammatory skin diseases [85, 155]. This comprehensive approach not only improves the understanding of skin health but also facilitates the development of targeted therapies that can be tested using AI-driven simulations, further reducing the need for extensive human trials [151, 152].

Applications in Beauty Therapy

Beauty therapists can integrate AI and machine learning tools into their practices to elevate client services, streamline consultations, and deliver more personalized treatments. For instance, tools like SkinID by Neutrogena, L'Oreal Skin Genius, and the HiMirror smart mirror allow therapists to conduct detailed skin assessments during consultations. These tools provide instant insights into skin issues such as dryness, uneven tone, fine lines, and dark spots, helping therapists recommend appropriate treatments or products. Additionally, smart mirrors can track a client's progress over multiple visits, ensuring that treatments are effective and achieving the desired results.

Virtual try-on tools, such as Sephora's Virtual Artist, enable beauty therapists to offer clients a preview of how makeup or skincare products will look or perform on their skin before application. This enhances the in-salon experience by allowing clients to make informed decisions about products or treatments. For example, therapists can use virtual try-on technology to demonstrate different makeup looks, helping clients choose the most flattering options without physically applying multiple products.

Therapists can also leverage personalized skincare platforms like Curology or Proven Skincare to design customized regimens for their clients. By guiding clients through uploading selfies or completing detailed skin history forms, therapists can use AI-generated recommendations to inform their treatments. These platforms also enable therapists to partner with labs to create custom formulations tailored to specific skin concerns, further enhancing their professional offerings and delivering a truly personalized service.

AI tools like Troveskin and Skintelli provide therapists with the ability to monitor a client's skin over time and predict potential issues such as dryness, breakouts, or sun damage. These tools track hydration levels and assess environmental impacts like pollution, allowing therapists to provide proactive solutions and maintain long-term relationships with clients through ongoing care and tailored recommendations. Predictive insights generated by these tools enable therapists to adapt skincare routines to evolving client needs.

In collaboration with dermatologists, beauty therapists can utilize tools like SkinVision and MoleMapper to identify and monitor skin conditions that require medical attention. While therapists may not diagnose conditions like melanoma, these tools enable them to refer clients to dermatologists for further evaluation, ensuring that potential risks are addressed early. This collaboration enhances the quality of care provided and strengthens the therapist-client relationship.

Beauty therapists can also collaborate with brands using platforms like Revieve and Atolla to offer cutting-edge products and services. These platforms analyse aggregated data from clients to identify common concerns, allowing therapists to recommend effective products aligned with individual needs. Custom serums developed through AI platforms can be offered as premium services, setting therapists apart from competitors and providing added value to clients.

Devices like the FOREO Luna Fofo and Opte Precision Skincare System can complement a therapist's services by enabling clients to maintain their skin at home. Therapists can recommend these devices as part of an aftercare plan to ensure continued results between visits. By teaching clients how to use these devices effectively, therapists enhance the value of their advice and establish themselves as trusted professionals in skincare.

Platforms like Skinsei and Facelytics can be integrated into virtual consultation services, allowing therapists to analyse a client's skin through selfies or questionnaires during remote sessions. AI-generated insights from these tools can guide therapists in creating personalized treatment plans for clients who cannot visit the salon in person, broadening their service reach and accessibility.

For therapists who sell skincare products, AI-powered kiosks and chatbots like those used by Walmart and Dermstore can streamline product recommendations. An in-salon AI kiosk, for example, could allow clients to scan their skin and instantly receive product suggestions tailored to their treatment plans. This integration enhances the retail aspect of a therapist's business, increasing sales and improving client satisfaction.

Finally, research tools like ModiFace enable therapists to stay informed about the efficacy of new products and treatments before introducing them to their clients. By simulating how products interact with the skin, therapists can confidently recommend effective solutions. These tools also allow therapists to test emerging technologies and treatments in a controlled environment, ensuring they deliver the best possible results to their clients.

Incorporating AI and machine learning tools into their practice, beauty therapists can elevate the level of care they provide, offer more personalized and effective services, and stay ahead in a competitive industry. These tools not only enhance the client experience but also help therapists build trust, improve outcomes, and establish themselves as experts in their field.

Applications for Consumers

Consumers can leverage AI and machine learning tools to make more informed decisions about their skincare, personalize their routines, and monitor their skin health conveniently from home. These tools empower individuals by providing accurate, tailored insights and recommendations that cater to their unique needs.

AI-powered skin diagnostic tools like SkinID by Neutrogena and L'Oreal Skin Genius allow consumers to conduct detailed skin assessments using just a smartphone camera. These tools analyse issues such as dryness, uneven tone, and acne, providing instant feedback and personalized recommendations for skincare products or routines. Similarly, the HiMirror smart mirror enables users to track their skin's progress daily, identifying changes such as fine lines or dark spots, which helps them evaluate the effectiveness of their current skincare regimen.

Virtual try-on and augmented reality (AR) applications, such as Sephora's Virtual Artist, allow consumers to experiment with makeup and skincare products before purchasing. These tools use AI to scan the user's face, evaluate skin tone and condition, and recommend suitable products. Consumers can virtually "try on" makeup looks or see how skincare products might improve their appearance, making the shopping experience more engaging and personalized while reducing the risk of buying unsuitable products.

Personalized skincare platforms like Curology and Proven Skincare take customization a step further by creating tailored skincare solutions. Consumers upload selfies and provide detailed information about their skin concerns and history. AI algorithms, combined with dermatologist expertise, then generate customized formulations that target specific issues. These platforms save time and effort by delivering products designed specifically for the individual, offering an elevated level of care.

Predictive skin analysis tools such as Troveskin and Skintelli enable consumers to monitor their skin health over time and take preventive measures. These apps analyse factors like hydration levels, UV exposure, and sleep patterns, providing actionable recommendations to address potential issues such as dryness, breakouts, or sun damage. By offering insights into how lifestyle and environmental factors affect their skin, these tools help users adapt their routines for better results.

AI tools like SkinVision and MoleMapper allow consumers to monitor their skin for potential health risks, such as skin cancer or melanoma. By analyzing moles and lesions, these apps provide early warnings and encourage users to seek professional medical advice when necessary. This empowers individuals to take control of their skin health and potentially catch issues at an early, treatable stage.

Smart home skincare devices, such as the FOREO Luna Fofo and the Opte Precision Skincare System, bring professional-grade care into consumers' homes. These devices use AI to analyse skin hydration, recommend cleansing routines, and deliver precise amounts of pigment or serum to treat specific concerns. They allow users to maintain their skincare routines effectively and conveniently, enhancing their overall skin health.

AI-powered online skin advisors like Skinsei and Facelytics provide consumers with personalized skincare regimens based on their lifestyle, environment, and skin concerns. These platforms analyse selfies or questionnaires to recommend products and corrective solutions, offering convenience and accessibility for those who prefer virtual consultations or cannot visit a professional.

AI integration in retail and e-commerce further enhances the consumer experience. In-store AI-powered kiosks, such as those used by Walmart, allow users to scan their skin and receive instant product recommendations. Online platforms like Dermstore employ chatbots that guide customers through personalized skincare purchases, making the shopping process seamless and tailored to individual needs.

Research tools like ModiFace allow consumers to stay informed about the efficacy of skincare products before purchasing. By simulating how a product will interact with their skin, consumers can make confident decisions about whether a product will meet their needs. This eliminates the guesswork and reduces the likelihood of buying products that fail to deliver results.

By using these AI and machine learning tools, consumers can take greater control of their skincare routines, access highly personalized solutions, and monitor their skin health more effectively. These technologies not only enhance convenience and confidence but also enable smarter, data-driven decisions that promote healthier and more radiant skin.

Virtual Reality (VR) for Client Consultations

The integration of Virtual Reality (VR) in cosmetology represents a significant advancement in client consultations, enhancing the overall experience through immersive and interactive technologies. By utilizing 3D visualizations, VR allows clients to preview potential treatments and outcomes, thereby improving communication and managing expectations effectively. This innovative approach not only personalizes the consultation process but also fosters a more engaging environment for clients, which is crucial in the beauty industry where visual outcomes are paramount [156, 157].

One of the primary benefits of VR in cosmetology is its ability to simulate various beauty services, such as hair colouring, hairstyling, and skincare treatments. For instance, clients can "try on" different hairstyles or colours in real-time, significantly reducing the uncertainty associated with drastic changes in appearance [156, 157]. This capability is particularly valuable for services like chemical peels or facials, where VR can provide a realistic preview of post-treatment results, thereby enabling clients to make informed decisions [156, 157]. Such simulations not only enhance client satisfaction but also build trust between clients and professionals, as clients feel more involved in the decision-making process [157].

VR technology streamlines consultations by offering detailed visual representations of procedures. In cosmetic tattooing or microblading, for example, VR can display the exact shape and style of eyebrows before any pigment is applied, minimizing misunderstandings and aligning client preferences with professional recommendations [156, 157]. This precision is essential in the cosmetology field, where the alignment of client expectations with achievable results is critical for satisfaction [157]. Furthermore, VR can serve as an educational tool, helping clients understand complex treatments like laser therapy by visualizing the process step-by-step, which can alleviate concerns and enhance their overall experience [156, 157].

The personalization of consultations is further enhanced through the integration of AI and machine learning within VR systems. These technologies can analyse individual client features—such as facial structure, skin tone, and hair texture—to provide tailored recommendations for products and techniques [157]. This level of customization not only improves the client experience but also positions cosmetologists as knowledgeable professionals who can offer expert advice based on advanced technological insights [157].

In addition to enhancing client consultations, VR also facilitates immersive educational experiences. Clients can engage in virtual tutorials on skincare routines or makeup applications, allowing them to practice techniques in a risk-free environment [156, 157]. This hands-on experience builds confidence and encourages clients to maintain their beauty regimens at home, further solidifying the relationship between the client and the cosmetologist [156, 157].

Despite the numerous advantages, the implementation of VR in cosmetology does require significant investment in technology and training. However, as VR technology becomes more accessible and affordable, its adoption is likely to increase, making it a standard tool in client consultations [156, 157]. Additionally, the ability to conduct virtual consultations remotely expands access to expert advice, particularly for clients who may face barriers to in-person visits due to time constraints or mobility issues [156, 157].

To implement Virtual Reality (VR) for client consultations in cosmetology, specific equipment and tools are necessary to create an immersive, engaging, and effective experience. A high-quality VR headset is central to this setup, as it enables clients to enter a virtual environment where they can visualize treatments and results in real time. Options like the Meta Quest 2 are popular for their affordability and standalone design, making them ideal for salons and spas. For more advanced and detailed beauty simulations, high-end devices like the HTC Vive Pro or Valve Index offer superior resolution and interactivity. Consumer-level devices like the PlayStation VR can also be used for less intensive applications, offering versatility for various salon needs.

Figure 3: Use of VR Headset. CC0, via Pickpik.

In addition to the headset, a VR-ready computer or gaming console is often required for advanced systems to process high-quality graphics and run applications smoothly. These systems typically need a powerful GPU, such as an NVIDIA RTX 30-series, paired with a high-speed processor like an Intel i7/i9 or AMD Ryzen 7/9. At least 16GB of RAM is recommended to ensure seamless performance. Some standalone headsets, like the Meta Quest, eliminate the need for external hardware but may have lower processing power compared to PC-powered systems.

Specialized VR software tailored to cosmetology is essential for providing realistic simulations and enhancing the client experience. This software should include tools for hair and makeup simulations, 3D modelling for skincare treatments or cosmetic tattoo previews, and tutorials for client education.

Advances in Cosmetology

Many of these platforms are proprietary to specific industries, requiring salons to collaborate with developers or consult VR content creators to access the most suitable applications for their needs.

To ensure accurate and personalized consultations, 3D scanning devices or cameras are often integrated into the setup. Devices like the Structure Sensor or Occipital 3D Scanner capture precise details of a client's facial structure, skin tone, and hair texture, enabling the creation of realistic 3D models. High-resolution cameras, such as DSLRs or advanced smartphone cameras, may also be used for face mapping or skin analysis. These tools capture fine details, including imperfections and contours, for seamless integration into VR simulations.

Reliable internet connectivity is vital for cloud-based VR applications or remote consultations. A stable, high-speed connection ensures smooth delivery of VR experiences, whether streamed in-house or over video platforms for clients participating from home. This connectivity enables salons to expand their services to a broader audience without compromising quality.

Accessories like VR controllers, haptic gloves, and body sensors enhance the interactivity of the VR experience. Controllers allow clients to manipulate virtual tools, such as brushes or hair colours, within the simulation, while haptic gloves provide tactile feedback that simulates the feel of products or treatments. Body sensors can track movements, offering a more realistic sense of immersion in the virtual environment.

AI integration is a critical component of VR in cosmetology, as it allows systems to deliver personalized recommendations. Software powered by artificial intelligence and machine learning analyses data such as facial features, skin conditions, or hair type to provide tailored results. This technology ensures that consultations are not only interactive but also highly customized to meet individual client needs.

Training materials are essential for professionals to effectively utilize VR in their practice. These resources include tutorials on operating the system, guidance on using 3D scanning tools, and educational content for integrating VR seamlessly into consultations. Proper training ensures that cosmetologists can maximize the potential of VR technology while delivering a superior client experience.

A designated space within the salon or spa is necessary for setting up the VR equipment. This area should be free of obstructions and spacious enough to allow clients to move comfortably while wearing the headset. Creating a dedicated space ensures a professional and immersive experience, enhancing the overall impact of the technology.

Hygiene and maintenance are critical considerations for using VR equipment in a salon setting. Since headsets and accessories come into direct contact with clients, it is essential to maintain cleanliness by using disposable headset covers, sanitizing wipes, and regular cleaning routines. These practices prioritize client safety and comfort while ensuring that the equipment remains in optimal condition.

By integrating these tools and equipment, salons and beauty professionals can transform their consultation process with state-of-the-art VR technology. This not only builds client trust and confidence but also improves decision-making and sets the business apart as a leader in innovative cosmetology. Through immersive, personalized, and hygienic experiences, VR enhances the overall quality and professionalism of client interactions.

Currently, there are several commercial systems available for Virtual Reality (VR) in client consultations within the cosmetology industry. These systems leverage advanced technologies like VR headsets, AI integration, and 3D modelling to offer immersive and interactive experiences. Below is an overview of the most popular and commercially available systems tailored for cosmetology consultations:

1. Perfect Corp – YouCam Makeup and Virtual Beauty: Perfect Corp's **YouCam Makeup** is an AI-powered virtual beauty platform widely used in salons and by beauty professionals for consultations. While it primarily utilizes augmented reality (AR), the technology has been adapted to integrate VR capabilities for client consultations. The system allows clients to virtually try on makeup, experiment with different hair colours, and visualize how skincare treatments may impact their appearance. It uses AI and facial mapping technology to deliver accurate and realistic results. YouCam is accessible through mobile apps or integrated into salon systems, making it a versatile choice for businesses.

2. Modiface by L'Oréal: L'Oréal's Modiface is a leading VR and AR platform specifically designed for beauty consultations. This system offers tools for virtual makeup application, hair colour previews, and skincare analysis. It is compatible with VR headsets, allowing salons to provide fully immersive experiences where clients can explore different beauty options in a virtual environment. Modiface also features advanced AI algorithms that analyse skin tone, texture, and facial features to recommend personalized products and treatments. It is often used in retail and professional settings, with brands like Maybelline and Lancôme integrating the technology into their consultations.

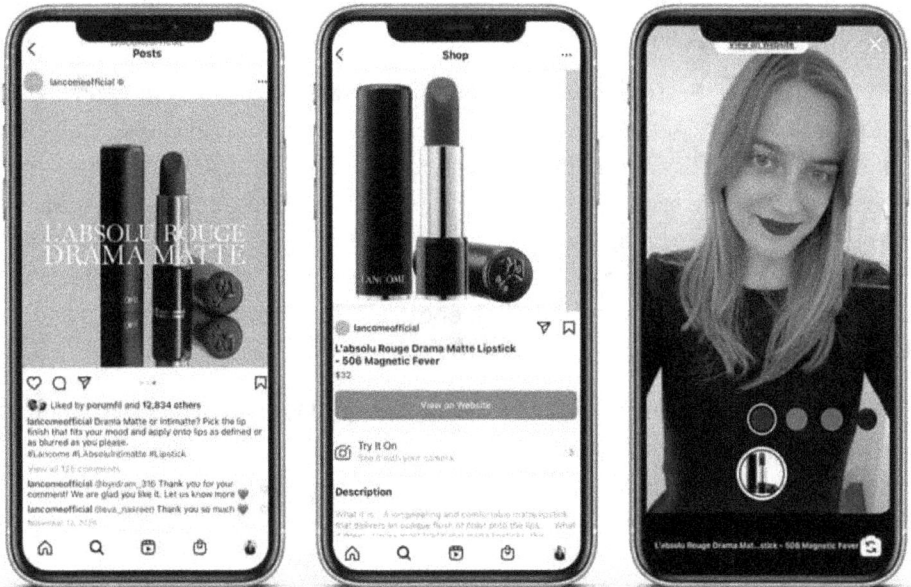

Figure 4: Instagram shoppers can now virtually try on Lancôme lipsticks thanks to ModiFace. L'Oreal, CC BY 4.0, via FMT.

3. Skin Consult AI by L'Oréal: L'Oréal's **Skin Consult AI** is an advanced tool designed for personalized skincare consultations. While not strictly VR-focused, it complements VR systems by using AI to analyse skin conditions like

47

wrinkles, fine lines, and uneven tone. This data can then be visualized through VR headsets, providing clients with an immersive view of their skin concerns and potential improvements after treatments. Skin Consult AI is often integrated into broader salon VR systems, allowing professionals to combine cutting-edge diagnostics with immersive virtual simulations.

4. Revieve Skincare Advisor: The Revieve Skincare Advisor combines AI, AR, and VR technology to create a holistic beauty consultation system. It uses facial scanning and advanced algorithms to analyse skin and recommend personalized products or treatments. Revieve integrates seamlessly with VR headsets, enabling clients to visualize the effects of skincare regimens or professional treatments in an immersive environment. It also provides interactive tutorials for skincare application, making it a comprehensive tool for both at-home and salon use.

5. Schwarzkopf Professional – SalonLab Smart Analyzer: Schwarzkopf's SalonLab Smart Analyzer is an innovative system designed for hair consultations. This system uses advanced sensors and AI to analyse hair structure, moisture levels, and colour history. The collected data is visualized using VR or AR platforms, allowing clients to see potential results of different hair treatments, such as colouring or conditioning. The immersive technology helps clients feel confident about their choices by offering a detailed preview of the expected outcomes.

6. VIVE Pro by HTC: The HTC VIVE Pro is a high-end VR headset widely used in various industries, including cosmetology. Although it is not a dedicated beauty system, it serves as a platform for beauty professionals to run custom VR applications. Many salons and beauty tech providers use VIVE Pro to deliver detailed simulations of makeup looks, skincare treatments, and hair transformations. Its high-resolution display and precise tracking ensure an immersive and realistic experience for clients.

Advances in Cosmetology

Figure 5: HTC RE Vive. Maurizio Pesce, CC BY 2.0, via Wikimedia Commons.

7. Oculus Quest 2 (Meta Quest 2): The **Meta Quest 2** is a standalone VR headset that is increasingly being adopted by cosmetology businesses for consultations. Its affordability and ease of use make it a practical choice for salons looking to offer VR services without investing in extensive hardware. Beauty professionals can use third-party VR applications compatible with Quest 2 to simulate hair, makeup, or skincare transformations. Its wireless design also provides flexibility for in-salon or remote consultations.

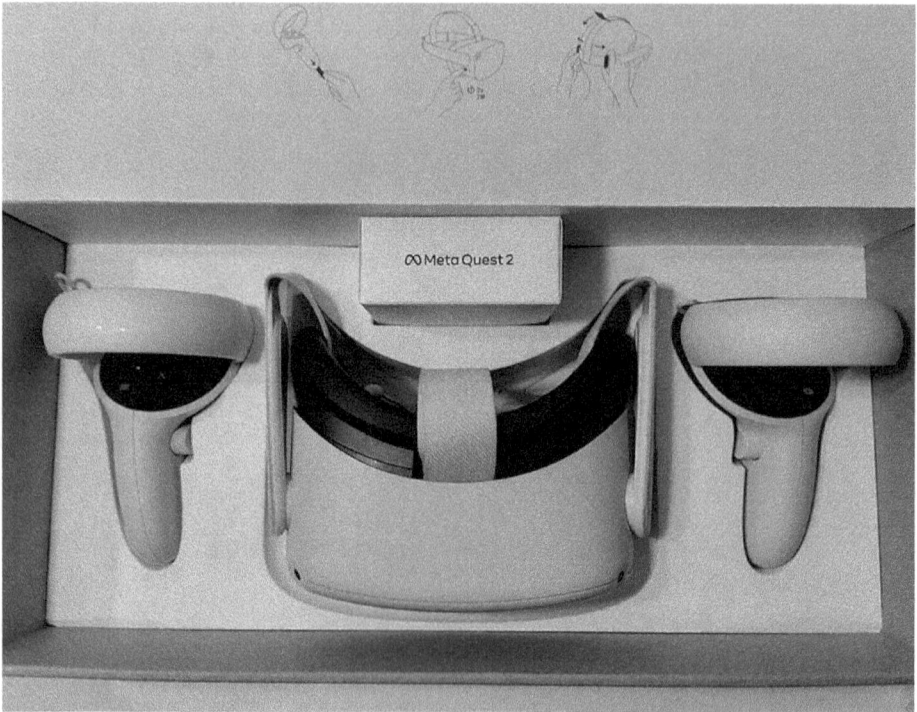

Figure 6: Meta Quest 2. Wasiul Bahar, CC BY-SA 4.0, via Wikimedia Commons.

8. MirrorMe3D: MirrorMe3D specializes in 3D facial imaging and VR applications for cosmetic and beauty consultations. It creates detailed 3D models of a client's face using advanced scanning technology, which can then be used in VR environments to showcase potential changes from treatments like facials, Botox, or contouring. This system is particularly popular in high-end salons and aesthetic clinics, where precision and personalization are critical.

9. Hololens by Microsoft

Microsoft's Hololens is a mixed-reality headset that integrates AR and VR capabilities. It is often used in cosmetology for training and client consultations. Hololens allows beauty professionals to overlay virtual makeup, hair colours, or skincare effects onto a client's real-world image. This system provides a hybrid experience, blending the real and virtual worlds for a seamless and interactive consultation.

10. ModiFace Virtual Beauty Advisor: ModiFace's Virtual Beauty Advisor offers a cloud-based system for both AR and VR beauty consultations. It is used by major beauty brands and salons to allow clients to explore a wide range of options, from makeup looks to skincare treatments. ModiFace supports integration with VR headsets, enabling immersive client experiences. It also uses AI to analyse facial features and provide tailored product recommendations, enhancing the precision of consultations.

11. HiMirror Smart Beauty Mirror: The **HiMirror** is an advanced beauty device that integrates AR and VR technologies to provide clients with a comprehensive skin analysis and virtual try-on options. It scans the client's face to detect issues like fine lines, wrinkles, and discoloration, then uses VR capabilities to simulate the effects of various treatments. HiMirror is a popular choice for salons and individual beauty professionals looking for an all-in-one consultation system.

Figure 7: CES2017 HiMirror SmartMirror im use in salon. ETC-USC, CC BY 2.0, via Flickr.

Table 1 provides an in-depth comparison of Virtual Reality (VR) systems and technologies tailored to cosmetology, focusing on their costs, functionality, and implementation requirements. Each column in the table highlights a critical aspect of these systems, offering valuable insights into their capabilities and suitability for salons or spas looking to enhance client consultations with advanced technology.

Table 1: VR Cosmetology Technologies Costs (Approx. as at January, 2025).

Technology/ System	Setup Costs (Approx.)	Annual Maintenance/Subscription Costs (Approx.)	Additional Requirements
Perfect Corp – YouCam Makeup and Virtual Beauty	$1,000 - $5,000 (software licenses, initial setup)	$500 - $2,000	Camera for facial analysis, high-speed internet
Modiface by L'Oréal	$5,000 - $10,000 (customized platform, integrations)	$1,000 - $3,000	VR-ready PC, camera for integrations
Skin Consult AI by L'Oréal	$10,000 - $20,000 (AI diagnostics, hardware integration)	$2,000 - $5,000	VR/AR headsets, integration with salon software
Revieve Skincare Advisor	$2,000 - $7,000 (license and customization)	$500 - $1,500	Facial scanner, salon system integration
Schwarzkopf Professional – SalonLab Smart Analyzer	$5,000 - $15,000 (hardware, sensors, setup)	$1,000 - $3,000	Moisture analysers, VR-compatible devices
HTC VIVE Pro	$1,200 - $1,500 (hardware only)	$200 - $500	VR-ready PC, VR applications
Meta Quest 2 (Oculus Quest 2)	$299 - $399 (standalone VR headset)	$0 - $100	None (standalone system)
MirrorMe3D	$3,000 - $6,000 (3D imaging setup)	$500 - $1,000	3D scanner, VR headset for visualization
Microsoft Hololens	$3,500 - $5,000 (hardware only)	$500 - $2,000	High-speed internet, compatible software

Technology/ System	Setup Costs (Approx.)	Annual Maintenance/Sub scription Costs (Approx.)	Additional Requirements
ModiFace Virtual Beauty Advisor	$5,000 - $10,000 (cloud-based license and hardware)	$1,000 - $2,500	VR-ready PC, salon software integration
HiMirror Smart Beauty Mirror	$1,500 - $2,500 (smart beauty mirror)	$200 - $500	Facial scanning capabilities, internet connectivity

The first column lists the various VR systems and tools available in the cosmetology industry, ranging from AI-driven beauty applications to high-end VR hardware. These systems serve diverse purposes, including virtual makeup try-ons, skincare analysis, and fully immersive consultations. Examples include Perfect Corp's YouCam Makeup for virtual beauty applications, HTC VIVE Pro for high-resolution and interactive simulations, and Microsoft Hololens for mixed-reality experiences. These options reflect the breadth of technology available to meet the unique needs of cosmetology professionals.

The setup costs associated with implementing these systems vary significantly based on their complexity and functionality. Entry-level systems, such as the Meta Quest 2, are affordable, with costs ranging between $299 and $399, making them accessible to smaller salons or those new to VR technology. Mid-range systems like Revieve Skincare Advisor, priced between $2,000 and $7,000, or MirrorMe3D, costing $3,000 to $6,000, require additional equipment such as facial scanners or VR-compatible devices, resulting in higher initial investments. High-cost systems like Skin Consult AI by L'Oréal and Schwarzkopf Professional – SalonLab Smart Analyzer demand more substantial investments, ranging from $5,000 to $20,000. These advanced solutions often include custom hardware, software integrations, and extensive capabilities, making them ideal for high-end salons aiming to deliver premium experiences.

Annual maintenance and subscription costs reflect the ongoing expenses associated with these technologies. Basic systems such as the HiMirror Smart

Beauty Mirror, with maintenance costs between $200 and $500, and the Meta Quest 2, with minimal upkeep costs of $0 to $100, are cost-effective options for salons. Mid-range solutions like YouCam Makeup and Revieve Skincare Advisor incur manageable subscription fees of $500 to $2,000 annually. However, more sophisticated platforms, such as Modiface by L'Oréal and Skin Consult AI, have higher recurring costs, ranging from $1,000 to $5,000. These fees cover essential services like software updates, customer support, and cloud-based functionality, ensuring the systems remain up-to-date and efficient.

The additional requirements column outlines the specific tools and infrastructure needed to operate each system effectively. Standalone systems like Meta Quest 2 and HiMirror Smart Beauty Mirror are self-contained and require minimal additional setup, making them easy to integrate into existing salon workflows. Integrated systems, such as Schwarzkopf Professional – SalonLab Smart Analyzer, necessitate specialized hardware like moisture analyzers, while MirrorMe3D requires 3D scanners and VR headsets to deliver detailed and personalized consultations. Many systems, including Modiface and Skin Consult AI, depend on AI-powered algorithms and high-speed internet for seamless operation. Advanced technologies like Microsoft Hololens and HTC VIVE Pro often require VR-ready PCs and tailored software configurations, adding to their complexity but offering unparalleled functionality.

The table highlights the versatility of VR systems, catering to different salon sizes, budgets, and objectives. Entry-level options like Meta Quest 2 and HiMirror are affordable, user-friendly, and suitable for smaller businesses or those exploring VR technology for the first time. Mid-range solutions such as Revieve Skincare Advisor and Modiface strike a balance between cost and functionality, offering advanced features like AI-driven recommendations without excessive investments. Premium systems, including Skin Consult AI and Schwarzkopf SalonLab, are designed for high-end salons seeking cutting-edge tools with extensive customization and diagnostic capabilities. Many systems also require training and customization to align with salon workflows, particularly for AI-integrated or hardware-intensive platforms.

Advanced Diagnostic Tools in Skin Care

Diagnosis in skincare is a critical component that underpins effective and personalized treatment strategies. The complexity of the skin as an organ, influenced by various internal and external factors, necessitates a thorough understanding of individual conditions to ensure that skincare professionals can accurately and safely address client needs. This response synthesizes the importance of diagnosis in skincare across several key areas.

A proper diagnosis is essential for understanding the underlying causes of skin issues rather than merely treating symptoms. For example, acne can stem from hormonal imbalances, clogged pores, or lifestyle factors such as diet and stress [158]. Without identifying these root causes, treatments may only provide temporary relief, failing to resolve the issue at its source [159]. Accurate diagnosis enables professionals to develop targeted treatment plans that lead to lasting improvements in skin health [160].

Each individual's skin is unique, with variations in texture, tone, and sensitivity. Diagnosis allows professionals to assess these differences and tailor treatments accordingly. For instance, a hydration analysis may reveal that a client has extremely dry skin, necessitating a regimen with hydrating serums and occlusive moisturizers [161]. Conversely, someone with oily, acne-prone skin may benefit from treatments containing salicylic acid or clay-based masks [162]. This personalized approach maximizes treatment efficacy and minimizes the risk of adverse reactions [98].

Thorough diagnostic processes can uncover skin concerns that are not immediately visible, such as early signs of sun damage or hyperpigmentation [163]. Advanced diagnostic tools, including UV imaging and AI-powered systems, can detect these underlying issues, allowing for timely preventive measures [98]. Early intervention can significantly improve long-term skin health by addressing concerns before they escalate [164].

Skin conditions often share similar symptoms, which can lead to misdiagnosis if not properly analysed. For example, redness could indicate rosacea, eczema, or an allergic reaction, each requiring a different treatment approach [165]. Accurate diagnosis helps prevent the application of incorrect treatments, which could exacerbate the problem and lead to client dissatisfaction [166]. This reduces the trial-and-error approach, saving time and resources for both clients and professionals [160].

Diagnosis is an ongoing process that aids in tracking treatment effectiveness. Regular evaluations allow professionals to compare baseline results with progress over time [167]. For instance, if a client undergoes a series of chemical peels for pigmentation, diagnostic scans can reveal whether the dark spots are fading [168]. This data-driven approach ensures treatments are effective and allows for necessary adjustments, enhancing overall outcomes [164].

A detailed diagnosis empowers clients to understand their skin and its needs better. When professionals utilize diagnostic tools to visually showcase skin conditions, clients gain clarity regarding their concerns and the rationale behind specific treatments [169]. This transparency fosters trust, encouraging adherence to recommended products and routines, ultimately leading to better results [160].

Diagnosis is crucial for recommending appropriate products tailored to a client's skin type and concerns. For example, analysing sebum levels might indicate a need for oil-free products, while sensitivity tests could suggest hypoallergenic formulations [159]. Aligning product choices with diagnostic insights ensures clients invest in products that genuinely benefit their skin [98].

In some cases, a skincare diagnosis can reveal issues requiring medical attention, such as suspicious moles or severe acne [170]. Professionals trained in skin analysis can identify these concerns early and refer clients to dermatologists for further evaluation, which can be life-saving in serious conditions like melanoma [160].

Without a proper diagnosis, treatments may lead to irritation or allergic reactions. For instance, applying strong exfoliants on sensitive skin can cause significant discomfort [160]. Diagnosis ensures that treatments are suitable for the client's skin condition and tolerance levels, minimizing the risk of adverse outcomes [166].

A thorough diagnosis helps professionals educate clients about preventive measures to maintain healthy skin. By identifying risk factors such as dehydration or sun exposure, professionals can recommend proactive steps like using sunscreen or antioxidants [160]. Preventive skincare extends the longevity of healthy skin and reduces the likelihood of developing severe concerns in the future [164].

Advanced diagnostic tools in skin care represent a significant leap forward in the assessment and analysis of skin conditions, utilizing cutting-edge technologies to provide precise insights into individual skin health. These tools are essential for dermatologists, aestheticians, and skincare professionals, enabling them to create highly personalized treatment plans based on detailed analyses of skin conditions.

Advanced skin diagnostic tools employ a combination of visual imaging, data analysis, and predictive modelling to assess the skin's condition beyond superficial observations. For instance, tools such as optical coherence tomography (OCT) and reflectance confocal microscopy (RCM) allow for the evaluation of skin texture, elasticity, pore size, and underlying health issues, facilitating targeted treatment recommendations [171, 172]. The integration of these technologies enables practitioners to anticipate potential future skin concerns, thus enhancing the overall effectiveness of skincare regimens [173].

Key technologies used include:

High-Resolution Imaging Systems: High-definition cameras and multispectral imaging devices, such as dermatoscopes, provide detailed images of the skin's surface. These systems can reveal fine lines, pigmentation, and uneven texture, offering a comprehensive view of skin conditions [174]. Recent advancements in three-dimensional (3D) imaging techniques have further improved the accuracy of skin assessments, allowing for the identification of subtle variations in skin characteristics [175, 176].

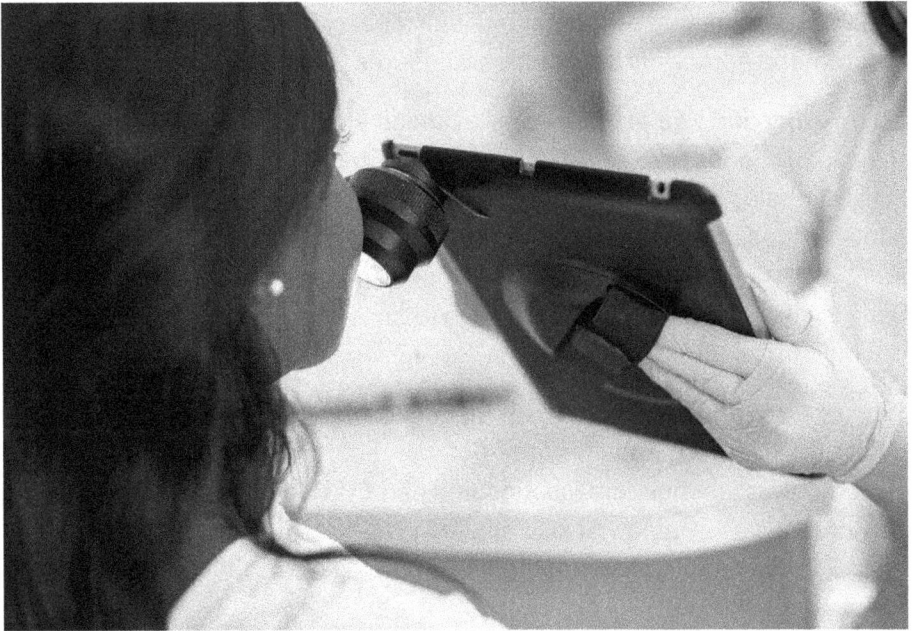

Figure 8: A Tablet with a Magnifier. Gustavo Fring, CC0, via Pexels.

AI and Machine Learning: Artificial intelligence (AI) and machine learning (ML) play a pivotal role in skin diagnostics by analysing extensive datasets to identify patterns in skin conditions. For example, tools like ModiFace and Skin Consult AI utilize AI algorithms to compare user data with global benchmarks, generating tailored treatment recommendations [177, 178]. These technologies enhance diagnostic accuracy and enable the identification of a wide range of skin issues, including acne, pigmentation disorders, and signs of aging [178].

UV and Infrared Analysis: Some diagnostic devices utilize UV light and infrared imaging to detect sun damage and underlying pigmentation, which are often invisible to the naked eye. These tools are particularly valuable for assessing the long-term effects of sun exposure and formulating preventive strategies [179]. By analysing skin responses to UV exposure, practitioners can better understand individual skin sensitivities and recommend appropriate protective measures [179].

3D Imaging and Facial Mapping: Advanced 3D scanners create detailed maps of a client's face, identifying variations in skin texture and pore size. This technology is crucial for precise analysis and treatment planning, allowing for a more individualized approach to skincare [175, 176]. The ability to visualize skin in three dimensions enhances the understanding of facial symmetry and problem areas, leading to more effective interventions [180].

Sensor-Based Tools: Devices equipped with sensors measure skin hydration, oil levels, and elasticity. For instance, the Visia Skin Analysis system assesses moisture balance and detects fine lines, providing a comprehensive overview of skin health [178]. These measurements are critical for developing personalized skincare regimens that address specific skin needs.

Biometric Data Collection: Some advanced diagnostic tools incorporate biometric measurements, such as temperature and pH levels, to provide a holistic view of skin health. This integration of data allows for a more thorough understanding of individual skin conditions and the factors influencing them [177].

The application of advanced diagnostic tools in skincare has revolutionized the way professionals approach treatment and client education. These tools enable the creation of personalized treatment plans tailored to the unique needs of each client. For instance, hydration analysis can reveal the necessity for moisturizers containing hyaluronic acid, while assessments of UV damage can lead to recommendations for specific SPF products or repair serums [179, 181]. Personalized skincare is increasingly recognized as essential in enhancing treatment efficacy and client satisfaction, as it allows for a more targeted approach to skincare regimens [182, 183].

These diagnostic tools facilitate the early detection of skin issues, such as acne-prone areas, sun damage, and signs of premature aging. By identifying these concerns before they become visible, skincare professionals can implement proactive treatment strategies that prevent further deterioration of the skin [163, 184]. This proactive approach is crucial in managing conditions like acne, where timely intervention can significantly improve outcomes and reduce the risk of scarring [163, 182].

Tracking treatment progress is another critical application of these diagnostic devices. They allow skincare professionals to monitor the effectiveness of treatments over time by comparing baseline measurements with follow-up scans. This capability not only aids in assessing the success of a skincare regimen but also provides valuable feedback for adjusting treatment plans as necessary [185, 186]. Such continuous monitoring fosters a dynamic relationship between clients and professionals, enhancing trust and adherence to recommended treatments [186].

Enhanced client education is a significant benefit derived from the use of diagnostic tools. By visually demonstrating skin concerns and potential improvements, these tools empower clients to understand their skin better. This understanding is vital for building trust and promoting adherence to treatment plans, as clients are more likely to follow recommendations when they comprehend the rationale behind them [181, 186]. Furthermore, many diagnostic systems are integrated with product databases, enabling them to suggest specific products based on the client's unique skin profile. For example, AI-driven platforms can recommend tailored cleansers, serums, or masks, thereby optimizing the skincare routine for individual needs [186, 187].

Chapter 3

Revolutionary Treatments

Non-Invasive Procedures: Laser, Cryotherapy, and Ultrasound

Laser Technology

Laser technology in cosmetology has revolutionized the beauty and skincare industry by offering precise, effective, and non-invasive solutions for a wide range of aesthetic concerns. Lasers are used for hair removal, skin rejuvenation, pigmentation correction, acne treatment, scar reduction, and more. By targeting specific skin layers with controlled wavelengths of light, lasers deliver remarkable results while minimizing downtime. Here's a detailed overview of the use of lasers in cosmetology:

Lasers in cosmetology operate by emitting a focused beam of light that penetrates the skin to target specific structures or issues. The light energy is absorbed by chromophores in the skin, such as melanin (pigment) or haemoglobin (blood), and is converted into heat. This heat selectively destroys the targeted cells or tissues without damaging the surrounding areas, making lasers highly effective and safe for cosmetic applications.

Advances in Cosmetology

The type of laser used depends on the intended treatment, as different lasers emit light at specific wavelengths that interact with various skin components. Common types include ablative lasers, non-ablative lasers, and fractional lasers, each suited for specific purposes.

Laser technology has become an essential tool in cosmetology, offering precise and effective treatments for a variety of aesthetic concerns. One of the most popular applications is laser hair removal, a procedure that targets melanin within hair follicles to destroy them and prevent further growth. Devices such as diode lasers, alexandrite lasers, and Nd:YAG lasers are commonly used for this purpose, providing long-term hair reduction. This method is considered safe for most skin types, although darker skin tones require specific laser technologies, like the Nd:YAG laser, to minimize risks of burns or pigmentation changes.

Skin rejuvenation is another widely used application of laser technology, aimed at improving skin texture, tone, and elasticity. By stimulating collagen production, lasers help reduce the appearance of wrinkles, fine lines, and sagging skin. Non-ablative lasers, such as Nd:YAG or pulsed dye lasers, work beneath the surface of the skin to achieve these results with minimal downtime. For deeper resurfacing and more dramatic results, ablative lasers like CO_2 or erbium lasers remove the outer layers of skin, effectively addressing more severe signs of aging and imperfections.

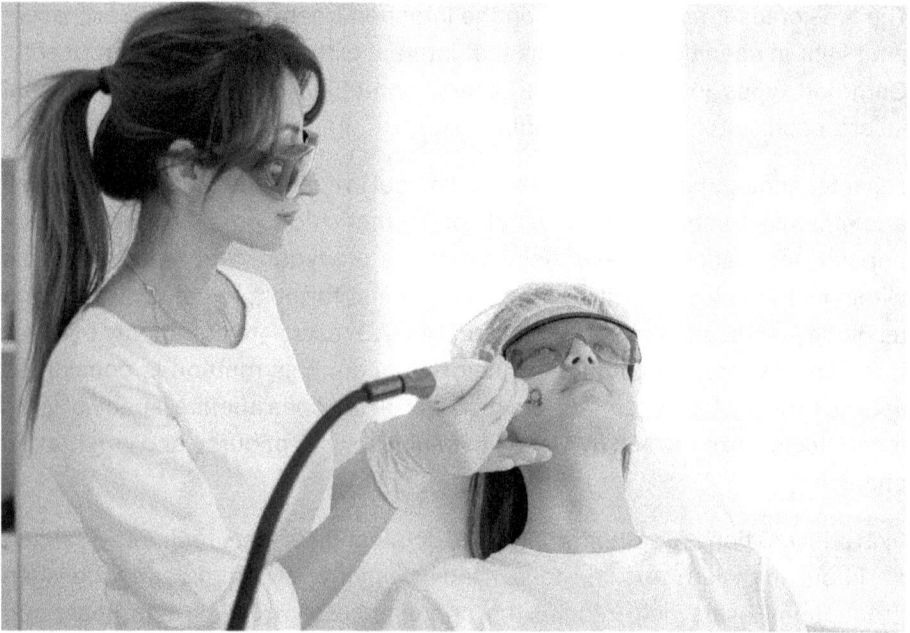

Figure 9: Cosmetologist Performing Scar Whitening with laser. Anna Shvets, CCO. Via Pexels.

Pigmentation correction is a critical area where lasers excel. They are highly effective in treating hyperpigmentation, age spots, melasma, and sun damage by targeting the excess melanin in the skin. Devices like Q-switched and picosecond lasers deliver precise bursts of energy to break down pigment particles, which are then naturally eliminated by the body. This process helps restore an even skin tone and enhances overall brightness, making these treatments particularly appealing for individuals seeking a clear and radiant complexion.

Laser technology also plays a pivotal role in acne treatment, addressing both active acne and the scars it leaves behind. Blue light lasers specifically target acne-causing bacteria (P. acnes), reducing inflammation and preventing future breakouts. Additionally, fractional lasers stimulate collagen production to repair and smooth acne scars. This dual-action approach not only treats immediate concerns but also promotes long-term skin health.

For scar reduction, laser therapy is highly effective in minimizing the appearance of various types of scars, including surgical scars, acne scars, and stretch marks. Fractional CO_2 and erbium lasers create microscopic injuries in the skin to trigger the body's natural healing process. This stimulates the production of new, healthy skin cells, gradually reducing the visibility of scars and improving overall skin texture.

Tattoo removal has seen significant advancements with the use of Q-switched and picosecond lasers. These devices emit rapid pulses of energy to break down tattoo ink particles into smaller fragments, allowing the body's immune system to clear them over time. The number of sessions required depends on factors such as the size, colour, and age of the tattoo, but the precision of these lasers ensures effective results with minimal impact on the surrounding skin.

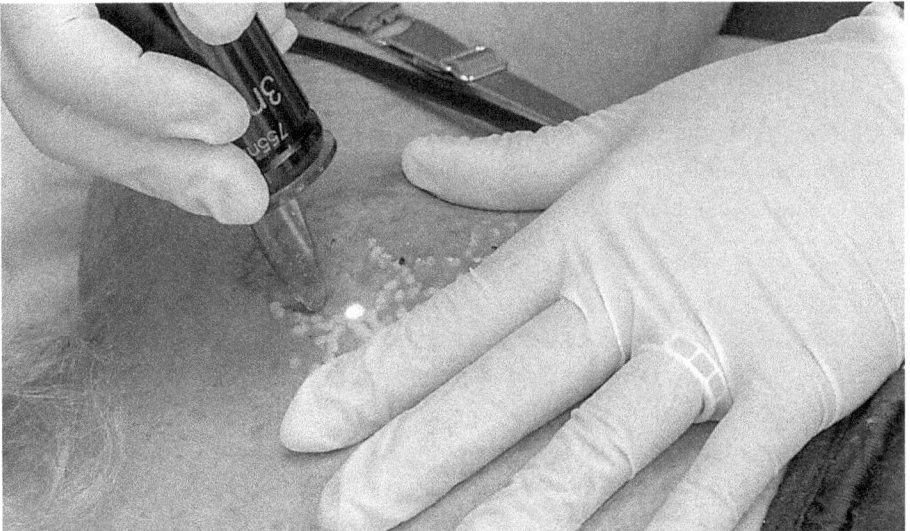

Figure 10: Laser tattoo removal using Q-switch laser. Alice Pien, MD, CC BY-SA 4.0, via Wikimedia Commons.

Lasers are also extensively used to treat vascular lesions such as spider veins, rosacea, and broken capillaries. Pulsed dye lasers and Nd:YAG lasers target haemoglobin in blood vessels, generating heat that causes the vessels to collapse and fade. This non-invasive approach is particularly effective for reducing redness and improving the skin's overall appearance without significant downtime.

Skin tightening is another highly sought-after application of laser technology. Using infrared or radiofrequency energy, lasers heat the deeper layers of the skin to stimulate collagen production and tighten existing collagen fibres. This non-surgical procedure results in firmer, more youthful-looking skin and is often performed with Nd:YAG and fractional lasers, which deliver effective results with minimal discomfort.

Lastly, laser technology is frequently used to remove benign skin lesions such as warts, moles, and skin tags. Ablative lasers like CO2 are especially effective in vaporizing these growths with precision, leaving surrounding tissue unharmed and minimizing the risk of scarring. This approach is both efficient and safe, making it a preferred choice for addressing such concerns.

In cosmetology, different types of lasers are utilized to address various skin and aesthetic concerns, each offering unique capabilities tailored to specific treatments. Understanding the distinctions between these laser technologies is essential for selecting the most appropriate option for individual needs.

Ablative lasers are powerful tools designed to remove the outer layers of the skin, making them particularly effective for deep resurfacing and scar treatment. These lasers, such as CO_2 and erbium lasers, target damaged skin cells on the surface while stimulating collagen production in deeper layers. The process results in dramatic improvements in skin texture, tone, and elasticity, making them ideal for treating severe wrinkles, deep scars, and sun-damaged skin. However, because ablative lasers remove the outermost layer of the skin, the recovery time can be significant. Clients undergoing this treatment may experience redness, swelling, and peeling as the skin heals, but the results are long-lasting and transformative.

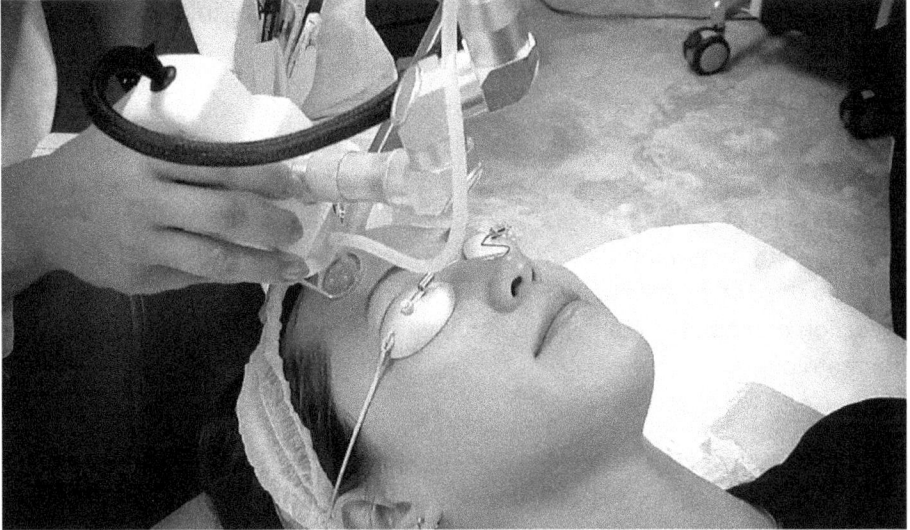

Figure 11: Doctor performing CO2 Fractional laser resurfacing on a patient. Alice Pien, MD, CC BY-SA 4.0, via Wikimedia Commons.

Non-ablative lasers, on the other hand, work beneath the skin's surface without causing damage to the outer layer. These lasers, such as Nd:YAG and pulsed dye lasers, are commonly used for skin rejuvenation, pigmentation correction, and treating vascular issues like spider veins or rosacea. By heating the deeper layers of the skin, non-ablative lasers stimulate collagen production and improve overall skin tone and texture. The advantage of these lasers is their minimal downtime, as the skin's surface remains intact, making them a popular choice for clients seeking effective results without extended recovery periods.

Fractional lasers represent a hybrid approach, combining the benefits of both ablative and non-ablative technologies. These lasers create microscopic zones of thermal damage in the skin while leaving the surrounding tissue untouched. This precise targeting allows the skin to heal more quickly and reduces the risk of side effects compared to fully ablative treatments. Fractional lasers are effective for treating a range of concerns, including scars, wrinkles, and pigmentation issues. They are often used for clients seeking significant improvements with a shorter recovery time compared to traditional ablative lasers.

Q-switched lasers are specialized devices that emit high-intensity pulses of light in extremely short durations. This technology makes them particularly effective for pigmentation treatments and tattoo removal. The laser energy targets melanin or tattoo ink particles, breaking them into smaller fragments that the body's immune system naturally clears over time. Q-switched lasers are also used to treat conditions like age spots, freckles, and melasma. Their precision and ability to target specific pigments make them a versatile tool in cosmetology.

Picosecond lasers take precision and speed to the next level, operating at incredibly fast speeds to deliver light energy to the skin. These lasers are especially effective for breaking down pigment particles, such as those in tattoos or areas of hyperpigmentation, more efficiently than traditional lasers. The rapid pulses reduce heat damage to the surrounding skin, minimizing side effects and improving patient comfort. Picosecond lasers also require fewer sessions to achieve results compared to Q-switched lasers, making them an advanced option for clients seeking faster outcomes with less disruption.

Each of these laser technologies plays a critical role in modern cosmetology, offering tailored solutions for a wide range of skin concerns. Whether for deep resurfacing, non-invasive rejuvenation, or precise pigment targeting, these lasers provide effective and often transformative results. The choice of laser depends on the client's specific needs, desired outcomes, and tolerance for recovery, allowing skincare professionals to deliver highly personalized treatments.

Laser treatments are highly precise, targeting specific areas without affecting surrounding tissues. This precision reduces downtime and ensures safer procedures. Lasers are also versatile, addressing a wide range of aesthetic concerns from hair removal to advanced skin resurfacing. Most treatments are non-invasive or minimally invasive, providing effective results with little to no recovery time. Additionally, lasers stimulate natural processes like collagen production, offering long-term benefits for skin health.

While lasers are highly effective, they are not suitable for everyone. Factors like skin type, existing medical conditions, and the nature of the concern must be carefully evaluated. Certain lasers, particularly those targeting melanin, can pose a risk of hyperpigmentation or burns in darker skin tones if not used correctly. It's crucial for practitioners to be well-trained and for clients to follow pre- and post-treatment care instructions to minimize risks and maximize results.

Setting up laser systems in a cosmetology setting involves significant costs that vary based on the type of laser, its capabilities, and additional requirements such as training, facility upgrades, and ongoing maintenance. Below is a detailed breakdown of the costs associated with setting up each type of laser system (Approximate costs in USD in 2024/25):

Ablative Lasers (e.g., CO2 and Erbium Lasers): Ablative lasers are high-powered systems used for deep resurfacing and scar treatments. They require advanced technology and precise calibration, which translates into higher initial and operational costs.

- **Equipment Costs**: The purchase price for ablative lasers ranges from $50,000 to $150,000, depending on the brand, model, and additional features such as dual-mode functionality (ablative and fractional capabilities).

- **Facility Requirements**: Ablative laser treatments require a sterile and controlled environment. Upgrading treatment rooms to meet these standards can cost between $5,000 and $20,000, including proper ventilation systems and medical-grade equipment.

- **Training**: Proper training for ablative lasers is essential due to their intensity and potential risks. Training programs for staff can range from $1,000 to $5,000 per person, depending on the certification and depth of the course.

- **Maintenance**: Annual maintenance contracts typically cost $5,000 to $10,000, covering calibration, software updates, and routine inspections.

- **Consumables**: Some ablative lasers require specific consumables such as cooling gels or handpiece components, costing around $500 to $1,000 per month.

Non-Ablative Lasers (e.g., Nd:YAG and Pulsed Dye Lasers): Non-ablative lasers are less invasive and target deeper skin layers without damaging the surface, making them a versatile option for skin rejuvenation and pigmentation treatments.

- **Equipment Costs**: These systems generally cost between $30,000 and $100,000, with variations based on the wavelength range and additional features.

- **Facility Requirements**: Non-ablative lasers require less stringent environmental controls than ablative lasers, but upgrading treatment rooms to accommodate the equipment may still cost $3,000 to $10,000.

- **Training**: Staff training for non-ablative lasers typically costs $500 to $2,500 per person, as the technology is easier to operate compared to ablative lasers.

- **Maintenance**: Annual maintenance costs range from $3,000 to $7,000, depending on the complexity of the system.

- **Consumables**: Non-ablative lasers may require fewer consumables than ablative lasers, with monthly costs ranging from $200 to $500.

Fractional Lasers (Ablative and Non-Ablative Types): Fractional lasers combine the benefits of ablative and non-ablative technologies, making them effective yet versatile. They are commonly used for scars, wrinkles, and pigmentation.

- **Equipment Costs**: Fractional laser systems typically cost between $50,000 and $120,000. Dual-mode systems that can switch between ablative and non-ablative modes tend to be on the higher end of this range.

Advances in Cosmetology

- **Facility Requirements**: Setting up for fractional lasers requires moderate room modifications, costing between $5,000 and $15,000 to ensure compliance with safety standards.

- **Training**: Training costs for fractional lasers are generally between $1,000 and $3,000 per person, as these systems require knowledge of dual functionalities.

- **Maintenance**: Maintenance contracts for fractional lasers cost around $4,000 to $8,000 annually.

- **Consumables**: Consumables for fractional lasers, such as disposable tips and cooling agents, typically cost $300 to $800 per month.

Q-Switched Lasers: Q-switched lasers are primarily used for pigmentation treatments and tattoo removal. They deliver short, high-intensity pulses to break down pigments effectively.

- **Equipment Costs**: Q-switched lasers are priced between $40,000 and $100,000, depending on the power, pulse duration, and wavelength flexibility.

- **Facility Requirements**: Minimal room upgrades are needed, costing around $2,000 to $8,000, as these lasers are less invasive.

- **Training**: Training costs range from $500 to $2,000 per person, focusing on safe and effective use for pigmentation and tattoo removal.

- **Maintenance**: Annual maintenance fees are typically $3,000 to $6,000.

- **Consumables**: Monthly consumable costs, such as cooling accessories and protective eyewear, range between $200 and $400.

Picosecond Lasers: Picosecond lasers are advanced systems used for tattoo removal and pigmentation correction, delivering faster and more precise results than Q-switched lasers.

- **Equipment Costs**: Picosecond lasers are among the most expensive, with prices ranging from $100,000 to $250,000. Their advanced technology justifies the high upfront cost.

- **Facility Requirements**: Room modifications for picosecond lasers cost approximately $5,000 to $15,000, ensuring compliance with safety standards for high-power systems.

- **Training**: Training costs for picosecond lasers range from $1,000 to $3,000 per person, as these systems require specialized knowledge for optimal use.

- **Maintenance**: Maintenance contracts cost between $6,000 and $12,000 annually, reflecting the sophistication of the technology.

- **Consumables**: Consumables for picosecond lasers, including replacement handpieces and filters, cost around $500 to $1,000 per month.

Table 2: Summary of costs associated with laser systems.

Laser Type	Equipment Cost	Facility Upgrades	Training	Maintenance	Monthly Consumables
Ablative Lasers	$50,000 - $150,000	$5,000 - $20,000	$1,000 - $5,000	$5,000 - $10,000	$500 - $1,000
Non-Ablative Lasers	$30,000 - $100,000	$3,000 - $10,000	$500 - $2,500	$3,000 - $7,000	$200 - $500
Fractional Lasers	$50,000 - $120,000	$5,000 - $15,000	$1,000 - $3,000	$4,000 - $8,000	$300 - $800
Q-Switched Lasers	$40,000 - $100,000	$2,000 - $8,000	$500 - $2,000	$3,000 - $6,000	$200 - $400
Picosecond Lasers	$100,000 - $250,000	$5,000 - $15,000	$1,000 - $3,000	$6,000 - $12,000	$500 - $1,000

Advances in Cosmetology

This detailed breakdown helps cosmetology professionals evaluate the financial commitment associated with each laser system and choose the one that aligns best with their business goals and client needs.

Cryotherapy in Cosmetology

Cryotherapy, defined as "cold therapy," has emerged as a treatment in cosmetology, utilizing extremely low temperatures to enhance skin health and address various skin conditions. This non-invasive approach has gained traction within the beauty industry due to its rapid and effective results, including improvements in skin tone, reduction of puffiness, and overall skin rejuvenation [188]. The applications of cryotherapy can be categorized into local and whole-body treatments, each serving distinct purposes depending on the desired aesthetic outcomes.

The mechanism of cryotherapy involves exposing the skin to temperatures typically ranging from -100°C to -180°C for brief periods. Local cryotherapy utilizes devices such as cryo wands or sprays to deliver controlled bursts of cold air or liquid nitrogen to specific skin areas. This exposure induces vasoconstriction, reducing inflammation and triggering a natural healing response [189]. Upon rewarming, blood vessels dilate, facilitating the flow of oxygen and nutrient-rich blood to the treated area, which aids in skin repair and rejuvenation [188]. Whole-body cryotherapy, conversely, involves standing in a cryotherapy chamber where the entire body is subjected to sub-zero temperatures for two to four minutes. While primarily utilized for general wellness, this method also offers cosmetic benefits, such as enhanced skin elasticity and reduced inflammation [190].

Research supports the efficacy of cryotherapy in treating various dermatological conditions. For instance, a study comparing cryotherapy with electrosurgery demonstrated that both methods are safe and effective for treating sebaceous hyperplasia, seborrheic keratosis, cherry angiomas, and skin tags [191]. Additionally, cryotherapy has been shown to be beneficial in managing keloids, particularly those with higher blood flow, which respond more favourably to treatment [192]. The combination of cryotherapy with topical treatments, such as ingenol mebutate for actinic keratosis, has also been explored, indicating that cryotherapy can enhance the absorption and efficacy of these medications [193].

Whole-body cryotherapy has been investigated for its impact on skin conditions like atopic dermatitis, where it was found to reduce skin irritations and inflammation without adverse effects [190]. The immunological responses triggered by cryotherapy further support its application in treating immune-related skin diseases [194]. The standardization of cryotherapeutic techniques has minimized adverse events, reinforcing its safety and efficacy across various skin disorders [195].

Figure 12: Cryotherapy chamber is an individual, tube-shaped enclosure that covers a person's body with an open-top to keep the head at room temperature. ВитяВетер, CC BY 4.0, via Wikimedia Commons.

Cryotherapy has a wide range of applications in cosmetology, offering effective, non-invasive solutions for improving skin health and addressing aesthetic concerns. One of its most sought-after uses is in skin rejuvenation and anti-aging treatments. Cryotherapy stimulates collagen production, a key component of youthful and elastic skin. As collagen levels increase, the skin becomes firmer, reducing the appearance of fine lines and wrinkles. The cold exposure also tightens pores and boosts circulation, delivering oxygen and nutrients to the skin. These effects combine to enhance overall skin tone and texture, giving the skin a radiant, refreshed, and more youthful appearance.

Another significant application of cryotherapy is in reducing puffiness and dark circles, particularly around the eyes. By constricting blood vessels, cold therapy helps reduce swelling and inflammation in targeted areas. This not only alleviates puffiness but also minimizes the appearance of dark circles under the eyes. Cryotherapy's ability to calm inflammation makes it a quick and effective solution for individuals looking to improve their appearance before important events or occasions.

Cryotherapy is also an effective treatment for managing acne. The cold temperatures reduce inflammation and soothe irritated skin, helping to calm active breakouts. Additionally, cryotherapy targets overactive sebaceous glands, which are often responsible for excess oil production and clogged pores. The cold exposure also kills acne-causing bacteria on the skin's surface, making cryotherapy a comprehensive solution for managing both active acne and preventing future breakouts.

For individuals with chronic skin conditions like eczema, psoriasis, or dermatitis, cryotherapy provides much-needed relief. The cold exposure reduces inflammation, calms irritated skin, and alleviates redness, itching, and discomfort. By targeting the underlying inflammatory processes associated with these conditions, cryotherapy offers a non-invasive and drug-free alternative for managing symptoms. Many clients report significant improvements in their skin's appearance and comfort after regular cryotherapy sessions.

Cryotherapy has also found a prominent place in body contouring through a process known as cryolipolysis, commonly referred to as "fat freezing." This treatment targets localized fat deposits in areas such as the abdomen, thighs, and arms. Devices like CoolSculpting expose fat cells to freezing temperatures, causing them to crystallize and break down. Over time, the body naturally eliminates these fat cells, resulting in a slimmer and more contoured appearance. This non-invasive method is especially appealing to clients seeking fat reduction without the risks and downtime associated with surgical procedures.

Localized cryotherapy is highly effective in removing benign skin growths like skin tags and warts. Using liquid nitrogen, the procedure involves applying extreme cold to the abnormal tissue, which causes it to freeze and eventually fall off naturally. This method is precise, quick, and minimally invasive, making it a popular choice for addressing minor skin imperfections in a cosmetology setting.

Cryotherapy also plays a role in improving skin hydration. The treatment enhances the skin's ability to absorb serums and moisturizers applied during or after a session. By tightening the skin and boosting its moisture retention capabilities, cryotherapy leaves the skin feeling supple, smooth, and deeply hydrated. This application is particularly beneficial for individuals with dry or dehydrated skin, as it helps restore and maintain optimal hydration levels.

Finally, cryotherapy extends its benefits to scalp therapy, where it improves circulation and stimulates hair follicles. By increasing blood flow to the scalp, cryotherapy promotes healthier hair growth and helps reduce inflammation associated with scalp conditions. Clients seeking solutions for thinning hair or an irritated scalp can benefit from cryotherapy treatments, which contribute to improved hair health and appearance over time.

Cryotherapy has gained significant attention in the field of cosmetology due to its numerous benefits, which include being a non-invasive and safe procedure, providing immediate results, and offering a wide range of applications.

Cryotherapy is recognized as a non-surgical procedure with minimal risks and no downtime, making it an appealing choice for clients seeking quick and effective results. The safety profile of cryotherapy is highlighted in various studies, which indicate that it can be performed with minimal complications, particularly in patients with lighter skin types who are less prone to post-inflammatory hyperpigmentation (PIH) [196, 197]. However, it is important to note that post-cryotherapy hypopigmentation can occur, especially in individuals with darker skin types [196]. Moreover, cryotherapy has been shown to be effective in treating various skin conditions without the need for invasive techniques, thus reducing the risk associated with surgical interventions [198].

Many clients report immediate improvements in skin tone and reduction in puffiness following a single cryotherapy session. This is supported by findings that indicate cryotherapy can enhance the skin's appearance rapidly, with some studies noting that patients experience significant cosmetic improvements after just one treatment [198]. Additionally, the long-term benefits of cryotherapy, such as increased collagen production, become more pronounced with repeated treatments, contributing to sustained skin rejuvenation [195].

Cryotherapy is versatile and can be applied to various cosmetic concerns, including anti-aging, acne treatment, and fat reduction. For instance, studies have demonstrated its efficacy in treating conditions such as sebaceous hyperplasia and actinic keratoses, showcasing its broad applicability in dermatological and cosmetic practices [198, 199]. Furthermore, the use of cryotherapy in combination with other treatments, such as lasers, has been explored, indicating its potential to enhance the overall effectiveness of cosmetic procedures [200].

Cryotherapy has been shown to improve circulation by boosting blood flow and oxygen delivery to the skin, which enhances overall skin health and appearance. Research indicates that cryotherapy can lead to initial vasoconstriction followed by vasodilation, resulting in improved microcirculation and nutrient delivery to the skin [201]. This physiological response not only aids in skin rejuvenation but also contributes to the healing of various skin conditions, further emphasizing the therapeutic benefits of cryotherapy in cosmetology [201].

Beyond its cosmetic benefits, cryotherapy sessions often leave clients feeling refreshed and invigorated, contributing to overall mental and physical well-being. The cooling effect of cryotherapy can induce a state of relaxation, which may help alleviate stress and promote a sense of wellness [202]. This aspect of cryotherapy is particularly appealing to clients seeking holistic treatments that address both aesthetic and psychological needs.

Advances in Cosmetology

Cryotherapy in cosmetology is performed using a range of specialized equipment, each tailored to specific applications and treatment goals. The choice of equipment depends on whether the procedure involves whole-body cryotherapy, localized skin treatments, or body contouring through fat reduction.

Cryotherapy chambers are commonly used for whole-body treatments. These chambers expose the entire body, excluding the head, to extremely cold temperatures ranging from -100°C to -180°C. The client stands in the chamber for a short duration, typically two to four minutes. This process triggers vasoconstriction, followed by vasodilation when the body returns to normal temperature, promoting circulation and oxygen delivery to the skin. Whole-body cryotherapy is often used for general wellness, skin rejuvenation, and reducing inflammation. These chambers are sophisticated and require precise calibration and safety mechanisms to ensure the controlled delivery of cold exposure without causing discomfort or harm.

For localized treatments, cryo wands or cryo sprays are commonly employed. These handheld devices allow professionals to deliver targeted bursts of cold air or liquid nitrogen directly to specific areas of the skin. They are particularly effective for addressing puffiness, inflammation, and localized concerns such as dark circles, acne, or skin tags. The devices are highly versatile and can be adjusted to treat different areas with varying levels of intensity. Their precision ensures that the cold exposure is confined to the target area, minimizing any impact on surrounding skin. Cryo wands and sprays are compact and user-friendly, making them a staple in many cosmetology practices.

Cryolipolysis devices, such as CoolSculpting, are designed specifically for fat reduction and body contouring. These devices use applicators that are placed on targeted areas like the abdomen, thighs, or arms. The applicators cool the fat cells to freezing temperatures, causing them to crystallize and break down without affecting surrounding tissues. Over the following weeks, the body naturally eliminates the destroyed fat cells, resulting in a slimmer appearance. Cryolipolysis is a non-invasive alternative to surgical fat reduction, offering clients a safer and more convenient option with minimal downtime. These devices are more complex and require proper training to operate, as well as thorough consultations to ensure the client is a suitable candidate.

Cryotherapy treatments are typically quick, with sessions lasting between 5 and 30 minutes, depending on the type and scope of the procedure. Whole-body treatments are shorter, usually not exceeding four minutes, to prevent overexposure to extreme cold. Localized treatments may take longer, particularly if multiple areas are being addressed. Cryolipolysis sessions, on the other hand, can last up to an hour as the applicators need time to effectively freeze the fat cells. Despite the varying durations, the procedures are efficient and designed to fit seamlessly into clients' schedules.

A trained professional is always responsible for administering cryotherapy treatments to ensure the client's safety and comfort. The professional begins by assessing the client's skin or body condition and determining the appropriate treatment plan. During the procedure, they monitor the client closely to ensure the cold exposure is applied effectively without causing discomfort or adverse effects. Proper training is essential for the operator, especially for advanced equipment like cryolipolysis devices and cryotherapy chambers, as improper use could lead to skin damage or other complications.

While cryotherapy is generally safe, it may cause temporary redness, numbness, or irritation in some clients. It is not recommended for individuals with certain conditions, such as Raynaud's disease, severe cold sensitivity, or circulatory disorders. A thorough consultation and skin assessment should be conducted before the treatment to ensure its suitability for the client.

The costs associated with cryotherapy in cosmetology vary widely depending on the type of treatment provided, the equipment used, and the scope of the procedure. For clients, the pricing for individual sessions is generally determined by the type of cryotherapy they undergo, while for salons and spas, the cost to implement cryotherapy services depends on the type of equipment purchased and the infrastructure required.

Local cryotherapy is one of the more affordable options for clients, with treatments typically ranging from $50 to $150 per session. These treatments focus on specific areas of the body or face, such as reducing puffiness around the eyes, alleviating inflammation, or targeting acne. The cost reflects the shorter duration and localized nature of these procedures, making them an accessible option for clients seeking quick and effective results for targeted concerns.

Advances in Cosmetology

Whole-body cryotherapy is another popular service offered by many wellness centers and spas. The cost for a single session of whole-body cryotherapy generally falls between $30 and $100. Clients step into a cryotherapy chamber where their entire body is exposed to sub-zero temperatures for a few minutes. This type of treatment is often less expensive than localized or fat-reduction cryotherapy because it is designed for broader benefits, such as improved circulation, skin rejuvenation, and overall wellness. Many providers offer package deals or memberships for clients who want to undergo regular sessions, further reducing the per-session cost.

Cryolipolysis, or fat freezing, is the most expensive form of cryotherapy due to its specialized equipment and the time-intensive nature of the procedure. The cost for a single session of cryolipolysis typically ranges from $600 to $1,500, depending on the area being treated and the number of applicators used. Larger areas like the abdomen or thighs may require higher costs, while smaller areas like the chin may fall on the lower end of the pricing spectrum. Despite the higher cost, cryolipolysis is a popular choice for clients seeking non-invasive body contouring, as it eliminates fat cells without the risks or recovery time associated with surgical procedures.

For salons and spas looking to offer cryotherapy services, the initial investment in equipment represents a significant cost. Cryotherapy chambers, which are used for whole-body treatments, typically range from $30,000 to $100,000, depending on their size, features, and manufacturer. These chambers are sophisticated pieces of equipment designed to safely and effectively deliver sub-zero temperatures while ensuring client comfort and safety.

Localized cryotherapy devices, such as cryo wands or sprays, are more affordable, with prices ranging from $10,000 to $30,000. These devices are ideal for salons or spas that want to offer targeted treatments without the high investment required for a full-body chamber. Cryolipolysis devices, such as CoolSculpting machines, are among the most expensive, with prices ranging from $50,000 to $100,000 or more. These systems require multiple applicators and advanced cooling technology to achieve their fat-reduction effects, contributing to their higher cost.

Beyond the purchase of equipment, salons and spas must also account for additional costs, such as staff training, facility upgrades, and maintenance.

Training programs for cryotherapy equipment typically cost between $1,000 and $5,000, depending on the complexity of the device and the level of certification required. Facility upgrades may include installing proper ventilation systems, purchasing safety equipment, or creating dedicated treatment rooms, with costs ranging from $5,000 to $20,000. Maintenance fees for cryotherapy machines, including routine servicing and repairs, can range from $2,000 to $10,000 annually, depending on the type and frequency of use.

In summary, the costs associated with cryotherapy treatments and implementation depend on the specific type of procedure and equipment. Clients can expect to pay between $30 and $1,500 per session, depending on the scope of the treatment, while salons and spas must be prepared to invest between $10,000 and $100,000 for the equipment, along with additional costs for training and maintenance. Despite the upfront investment, cryotherapy services offer significant potential for revenue generation and client satisfaction, making them a worthwhile addition to many cosmetology and wellness businesses.

Ultrasound in Cosmetology

Ultrasound technology has emerged as a significant advancement in cosmetology, providing non-invasive solutions for various skin and aesthetic treatments. By employing high-frequency sound waves, typically ranging from 1 MHz to 10 MHz, ultrasound devices deliver targeted energy into the deeper layers of the skin and underlying tissues. This process stimulates cellular activity, enhances circulation, and promotes collagen production, making ultrasound a versatile tool in the beauty and skincare industry [203, 204].

The mechanism of ultrasound in cosmetology involves the generation of vibrations that create both heat and micro-massage effects within the targeted tissues. This energy penetrates the skin without damaging the outer layers, ensuring safe and precise treatments [204, 205]. The ability to adjust the intensity, depth, and frequency of the ultrasound waves allows practitioners to tailor treatments for specific outcomes, such as skin tightening, fat reduction, or enhanced absorption of skincare products [205, 206]. Furthermore, ultrasound is often combined with other technologies, such as radiofrequency (RF) or microcurrents, to enhance its effectiveness [203, 204].

In terms of applications, ultrasound is widely recognized for its efficacy in skin rejuvenation and tightening. Treatments utilizing ultrasound, such as Ultherapy, effectively lift sagging skin on the face, neck, and décolletage by stimulating collagen and elastin production [203, 204]. Clinical studies have demonstrated that ultrasound-based treatments lead to noticeable improvements in skin elasticity and texture over time, with results continuing to enhance as collagen production increases [203, 206].

Ultrasound devices are effective for deep cleansing and exfoliation. The vibrations generated by ultrasound help dislodge dirt, oil, and dead skin cells from the pores, resulting in a thorough yet gentle cleansing process suitable for sensitive skin types [204, 206]. This deep cleansing prepares the skin for better absorption of active ingredients in skincare products, a process known as sonophoresis, which significantly enhances the efficacy of topical treatments [203, 204].

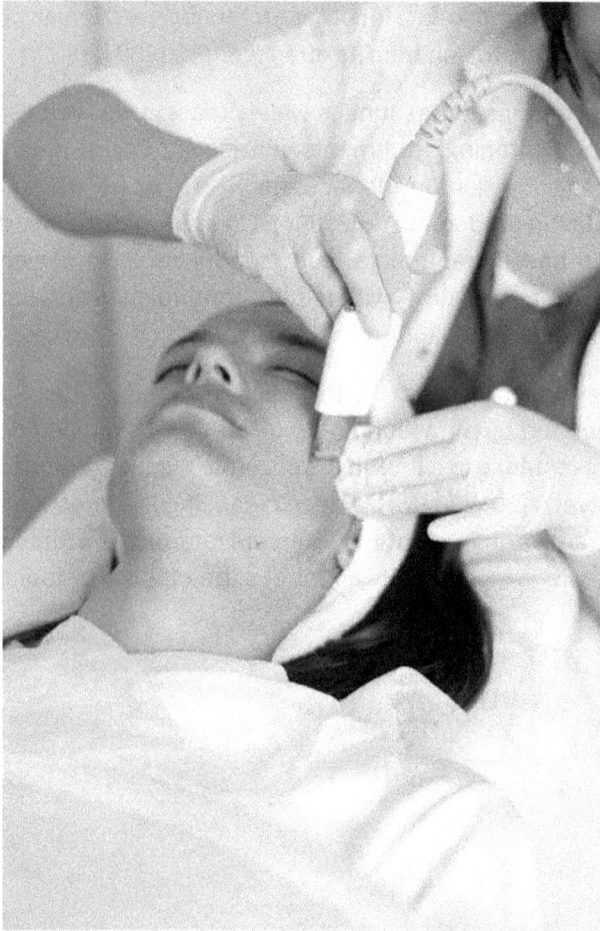

Figure 13: Client receiving cleansing therapy with professional ultrasonic equipment. Anna Shvets, CC0, via Pexels.

Ultrasound technology is also employed for non-invasive fat reduction and body contouring. High-intensity focused ultrasound (HIFU) specifically targets fat cells beneath the skin, leading to their breakdown without affecting surrounding tissues [207]. This method has gained popularity for its effectiveness in sculpting areas such as the abdomen, thighs, and upper arms, with the body naturally eliminating the destroyed fat cells over time [207].

Advances in Cosmetology

Additionally, ultrasound therapy has shown promise in treating acne and promoting skin healing by increasing blood circulation and reducing inflammation, thus supporting the skin's natural repair processes [204, 206].

The benefits of ultrasound in cosmetology are manifold. Treatments are non-invasive and painless, requiring no downtime, which appeals to clients seeking effective results without discomfort [203, 204]. The precision of ultrasound technology allows for targeted treatment of specific skin layers or fat deposits, minimizing the risk of damage to surrounding tissues [204, 206]. Furthermore, ultrasound's versatility enables it to address a wide range of concerns, from anti-aging and skin tightening to acne management and fat reduction [203, 204]. Immediate results, such as smoother skin and improved hydration, can be observed, while longer-term benefits, such as enhanced collagen production and fat reduction, continue to develop over time [203, 204].

Ultrasound devices in cosmetology come in various types, each specifically designed to address different skin and body concerns. These devices leverage advanced ultrasound technology to deliver targeted treatments that are effective, non-invasive, and safe. By using sound waves to penetrate deep into the skin or underlying tissues, they provide a wide range of aesthetic benefits, from lifting and tightening to deep cleansing and fat reduction. Each type of device has unique features and applications that make it suitable for specific cosmetology treatments.

Ultherapy is one of the most recognized ultrasound devices in the field of cosmetology. As a high-intensity focused ultrasound (HIFU) system, it is widely used for non-surgical skin lifting and tightening. Ultherapy works by delivering focused ultrasound energy to the deeper layers of the skin, specifically targeting the dermis and the superficial muscular aponeurotic system (SMAS) layer. This stimulates the production of collagen and elastin, resulting in firmer, more lifted skin over time. Ultherapy is commonly used to treat sagging skin on the face, neck, and décolletage, offering a natural-looking lift without the need for surgery or downtime. Its precision and effectiveness have made it a preferred choice for clients seeking a youthful appearance.

Skin scrubbers are another category of ultrasound devices, designed primarily for deep cleansing and exfoliation. These portable devices use ultrasonic vibrations to remove dirt, oil, and dead skin cells from the surface of the skin.

The gentle yet effective exfoliation process helps unclog pores, leaving the skin refreshed and revitalized. Skin scrubbers are often incorporated into facial treatments to prepare the skin for better absorption of serums and moisturizers. Their compact design and ease of use make them a staple in many cosmetology practices, particularly for clients with sensitive or acne-prone skin.

For body contouring, devices like Liposonix and UltraShape use high-intensity focused ultrasound to target and reduce fat deposits. These machines deliver ultrasound energy to specific areas, such as the abdomen, thighs, or flanks, without affecting the surrounding tissues. The focused energy causes the fat cells to break down, which are then naturally eliminated by the body over time. Body contouring ultrasound devices are popular for non-invasive fat reduction and body shaping, offering clients a safe alternative to surgical procedures like liposuction. They are particularly effective for individuals who struggle with stubborn fat that does not respond to diet or exercise.

Facial ultrasound devices are smaller, more portable systems designed to enhance product absorption and rejuvenate facial skin. These devices use ultrasound waves to create microchannels in the skin, allowing active ingredients in serums and creams to penetrate deeper into the dermis. This process, known as sonophoresis, ensures that the skin receives maximum benefits from the applied products. Additionally, the gentle vibrations stimulate blood circulation and lymphatic drainage, improving skin texture and radiance. Facial ultrasound devices are a versatile tool in cosmetology, often used in combination with other treatments to enhance their effectiveness and provide a comprehensive approach to skincare.

Each type of ultrasound device plays a crucial role in modern cosmetology, addressing a wide range of client needs with precision and efficiency. From non-surgical lifting and tightening with Ultherapy to deep cleansing with skin scrubbers, body contouring with HIFU machines, and product penetration with facial ultrasound devices, these technologies are essential for delivering high-quality aesthetic treatments. Their versatility and effectiveness have made ultrasound devices a cornerstone of cosmetology, providing clients with innovative solutions for enhancing their appearance and achieving their beauty goals.

Advances in Cosmetology

Ultrasound refers to sound waves with frequencies above 20 kHz, exceeding the upper limit of the human audible range, which is 20 Hz to 20,000 Hz. In cosmetic applications, high-frequency ultrasound treatments typically operate in the range of 1 MHz to 10 MHz. This frequency range allows ultrasound waves to penetrate different layers of the skin with precision, making it suitable for a variety of treatments such as rejuvenation, tightening, deep cleansing, and product penetration.

The generation of ultrasound waves relies on a piezo-ceramic transducer system, which utilizes the reverse piezoelectric effect. In this process, a piezo-ceramic element, often made of quartz crystals, is subjected to alternating current (AC) voltage. The application of this voltage causes the atoms within the crystal to move, generating ultrasound waves. This sophisticated mechanism ensures a consistent and controlled delivery of ultrasound energy during cosmetic treatments.

For ultrasound to effectively penetrate the skin, a coupling medium is essential, as air acts as an excellent dampener of ultrasound waves. Liquids, on the other hand, facilitate the rapid transmission of these waves. A gel is the most suitable coupling medium, as it stays on the skin for the duration of the treatment and ensures optimal transmission of the ultrasound waves. To enhance precision and safety, many devices incorporate a skin contact detection sensor, such as in the IONTO-SONO Intense handpiece. These sensors ensure that ultrasound waves are emitted only when proper skin contact is established, indicated by a continuously lit LED strip on the device. The higher the frequency of the program being used, the more sensitive the skin contact detection sensor becomes, highlighting the importance of maintaining an airtight coupling for effective results.

The efficacy and depth of ultrasound penetration during treatments depend on several parameters: frequency, intensity, mode, and duration. Frequency, measured in hertz (Hz), determines the number of oscillations emitted per second. In cosmetic applications, frequencies of 1 MHz, 3 MHz, and 10 MHz are commonly used, each with distinct penetration depths. For example, a 1 MHz frequency produces a wavelength of 1.5 mm and penetrates approximately 3.0 cm into the skin, making it suitable for deep tissue treatments. A 3 MHz frequency generates a smaller wavelength of 0.5 mm and penetrates up to 1.0

cm, ideal for mid-layer treatments. A 10 MHz frequency has a wavelength of 0.15 mm and penetrates just 0.3 cm, targeting superficial layers of the skin.

Intensity, measured as acoustic power per unit area in watts per square centimetre (W/cm^2), influences both the penetration depth and the amount of heat generated during treatment. Low-intensity settings (0.1–0.3 W/cm^2) generate minimal heat, while high-intensity settings (0.8–2.0 W/cm^2) produce significant thermal effects, which can enhance blood circulation and metabolism in the skin.

The mode of ultrasound emission refers to whether the sound waves are delivered continuously or in pulses. Continuous mode provides a steady stream of ultrasound waves, creating intense thermal action that is beneficial for robust or atrophic skin types. Pulsed mode introduces controlled pauses between sound waves, reducing the thermal effects and making it suitable for sensitive skin or conditions such as blemishes and couperose. Different pulse ratios, such as 1:3 or 1:10, are programmed based on the treatment type and the client's skin condition to ensure safe and effective application.

The action of ultrasound in cosmetic treatments can be categorized into three primary effects: thermal, mechanical, and biochemical. The thermal effect increases blood flow and activates cellular metabolism, promoting overall skin health. The mechanical effect occurs through alternating pressure and vacuum phases, creating micro-massages that stimulate the fibroblasts responsible for collagen production. This stimulation helps improve skin elasticity and firmness. The biochemical effect enhances the absorption of active substances into the skin by increasing the permeability of the skin's barrier. This allows skincare products to penetrate deeper into the dermal layers, maximizing their efficacy.

The use of three standard frequencies—1 MHz, 3 MHz, and 10 MHz—ensures a versatile approach to treating various skin concerns. Lower frequencies are used for deeper tissue stimulation, while higher frequencies target superficial layers with precision. This versatility makes ultrasound a powerful tool in cosmetology, offering a triple effect that addresses multiple skin concerns in a single treatment.

Advances in Cosmetology

The procedure for ultrasound treatment in cosmetology is a meticulously structured process that emphasizes client comfort, safety, and the attainment of optimal results. Initially, the process begins with a comprehensive consultation between the client and the practitioner. This step is crucial as it allows the practitioner to evaluate the client's skin condition, identify specific needs, and discuss treatment goals. Such consultations are essential for tailoring the procedure to address unique concerns, including skin tightening, rejuvenation, deep cleansing, or enhanced product absorption [208, 209].

Following the consultation, the skin undergoes a thorough cleansing to eliminate makeup, oils, and impurities that could hinder the treatment's effectiveness. Proper skin preparation is vital to ensure that the ultrasound waves penetrate effectively while minimizing the risk of irritation [210]. After cleansing, a conductive gel is applied to the treatment area. This gel not only facilitates the smooth movement of the ultrasound applicator but also enhances the transmission of ultrasound waves into the skin and prevents friction or discomfort during the procedure. Additionally, it acts as a protective barrier, ensuring that the skin remains hydrated and soothed throughout the session [208, 209].

The practitioner then utilizes an ultrasound applicator to deliver the treatment, moving the handheld device systematically across the skin to ensure even coverage of the targeted area. The settings on the ultrasound device—such as frequency, intensity, and mode—are adjusted according to the client's specific needs and the depth of treatment required. For example, lower frequencies are typically employed for deeper tissue stimulation, while higher frequencies are reserved for more superficial skin layers. Continuous monitoring of the device's performance and the client's comfort level allows the practitioner to make necessary adjustments to optimize results [211-213].

The duration of the treatment can vary based on the size and scope of the area being treated. Smaller areas, such as the face or neck, generally require about 30 minutes, whereas larger areas, like the abdomen or thighs, may necessitate up to an hour of treatment. Despite the precision and intensity of the ultrasound waves, the procedure is typically painless, with clients often reporting a gentle warming sensation as the ultrasound energy penetrates their skin. This warmth results from the thermal effects generated by the sound waves, which stimulate circulation and collagen production, contributing to a relaxing experience akin to a soothing facial massage [209, 211, 212].

One of the significant advantages of ultrasound treatments is the absence of downtime. Clients can immediately resume their daily activities post-treatment, making it a convenient option for those with busy schedules. The effects of the treatment, including improved skin texture, firmness, and hydration, are often visible shortly after the session. For procedures aimed at skin tightening or collagen stimulation, results may continue to enhance over the following weeks as the skin regenerates and produces new collagen [208, 209, 211].

The costs associated with ultrasound treatments in cosmetology can vary significantly depending on the type of treatment, the complexity of the procedure, and the area being treated. For clients, these treatments represent an investment in non-invasive, effective cosmetic solutions tailored to a variety of aesthetic concerns. For businesses, such as salons and spas, the upfront costs of equipment and the ongoing expenses required to maintain the technology play a significant role in determining their offerings.

Facial rejuvenation and tightening treatments using ultrasound typically cost between $300 and $1,500 per session. The price variation depends on factors such as the specific device used, the expertise of the practitioner, and the complexity of the treatment area. These sessions often focus on stimulating collagen production and lifting sagging skin, making them a popular choice for clients seeking non-surgical anti-aging solutions. While the initial cost may seem high, many clients find the results worthwhile, particularly as these treatments require little to no downtime and offer visible improvements over time.

Body contouring treatments that use high-intensity focused ultrasound (HIFU) technology are more expensive, with prices ranging from $1,000 to $4,000 per session. These treatments are designed to reduce localized fat deposits and sculpt the body, targeting areas such as the abdomen, thighs, or upper arms. The cost depends on the size of the area being treated, as larger areas require more time and energy to achieve desired results. Body contouring with ultrasound is a non-invasive alternative to surgical procedures like liposuction, making it an attractive option for clients seeking effective fat reduction without the risks or recovery time associated with surgery.

For less intensive treatments, such as deep cleansing or exfoliation, the cost is significantly lower, typically ranging from $50 to $150 per session. These procedures are often included as part of a broader facial treatment and focus on removing dirt, oil, and dead skin cells to leave the skin refreshed and prepped for further skincare. The affordability of these treatments makes them a common choice for regular maintenance or as an add-on service in spas and salons.

For salons and spas looking to offer ultrasound treatments, the initial investment in equipment can vary widely, depending on the type of device and its features. Basic ultrasound devices designed for facial treatments and product absorption can cost as little as $5,000. Advanced devices, such as those used for body contouring or multi-functional systems that combine ultrasound with other technologies like radiofrequency, can cost upwards of $100,000. The choice of equipment depends on the range of services a business intends to offer and its target clientele.

In addition to the initial purchase, businesses must consider ongoing expenses associated with maintaining ultrasound equipment. Regular maintenance is essential to ensure the devices function optimally and comply with safety standards, with annual maintenance costs ranging from $1,000 to $5,000 depending on the complexity of the equipment. Consumables, such as conductive gels, represent another recurring cost. These gels are crucial for facilitating the effective transmission of ultrasound waves into the skin and are typically priced between $10 and $50 per treatment session, depending on the size of the treated area.

Overall, the cost structure of ultrasound treatments reflects the balance between their effectiveness, convenience, and non-invasive nature. For clients, these treatments offer a worthwhile investment in achieving their aesthetic goals. For salons and spas, the initial and ongoing costs of implementing ultrasound technology are offset by the potential for high demand and client satisfaction, making it a valuable addition to their service portfolio. As technology advances and becomes more accessible, ultrasound treatments are likely to remain a key component of modern cosmetology.

Richard Skiba

While ultrasound treatments are generally safe, improper use can lead to minor side effects such as temporary redness or swelling. It is essential that practitioners receive proper training and certification to ensure safe and effective application. Clients with certain medical conditions, such as pacemakers or severe skin disorders, should consult a doctor before undergoing ultrasound treatments.

Ultrasound in cosmetology is a versatile and effective technology that offers solutions for a wide range of skin and aesthetic concerns. Its non-invasive nature, combined with its ability to rejuvenate, tighten, cleanse, and contour, makes it a valuable addition to any beauty practice. With continuous advancements in ultrasound technology, its role in cosmetology is set to expand, providing even more innovative and effective treatments for clients.

Regenerative Techniques: Stem Cell Therapy, Microneedling and PRP

Regenerative techniques in cosmetology refer to advanced treatments and procedures designed to stimulate the body's natural ability to repair, renew, and regenerate skin and tissues. These techniques leverage cutting-edge science and technology to promote cellular regeneration, improve skin texture, reduce signs of aging, and address other cosmetic concerns. Unlike traditional treatments that focus on masking or temporarily improving imperfections, regenerative techniques work at a deeper level to enhance the skin's intrinsic repair mechanisms.

Regenerative techniques in cosmetology aim to leverage the body's intrinsic healing and repair mechanisms to rejuvenate the skin, enhance its appearance, and address various aesthetic concerns. Unlike traditional cosmetic treatments that often provide only temporary solutions, regenerative methods focus on stimulating natural biological processes, such as collagen production, tissue repair, and cellular turnover. This approach is designed to restore and improve skin health over the long term, promoting a more youthful and natural appearance that evolves positively over time [214-216].

Advances in Cosmetology

The increasing popularity of regenerative techniques can be attributed to several factors. Primarily, these treatments offer non-invasive or minimally invasive alternatives to conventional procedures like facelifts or chemical peels, which often require significant downtime and carry higher risks. Techniques such as platelet-rich plasma (PRP) therapy, stem cell treatments, and microneedling enable clients to tackle issues like fine lines, wrinkles, uneven skin tone, and sagging skin without the need for surgical intervention [217-219]. For instance, PRP therapy has been shown to enhance collagen expression and fibroblast proliferation, which are critical for skin rejuvenation [219, 220].

Further, regenerative treatments are favoured for their ability to yield more natural and subtle results. By stimulating the body's own regenerative processes, these techniques typically produce outcomes that appear more authentic and age-appropriate compared to synthetic alternatives. The gradual nature of these treatments allows for improvements in skin texture, tone, and elasticity over time, thereby avoiding the "overdone" appearance that can sometimes accompany more invasive procedures [221-223]. For example, studies have demonstrated that microneedling combined with stem cell-derived media can significantly enhance skin rejuvenation effects, leading to improved brightness and texture [222, 224].

Additionally, regenerative techniques are particularly effective for individuals with specific skin concerns, such as acne scars, pigmentation issues, or skin laxity. These treatments promote healing and tissue regeneration at the cellular level, addressing the underlying causes of skin imperfections rather than merely masking them. Research indicates that stem cell therapies and their secretomes can significantly improve skin conditions by promoting the regeneration of damaged tissues [224-226]. The ability of these treatments to foster long-term improvements not only enhances physical appearance but also boosts self-confidence among clients [227].

Ultimately, the appeal of regenerative techniques lies in their combination of safety, effectiveness, and longevity. Clients are increasingly attracted to the prospect of enhancing their beauty through the body's natural healing capabilities, resulting in healthier, more radiant skin that continues to improve over time. This trend reflects a broader shift in the cosmetology industry towards innovative solutions that prioritize natural results and minimal invasiveness [228-230].

As technology advances, regenerative techniques are becoming increasingly sophisticated and accessible. Innovations in stem cell research, biomaterials, and growth factor delivery are expected to further enhance the effectiveness of these treatments. Personalized regenerative therapies tailored to an individual's unique skin biology will likely become a standard in cosmetology, offering even more targeted and transformative results. These advancements will solidify the role of regenerative techniques as a cornerstone of modern cosmetic treatments.

Platelet-rich plasma (PRP) therapy is one of the most widely recognized regenerative techniques in cosmetology. Often referred to as the "vampire facial," this treatment involves extracting a small amount of the client's blood, processing it to concentrate the platelets, and reinfusing the plasma back into the skin through injection or microneedling. Platelets are abundant in growth factors that stimulate collagen production, promote wound healing, and encourage cellular turnover. This therapy is highly effective for addressing fine lines, wrinkles, acne scars, and uneven skin tone. Beyond facial rejuvenation, PRP is also used for hair restoration when applied to the scalp, helping to stimulate dormant hair follicles and encourage regrowth.

Stem cell therapy is another cutting-edge regenerative approach in cosmetology, utilizing stem cells derived from sources like plants, adipose tissue, or bone marrow to revitalize the skin. Stem cells possess the remarkable ability to differentiate into various cell types while releasing growth factors that promote collagen synthesis, tissue repair, and improved skin elasticity. This therapy is particularly effective in combating the signs of aging, improving skin texture, and addressing scars or pigmentation issues. Many professional treatments incorporate stem cell technology, and stem cell-based serums and creams are also available for at-home care, providing clients with ongoing regenerative benefits.

Microneedling, a minimally invasive technique that creates micro-injuries in the skin using fine needles, becomes even more effective when combined with growth factors or peptide-rich serums. The microchannels created during microneedling allow these substances to penetrate deeper into the skin, significantly amplifying the regenerative process. This combination stimulates collagen production, reduces the appearance of scars, and enhances skin firmness. It is an ideal treatment for clients seeking to rejuvenate dull, tired, or aging skin while achieving long-lasting improvements in texture and elasticity.

Laser skin resurfacing is a popular regenerative treatment that employs advanced technologies such as fractional CO_2 lasers or erbium lasers to rejuvenate the skin. These lasers target deeper layers of the skin, creating controlled thermal injuries that activate the body's natural healing response. The result is enhanced collagen and elastin production, which smoothens wrinkles, reduces scars, and evens out pigmentation. Laser skin resurfacing delivers dramatic results with relatively minimal downtime, making it a sought-after choice for those seeking transformative skin rejuvenation.

High-intensity focused ultrasound (HIFU) is a non-invasive technique that uses ultrasound energy to penetrate deep into the skin, stimulating the production of collagen and elastin. This treatment is particularly effective for tightening sagging skin on the face, neck, and body, providing a lifting effect without the need for surgery. Over time, as the body generates new collagen, clients notice firmer, more lifted skin with improved elasticity and texture, making HIFU a popular choice for non-surgical skin tightening.

Radiofrequency (RF) microneedling combines the mechanical benefits of traditional microneedling with the regenerative effects of radiofrequency energy. The RF energy heats the skin's deeper layers, stimulating collagen remodeling and tissue repair. This dual-action approach is highly effective for treating a range of concerns, including wrinkles, acne scars, stretch marks, and skin laxity. By addressing both the surface and deeper layers of the skin, RF microneedling delivers comprehensive and long-lasting rejuvenation.

Exosome therapy represents a groundbreaking advancement in regenerative cosmetology. This technique utilizes extracellular vesicles derived from stem cells, known as exosomes, which contain growth factors, cytokines, and bioactive molecules that accelerate skin repair and rejuvenation. Exosomes are applied topically or infused into the skin during treatments like microneedling or laser therapy. They work to reduce inflammation, stimulate collagen production, and enhance skin texture and tone, offering transformative results for clients seeking cutting-edge skin regeneration.

Cryotherapy, or cold therapy, is another regenerative treatment that stimulates the skin's natural repair mechanisms by exposing it to extremely low temperatures. This exposure improves blood circulation, reduces inflammation, and encourages collagen production, making it an effective solution for skin tightening, reducing puffiness, and achieving a rejuvenated appearance. Cryotherapy treatments are non-invasive and deliver visible results in a short amount of time, making them highly appealing to clients.

Hydrafacial treatments enhanced with regenerative boosters provide a multi-faceted approach to skincare. After the skin is exfoliated and cleansed, boosters containing peptides, growth factors, or stem cell-based serums are infused into the skin. These regenerative boosters promote deep hydration, stimulate cellular renewal, and improve skin texture, radiance, and elasticity. This combination treatment is ideal for clients looking to achieve a glowing, revitalized complexion while supporting long-term skin health.

Regenerative techniques in cosmetology represent the forefront of skincare innovation, offering solutions that go beyond surface-level improvements. Each method is designed to harness the body's natural processes, providing clients with safe, effective, and long-lasting results that enhance both their appearance and confidence.

Platelet-Rich Plasma (PRP) Therapy

Platelet-rich plasma (PRP) therapy, often referred to as the "vampire facial," has emerged as a prominent regenerative technique in cosmetology, leveraging the natural healing properties of platelets derived from the client's own blood. This innovative procedure capitalizes on the high concentration of growth factors found in platelets, which are essential for stimulating collagen production, promoting tissue repair, and enhancing cellular turnover. These growth factors, including platelet-derived growth factor (PDGF) and vascular endothelial growth factor (VEGF), play a pivotal role in the skin's rejuvenation process, making PRP a versatile treatment for various cosmetic concerns such as fine lines, wrinkles, and acne scars [231-233].

The PRP process begins with a blood draw from the client, typically from the arm. The collected blood is then subjected to centrifugation, a technique that separates the blood components based on density. This process isolates the platelet-rich plasma from red and white blood cells, resulting in a concentrated solution rich in growth factors and proteins that facilitate skin rejuvenation and tissue repair [231-233]. The efficacy of PRP in enhancing skin texture and appearance has been supported by numerous studies, which demonstrate significant improvements in atrophic scars and overall skin quality when PRP is applied, either through injections or in conjunction with microneedling [234, 235].

Once prepared, PRP can be administered in various ways. One common method involves injecting the plasma into targeted areas of the skin using fine needles, allowing for direct delivery of its regenerative properties to areas affected by cosmetic concerns. Another effective application method is microneedling, where PRP is applied topically and then worked into the skin through micro-injuries created by the microneedling device. This dual approach not only enhances the absorption of PRP but also maximizes its effectiveness by promoting deeper penetration of growth factors into the dermis [235-237]. Studies have shown that combining microneedling with PRP significantly improves outcomes for acne scars and skin rejuvenation compared to microneedling alone [235, 237, 238].

PRP therapy is particularly effective for treating fine lines and wrinkles, as it stimulates collagen production, which helps to plump and firm the skin. Additionally, it has been widely utilized for improving the appearance of acne scars, with growth factors encouraging the regeneration of damaged tissue [231, 234, 236]. For clients with uneven skin tone or texture, PRP promotes cellular turnover, leading to smoother, more radiant skin over time [231-233]. Beyond facial rejuvenation, PRP therapy has gained popularity in hair restoration treatments. When injected into the scalp, PRP stimulates dormant hair follicles, improves blood circulation, and promotes the growth of thicker, healthier hair, making it particularly beneficial for individuals experiencing thinning hair or early-stage hair loss [239, 240].

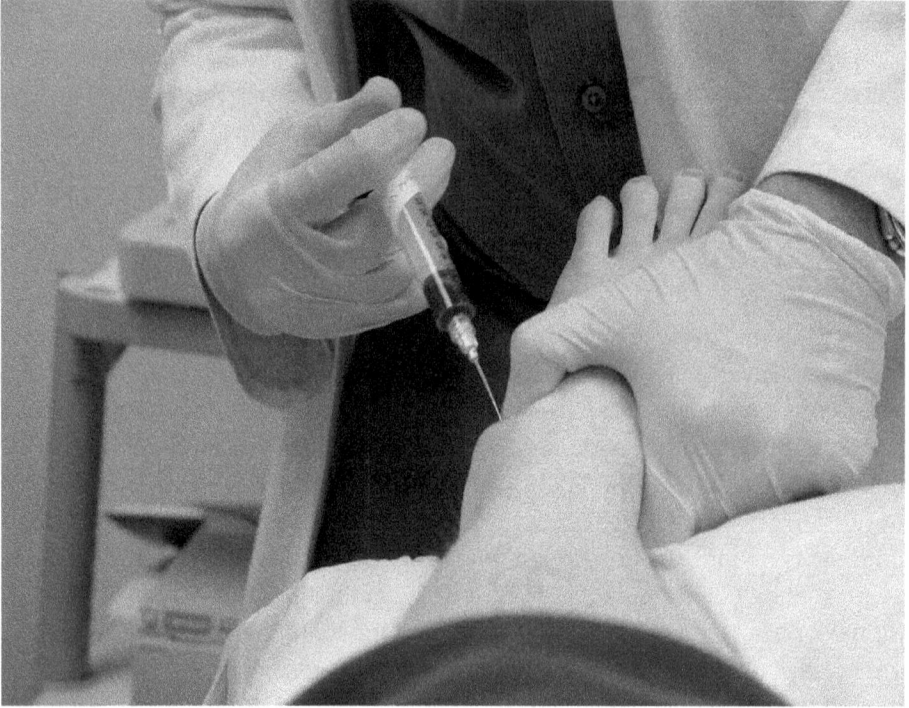

Figure 14: PRP Treatment. Lisle Boomer, CC BY-ND 2.0, via Flickr.

One of the key advantages of PRP therapy is its safety profile, as it utilizes the client's own blood, thereby minimizing the risk of allergic reactions, infections, or other complications often associated with synthetic fillers or external substances [231, 240]. Furthermore, PRP is a minimally invasive procedure with little to no downtime, making it a convenient option for clients seeking noticeable results without the recovery period associated with more invasive cosmetic procedures [231, 240]. PRP therapy represents a cutting-edge regenerative treatment that harnesses the body's natural healing processes to rejuvenate the skin and promote hair growth. Its ability to address multiple cosmetic concerns, combined with its safety and effectiveness, has solidified its status as one of the most popular and trusted techniques in modern cosmetology [231, 240].

Advances in Cosmetology

To offer platelet-rich plasma (PRP) therapy in a cosmetology or medical practice, specific equipment and tools are required to ensure the procedure is performed safely and effectively. Each piece of equipment serves a vital role in the preparation and application of the platelet-rich plasma, facilitating optimal results while maintaining safety and hygiene standards.

The centrifuge is the cornerstone of PRP therapy. This device is designed to spin blood samples at high speeds, separating the components of the blood to isolate the platelet-rich plasma from the red and white blood cells. For PRP therapy, the centrifuge must be specifically tailored for medical or cosmetic use and approved by regulatory bodies such as the FDA or CE. The cost of a PRP-specific centrifuge ranges between $1,500 and $10,000, depending on its speed, capacity, and programmable features.

Sterile blood collection kits are also essential for safely drawing blood from the client. These kits typically include vacuum-sealed blood tubes, syringes, and needles. PRP-specific blood collection tubes are often treated with anticoagulants to prevent clotting and maximize platelet recovery. These disposable kits typically cost between $10 and $30 each, depending on the brand and type.

Injection needles and syringes are required for delivering PRP into targeted areas of the skin or scalp. The sizes of the needles vary based on the application. For facial injections, thin needles (30G to 34G) are used to minimize discomfort, while slightly larger needles are employed for scalp treatments. These consumables cost approximately $1 to $5 per needle or syringe and are a recurring expense.

For practices that use microneedling to enhance PRP delivery, a microneedling device is necessary. These devices, such as pens or rollers, create micro-injuries in the skin, allowing the PRP to penetrate more effectively. Professional-grade microneedling devices can cost between $500 and $5,000, with features like adjustable needle depth, varying speed settings, and disposable cartridges influencing the price.

Some PRP systems are available as complete kits, which include tubes, needles, syringes, and centrifuge adapters. These kits streamline the procedure and ensure consistent results. The cost of these comprehensive kits ranges from $50 to $200 per treatment, depending on the brand and whether a single-spin or dual-spin system is used to process the PRP.

In cases where PRP is applied via microneedling, a conductive gel or serum is used to facilitate the smooth operation of the device and enhance the effectiveness of the treatment. High-quality conductive gels typically cost between $20 and $50 per session.

A sterile and organized workspace is essential for safely handling blood samples and preparing PRP injections. This includes a medical-grade trolley or preparation area, which can cost between $500 and $2,000, depending on the setup. Maintaining hygiene is critical during the procedure, which is why personal protective equipment (PPE), such as gloves, face masks, and disposable gowns, is required. PPE typically costs $5 to $10 per session, representing a recurring expense.

The total cost to set up PRP therapy services depends on the quality of the equipment, the scale of the practice, and the additional services offered. Below, Table 3, is a cost estimate for setting up a PRP service.

Table 3: Cost to set up PRP therapy services.

Category	Estimated Cost
Centrifuge	$1,500 – $10,000
Blood Collection Kits (initial supply)	$300 – $500 (for 20-50 treatments)
Microneedling Device (optional)	$500 – $5,000
PRP Injection Kits	$1,000 – $2,000 (initial stock)
Conductive Gel	$100 – $200 (initial supply)
Storage/Preparation Equipment	$500 – $2,000
PPE and Consumables (initial supply)	$200 – $500
Practitioner Training	$1,500 – $3,500

Advances in Cosmetology

Category	Estimated Cost
Total Estimated Cost	$5,600 – $23,700

Additional Considerations

1. **Maintenance Costs:** Centrifuge calibration, device servicing, and replenishment of consumables represent ongoing expenses. Annual maintenance costs may range from $500 to $2,000.

2. **Regulatory Compliance:** Depending on the country, you may need additional certifications, inspections, or licensing to offer PRP therapy legally. Costs vary but can add an extra $500 to $1,500.

3. **Marketing Costs:** To promote PRP services, clinics may invest in advertising, which could range from $1,000 to $5,000 for initial campaigns.

By investing in the right equipment, training, and setup, clinics can offer PRP therapy as a highly effective and profitable service, with individual treatment costs for clients typically ranging from $300 to $1,500 per session. This setup ensures that practitioners meet high standards of safety and efficacy while catering to the growing demand for regenerative cosmetic treatments.

Practitioners must also undergo specialized training in PRP therapy to ensure the procedure is performed safely and effectively. Training programs, which often include hands-on practice, can cost between $1,500 and $3,500, depending on the provider and location. This certification not only ensures client safety but also enhances the credibility and reputation of the practice.

Stem Cell Therapy

Stem cell rejuvenation represents a pioneering approach in cosmetic procedures aimed at restoring and enhancing the skin's natural functions by leveraging the regenerative capabilities of stem cells. Stem cells are unique biological entities that possess the ability to differentiate into various cell types and facilitate the repair of damaged tissues. In the context of skin rejuvenation, stem cells are typically harvested from the patient's own body, most commonly from adipose tissue or blood, and subsequently reintroduced into the skin to stimulate healing and regeneration [241, 242]. This process is particularly effective in revitalizing the skin by promoting the production of collagen and elastin, two critical proteins that play a vital role in maintaining a youthful and healthy appearance [218].

The application of stem cells in cosmetic procedures has been shown to significantly improve skin elasticity, tone, and texture while effectively reducing the appearance of wrinkles, fine lines, and age spots [218]. Various methods of delivering stem cells for rejuvenation exist, including intravenous injections, localized injections, and facial treatments. These minimally invasive interventions are generally considered safe and effective when performed by qualified medical professionals who can evaluate individual needs and contraindications to determine the most suitable approach [243]. The use of adipose-derived stem cells (ADSCs) is particularly notable, as they are easily accessible and have demonstrated the potential to differentiate into multiple cell types, making them a preferred choice in cosmetic surgery [241, 242].

Research has indicated that the regenerative properties of stem cells can enhance skin healing and rejuvenation through various mechanisms. For instance, mesenchymal stem cells (MSCs) have been shown to secrete bioactive factors that promote tissue repair and modulate immune responses, thereby facilitating the healing process [244, 245]. Additionally, studies have highlighted the role of conditioned media derived from stem cells, which can enhance skin rejuvenation characteristics by delivering growth factors and cytokines that support skin health [218, 246]. The integration of these advanced techniques into cosmetic practices reflects a growing trend towards utilizing biotechnological advancements in the field of dermatology and aesthetic medicine [247].

Stem cells are highly versatile, making them suitable for a range of cosmetic and medical applications. In rejuvenation procedures, they can regenerate damaged tissues and improve the appearance of aging or compromised skin. Beyond cosmetic uses, stem cell therapy is a promising treatment for numerous medical conditions. For example, haematological diseases like leukemia and severe sickle cell anaemia benefit from bone marrow transplants, where stem cells replace damaged blood cells. Neurological disorders such as Parkinson's and multiple sclerosis have shown potential for improvement through stem cell therapy, though this remains in the experimental stages. Autoimmune diseases, cardiovascular conditions, and even organ transplantation are other fields where stem cells demonstrate immense potential.

In the realm of cosmetology, stem cell treatments have gained significant traction due to their ability to rejuvenate skin, repair scars, and even restore hair growth. They also show promising results in treating various skin conditions and pigmentation issues, offering patients a non-invasive or minimally invasive alternative to surgical procedures.

Stem cells used in rejuvenation and other medical therapies can be sourced from several origins. Embryonic stem cells are pluripotent, meaning they can differentiate into any cell type in the body, but their use raises ethical concerns and is highly regulated. Adult stem cells, derived from tissues like bone marrow, adipose tissue, or blood, are multipotent, capable of differentiating into specific cell types. Induced pluripotent stem cells (iPSCs), created by reprogramming adult cells into a pluripotent state, offer an ethical and highly versatile option for research and treatments. Additionally, cord blood stem cells, extracted from the umbilical cord and placenta after childbirth, are gaining popularity due to their regenerative properties and effectiveness in treating various conditions.

For cosmetic procedures, adult stem cells, particularly those from adipose tissue or venous blood, are commonly used. These cells can be collected from the patient's body, processed, and then reintroduced into targeted areas to stimulate regeneration. Plant-derived stem cells are also frequently used in cosmetic products, as they exhibit antioxidant properties that help protect the skin from environmental damage and support collagen and elastin production.

The collection of stem cells depends on their source. For hematopoietic stem cells (HSCs) found in bone marrow, extraction typically involves using a needle to withdraw a sample from the pelvic bone under general anaesthesia. Peripheral blood stem cells (PBSCs), on the other hand, are collected through a less invasive process in which the donor is given a growth factor to stimulate stem cell release into the bloodstream. The blood is then drawn, and stem cells are separated using specialized machines.

For cosmetic applications, adult stem cells are usually derived from venous blood or adipose tissue, making the procedure less invasive. Once collected, stem cells are processed and immediately injected into the targeted area. The injected stem cells then migrate to damaged tissues and differentiate into the necessary cell types to repair and rejuvenate the skin.

In cosmetology, stem cells serve as a revolutionary tool to enhance skin health and appearance. While medical treatments rely on specific cell types, cosmetic applications often use plant or patient-derived stem cells. Cosmetic products infused with stem cell extracts boast anti-aging benefits, offering improvements in skin elasticity, wrinkle reduction, and overall texture. In professional cosmetic treatments, stem cells derived from the patient's venous blood are most commonly used, as their collection is minimally invasive. More complex procedures involving adipose or bone marrow-derived cells are rare due to their invasive nature and are reserved for specific medical contexts.

Once collected, stem cells can either be used immediately for procedures or stored in specialized stem cell or cord blood banks. For long-term storage, cells are cryopreserved to maintain their viability for future use. Banks store stem cells not only for cosmetic purposes but also for medical treatments of conditions like cancer, autoimmune disorders, and genetic diseases. For cosmetic procedures, stem cells are typically used fresh to maximize their regenerative potential.

In most cases, stem cells used in cosmetology are autologous, meaning they are derived from the patient's own body. This reduces the risk of rejection or adverse reactions. However, in certain medical scenarios, donor stem cells may be used. Known as allogeneic stem cell transplantation, this approach is common in treating conditions like leukemia and severe aplastic anaemia. In cosmetology, donor stem cells are used only in rare cases where patient-derived cells are unsuitable.

Stem cells can be administered using various techniques, carefully chosen based on the therapy's purpose, the condition being treated, and the target area of the body. The method of administration is critical to ensuring the stem cells reach the intended tissue and achieve maximum therapeutic efficacy.

Intravenous (IV) administration is one of the most common methods, involving the delivery of stem cells directly into the bloodstream via an IV line. This technique is primarily used for systemic therapies aimed at treating autoimmune diseases, neurological disorders, or general tissue regeneration. Once in the bloodstream, the stem cells naturally migrate to areas of inflammation or damage, guided by chemical signals released by the affected tissues. IV administration is minimally invasive and ideal for conditions requiring widespread distribution of stem cells throughout the body.

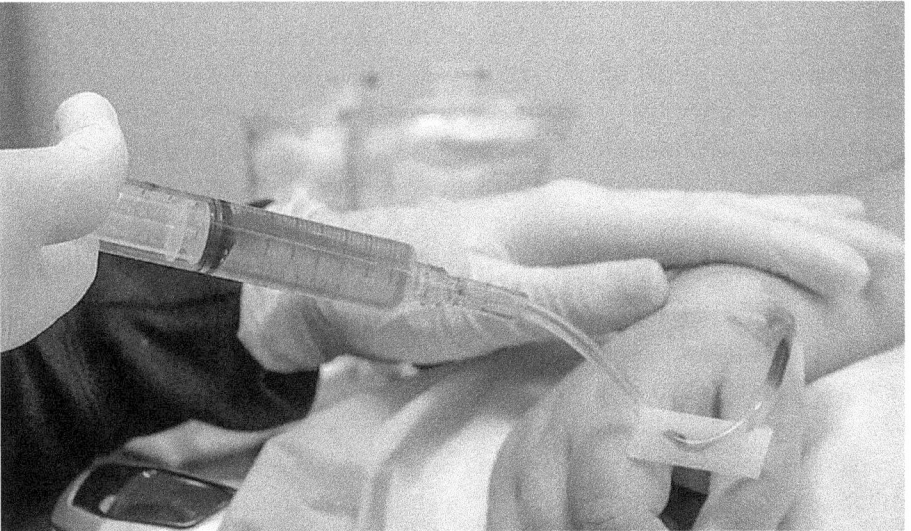

Figure 15: Stem cell IV administration. Alice Pien, MD, CC BY-SA 4.0, via Wikimedia Commons.

Cell therapy, particularly stem cell therapy, has emerged as a promising avenue for treating various medical and cosmetic conditions. However, it is crucial to recognize the potential dangers and side effects associated with these therapies. Understanding these risks is essential for both practitioners and patients to ensure informed decision-making.

One of the primary risks associated with cell therapy is the possibility of an immune response. When cells are transplanted from a donor (allogeneic cells), the recipient's immune system may recognize them as foreign, leading to an immune attack. This can result in inflammation, tissue damage, and other complications [248]. In contrast, autologous cells, which are derived from the patient's own body, significantly reduce the risk of such immune-related issues [248]. However, even with autologous cells, there are still concerns regarding the potential for immune reactions, particularly in the context of poorly characterized or manipulated cells [249].

Infection is another significant risk linked to cell therapy. The process of injecting or transplanting cells often involves breaking the skin barrier, which can introduce pathogens into the body. This risk is heightened in environments where sterile conditions are not strictly maintained, leading to potential infections that can range from mild to severe [250]. The handling of equipment and the training of personnel play critical roles in mitigating this risk [249]. Furthermore, the use of contaminated stem cell preparations can lead to the transmission of infectious diseases, underscoring the importance of stringent safety protocols [250].

Rejection of transplanted cells is a further challenge in cell therapy. Even when donor cells are closely matched, there is no guarantee of successful integration with the recipient's tissues. This incompatibility can lead to cell rejection, resulting in ineffective treatment and potential complications such as local inflammation or scarring [249]. In aesthetic applications, such as skin rejuvenation, improper integration may yield uneven results or other unwanted side effects [249].

The unregulated nature of some cell therapy practices exacerbates these dangers. Clinics may offer experimental treatments without adequate scientific validation or regulatory oversight, increasing the likelihood of adverse effects [251]. Patients are advised to seek care only from reputable providers to minimize these risks [249]. The lack of regulation can lead to the proliferation of untested therapies that may pose significant health risks.

Long-term effects of cell therapy also warrant consideration. The behaviour of transplanted cells over time can be unpredictable, particularly with emerging therapies like induced pluripotent stem cells (iPSCs). There is a theoretical risk that these cells could proliferate uncontrollably, potentially leading to tumour formation [252]. Although this risk is generally lower with multipotent cells compared to pluripotent cells, it remains a concern that necessitates careful monitoring [252].

Setting up stem cell therapy services requires advanced equipment to ensure the safety, precision, and effectiveness of the procedures. The type of equipment and infrastructure needed depends on the source of stem cells—such as adipose tissue, blood, bone marrow, or umbilical cord—and the delivery method, whether through injections or topical applications.

A centrifuge is the cornerstone of stem cell therapy. This device processes collected samples, such as blood or adipose tissue, to separate stem cells from other components. Medical-grade centrifuges approved by regulatory bodies like the FDA or CE are essential for maintaining precision and safety during this critical step. These centrifuges range in cost from $5,000 to $20,000, depending on features such as capacity and speed.

Cell isolation kits are required for extracting stem cells from specific sources. These kits include reagents, filters, and specialized containers for processing samples. Depending on the type of stem cells being isolated, kits can cost between $100 and $500 per procedure. If adipose tissue is the source, additional equipment like liposuction devices and microcannulas is needed to collect fat while preserving cell viability. Liposuction equipment costs range from $2,000 to $10,000, and microcannulas cost approximately $50 to $150 each.

Flow cytometers or cell counters are vital for analysing and quantifying stem cells in the isolated sample, ensuring accurate therapeutic dosing. These devices range from $10,000 to $100,000, depending on the level of sophistication and features. For clinics offering long-term storage options for stem cells, cryopreservation equipment is essential. This includes cryogenic freezers, storage tanks, and liquid nitrogen supplies to store stem cells at temperatures as low as -196°C. Cryopreservation systems cost between $5,000 and $30,000, with recurring expenses for liquid nitrogen.

Maintaining a sterile environment is critical for preventing contamination during stem cell processing. This is achieved through laminar flow hoods or cleanroom setups, which cost between $10,000 and $50,000. Additionally, sterile syringes and needles are required for delivering stem cells into the target area, costing $1 to $5 each. In more advanced treatments, such as orthopaedic applications, imaging equipment like ultrasound or MRI may be necessary to guide the injections. These systems can range from $50,000 to $150,000.

Practitioners must undergo specialized training to administer stem cell therapy safely and effectively. Certification programs and workshops typically cost $2,000 to $5,000 per practitioner. This ensures that professionals are equipped with the skills and knowledge to handle stem cells and deliver high-quality care.

The total cost to establish stem cell therapy services varies based on the scope of the clinic, the quality of equipment, and the level of service offered. A basic setup focused on cosmetic applications, such as skin rejuvenation, may cost around $50,000, while a full-scale facility offering medical-grade treatments can require an investment of up to $250,000.

The cost of stem cell therapy for patients depends on the type of treatment. Cosmetic treatments, such as skin rejuvenation and anti-aging, typically cost between $1,000 and $10,000 per session, with lower costs for platelet-rich plasma (PRP)-based treatments and higher costs for adipose-derived or bone marrow-derived therapies. Hair restoration using stem cells is priced between $1,500 and $7,000 per session, while orthopaedic treatments for joint pain or injuries cost between $3,000 and $10,000 per session. Clinics offering cryopreservation services charge an initial processing fee of $1,000 to $2,500 and annual storage fees of $200 to $500.

Ongoing expenses for stem cell therapy services include consumables such as syringes, isolation kits, and reagents, which cost $500 to $1,000 per month. Liquid nitrogen for cryopreservation requires an annual budget of $1,000 to $2,000. Equipment maintenance and calibration costs range from $5,000 to $10,000 per year, while staff salaries and training costs depend on the size and expertise of the team.

Setting up stem cell therapy services demands a significant investment in advanced equipment, sterile facilities, and staff training. However, the high demand for regenerative and cosmetic treatments, combined with premium service charges, makes this a lucrative option for clinics. By ensuring adherence to safety standards, maintaining high-quality equipment, and staying updated on advancements in stem cell research, clinics can attract a diverse clientele seeking innovative solutions for anti-aging, hair restoration, and other medical or aesthetic concerns.

Microneedling with Growth Factors

Microneedling with growth factors represents a significant advancement in aesthetic dermatology, combining the mechanical stimulation of the skin through microneedling with the biochemical benefits of growth factors. This dual approach enhances skin rejuvenation by promoting collagen production and facilitating cellular repair, making it a popular choice for addressing various skin concerns, including acne scars, fine lines, and overall skin texture.

Microneedling, also known as collagen induction therapy, utilizes a device with fine needles to create micro-injuries in the skin. This process triggers the body's natural healing response, leading to increased production of collagen and elastin, which are vital for maintaining youthful skin [238]. When combined with growth factors, the efficacy of microneedling is significantly enhanced. Growth factors, which are proteins that regulate cell growth and tissue repair, are delivered deeper into the skin through the microchannels created by the microneedling process. This synergistic effect amplifies the skin's regenerative capabilities, promoting a more effective healing response [253, 254].

The growth factors used in conjunction with microneedling can be derived from several sources, including Platelet-Rich Plasma (PRP), synthetic formulations, and plant-derived extracts. PRP, often referred to as the "vampire facial," is obtained from the patient's own blood and is rich in growth factors such as epidermal growth factor (EGF) and platelet-derived growth factor (PDGF) [255, 256]. These proteins play a crucial role in wound healing and skin regeneration, enhancing the overall effectiveness of the microneedling procedure [257]. Synthetic growth factors, engineered through recombinant DNA technology, are also utilized in some treatments, providing a consistent and compatible option for skin rejuvenation [258]. Additionally, plant-derived growth factors offer bioactive properties that can further support skin healing and regeneration [259].

The combination of microneedling and growth factors provides numerous benefits for patients seeking skin rejuvenation. Key advantages include:

- **Enhanced Collagen Production:** Microneedling induces controlled micro-injuries to the skin, which triggers a wound healing response that significantly boosts collagen and elastin production. Studies have shown that this technique leads to substantial clinical improvements in skin appearance, particularly in reducing wrinkles and fine lines [260]. The addition of growth factors, such as those derived from platelet-rich plasma (PRP), further amplifies this effect by enhancing the proliferation of fibroblasts and the deposition of collagen and elastic fibres [237]. This synergistic effect underscores the importance of combining microneedling with growth factors for optimal results in skin rejuvenation.

- **Improved Skin Texture and Tone:** The application of growth factors during microneedling has been shown to effectively target pigmentation issues, acne scars, and uneven skin tone. Research indicates that the combination of microneedling with topical agents, including antioxidants and growth factors, leads to significant improvements in skin elasticity, hydration, and overall texture [261]. Furthermore, the microchannels created by microneedling facilitate deeper penetration of these therapeutic agents, enhancing their efficacy [262]. This results in a more uniform skin tone and smoother texture, addressing common concerns such as hyperpigmentation and rough patches.

- **Minimized Pores:** Microneedling promotes collagen remodelling around the pores, which can lead to a noticeable reduction in their size. The mechanical stimulation from microneedling, coupled with the regenerative properties of growth factors, helps to refine the skin's appearance, resulting in a polished and youthful look [263]. This effect is particularly beneficial for individuals with enlarged pores, as it addresses both the structural and functional aspects of skin health.

- **Accelerated Healing:** The incorporation of growth factors into microneedling treatments not only enhances the aesthetic outcomes but also accelerates the healing process. Studies have demonstrated that the presence of growth factors can significantly reduce post-procedural redness and swelling, leading to shorter recovery times compared to microneedling alone [264]. This rapid healing is crucial for patients seeking effective yet minimally invasive treatments, as it allows them to return to their daily activities sooner.

- **Increased Hydration and Radiance:** Microneedling has been associated with improved skin hydration levels, which is further enhanced by the application of growth factors. The micro-injuries created during the procedure allow for better absorption of hydrating agents, leading to plumper and more radiant skin [265]. Research indicates that treatments combining microneedling with hyaluronic acid and other hydrating compounds yield significant improvements in skin moisture content and overall radiance [266].

The versatility of microneedling with growth factors makes it suitable for a wide range of skin concerns, including fine lines, acne scars, hyperpigmentation, enlarged pores, stretch marks, sun damage, and dull skin. This treatment can be performed on various body areas, including the face, neck, and décolletage, making it a comprehensive solution for skin rejuvenation [267]. The ability to address multiple skin issues simultaneously enhances its appeal among patients seeking effective cosmetic interventions.

The procedure begins with a consultation to assess the patient's skin type, concerns, and treatment goals. During the session, the skin is cleansed, and a numbing cream may be applied to minimize discomfort. A microneedling device is then used to create microchannels in the skin. Growth factors, either in the form of PRP or a specialized serum, are applied during or immediately after the microneedling process to ensure maximum absorption.

The treatment typically takes 30 to 60 minutes, depending on the area being treated. Most patients experience mild redness and sensitivity for one to three days post-treatment, with noticeable improvements in skin texture and tone within a week. For optimal results, multiple sessions spaced four to six weeks apart are often recommended.

Microneedling with growth factors is generally safe when performed by a trained professional in a sterile environment. However, patients may experience temporary redness, mild swelling, and slight irritation post-treatment. Rarely, those with sensitive skin may experience minor bruising or prolonged redness. It is essential to follow aftercare instructions, such as avoiding direct sunlight and using gentle skincare products, to ensure proper healing.

The cost of microneedling with growth factors can vary significantly depending on several factors, including the source of the growth factors, the size of the treatment area, and the geographic location of the clinic offering the procedure. The specific type of growth factors used plays a significant role in determining the overall expense, as does the complexity of the preparation and application process.

When platelet-rich plasma (PRP) is used as the growth factor source, the cost is generally higher due to the additional steps involved in the treatment. PRP is derived directly from the patient's blood, requiring a blood draw and subsequent processing using a centrifuge to isolate the platelet-rich plasma. This additional step not only requires specialized equipment but also adds to the time and expertise needed to perform the procedure effectively. As a result, PRP-based microneedling treatments typically range from $500 to $1,500 per session. The final cost may also depend on the clinic's reputation, the practitioner's experience, and the extent of the treatment area.

Alternatively, microneedling treatments that incorporate synthetic or botanical growth factors tend to be less expensive. These growth factors are typically pre-formulated in specialized serums and do not require additional preparation steps, such as blood processing. Synthetic growth factors are often developed in laboratories to mimic natural proteins, while botanical growth factors are derived from plants and offer regenerative properties similar to their human counterparts. The cost for treatments using these types of growth factors generally ranges from $300 to $800 per session. The variation in price within this range can depend on the quality and potency of the growth factor serum, as well as the clinic's location and level of service.

In addition to the cost of individual sessions, clinics may offer packages for multiple treatments, which can provide some savings for patients seeking long-term results. The size of the treatment area also affects pricing, as larger areas or multiple zones require more time, effort, and growth factor serum. Patients are encouraged to consult with their practitioner to understand the specifics of their chosen treatment and receive a detailed breakdown of associated costs.

Setting up microneedling with growth factors in a clinic or spa requires specialized equipment and materials to ensure the safety, effectiveness, and professional quality of the treatment. The costs associated with this setup vary depending on the type of microneedling device, the source of growth factors, and the scale of operations. Below is a detailed explanation of the equipment required and the estimated costs for implementing this service.

The microneedling device is the cornerstone of the procedure. These devices create controlled micro-injuries in the skin, which stimulate collagen production and allow for the enhanced absorption of growth factors. While basic rollers are available, professional microneedling pens are the preferred option for clinical use. These pens feature adjustable needle depths and multiple speed settings, enabling precise and customizable treatments. The cost of these devices ranges from $500 to $5,000, depending on the brand and technology, with popular options including Dermapen and SkinPen.

Sterile microneedling cartridges are essential for maintaining hygiene and preventing cross-contamination. These single-use cartridges, which attach to the microneedling device, contain fine needles designed to penetrate the skin effectively. Depending on the brand and the number of needles, these cartridges cost between $2 and $10 each.

The choice of growth factors significantly influences the setup costs. Clinics may opt for platelet-rich plasma (PRP), synthetic growth factors, or botanical growth factors. PRP requires processing the patient's blood and involves additional steps such as blood collection and centrifugation. PRP kits, which include blood collection tubes, syringes, and anticoagulants, cost approximately $100 to $200 per session. Alternatively, synthetic or botanical growth factors are pre-formulated serums that do not require additional processing. These serums cost between $50 and $300 per bottle, depending on their quality and potency.

If PRP is chosen as the growth factor source, a medical-grade centrifuge is necessary for processing blood to isolate the platelet-rich plasma. These centrifuges are designed for precision and safety, with costs ranging from $1,500 to $10,000, depending on the model and capacity. Alongside the centrifuge, sterile blood collection kits are required for safely drawing and processing blood samples. These kits typically cost $10 to $30 per treatment.

Conductive serum or gel is applied during microneedling to enhance the device's glide and ensure even absorption of growth factors. This product also provides hydration and additional active ingredients to the skin during the procedure. The cost of these serums or gels is typically $20 to $50 per session, depending on the product used. To ensure patient comfort, numbing cream is applied to minimize pain and discomfort caused by the microneedling needles. The cost of a numbing cream varies between $30 and $100, depending on the brand and size.

Maintaining proper hygiene is critical for microneedling treatments. Sterile gloves, face masks, and disposable gowns are required to create a clean and safe environment for both the practitioner and the patient. These protective supplies cost approximately $5 to $10 per session. Additionally, the treatment area must be thoroughly cleansed and disinfected using alcohol wipes or medical-grade cleansers. Bulk supplies of these cleaning materials cost between $20 and $50.

A sterile and organized workspace is essential for preparing and conducting microneedling treatments. This setup may include a medical-grade trolley or counter for organizing tools, as well as a sterilization unit for reusable equipment if applicable. Setting up such a workspace typically costs between $500 and $2,000, depending on the size and requirements of the clinic.

The total cost of setting up microneedling with growth factors depends on the choice of equipment and the type of growth factors used. A basic setup that includes synthetic or botanical growth factors can cost between $2,000 and $5,000, covering the microneedling device, disposable cartridges, and serums. For clinics offering PRP-based treatments, the costs are higher due to the additional need for a centrifuge, blood collection kits, and related consumables. The investment for such advanced setups typically ranges from $10,000 to $25,000.

In conclusion, setting up microneedling with growth factors requires an initial investment in specialized equipment and consumables, with costs varying based on the complexity and scope of services offered. By investing in the right tools and materials, clinics can provide safe and effective treatments that meet the growing demand for this innovative skincare procedure.

Microneedling with growth factors is a highly effective treatment that combines the best of regenerative medicine and advanced skincare technology. By enhancing collagen production, promoting skin repair, and improving overall skin health, it addresses a variety of aesthetic concerns with minimal downtime. Whether for anti-aging, scar reduction, or skin rejuvenation, this treatment offers noticeable, long-lasting results and is a valuable addition to any cosmetic or dermatological practice.

Radiofrequency (RF) Microneedling

Radiofrequency (RF) microneedling is an innovative skin rejuvenation technique that combines microneedling with radiofrequency energy to enhance skin appearance and texture. This minimally invasive procedure is effective in treating various skin concerns, including wrinkles, fine lines, acne scars, and skin laxity. The mechanism of RF microneedling involves the use of a specialized device that creates micro-injuries in the skin while simultaneously delivering RF energy to the deeper dermal layers. This dual action promotes collagen and elastin production, resulting in firmer and smoother skin [268-270].

The RF microneedling device employs ultrafine needles to penetrate the skin at controlled depths, allowing for the precise delivery of RF energy. This energy generates heat within the dermis, stimulating fibroblasts—cells responsible for collagen and elastin synthesis. The controlled heating effect enhances collagen remodelling and tightens the skin, addressing both superficial and deeper skin issues [268, 271]. Unlike traditional microneedling, RF microneedling preserves the epidermis, which minimizes downtime and reduces the risk of adverse effects, making it a more appealing option for patients seeking skin rejuvenation [268, 269, 272].

The benefits of RF microneedling include tightening the skin by stimulating collagen contraction and remodelling, reducing the appearance of fine lines and wrinkles, and improving skin tone and texture by addressing issues such as enlarged pores and roughness [268, 269, 273]. Additionally, RF microneedling has been shown to be particularly advantageous for treating acne scars, as it promotes new collagen growth in scarred areas, leading to improved skin appearance [268, 269]. The procedure is also recognized for its minimal downtime compared to other resurfacing treatments, such as laser therapy, and serves as a non-surgical alternative for individuals seeking skin rejuvenation [268, 269, 272].

RF microneedling is versatile and can be applied to various areas of the body, including the face, neck, and other regions. Its applications range from reducing fine lines and wrinkles around sensitive areas like the eyes and mouth to tightening sagging skin on the jawline and neck. Furthermore, it can effectively treat surgical scars and stretch marks, enhance skin tone, and minimize hyperpigmentation [268, 269, 273]. The customization of the procedure, based on individual skin types and concerns, further enhances its appeal, making RF microneedling a popular choice among both practitioners and patients [268-270].

The RF microneedling procedure typically begins with a consultation to assess the patient's skin concerns and treatment goals. Before the treatment, a numbing cream is applied to the skin to ensure comfort during the procedure. The practitioner then uses an RF microneedling device to deliver controlled micro-injuries and RF energy to the target areas. The entire procedure usually takes 30 to 60 minutes, depending on the size of the treatment area.

After the procedure, patients may experience mild redness, swelling, or sensitivity, which typically subsides within 24 to 48 hours. Full results become visible over the following weeks as the skin produces new collagen and elastin. Multiple sessions, spaced four to six weeks apart, are often recommended for optimal results.

Radiofrequency (RF) microneedling relies on advanced devices specifically engineered to combine the benefits of microneedling and RF energy. These devices are critical for delivering controlled micro-injuries to the skin while simultaneously applying RF energy to the deeper dermal layers. Each device has unique features that cater to specific treatment needs, making them essential tools for practitioners offering RF microneedling services.

The Morpheus8 is a well-known RF microneedling device renowned for its deep fractional RF delivery, which penetrates the skin more deeply than many other devices. This capability makes it particularly effective for skin tightening and contouring, addressing concerns like sagging skin on the face, neck, and body. The device allows practitioners to treat deeper layers of tissue, making it suitable for advanced anti-aging and sculpting treatments.

The Vivace RF microneedling device is a versatile option that combines microneedling, RF energy, and LED light therapy. This combination enhances the overall skin rejuvenation process by addressing multiple skin concerns simultaneously, such as wrinkles, fine lines, and uneven texture. The inclusion of LED light therapy provides additional benefits, such as reducing inflammation and stimulating healing, making it a popular choice for clinics seeking to offer comprehensive treatments.

The Secret RF device is another advanced option that offers adjustable needle depths and customizable RF energy settings. This level of precision allows practitioners to tailor treatments to each patient's unique skin type and concerns. The device is particularly effective for addressing acne scars, stretch marks, and skin laxity, as the adjustable settings enable targeted treatment of various skin conditions.

The Sylfirm X is specifically designed for individuals with sensitive skin and unique concerns, such as pigmentation and vascular issues. This device stands out for its ability to target pigmentation irregularities, rosacea, and other vascular conditions while also delivering the benefits of RF microneedling. It is a preferred option for patients who require a gentle yet effective treatment approach.

Each of these devices represents an investment in state-of-the-art technology, allowing clinics to deliver safe, effective, and customizable RF microneedling treatments. The choice of device depends on the clinic's budget, the types of treatments offered, and the specific needs of the patient population. By incorporating one or more of these devices into their practice, clinics can provide advanced skin rejuvenation solutions that meet the growing demand for minimally invasive aesthetic treatments.

The cost of offering RF microneedling treatments varies widely depending on several factors, including the device selected, the geographic location of the clinic, the expertise of the practitioner, and the size or scope of the treatment area. Both patients and clinics must consider these financial aspects when evaluating the procedure or implementing it as a service.

For patients, the per-session cost of RF microneedling generally ranges from $500 to $2,500. The price is influenced by the complexity of the treatment, the type of device used, and the size of the treatment area. Treatments targeting small areas, such as the face or neck, are typically less expensive, whereas larger areas like the abdomen or thighs can cost significantly more due to the additional time and consumables required. Clinics that use cutting-edge devices like Morpheus8 or Vivace often charge higher rates due to the superior technology and results these devices provide.

From a clinic's perspective, the setup costs for RF microneedling services are substantial. The initial investment in an RF microneedling device can range from $30,000 to $150,000, depending on the brand, features, and level of sophistication. Devices with advanced functionalities, such as adjustable needle depths, fractional RF delivery, or integrated LED therapy, are on the higher end of the price spectrum. This upfront cost also includes training for practitioners, which is often provided by the device manufacturer.

In addition to the initial investment, clinics must account for ongoing consumables and maintenance expenses. Single-use cartridges, which house the needles for microneedling, are a significant recurring cost. These cartridges are essential for maintaining hygiene and safety during each treatment and typically cost between $50 and $150 per session. The exact price depends on the brand of the device and the number of needles in the cartridge. Maintenance costs for the device itself, including regular servicing, calibration, and potential repairs, should also be factored into the overall operational expenses.

Overall, while the financial commitment to offering RF microneedling services is significant, it is a highly lucrative investment for clinics due to the growing demand for minimally invasive skin rejuvenation treatments. For patients, the procedure offers a non-surgical solution to a variety of skin concerns, with costs reflecting the advanced technology and expertise involved in delivering effective results.

Exosome Therapy

Exosome therapy represents a novel approach in regenerative medicine, utilizing exosomes—small extracellular vesicles secreted by cells—to facilitate healing and rejuvenation. These vesicles are pivotal in intercellular communication, carrying a diverse array of bioactive molecules, including proteins, lipids, and RNA, which influence the behaviour of recipient cells [274, 275]. In the context of cosmetology, exosome therapy is gaining traction for its potential to enhance skin rejuvenation, improve texture and tone, and expedite recovery from cosmetic procedures [276, 277].

Exosomes are primarily derived from mesenchymal stem cells (MSCs), which are known for their regenerative properties. Unlike traditional stem cell therapies that involve the use of live cells, exosome therapy circumvents ethical and logistical challenges by employing cell-free products. This characteristic not only simplifies the therapeutic process but also minimizes risks associated with cell-based therapies, such as tumorigenicity [278]. The therapeutic efficacy of exosomes is attributed to their rich content of growth factors, cytokines, and signalling molecules that activate the body's natural regenerative processes [279].

The mechanism of action for exosome therapy involves the delivery of bioactive molecules into target tissues, particularly the skin. Upon application, exosomes penetrate the dermis, where they stimulate fibroblasts to produce collagen and elastin, reduce inflammation, and enhance cellular turnover. This cascade of events leads to improved skin elasticity, diminished wrinkles, and overall rejuvenation [280]. In aesthetic procedures, exosomes are typically administered through techniques such as microneedling or laser treatments, which create microchannels in the skin, facilitating deeper penetration of the exosomal cargo [277].

The applications of exosome therapy in cosmetology are diverse. It is effectively employed for skin rejuvenation, where it aids in enhancing skin tone and texture while reducing signs of aging such as wrinkles and sagging [276, 277]. Additionally, exosome therapy shows promise in scar reduction by promoting cellular regeneration and minimizing inflammation, thus improving the appearance of acne scars and surgical marks [277]. Furthermore, it accelerates recovery from cosmetic procedures, reducing redness and swelling, which enhances overall treatment outcomes [276, 277]. In the realm of hair restoration, exosomes are injected into the scalp to stimulate hair follicles, promoting healthier and thicker hair growth, making it a viable option for individuals facing hair thinning [277].

Exosome therapy offers several unique benefits that can make it a preferred choice for regenerative treatments. It is non-invasive, safe, and highly effective, with minimal downtime compared to other procedures. Since exosomes are cell-free, there is no risk of cell rejection or immune responses, making the treatment suitable for a wide range of patients. Additionally, exosome therapy is compatible with various cosmetic procedures, enhancing their efficacy and reducing recovery time.

An exosome therapy session typically begins with a consultation to assess the patient's needs and goals. If used in conjunction with a cosmetic procedure, such as microneedling or laser resurfacing, the exosome solution is applied to the treatment area immediately after creating microchannels in the skin. For standalone treatments, exosomes may be delivered through direct injection into the skin or scalp.

The procedure usually lasts between 30 minutes to an hour, depending on the treatment area. Patients may experience mild redness or swelling immediately after the procedure, but these effects subside within a day or two. Results start to become visible within a few weeks, with full effects developing over several months as the skin or hair undergoes repair and rejuvenation.

The costs associated with exosome therapy reflect its status as a premium, cutting-edge treatment that relies on advanced biotechnology and rigorous research. The expenses for patients can vary significantly based on the type of treatment, the size of the target area, and whether the therapy is performed independently or in combination with other procedures.

Advances in Cosmetology

For skin rejuvenation treatments, the cost typically ranges from $1,500 to $3,500 per session. These treatments are focused on improving skin tone, texture, and elasticity while addressing issues such as wrinkles, fine lines, and uneven pigmentation. The cost reflects the precision of the therapy, the expertise of the practitioner, and the high-quality exosome products used.

In hair restoration treatments, exosome therapy is slightly more expensive, ranging from $2,000 to $5,000 per session. These treatments are designed to stimulate hair follicles, improve scalp health, and promote the growth of thicker, healthier hair. The higher cost is influenced by the larger treatment area and the higher volume of exosomes often required for optimal results.

When exosome therapy is added as a post-procedure recovery enhancement, such as following microneedling, laser resurfacing, or chemical peels, the cost is typically between $500 and $1,000. In this context, exosomes accelerate healing, reduce inflammation, and enhance the effectiveness of the primary treatment, making it a valuable add-on for patients seeking faster recovery and superior outcomes.

For clinics offering exosome therapy, the initial setup and recurring costs are substantial. Exosome products, which are typically sourced in vials, cost between $500 and $1,500 each, depending on the brand, quality, and source of the exosomes. These products must meet strict regulatory standards to ensure their safety and efficacy. Clinics must also account for staff training to safely and effectively administer the therapy, which may involve certification programs or workshops. Additional investments may include integrating exosome therapy into existing procedures and ensuring compatibility with equipment like microneedling pens or injection tools.

Overall, the high costs of exosome therapy for both patients and clinics are justified by the treatment's innovative nature, the extensive research required to develop it, and the impressive regenerative results it delivers. This makes exosome therapy an appealing option for clients seeking advanced solutions for skin and hair concerns and a lucrative addition for clinics aiming to offer state-of-the-art treatments.

Exosome therapy, while promising in the field of regenerative medicine, faces several challenges that must be addressed to ensure its safe and effective application. One of the primary concerns is the need for stringent quality control during the production of exosomes. This is crucial to guarantee their safety and efficacy, as variations in production methods can lead to inconsistencies in the therapeutic properties of exosomes. For instance, the manufacturing and characterization of exosomes derived from mesenchymal stem cells (MSCs) require adherence to good manufacturing practices (GMP) to ensure that the final product is suitable for clinical use [281]. Additionally, the sourcing of exosomes from reputable suppliers who comply with regulatory standards is essential to mitigate risks associated with contamination and variability in exosome quality [282].

While current studies indicate that exosome therapy is generally safe, the long-term effects of such treatments remain inadequately understood, as this field is still relatively nascent. Research has shown that exosomes can modulate immune responses and have therapeutic potential in various conditions, but comprehensive studies examining their long-term safety and efficacy are still ongoing [283, 284]. The limited understanding of the mechanisms through which exosomes exert their effects further complicates the development of standardized protocols for their clinical application [285]. This uncertainty underscores the importance of consulting trained professionals who can evaluate the appropriateness of exosome therapy for individual patients based on their specific medical needs and conditions [286].

Hydrafacial with Regenerative Boosters

Hydrafacial with regenerative boosters is an innovative skin treatment that integrates the foundational aspects of a Hydrafacial with specialized serums or boosters aimed at addressing specific skin issues. This advanced procedure enhances the traditional Hydrafacial experience by incorporating regenerative ingredients such as growth factors, peptides, stem cell-derived serums, and hyaluronic acid-based formulations, which are known to promote deeper skin repair, hydration, and anti-aging effects [287, 288].

This treatment is particularly effective for clients dealing with visible signs of aging, such as fine lines and wrinkles. By incorporating regenerative boosters like growth factors and peptides, the treatment stimulates collagen and elastin production, helping to reduce the appearance of these aging markers. Clients who want to achieve a more youthful and revitalized look often benefit significantly from this advanced skincare option.

Individuals struggling with dry, dull, or uneven skin tone are also excellent candidates for this treatment. The Hydrafacial's multi-step process, combined with the infusion of regenerative serums, deeply hydrates the skin and enhances its natural glow. Brightening agents and hyaluronic acid-based boosters address pigmentation issues and replenish moisture, leaving the skin radiant, plump, and visibly healthier.

For those looking to improve their skin's elasticity and firmness, Hydrafacial with regenerative boosters is a top choice. By targeting the deeper layers of the skin with bioactive ingredients, the treatment promotes cell renewal and strengthens the skin's structural integrity. This is especially beneficial for clients experiencing sagging or loss of elasticity due to aging or environmental factors.

This treatment is also ideal for individuals preparing for special events, such as weddings, parties, or professional engagements. The non-invasive nature of the Hydrafacial means there is no downtime, and clients can enjoy an immediate improvement in their skin's texture, tone, and radiance. It provides a quick, effective solution for achieving a glowing complexion in time for important occasions.

Hydrafacial with regenerative boosters is also highly beneficial for clients managing acne or post-acne marks. The deep-cleansing and exfoliation phases of the Hydrafacial help clear out clogged pores and reduce inflammation, while the regenerative serums promote healing and skin repair. This dual approach not only improves active breakouts but also reduces the appearance of scars and discoloration left behind by previous acne.

The Hydrafacial process itself is a multi-step procedure that involves cleansing, exfoliating, extracting impurities, and hydrating the skin through a patented Vortex-Fusion delivery system. The addition of regenerative boosters allows for the introduction of concentrated bioactive compounds that penetrate deeply into the skin, stimulating collagen and elastin production while reducing inflammation and improving overall skin texture and tone [289, 290]. This personalized approach not only enhances the efficacy of the treatment but also caters to individual skin concerns, making it a versatile option for various skin types [291].

The treatment begins with a thorough consultation to evaluate the client's skin type and concerns, followed by the application of the Hydrafacial steps. The process includes cleansing and exfoliation, where dead skin cells are removed, preparing the skin for optimal absorption of the regenerative booster. A gentle chemical peel is then applied to loosen dirt and impurities, followed by the extraction of blackheads and sebum using the Vortex-Fusion technology. The selected regenerative booster is infused into the skin, promoting cellular renewal and addressing specific concerns such as fine lines, pigmentation, or dullness. Finally, the treatment concludes with hydrating serums and antioxidants to protect and nourish the skin [287, 288].

Regenerative boosters used in Hydrafacial treatments include growth factors, peptides, stem cell-derived serums, and hyaluronic acid formulations. Growth factors stimulate collagen and elastin production, aiding in skin regeneration and reducing the appearance of fine lines and wrinkles. Peptide-based boosters enhance skin elasticity and repair damaged skin, while stem cell-derived serums support cellular repair and renewal, improving overall skin health. Hyaluronic acid boosters provide intense hydration, plumping the skin and reducing dryness and fine lines [292]. Additionally, brightening agents such as vitamin C can target pigmentation issues, further enhancing skin tone and clarity [289].

The applications of Hydrafacial with regenerative boosters are extensive, offering numerous benefits such as anti-aging effects, improved hydration, enhanced skin texture and tone, and effective acne management. The treatment is particularly appealing due to its non-invasive nature and the absence of downtime, allowing clients to achieve immediate results without recovery time [291]. This makes it an ideal choice for individuals seeking both short-term and long-term skin improvements, particularly before events or as part of a regular skincare regimen [288].

The cost of Hydrafacial with regenerative boosters varies depending on several factors, including the type of booster used, the clinic's location, and the level of expertise of the practitioner administering the treatment. This pricing structure reflects the added value of incorporating advanced regenerative ingredients into the standard Hydrafacial procedure, enhancing its efficacy and appeal.

The cost of a standard Hydrafacial session typically ranges between $150 and $300. This price covers the base treatment, which includes cleansing, exfoliation, extraction, and hydration. However, when regenerative boosters are incorporated into the procedure, the price increases to account for the specialized serums and their enhanced results. On average, a Hydrafacial with regenerative boosters costs between $300 and $600 per session. The final price within this range depends on the type of booster selected and its specific ingredients. Boosters containing advanced formulations, such as growth factors or stem cell-derived serums, generally fall on the higher end of the spectrum due to their potency and effectiveness.

For clinics offering Hydrafacial with regenerative boosters, the cost of purchasing these boosters is an important factor in determining the overall pricing structure. High-quality regenerative boosters typically cost between $50 and $150 per treatment vial. These serums are sourced from reputable manufacturers and are designed to address specific skin concerns, such as anti-aging, hydration, or pigmentation. The price of the booster often reflects the complexity of its formulation and the research involved in its development.

Introducing Hydrafacial with regenerative boosters to a clinic's menu involves minimal setup costs, especially for facilities that already offer Hydrafacial treatments. The primary investment is in sourcing the regenerative boosters themselves and providing training for practitioners to ensure they are skilled in selecting and applying the most appropriate booster for each client's needs. Additional costs may include marketing efforts to promote the upgraded service and educating clients about the benefits of regenerative boosters.

Legality and Regulatory Status of Regenerative Techniques

The legality and regulatory status of regenerative techniques in cosmetology, such as Platelet-Rich Plasma (PRP) therapy, stem cell therapy, and other treatments, vary significantly across the world. Factors influencing legality include safety concerns, scientific validation, the source of materials (e.g., stem cells), and the level of medical expertise required for administration.

Below is a detailed explanation of the legal status of these treatments in different countries and the reasons behind their regulation or acceptance.

Platelet-Rich Plasma (PRP) Therapy: PRP therapy is legal and widely used in many countries, including the United States, Canada, the United Kingdom, Australia, and much of Europe. It is regulated as a minimally invasive procedure that uses the patient's own blood, which minimizes risks such as rejection or allergic reactions. PRP's popularity stems from its versatility, being used in both cosmetic and medical fields, such as orthopaedics and sports medicine.

In countries like India, South Korea, and Japan, PRP therapy is also legal and commonly practiced. However, some regions, such as China and parts of the Middle East, have stricter oversight of PRP due to concerns over practitioner qualifications and equipment sterilization. The treatment is generally regulated to ensure that sterile techniques and FDA-approved devices are used.

Stem Cell Therapy: Stem cell therapy in cosmetology is subject to stricter regulations compared to PRP, given the ethical concerns and potential risks associated with stem cells. In the United States, the FDA heavily regulates stem cell-based cosmetic treatments. Autologous stem cells (from the client's own body) may be used, but the process must meet stringent guidelines. Stem cell products that involve significant manipulation or are derived from embryonic sources often require extensive approval and clinical validation, which limits their availability.

In Europe, the use of stem cells in cosmetology is legal but tightly controlled, with a focus on adult or adipose-derived stem cells for rejuvenation. Countries like Switzerland and Germany are leaders in stem cell research and offer advanced cosmetic treatments, but only under strict medical supervision. In contrast, regions like South Korea, Japan, and Thailand are more permissive, allowing a broader range of stem cell applications due to their progressive medical regulations and high demand for anti-aging treatments. These countries, however, maintain oversight to ensure safety and efficacy.

Many countries, particularly in the Middle East and parts of Africa, restrict stem cell therapy in cosmetology due to ethical concerns, insufficient regulation, or a lack of scientific consensus on its long-term safety.

Advances in Cosmetology

Microneedling with Growth Factors: Microneedling is widely legal and practiced globally, including in the United States, Canada, Europe, and Asia. When combined with growth factors, it is typically regulated as a cosmetic procedure, provided the serums or peptides used are FDA-approved or meet local regulatory standards. However, in some countries, stricter oversight applies to ensure that microneedling pens or devices are safe, sterile, and used by qualified practitioners.

In countries like Australia and the UK, microneedling is permitted for aesthetic use, but treatments involving deeper penetration or the use of certain biologics (e.g., autologous growth factors) may require medical supervision. The regulatory focus is on ensuring that the equipment is properly calibrated and that practitioners are trained to avoid adverse outcomes like infection or scarring.

Laser Skin Resurfacing: Laser skin resurfacing is legal and highly popular worldwide, including in the United States, Canada, Europe, Australia, and Asia. It is regulated as a medical or advanced cosmetic procedure, with specific licensing requirements for practitioners. Different lasers, such as fractional CO_2 and erbium lasers, are approved for cosmetic use, but their application is closely monitored to ensure that they are used safely and effectively.

In some regions, like the UAE and Saudi Arabia, laser treatments are heavily regulated to ensure that only licensed dermatologists or trained professionals perform them. Developing countries may face challenges with oversight, leading to variations in the quality and safety of laser treatments.

High-Intensity Focused Ultrasound (HIFU): HIFU is legal in most countries, including the United States, Canada, the UK, Australia, and much of Asia. The treatment is classified as a non-invasive cosmetic procedure, and the devices used are typically FDA-cleared or CE-marked in Europe. South Korea, in particular, is a global leader in HIFU technology and treatments, reflecting its advanced cosmetology industry.

While generally safe, HIFU is regulated to ensure proper training for practitioners and that only approved devices are used. In some regions, the treatment may be restricted to medical professionals to mitigate risks of improper use, such as skin burns or nerve damage.

Radiofrequency (RF) Microneedling: RF microneedling is widely legal and practiced in countries with established cosmetology markets, such as the United States, Canada, the UK, Australia, and South Korea. It is regulated similarly to standard microneedling, with added oversight due to the thermal effects of radiofrequency energy. FDA-cleared or equivalent-approved devices are required, and practitioners often need specialized training to operate them safely.

In some regions, such as parts of Southeast Asia and Latin America, access to RF microneedling may be less regulated, potentially leading to inconsistencies in safety standards.

Exosome Therapy: Exosome therapy is still emerging in the cosmetology field and is subject to varying levels of regulation. In the United States, exosomes are not FDA-approved for cosmetic use, as they are classified as biologics requiring extensive clinical trials. Despite this, some clinics offer exosome treatments under experimental or off-label use.

In countries like South Korea and Japan, where regenerative medicine is more advanced, exosome therapy is permitted under strict oversight. These regions have embraced exosomes for their potential to accelerate skin healing and regeneration. However, in Europe and many developing countries, exosome therapy is either restricted or not widely available due to a lack of regulatory frameworks.

Cryotherapy: Cryotherapy is legal and widely practiced globally, including in the United States, Europe, Canada, Australia, and Asia. It is regulated as a non-invasive wellness and cosmetic procedure. Whole-body cryotherapy chambers and localized devices must meet safety standards, and practitioners are required to follow protocols to avoid risks like frostbite or overexposure.

In some developing countries, cryotherapy may be less regulated, leading to variability in equipment quality and practitioner training.

Hydrafacial with Regenerative Boosters: Hydrafacial treatments are legal and commonly available worldwide, including in the United States, Canada, Europe, Australia, and Asia. The use of regenerative boosters, such as peptides or growth factors, is typically regulated as part of the cosmetic product category, provided the ingredients are approved by local authorities. As long as the Hydrafacial device is FDA-cleared or meets equivalent standards, and practitioners are trained, these treatments are widely accepted.

Table 4 summarises the legality of regenerative techniques in cosmetology across different countries and the reasons for their acceptance or restrictions.

Table 4: Summary of the legality of regenerative techniques in cosmetology across different countries.

Regenerative Technique	Legal Status	Countries Where Legal	Reasons for Regulation
Platelet-Rich Plasma (PRP) Therapy	Legal and widely practiced	United States, Canada, UK, Australia, South Korea, Japan, Europe, India	Considered safe due to the use of the client's own blood. Regulated to ensure sterile techniques and FDA/CE-approved devices.
Stem Cell Therapy	Legal with strict regulations in some countries; restricted or banned in others	South Korea, Japan, Thailand, Switzerland, Germany, United States, select EU countries	Regulated due to ethical concerns, potential risks, and the source of stem cells. Use of autologous or minimally manipulated stem cells is often allowed, while embryonic sources are heavily restricted.
Microneedling with Growth Factors	Legal with minimal restrictions	United States, Canada, UK, Australia,	Regulated to ensure that devices and serums used are FDA-approved or meet equivalent local

Regenerative Technique	Legal Status	Countries Where Legal	Reasons for Regulation
		Europe, South Korea	safety standards. Advanced penetration treatments may require medical supervision in some regions.
Laser Skin Resurfacing	Legal and widely practiced, subject to licensing requirements	United States, Canada, UK, Europe, Australia, South Korea	Requires training and licensing for practitioners to prevent misuse of high-intensity devices. Regulated for safety and compliance with local cosmetic or medical device laws.
High-Intensity Focused Ultrasound (HIFU)	Legal and widely practiced	United States, Canada, UK, South Korea, Australia, Japan, Europe	Approved as a non-invasive cosmetic procedure; regulated for safe use and to ensure only trained professionals operate the devices.
Radiofrequency (RF) Microneedling	Legal and widely practiced	United States, Canada, UK, South Korea, Australia	Requires certification or training to use RF devices due to their thermal effects. Equipment must be FDA-cleared or CE-marked to ensure safety.

Advances in Cosmetology

Regenerative Technique	Legal Status	Countries Where Legal	Reasons for Regulation
Exosome Therapy	Emerging and not widely approved	South Korea, Japan, experimental use in United States	Largely unregulated globally; requires approval as a biologic in regions like the US. Allowed under strict oversight in countries like South Korea and Japan for its regenerative potential.
Cryotherapy	Legal and widely practiced	United States, Canada, Europe, UK, Australia, South Korea	Regulated as a wellness or cosmetic procedure. Safety standards focus on preventing overexposure and ensuring proper equipment maintenance.
Hydrafacial with Regenerative Boosters	Legal and widely available	United States, Canada, Europe, Australia, South Korea	Regulated as a cosmetic treatment; boosters and serums must meet FDA or equivalent local safety and quality standards.

Matching Treatments to Clients: Suitability and Combinations

The suitability of various regenerative skincare treatments, including Hydrafacial with regenerative boosters, microneedling with growth factors, RF microneedling, and exosome therapy, is contingent upon a client's skin type, specific concerns, goals, and lifestyle. Each treatment offers unique benefits and can be combined strategically to enhance overall results.

Hydrafacial with Regenerative Boosters: This treatment is particularly advantageous for clients seeking a quick, non-invasive solution with minimal downtime. It is well-suited for individuals with dull, dehydrated skin or those exhibiting early signs of aging, such as fine lines and loss of elasticity. The gentle nature of Hydrafacial makes it an excellent option for sensitive skin types, providing an instant glow that is often desired before events [293, 294].

The efficacy of this treatment lies in its ability to deeply cleanse, exfoliate, and hydrate the skin while infusing customized regenerative serums. These serums, which may include growth factors or hyaluronic acid, significantly enhance the skin's reparative capabilities and hydration levels, leading to a restored youthful appearance [295, 296].

For optimal results, Hydrafacial can be effectively combined with microneedling with growth factors or exosome therapy. Performing a Hydrafacial first prepares the skin, allowing subsequent treatments to penetrate more effectively, thereby amplifying collagen production and skin rejuvenation [297, 298].

Microneedling with Growth Factors: Microneedling is particularly beneficial for clients dealing with acne scars, fine lines, and uneven skin texture. This treatment stimulates collagen production and improves skin tone, making it ideal for those with early aging signs. However, it is not recommended for individuals with active acne or severe skin conditions due to the potential for exacerbating these issues [271, 299].

The mechanism of microneedling involves creating micro-injuries that activate the skin's natural healing processes. When combined with growth factors, the healing and collagen production are significantly enhanced, resulting in more pronounced and lasting outcomes [291, 300].

Microneedling can be paired with RF microneedling for enhanced tightening effects or with Hydrafacial to prepare the skin beforehand. It is essential to space these treatments appropriately, as microneedling should follow a Hydrafacial after the skin has had time to heal [301, 302].

RF Microneedling: RF microneedling is particularly effective for clients experiencing moderate to severe skin laxity, deeper wrinkles, and stretch marks. It is a non-surgical option for those seeking skin tightening and lifting, although it may not be suitable for individuals with very thin or sensitive skin due to the intensity of the RF energy [303, 304].

This treatment synergistically combines the collagen-stimulating effects of microneedling with the skin-tightening benefits of radiofrequency energy. The RF energy heats deeper skin layers, promoting collagen remodelling and improving skin firmness over time [160, 305].

For enhanced results, RF microneedling can be alternated with exosome therapy, which aids in faster healing and improved outcomes. Following RF microneedling with Hydrafacial can help maintain hydration and refine skin texture, ensuring comprehensive rejuvenation [306, 307].

Exosome Therapy: Exosome therapy is suitable for clients seeking advanced regenerative treatments, particularly those with significant skin damage, including scars and pigmentation issues. It is also beneficial for individuals recovering from invasive procedures, as it accelerates healing and reduces inflammation [308, 309].

Exosomes, derived from stem cells, contain growth factors and bioactive molecules that stimulate cellular repair and renewal, enhancing collagen production and improving skin texture [273, 310]. When combined with microneedling or RF microneedling, the micro-injuries facilitate deeper absorption of exosomes, making this combination particularly effective for anti-aging and scar reduction [268, 311].

Cryotherapy: Cryotherapy is ideal for clients with puffiness, redness, or inflammation, offering a quick, non-invasive treatment for tightening and brightening the skin. It is also effective in reducing acne-related inflammation and stimulating circulation in dull skin [312].

The cold exposure from cryotherapy enhances blood flow and collagen synthesis, resulting in a firmer appearance. It serves as an excellent maintenance treatment for sensitive or rosacea-prone skin. Cryotherapy can complement Hydrafacial or exosome therapy to further reduce inflammation and optimize results, making it a suitable post-treatment care option after RF microneedling or microneedling with growth factors.

In summary, and as summarised in Table 5, the strategic combination of these advanced skincare treatments can address a variety of skin concerns effectively. Tailoring combinations based on individual client needs—such as anti-aging, scar reduction, pigmentation issues, or sensitive skin—can significantly enhance treatment outcomes and client satisfaction.

Table 5: Summary of regenerative treatment options.

Treatment	Who it's for	Why it works	Combination Recommendations
Hydrafacial with Regenerative Boosters	Ideal for clients with dull, dehydrated, or uneven skin, and mild signs of aging like fine lines or loss of elasticity. Perfect for event preparation or those with sensitive skin seeking a gentle yet effective solution.	This treatment deeply cleanses, exfoliates, and hydrates the skin while infusing customized regenerative serums tailored to the client's needs. Boosters like growth factors or hyaluronic acid enhance the skin's ability to repair itself and restore a youthful glow.	Pairs well with microneedling with growth factors or exosome therapy for deeper rejuvenation. Hydrafacial can prepare the skin by cleansing and hydrating before microneedling or exosome therapy amplifies repair and collagen production.
Microneedling with Growth Factors	Best for individuals with acne scars, fine lines, uneven texture, or enlarged pores. Ideal for those looking to	Microneedling creates micro-injuries that trigger the skin's repair processes, while growth factors enhance healing and	Can be combined with RF microneedling for enhanced tightening or Hydrafacial with regenerative boosters to prep the skin. These

Advances in Cosmetology

Treatment	Who it's for	Why it works	Combination Recommendations
	stimulate collagen production and improve skin tone, but not suitable for those with active acne or severe skin conditions.	collagen production, delivering pronounced and long-lasting results.	treatments should be spaced apart, with microneedling following after the skin heals from Hydrafacial.
RF Microneedling	Suitable for clients with moderate to severe skin laxity, deeper wrinkles, stretch marks, or acne scars. Ideal for non-surgical tightening and lifting of the face, neck, or body. Not recommended for very thin or sensitive skin due to the intensity of RF energy.	Combines microneedling's collagen-stimulating effects with radiofrequency energy for skin-tightening. RF heats deeper skin layers, promoting collagen remodeling and improving firmness over time.	Can be alternated with exosome therapy for faster healing and enhanced results. Hydrafacial with regenerative boosters several weeks later helps maintain hydration and further refine the skin's texture post RF microneedling.
Exosome Therapy	Perfect for clients seeking advanced regenerative treatments. Ideal for those with significant skin damage, including scars, pigmentation, and severe aging signs.	Exosomes contain growth factors, cytokines, and bioactive molecules that promote cellular repair, collagen production, and overall skin rejuvenation. They reduce	Pairs effectively with microneedling with growth factors or RF microneedling, as micro-injuries allow for deeper exosome absorption. Also follows Hydrafacial with regenerative boosters to hydrate and treat deeper skin

Treatment	Who it's for	Why it works	Combination Recommendations
	Recommended for recovery from invasive procedures due to its ability to speed healing and reduce inflammation.	redness, improve skin tone, and accelerate recovery after procedures.	issues simultaneously.
Cryotherapy	Ideal for clients with puffiness, redness, or inflammation, and those looking for quick tightening and brightening. Effective for reducing acne-related inflammation and stimulating circulation in dull skin.	Enhances blood flow, reduces swelling, and promotes collagen synthesis through cold exposure. This results in firmer, lifted skin and is particularly beneficial for maintenance in clients with sensitive or rosacea-prone skin.	Complements Hydrafacial with regenerative boosters or exosome therapy to reduce inflammation and optimize results. Cryotherapy is also excellent for post-treatment care after RF microneedling or microneedling with growth factors to soothe and accelerate recovery.

Tailored Combinations for Specific Concerns

For clients seeking anti-aging solutions to address wrinkles and skin laxity, a combination of treatments can deliver comprehensive results. Starting with a Hydrafacial infused with regenerative boosters provides deep hydration and gentle exfoliation, creating a refreshed and smooth surface. This prepares the skin for RF microneedling, which tightens and lifts sagging areas by stimulating collagen and elastin production through heat and controlled micro-injuries. To further enhance the anti-aging benefits, exosome therapy can be applied following RF microneedling. The exosomes accelerate collagen remodelling, improve elasticity, and promote cellular renewal for firmer, more youthful-looking skin.

For individuals aiming to reduce acne scars or stretch marks, microneedling with growth factors serves as an effective first step. This treatment targets scar tissue by creating micro-channels that stimulate collagen production and improve overall skin texture. Following microneedling, exosome therapy can be applied to speed up healing and amplify the regenerative effects. Exosomes deliver concentrated growth factors that repair damaged skin and enhance the results of microneedling. Later, a Hydrafacial can be introduced to refine the skin further, improving its brightness and tone while maintaining hydration.

Clients dealing with pigmentation issues or dull skin can benefit from starting their regimen with a Hydrafacial infused with brightening boosters. This treatment effectively exfoliates dead skin cells and addresses uneven skin tone, laying the groundwork for subsequent therapies. Microneedling with growth factors can then be performed to promote deeper skin rejuvenation and repair pigmentation at its source. To achieve the best results, exosome therapy can be incorporated to provide advanced cellular repair and reduce hyperpigmentation. Together, these treatments deliver a glowing, even complexion.

For those with sensitive or redness-prone skin, a gentler approach is essential to prevent irritation. Cryotherapy is an excellent starting point, as it calms inflammation, boosts circulation, and strengthens the skin's natural barrier. This can be paired with a Hydrafacial featuring regenerative boosters to hydrate the skin and gently exfoliate without causing redness or discomfort. RF-based treatments should be avoided for sensitive skin types, as the heat generated may aggravate inflammation or worsen redness.

Hair restoration is another area where tailored combinations can yield impressive results. Exosome therapy is a cutting-edge option for stimulating hair follicles and promoting regrowth. By delivering a concentrated dose of growth factors and bioactive molecules directly to the scalp, exosomes rejuvenate dormant follicles and improve scalp health. When combined with microneedling for the scalp, the effectiveness of the therapy is significantly enhanced. Microneedling creates micro-channels in the scalp, allowing the exosomes to penetrate deeply and target the root causes of hair thinning. This dual approach is ideal for clients experiencing hair loss or seeking to improve hair density and quality.

In all cases, combining treatments allows for a comprehensive and personalized approach to address specific skin or hair concerns. By leveraging the synergistic effects of multiple therapies, clients can achieve more dramatic and long-lasting improvements while addressing their unique needs.

Nanotechnology in Skincare Products

Nanotechnology, the science of manipulating materials at an incredibly small scale, has significantly transformed the skincare industry. By creating nanoparticles or nanosized carriers, scientists have enhanced the delivery, stability, and overall efficacy of active ingredients in skincare products. This advanced technology allows beneficial compounds to penetrate deeper layers of the skin, providing results that are often more pronounced and effective compared to traditional formulations. The application of nanotechnology in skincare has opened up new possibilities for addressing a wide range of skin concerns while offering innovative solutions for improving product performance.

Nanomaterials, defined as materials with dimensions ranging from 1 to 100 nanometres in at least one dimension, exhibit distinct properties that differ significantly from their bulk counterparts. This size-dependent behaviour is attributed to the increased surface area-to-volume ratio and quantum effects that become pronounced at the nanoscale. These unique properties enable the exploitation of nanomaterials in various applications, particularly in the cosmetic and skincare industries, where they are utilized to enhance product efficacy and safety [313-315].

The incorporation of nanomaterials into cosmetic formulations has led to the emergence of "nanocosmetics," which are designed to overcome the limitations of traditional cosmetic products. For instance, nanoparticles such as silver, gold, titanium dioxide, and zinc oxide are frequently employed due to their enhanced stability, improved penetration, and ability to encapsulate active ingredients effectively [313, 316, 317]. These innovations not only improve the delivery of active compounds but also enhance the sensory attributes of cosmetic products, making them more appealing to consumers [314, 315]. Moreover, the use of nanoparticles in formulations like nanoemulsions and liposomes allows for better solubility and stability of cosmetic ingredients, which is crucial for maintaining product quality over time [317-319].

The cosmeceutical industry, which merges cosmetic and pharmaceutical properties, is experiencing rapid growth, driven by advancements in nanotechnology. Research indicates that the use of nanomaterials in this sector is expanding, with a focus on developing products that offer targeted delivery and enhanced performance [319, 320]. For example, silver nanoparticles are recognized for their antibacterial properties, making them suitable for applications in skincare products aimed at acne treatment and wound healing [313, 321, 322]. Similarly, titanium dioxide and zinc oxide nanoparticles are popular in sunscreens due to their superior UV protection capabilities compared to larger particles, which often leave a visible residue on the skin [323-325].

However, the increasing use of nanomaterials in cosmetics raises concerns regarding safety and potential health risks. Studies have highlighted the need for thorough assessments of the skin absorption and systemic effects of nanoparticles, as their small size may facilitate deeper penetration into the skin layers [326-328]. Regulatory bodies are beginning to address these concerns, emphasizing the importance of safety evaluations before the commercial release of nanocosmetics [320, 329]. As the industry continues to evolve, balancing the benefits of nanotechnology with safety considerations will be crucial for consumer acceptance and regulatory compliance.

Nanotechnology is particularly valuable for enhancing the penetration of active ingredients. The outermost layer of the skin, the stratum corneum, acts as a natural barrier that limits the absorption of skincare products. Nanoparticles, due to their minuscule size, can effectively bypass this barrier and deliver active ingredients such as vitamins, peptides, and antioxidants directly to the deeper layers of the skin. This targeted delivery maximizes the efficacy of these compounds, allowing for better hydration, rejuvenation, and overall skin health. For instance, nanosized carriers like liposomes and solid lipid nanoparticles are commonly used to deliver retinoids and hyaluronic acid, ensuring optimal absorption and effectiveness.

Another significant advantage of nanotechnology in skincare is its ability to improve the stability of sensitive ingredients. Many active compounds, such as vitamin C and retinol, are prone to degradation when exposed to environmental factors like air, light, or heat. By encapsulating these ingredients within nanoparticles, their stability is preserved, ensuring they remain potent throughout the product's shelf life. This approach not only enhances the longevity of skincare formulations but also guarantees consistent results for the user.

Nanotechnology also enables the controlled and sustained release of active ingredients. This means that the compounds are delivered gradually over time, reducing the risk of irritation from potent ingredients and maintaining a consistent effect. This makes nanoparticle-based products particularly suitable for individuals with sensitive skin or those prone to adverse reactions from high concentrations of active ingredients.

One of the most notable applications of nanotechnology in skincare is its use in sunscreen formulations. Ingredients like zinc oxide and titanium dioxide, when converted into nanoparticle form, create sunscreens that are lightweight, transparent, and non-greasy. These nanoparticle-based sunscreens offer broad-spectrum UV protection without leaving the white residue commonly associated with traditional sunscreens, making them more appealing for everyday use.

Nanotechnology has also shown promise in antimicrobial and wound-healing applications. Nanoparticles with antimicrobial properties, such as silver nanoparticles, are incorporated into skincare products to target acne-causing bacteria, reduce inflammation, and promote faster wound healing. Their small size allows them to reach areas of infection or irritation with greater precision, enhancing their effectiveness.

In the realm of anti-aging skincare, nanotechnology plays a pivotal role in delivering peptides, growth factors, and stem cell derivatives deep into the skin. These active compounds stimulate collagen production, improve elasticity, and reduce the appearance of fine lines and wrinkles. Nanosized hyaluronic acid particles are especially popular for their ability to hydrate and plump the skin, providing a youthful and radiant appearance.

Safety Concerns

Nanotechnology in skincare, while offering remarkable advancements in product efficacy and innovation, also raises significant concerns and presents regulatory challenges that need to be addressed for safe and sustainable use. These concerns encompass safety, regulatory compliance, and environmental impact, each of which poses unique challenges for manufacturers, regulators, and consumers alike.

One of the primary concerns with nanotechnology in skincare is safety. Nanoparticles are engineered to be extremely small, allowing them to penetrate the skin's outer layers effectively. While this property enhances the delivery of active ingredients, it also raises the potential for unintended systemic absorption. Once nanoparticles enter the bloodstream, they could travel to various organs, raising questions about their impact on overall human health. Although current research has not conclusively demonstrated harmful long-term effects, the potential for nanoparticle accumulation in tissues remains a subject of ongoing study. This concern is particularly relevant for nanoparticles used in sunscreens, such as zinc oxide and titanium dioxide, which are applied in large amounts and may remain on the skin for extended periods.

Regulatory challenges further complicate the adoption of nanotechnology in skincare. In many regions, including the United States and the European Union, products containing nanoparticles are subject to additional scrutiny and safety assessments. Regulatory agencies require manufacturers to provide evidence of the safety of nanoparticles, including data on their size, composition, and behaviour when applied to the skin. These assessments aim to ensure that nanoparticles do not pose risks to consumers. However, the lack of standardized testing methods and the complexity of nanomaterials make compliance with these regulations a time-consuming and expensive process for manufacturers. This can slow down innovation and market entry for new products.

The environmental impact of nanoparticles is another critical concern. When skincare products containing nanoparticles are washed off, they can enter water systems and potentially harm aquatic ecosystems. Metallic nanoparticles, such as silver or titanium dioxide, are particularly problematic as they may accumulate in water sources and disrupt the balance of aquatic life. Studies have shown that certain nanoparticles can be toxic to microorganisms and fish, posing risks to biodiversity and water quality. These environmental challenges highlight the need for sustainable practices in the production, use, and disposal of nanotechnology-based skincare products.

Types of Nanoparticles Used in Skincare

Liposomes

Liposomes are one of the most widely used types of nanoparticles in skincare. These hollow, spherical vesicles are composed of phospholipids, which closely mimic the structure of natural cell membranes. This similarity allows liposomes to merge seamlessly with skin cells, making them highly effective carriers for active ingredients. Liposomes are particularly versatile as they can encapsulate both hydrophilic (water-soluble) and lipophilic (oil-soluble) compounds, such as vitamins, peptides, and antioxidants. This dual capability ensures that beneficial ingredients penetrate deep into the skin, bypassing the protective barrier of the stratum corneum. Liposomes also provide an added layer of protection for sensitive ingredients like retinol and vitamin C, shielding them from oxidation and degradation caused by environmental factors.

Liposomes have become a cornerstone in cosmetic and skincare applications due to their advanced structure and ability to deliver active ingredients deep into the skin. Their unique vesicular structure, composed of lipids or other amphiphilic molecules, allows them to enhance the penetration of beneficial compounds through biological membranes, improving the efficacy of skincare formulations. Below is a comprehensive explanation of liposomes in cosmetics, their structures, types, applications, and advantages, as well as their role in topical drug delivery systems.

The structure of liposomes is fundamental to their function in skincare. These are spherical vesicles formed by self-assembly in a solvent, and they consist of one or more lipid bilayers surrounding an aqueous core. This unique structure enables liposomes to encapsulate both hydrophilic (water-soluble) and lipophilic (oil-soluble) molecules, making them versatile carriers for various active ingredients. When applied to the skin, liposomes fuse with biological membranes, such as the stratum corneum, to deliver their contents into deeper layers of the skin, thereby enhancing transdermal delivery and the overall effectiveness of cosmetic products.

Different types of cosmetic liposomes have been developed to target specific skincare needs. For example, nanoliposomes are specially engineered to be ultra-small, improving their penetration capabilities and bioavailability. Ethosomes, which are made from phospholipids, ethanol, and water, excel at penetrating deeper skin layers, making them ideal for delivering active ingredients like antioxidants and peptides into the dermis. Another type, phytosomes, combines phospholipids with botanical extracts to enhance the absorption of plant-based compounds, improving skin hydration and radiance. Sphingosomes, made from ceramides, are particularly beneficial for repairing damaged skin and restoring the skin's natural barrier function, making them an excellent choice for dry or irritated skin.

Other types of liposomes cater to unique cosmetic and dermatological needs. For instance, invasomes, which contain ethanol and terpenes, are known for their high skin penetration properties, making them effective carriers for deep-acting treatments. Glycerosomes, a blend of glycerol and phospholipids, deliver active ingredients with added healing and moisturizing benefits. Oleosomes, natural liposomes rich in oils, vitamins, and pigments, serve as reservoirs for delivering antioxidants and nutrients, providing long-lasting hydration and improved skin texture.

The advantages of liposomes in cosmetics are manifold. They enhance the stability of encapsulated active ingredients, such as vitamin C and retinol, protecting them from oxidation and degradation caused by light, air, or heat. Liposomes also increase the efficacy and therapeutic index of these ingredients, allowing for controlled and sustained release over time. Furthermore, their biocompatible and biodegradable nature makes them safe for systemic and non-systemic applications, minimizing the risk of irritation or adverse reactions. By reducing the exposure of sensitive tissues to potentially toxic drugs, liposomes offer a targeted and gentle approach to skincare.

Despite their numerous advantages, liposomes do have some limitations. Their production cost is high due to the sophisticated technology required for their formulation, and they can suffer from stability issues such as oxidation or leakage of the encapsulated ingredients. Additionally, their short half-life and low solubility can limit their long-term effectiveness, making it essential to store and handle them carefully.

One of the most advanced applications of liposomes is in ethosomal drug delivery systems. Ethosomes, a type of liposome, are specially designed for topical drug delivery, overcoming the skin's natural barrier—the stratum corneum—which restricts the diffusion of active ingredients. Ethosomes contain ethanol, which enhances the permeability of the skin, allowing drugs to penetrate more effectively and reach systemic circulation. This innovation has proven especially useful for delivering anti-aging agents, anti-inflammatory drugs, and other therapeutic compounds directly to the site of action.

Cosmetic liposomes have emerged as a crucial technology in the formulation of skincare products, enhancing the efficacy, stability, and penetration of active ingredients. These vesicular structures facilitate the delivery of various compounds, including peptides, hyaluronic acid, and antioxidants, directly to the skin layers where they exert their beneficial effects. The following analysis synthesizes evidence from multiple studies to illustrate the role of liposomes in the highlighted cosmetic products.

Estée Lauder's Advanced Night Repair Synchronized Multi-Recovery Complex utilizes encapsulated hyaluronic acid and peptides in liposomes, which significantly enhances skin hydration and repair during the night. Research indicates that liposomes can improve the deposition of active ingredients within the skin, thereby maximizing their therapeutic effects [330, 331]. Similarly, Lancôme's Absolue Revitalizing Brightening Soft Cream employs liposomal delivery of Grand Rose Extracts, which has been shown to nourish and brighten the skin while improving elasticity through enhanced penetration of these bioactive compounds [331, 332].

Advances in Cosmetology

Drunk Elephant's Protini Polypeptide Cream contains a blend of peptides and amino acids encapsulated in liposomes, which are known to improve skin texture and firmness by facilitating deeper absorption into the skin layers [333, 334]. La Roche-Posay's Lipikar AP+M Body Balm also leverages liposomal technology to deliver prebiotic ingredients that restore the skin barrier, providing long-lasting hydration [335]. L'Oréal's Revitalift Laser X3 Day Cream incorporates pro-retinol and hyaluronic acid via liposomal encapsulation, which enhances the anti-aging benefits by ensuring stability and effective penetration [336].

Vichy LiftActiv Peptide-C Anti-Aging Ampoules utilize liposomal formulations to stabilize vitamin C and peptides, ensuring their enhanced penetration into the skin [332, 335]. SkinCeuticals C E Ferulic Serum features a similar liposomal formulation that combines vitamin C, vitamin E, and ferulic acid, known for their antioxidant properties and ability to brighten the skin [332, 336]. Clarins Double Serum Complete Age Control Concentrate combines both water- and oil-soluble actives in liposomes, which boosts hydration and targets signs of aging effectively [331, 337].

The Eucerin Hyaluron-Filler + Elasticity Day Cream employs liposomal hyaluronic acid for deep hydration and wrinkle reduction, demonstrating the effectiveness of liposomes in enhancing the delivery of hydrophilic compounds [333, 334]. Elemis Pro-Collagen Marine Cream, with its marine algae extracts in liposomal form, supports collagen synthesis and improves skin hydration, showcasing the versatility of liposomes in delivering various active ingredients [332, 335].

Nivea Q10 Plus Anti-Wrinkle Day Cream utilizes liposomal Q10 to enhance antioxidant protection and reduce fine lines, while Filorga NCEF Reverse Cream features a liposomal delivery system for hyaluronic acid and collagen boosters, promoting skin renewal [331, 332]. Chanel Hydra Beauty Micro Serum incorporates micro-liposomes to deliver camellia flower extract for deep hydration, illustrating the advanced formulation techniques in modern skincare [332, 335].

Clinique Moisture Surge 100H Auto-Replenishing Hydrator uses liposomal aloe bio-ferment to provide prolonged hydration and improve skin barrier function, while Dermalogica Age Smart Super Rich Repair includes encapsulated peptides and botanical extracts in liposomes for skin strengthening and hydration [332, 335]. Bioderma Sensibio AR Cream features liposomes containing anti-inflammatory ingredients to soothe sensitive skin, demonstrating the therapeutic potential of liposomal formulations [331, 332].

Shiseido Ultimune Power Infusing Concentrate encapsulates botanical extracts in liposomes to enhance skin defense mechanisms and boost radiance, while Medik8 C-Tetra Luxe Liposomal Vitamin C Serum employs liposomal vitamin C to protect the skin from oxidative stress [332, 335]. Avene PhysioLift Precision Wrinkle Filler contains retinaldehyde encapsulated in liposomes for targeted wrinkle reduction, and Neutrogena Hydro Boost Gel Cream infuses hyaluronic acid in liposomes for long-lasting hydration [332, 335].

Solid Lipid Nanoparticles

Solid lipid nanoparticles (SLNs) represent a significant advancement in skincare technology, offering a cutting-edge solution for enhancing the stability, bioavailability, and effectiveness of active ingredients. These nanoparticles are composed of biodegradable lipids that remain solid at room and body temperatures, creating a stable matrix that can encapsulate and protect delicate or easily degradable active compounds. This unique structure ensures that the active ingredients remain intact and potent until they are delivered to the deeper layers of the skin.

SLNs are particularly advantageous for protecting ingredients that are highly sensitive to environmental factors such as light, oxygen, and heat. For example, coenzyme Q10, a powerful antioxidant known for its role in reducing oxidative stress and promoting skin repair, often degrades when exposed to air or light. Similarly, plant extracts and vitamins like retinol or vitamin C can lose their efficacy over time in conventional formulations. Encapsulating these ingredients within SLNs provides a protective barrier that prevents degradation, ensuring they remain effective throughout the product's shelf life.

One of the key benefits of SLNs is their ability to provide a controlled and sustained release of active ingredients. This gradual release mechanism allows the skin to absorb the ingredients over an extended period, maximizing their benefits while minimizing potential irritation. For instance, in anti-aging products, SLNs ensure that ingredients like peptides or hyaluronic acid are continuously delivered to the skin, enhancing collagen production, improving elasticity, and reducing the appearance of fine lines and wrinkles. This sustained release not only increases the efficacy of the treatment but also enhances the overall experience for the user by providing long-lasting effects.

The solid structure of SLNs also contributes to their suitability for formulations targeting skin repair and rejuvenation. By creating a robust delivery system, these nanoparticles ensure that active ingredients penetrate the skin effectively, reaching the layers where they are most needed. This makes SLNs an ideal choice for advanced skincare products designed to address issues such as hyperpigmentation, scarring, or environmental damage. Additionally, their solid lipid matrix is biocompatible and biodegradable, making SLNs a safe and environmentally friendly option for skincare applications.

Solid lipid nanoparticles (SLNs) have emerged as a significant advancement in the formulation of skincare products, particularly for their ability to enhance the stability and efficacy of active ingredients. This technology is increasingly utilized in high-end skincare brands, which leverage SLNs for their controlled release properties, ensuring prolonged hydration and nourishment of the skin.

For instance, La Prairie's Skin Caviar Luxe Cream utilizes SLNs combined with caviar extract to improve skin firmness and elasticity. The encapsulation of active ingredients in SLNs allows for a controlled release, which is critical for maintaining hydration and delivering nutrients effectively to the skin [338]. Similarly, Estée Lauder's Advanced Night Repair Synchronized Multi-Recovery Complex employs SLNs to encapsulate antioxidants and peptides, facilitating deeper penetration into the skin and ensuring longer-lasting effects on fine lines and uneven skin tone [339].

L'Oréal Paris's Revitalift Triple Power Anti-Aging Moisturizer exemplifies the integration of SLNs with hyaluronic acid and retinol, enhancing the stability of these ingredients while providing a gradual release that minimizes irritation [340]. This is particularly important given the sensitivity often associated with retinol products. Nivea's Q10 Plus Anti-Wrinkle Day Cream also incorporates SLNs to protect coenzyme Q10 from degradation, ensuring a controlled delivery that effectively reduces wrinkles and rejuvenates the skin [341].

Vichy's LiftActiv Supreme Anti-Wrinkle and Firming Cream combines SLNs with rhamnose and antioxidants, prolonging the release of active ingredients for sustained hydration and anti-aging benefits [342]. Dr. Barbara Sturm's Anti-Aging Face Cream targets fine lines by encapsulating plant extracts and vitamins in SLNs, which allows for deep and sustained delivery of these beneficial compounds [338].

Eucerin's Hyaluron-Filler Day Cream utilizes SLNs to deliver hyaluronic acid deep into the skin layers, ensuring long-lasting moisture, while Lancôme's Absolue Revitalizing & Brightening Soft Cream protects botanical extracts and vitamins, enhancing their absorption and stability through SLN technology [338]. Chanel's Sublimage La Crème employs SLNs to improve the bioavailability of plant-based active ingredients, ensuring sustained skin regeneration [338].

The Ordinary's Granactive Retinoid Emulsion 2% offers a gentler alternative to traditional retinol formulations by utilizing SLNs to stabilize retinoid compounds and provide a slow-release effect, which helps reduce irritation [339]. Olay's Regenerist Micro-Sculpting Cream combines SLNs with niacinamide and peptides, enhancing skin firmness and hydration through increased penetration of these active ingredients [343]. Clinique's Smart Clinical Repair Wrinkle Correcting Cream also benefits from SLNs, providing a gradual release of peptides and antioxidants for prolonged action against wrinkles [338].

Bioderma's Atoderm Intensive Baume utilizes SLNs to enhance moisturizing properties and ensure a controlled release of lipids, effectively soothing extremely dry or sensitive skin [338]. Clarins' Double Serum incorporates SLNs to protect delicate plant extracts and vitamins, enhancing their absorption and effectiveness [338]. Lastly, Skinceuticals' A.G.E. Interrupter targets advanced signs of aging by encapsulating powerful antioxidants in SLNs, which helps reduce oxidative stress and improve skin elasticity [338].

Nanoemulsions

Nanoemulsions are fine dispersions of oil and water, either in oil-in-water or water-in-oil configurations, stabilized by surfactants. These nanoparticles are widely used in skincare to enhance the solubility of poorly water-soluble active ingredients, such as essential oils and ceramides. Nanoemulsions are characterized by their small droplet size, which enables them to penetrate the skin more efficiently and deliver active ingredients to deeper layers. They also create lightweight, non-greasy formulations, which are highly desirable for modern skincare products. Nanoemulsions are commonly found in moisturizers, sunscreens, and serums, where they provide hydration, UV protection, and improved skin texture.

Nanoemulsions represent a significant advancement in the formulation of skincare products, characterized as ultra-fine dispersions of oil and water stabilized by surfactants, which can form either oil-in-water (O/W) or water-in-oil (W/O) configurations. The droplet size of nanoemulsions typically ranges from 20 to 200 nanometers, distinguishing them from traditional emulsions and providing unique advantages in skincare formulations, such as improved delivery, stability, and effectiveness of active ingredients [344-346]. The small droplet size enhances the solubility and stability of poorly water-soluble active ingredients, including essential oils, ceramides, and certain vitamins, which are often hydrophobic and do not easily dissolve in water-based formulations. By encapsulating these ingredients within tiny oil droplets, nanoemulsions facilitate their effective integration into water-based products like serums and moisturizers [347, 348].

One of the primary benefits of nanoemulsions is their ability to enhance the penetration of active ingredients into the skin. Unlike traditional emulsions that may remain on the skin's surface, nanoemulsions allow active compounds to penetrate deeper layers, such as the epidermis and dermis, thereby improving the effectiveness of treatments aimed at hydration, anti-aging, and pigmentation [346, 349, 350]. This targeted delivery mechanism is crucial for maximizing the therapeutic potential of skincare ingredients, making nanoemulsions particularly valuable in formulations designed for specific skin concerns.

In addition to their delivery capabilities, nanoemulsions are favored for their lightweight, non-greasy texture, which is highly appealing in modern skincare. Traditional oil-based formulations can often feel heavy or sticky, leading to discomfort and reduced user compliance. In contrast, nanoemulsions provide a smooth, silky finish that hydrates the skin without clogging pores or leaving an oily residue, making them suitable for oily or acne-prone skin types and for use in hot or humid climates [348, 351]. This characteristic enhances user experience and compliance, which is essential for the success of skincare products.

Nanoemulsions are commonly incorporated into a variety of skincare products, including moisturizers, sunscreens, and serums. In moisturizers, they encapsulate hydrating agents like hyaluronic acid and ceramides, ensuring sustained release and improved absorption [352]. In sunscreens, nanoemulsions help disperse UV filters evenly, providing broad-spectrum protection while maintaining a light, non-whitening finish [346, 353]. Furthermore, in serums, nanoemulsions enhance the delivery of active ingredients such as retinol, peptides, and antioxidants, significantly boosting their efficacy in improving skin texture and reducing signs of aging [346, 354].

Nanoemulsions have emerged as a significant advancement in the formulation of cosmetic skincare products, primarily due to their ability to enhance the delivery and stability of active ingredients while providing a lightweight texture. Numerous high-end skincare brands have adopted this technology to improve the efficacy of their products. For instance, La Mer's Revitalizing Hydrating Serum utilizes nanoemulsion technology to effectively deliver its signature Miracle Broth™, which is rich in marine extracts and antioxidants, ensuring deep hydration and skin nourishment [355]. Similarly, Lancôme's Advanced Génifique Youth Activating Concentrate employs nanoemulsions to facilitate the deep penetration of probiotics and other active ingredients that target signs of aging and enhance skin texture [356]. Estée Lauder's Advanced Night Repair Serum also incorporates nanoemulsion technology to optimize the delivery of hyaluronic acid and antioxidants, promoting overnight skin repair and hydration [315].

Neutrogena's Hydro Boost Water Gel exemplifies the use of nanoemulsions to provide long-lasting hydration through the effective delivery of hyaluronic acid and glycerin, all while maintaining a non-greasy feel [315]. Kiehl's Daily Reviving Concentrate employs nanoemulsions to stabilize and deliver essential oils, such as ginger root and sunflower oil, which contribute to revitalized and glowing skin [357]. Furthermore, Dr. Jart+'s Ceramidin Cream utilizes nanoemulsions to encapsulate ceramides, ensuring deep penetration and prolonged hydration for dry or damaged skin [315].

Biossance's Squalane + Vitamin C Rose Oil showcases how nanoemulsions can enhance the stability and delivery of squalane and vitamin C, leading to improved skin brightness and elasticity [357]. Vichy's Aqualia Thermal Dynamic Hydration Serum also leverages nanoemulsion technology to effectively deliver minerals, hyaluronic acid, and thermal water, providing hydration and plumping effects [315]. SkinCeuticals' C E Ferulic serum benefits from nanoemulsions that enhance the stability and absorption of antioxidants, making it a powerful formulation against aging and environmental damage [357].

L'Oréal's Revitalift Triple Power Anti-Aging Moisturizer employs nanoemulsion technology to deliver pro-retinol and hyaluronic acid deep into the skin, effectively improving wrinkles and firmness [357]. Shiseido's Ultimune Power Infusing Concentrate incorporates nanoemulsions to stabilize botanical extracts and antioxidants, enhancing skin immunity and radiance [315]. Eucerin's Hyaluron-Filler + Elasticity Day Cream utilizes nanoemulsions to deliver hyaluronic acid and argan oil, providing intense hydration and anti-aging benefits [357].

Murad's Hydro-Dynamic Ultimate Moisture benefits from nanoemulsions that enhance the delivery of avocado oil and coconut extract for deep hydration and a soft skin texture [357]. Clarins' Double Serum employs a nanoemulsion-based dual-phase formula to encapsulate and deliver 21 active plant extracts, providing both anti-aging and hydration benefits [357]. Lastly, Amorepacific's Time Response Skin Renewal Serum uses nanoemulsions to stabilize and deliver green tea stem cell extracts, offering antioxidant protection and anti-aging effects [357].

Nanocrystals

Nanocrystals represent a cutting-edge application of nanotechnology in the skincare industry. These are active ingredients that are processed into nanometre-sized particles, typically less than 100 nanometres in size. By reducing the particle size to the nanoscale, the active ingredient's surface area is significantly increased. This size reduction improves the solubility and bioavailability of the compound, allowing it to penetrate the skin more effectively and deliver better results.

The primary advantage of nanocrystals lies in their ability to enhance the performance of active ingredients that are otherwise poorly soluble in water or oil. Many potent skincare compounds, such as certain antioxidants, anti-inflammatory agents, and vitamins, face challenges in formulation due to their limited solubility. Nanocrystals overcome this issue by improving the dispersion of the ingredient in the formulation, ensuring that it is effectively absorbed by the skin.

Nanocrystals are particularly valuable for delivering highly active but challenging compounds, such as retinoids, curcumin, and coenzyme Q10. These ingredients are known for their powerful anti-aging, anti-inflammatory, and antioxidant properties but often lose efficacy in traditional formulations due to poor stability or limited absorption. Nanocrystal technology not only preserves their effectiveness but also ensures consistent results across different skin types.

In addition to enhancing absorption, nanocrystals provide a controlled and sustained release of active ingredients. This allows the skin to receive a steady supply of the ingredient over time, reducing the risk of irritation or over-concentration in sensitive areas. As a result, skincare products formulated with nanocrystals are generally more suitable for clients with sensitive skin or those prone to reactions.

Nanocrystals also contribute to the stability of skincare formulations. By reducing the particle size of an active ingredient, nanocrystals prevent sedimentation or aggregation, ensuring a uniform and aesthetically pleasing product. This stability is particularly important in serums, creams, and lotions, where an even distribution of active ingredients is crucial for efficacy.

Applications of nanocrystals in skincare include anti-aging products, where they deliver ingredients like vitamin A (retinol) and coenzyme Q10 to improve skin elasticity, reduce fine lines, and protect against environmental damage. They are also widely used in brightening formulations, where they enhance the bioavailability of compounds like ascorbic acid (vitamin C) to combat pigmentation and promote an even skin tone. In addition, nanocrystals are increasingly incorporated into sunscreens to improve the dispersion of UV filters, providing more effective and even sun protection.

The incorporation of nanocrystals in cosmetic skincare products has emerged as a significant advancement in enhancing the delivery and effectiveness of active ingredients. Various brands have adopted this technology to improve the stability, absorption, and overall efficacy of their formulations. Below is a synthesis of notable examples of such products and their active ingredients, supported by relevant literature.

La Prairie's White Caviar Illuminating Pearl Infusion utilizes vitamin C in nanocrystal form, targeting pigmentation and dark spots while enhancing skin texture. The application of nanocrystals allows for improved penetration of vitamin C, which is known for its antioxidant properties and ability to brighten the skin [358]. Similarly, Estée Lauder's Advanced Night Repair Serum employs hyaluronic acid in nanocrystal form, providing deep hydration and supporting skin repair processes overnight. The nanocrystal formulation enhances the bioavailability of hyaluronic acid, facilitating better moisture retention and skin barrier function [358].

L'Oréal's Revitalift Derm Intensives Pure Vitamin C Serum features ascorbic acid nanocrystals, which are effective in brightening skin tone and reducing dark spots. The encapsulation of vitamin C in nanocrystals not only stabilizes the ingredient but also promotes its absorption into the skin [358]. Shiseido's Ultimune Power Infusing Concentrate incorporates botanical extracts stabilized with nanocrystal technology, which strengthens the skin barrier and enhances overall radiance. This approach leverages the unique properties of nanocrystals to deliver active compounds more effectively [358].

Chantecaille's Bio Lifting Serum+ contains peptides and antioxidants in nanocrystal form, aimed at reducing fine lines and wrinkles while firming the skin. The use of nanocrystals in this formulation enhances the delivery of these active ingredients, ensuring they reach deeper skin layers for optimal results [358]. Dr. Barbara Sturm's Brightening Serum employs antioxidants and botanical compounds as nanocrystals, promoting a luminous complexion by effectively targeting pigmentation issues [358].

Richard Skiba

Clarins' Double Serum features plant extracts like turmeric encapsulated in nanocrystal particles, which hydrate and revitalize the skin. The encapsulation technique allows for sustained release and better absorption of the active ingredients, contributing to a youthful appearance [358]. SkinCeuticals' C E Ferulic combines vitamin C and ferulic acid in a nanocrystal delivery system, neutralizing free radicals and improving skin texture through enhanced penetration of these potent antioxidants [358].

Vichy's LiftActiv Vitamin C Serum utilizes nanocrystallized vitamin C to improve skin radiance and reduce wrinkles. The nanocrystal formulation ensures that vitamin C remains stable and effective, providing significant anti-aging benefits [358]. Olay's Regenerist Retinol 24 Night Serum incorporates retinol nanocrystals, which work overnight to reduce fine lines and enhance skin tone, demonstrating the effectiveness of nanocrystal technology in delivering retinoids [358].

Lancôme's Advanced Génifique Serum employs probiotics and active ingredients delivered through nanocrystal technology, boosting skin barrier strength and hydration. This innovative approach enhances the efficacy of probiotics, which are beneficial for maintaining skin health [358]. Eucerin's Hyaluron-Filler Vitamin C Booster combines hyaluronic acid and vitamin C nanocrystals to fill fine lines and brighten the skin, showcasing the synergistic effects of these ingredients when delivered via nanocrystals [358].

Elizabeth Arden's Prevage Anti-Aging Daily Serum features antioxidants like idebenone in nanocrystal form, protecting against environmental damage while improving skin texture. The nanocrystal delivery system enhances the stability and absorption of idebenone, making it more effective in combating oxidative stress (Rao, 2024). Drunk Elephant's C-Firma Fresh Day Serum utilizes vitamin C stabilized with nanocrystal technology, which aids in fading dark spots and promoting skin radiance through improved delivery of active ingredients [358].

Finally, L'Occitane's Immortelle Reset Oil-in-Serum encapsulates immortelle essential oil in nanocrystals, reducing signs of fatigue and boosting hydration. The nanocrystal technology allows for better penetration of the essential oil, enhancing its rejuvenating effects on the skin [358].

154

Advances in Cosmetology

Metallic nanoparticles

Metallic nanoparticles, including silver and gold nanoparticles, have become prominent in modern skincare formulations due to their remarkable properties and multifunctional benefits. These nanosized particles offer unique advantages, ranging from antimicrobial and anti-inflammatory effects to enhanced delivery of active ingredients and skin-brightening capabilities.

Silver nanoparticles are widely recognized for their antimicrobial and anti-inflammatory properties. They are highly effective in targeting and neutralizing acne-causing bacteria, making them a valuable ingredient in products designed for acne-prone or irritated skin. The small size of silver nanoparticles allows them to penetrate the skin barrier, addressing inflammation at a deeper level. This makes them particularly beneficial for calming redness, reducing swelling, and supporting the healing of blemishes. Additionally, silver nanoparticles are used in wound-healing formulations due to their ability to reduce the risk of infection and accelerate tissue repair.

Gold nanoparticles are celebrated for their ability to brighten the skin and enhance the efficacy of other active ingredients. By improving the delivery of actives, such as peptides, vitamins, or botanical extracts, gold nanoparticles ensure these compounds penetrate deeper into the skin, maximizing their impact. Gold nanoparticles also possess antioxidant properties, protecting the skin from environmental stressors, free radicals, and oxidative damage. These benefits make gold nanoparticles particularly useful in anti-aging products, where they help reduce the appearance of fine lines and wrinkles, improve elasticity, and promote a more radiant complexion.

Both silver and gold nanoparticles exhibit antioxidant effects, neutralizing free radicals that contribute to skin aging and damage. Their anti-inflammatory properties are also crucial for soothing sensitive or irritated skin. These combined effects make metallic nanoparticles highly versatile, as they not only treat specific conditions like acne or dullness but also offer protective and restorative benefits for overall skin health.

Metallic nanoparticles are incorporated into a wide variety of skincare products, including serums, creams, masks, and cleansers. For acne-prone skin, silver nanoparticles are commonly found in spot treatments and anti-acne cleansers, where they work to kill bacteria and soothe inflammation. Gold nanoparticles, on the other hand, are featured in luxurious anti-aging serums, brightening creams, and radiance-boosting face masks. These nanoparticles are also used in sunscreen formulations, where they enhance UV protection and provide additional skin-soothing benefits.

While metallic nanoparticles offer many advantages, their safety remains a subject of ongoing research. Concerns exist regarding the potential for systemic absorption due to their small size, which could lead to unintended effects within the body. As a result, regulatory bodies often require thorough safety assessments for products containing metallic nanoparticles to ensure they are safe for human use. Despite these concerns, reputable brands use rigorously tested formulations and ensure that nanoparticles are stabilized to minimize risks.

Various brands have adopted this technology to improve the stability, absorption, and overall efficacy of their formulations. La Prairie's White Caviar Illuminating Pearl Infusion utilizes vitamin C in nanocrystal form, targeting pigmentation and dark spots while enhancing skin texture. The application of nanocrystals allows for improved penetration of vitamin C, which is known for its antioxidant properties and ability to brighten the skin (Rao, 2024). Similarly, Estée Lauder's Advanced Night Repair Serum employs hyaluronic acid in nanocrystal form, providing deep hydration and supporting skin repair processes overnight. The nanocrystal formulation enhances the bioavailability of hyaluronic acid, facilitating better moisture retention and skin barrier function (Rao, 2024).

Silver nanoparticles are widely recognized for their antimicrobial properties, making them effective in treating acne and skin irritations. For instance, the Silver Serum by Skin Shop targets acne by utilizing antimicrobial silver to combat bacteria associated with acne formation. Similarly, Silver Gel by ASAP Silver employs colloidal silver to soothe irritated skin, reducing redness and promoting healing, which is corroborated by studies highlighting silver's efficacy in wound healing and inflammation reduction [329, 359].

The Curativa Bay Healing Skin Cream and Skeyndor Clear Balance Purifying Factor also leverage silver nanoparticles for their anti-inflammatory and antibacterial effects, making them suitable for sensitive and acne-prone skin

[319]. The multipurpose Silversalve by Nature's Salve incorporates silver nanoparticles to aid in healing cuts and skin irritations, showcasing the versatility of silver in various formulations [326].

Gold nanoparticles are celebrated for their skin-enhancing properties, particularly in anti-aging formulations. The Orogold 24K Deep Moisturizer utilizes gold nanoparticles to improve hydration and reduce fine lines, a claim supported by research indicating that gold can enhance skin elasticity and radiance [346]. The Tatcha Gold Camellia Beauty Oil combines gold flakes with nourishing oils to provide antioxidant benefits, further emphasizing the role of gold in promoting skin health [315].

Premium products like the La Prairie Cellular Radiance Concentrate Pure Gold and Peter Thomas Roth 24K Gold Mask utilize gold nanoparticles to enhance skin firmness and luminosity, aligning with findings that suggest gold's potential in improving skin texture and appearance [346]. The Chantecaille Nano Gold Energizing Cream and Guerlain Orchidee Imperiale Black Cream also highlight gold's anti-aging and anti-inflammatory effects, promoting smoother and firmer skin [315].

Products that combine silver and gold nanoparticles, such as the NanoSilver Anti-Aging Cream by NanoBioLife and BioEffect Gold and Silver Eye Patches, leverage the unique properties of both metals to enhance skin health and address multiple concerns like acne, puffiness, and fine lines. The Silver-MSM Healing Cream by Akoma Skincare and Dr. Levy Switzerland Booster Cream further illustrate the versatility of these nanoparticles in specialty formulations aimed at healing and combating signs of aging.

The use of metallic nanoparticles in sunscreens and other specialty products, such as the Colloidal Silver Spray by Argentum Apothecary**, showcases their protective qualities against bacteria and environmental stressors, reinforcing the importance of these nanomaterials in modern skincare [329, 359].

Matching Treatments to Clients: Suitability and Combinations

The suitability of treatments utilizing liposomes, solid lipid nanoparticles (SLNs), nanoemulsions, nanocrystals, and metallic nanoparticles in skincare depends on the specific needs of the client, their skin type, and their individual concerns. Each of these advanced nanotechnology applications offers unique benefits, making them well-suited for addressing a variety of skin issues. Understanding their specific advantages allows for precise targeting of skin conditions, either as stand-alone treatments or in combination with other technologies, to optimize results.

Liposomes are particularly effective for clients with dry, sensitive, or aging skin, as well as those looking to address hyperpigmentation or dullness. These hollow, spherical vesicles are made of phospholipids that mimic the structure of natural cell membranes. This structural similarity allows liposomes to integrate seamlessly with the skin, delivering active ingredients like peptides, antioxidants, and vitamins deep into the dermis. This deeper delivery mechanism makes them ideal for enhancing hydration, brightening the complexion, and improving overall skin texture. Liposome-based treatments work exceptionally well when paired with hydrating serums, such as those containing hyaluronic acid, or brightening ingredients like vitamin C. For a comprehensive anti-aging routine, liposomes can be combined with SLNs to deliver long-term hydration, promote collagen production, and support skin renewal.

Solid lipid nanoparticles (SLNs) are best suited for clients seeking long-lasting hydration, protection against environmental stressors, or anti-aging effects. They are particularly effective for individuals with dry, aging, or environmentally damaged skin. Composed of biodegradable lipids, SLNs encapsulate and stabilize sensitive active ingredients, such as coenzyme Q10, retinol, or vitamin C, which are prone to degradation. This encapsulation not only protects the active ingredients but also allows for their controlled and sustained release over time, ensuring prolonged efficacy without overloading the skin. SLNs are particularly beneficial when combined with nanoemulsions in moisturizers or serums, providing both immediate hydration and long-term repair. Additionally, they pair effectively with metallic nanoparticles, such as gold, to amplify their anti-aging benefits.

Nanoemulsions are an excellent choice for clients with oily or acne-prone skin, those who prefer lightweight formulations, or individuals seeking sun protection and enhanced hydration. Their small droplet size improves the penetration and absorption of active ingredients without clogging pores, making them ideal for delivering oil-soluble compounds like essential oils, ceramides, and vitamins. Nanoemulsions are especially beneficial for enhancing hydration, improving skin texture, and providing lightweight UV protection. These formulations pair well with liposomes in hydrating and brightening products or with nanocrystals for addressing pigmentation and uneven skin tone. Nanoemulsions are also commonly included in sunscreens, particularly when combined with metallic nanoparticles to provide enhanced UV protection and a smooth, non-greasy finish.

Nanocrystals are particularly beneficial for clients with pigmentation issues, uneven skin tone, or advanced signs of aging. They are also well-suited for individuals seeking powerful antioxidant protection or a brighter, more even complexion. By reducing active ingredients to nanometer-sized particles, nanocrystals significantly enhance their solubility and bioavailability. This allows potent but poorly soluble ingredients, such as vitamin C or retinol, to penetrate more deeply into the skin, making them far more effective. Nanocrystals work synergistically with nanoemulsions and liposomes in brightening and anti-aging serums. They can also enhance the effects of gold nanoparticles in skin-brightening and rejuvenating products, offering a comprehensive solution for clients with advanced skin concerns.

Metallic nanoparticles, including silver and gold nanoparticles, provide unique benefits for specific skin types and concerns. Silver nanoparticles are best for clients with acne-prone, irritated, or sensitive skin due to their antimicrobial and anti-inflammatory properties. These nanoparticles are effective at targeting acne-causing bacteria, reducing redness, and promoting healing, making them a valuable component in acne treatments. Gold nanoparticles, on the other hand, are ideal for anti-aging and brightening treatments, as well as for clients with dull or mature skin. They enhance the delivery of active ingredients, brighten the complexion, and provide antioxidant protection against free radicals and environmental damage. Silver nanoparticles can be effectively combined with nanoemulsions or SLNs in acne treatments for added hydration and healing, while gold nanoparticles pair exceptionally well with liposomes and nanocrystals in anti-aging and brightening products to deliver comprehensive skin renewal and protection.

The application and suitability of these products is summarised in Table 6.

Table 6: Applications for nanotechnology in skincare products by type.

Nanoparticle Technology	Who It's For	Why It Works	Combination Recommendations
Liposomes	Clients with dry, sensitive, or aging skin, as well as those targeting hyperpigmentation or dullness.	Liposomes mimic the structure of skin cell membranes, merging seamlessly with the skin to deliver active ingredients like peptides, antioxidants, and vitamins to deeper layers. They boost hydration, brighten complexion, and improve skin texture.	Pair with hydrating serums (e.g., hyaluronic acid) or brightening ingredients (e.g., vitamin C). Complement SLNs in anti-aging routines for hydration, collagen production, and skin renewal.
Solid Lipid Nanoparticles (SLNs)	Clients seeking long-term hydration, protection from environmental stressors, or anti-aging effects. Ideal for dry, aging, or environmentally damaged skin.	SLNs encapsulate and stabilize sensitive active ingredients like coenzyme Q10, retinol, or vitamin C. They provide a controlled, sustained release of	Combine with nanoemulsions in moisturizers or serums for hydration and repair. Pair with metallic nanoparticles, such as gold, for enhanced anti-aging benefits.

160

Nanoparticle Technology	Who It's For	Why It Works	Combination Recommendations
		ingredients, ensuring long-lasting efficacy without overwhelming the skin.	
Nanoemulsions	Clients with oily or acne-prone skin, those who prefer lightweight formulations, or individuals seeking sun protection and enhanced hydration.	Nanoemulsions deliver oil-soluble active ingredients like essential oils, ceramides, and vitamins effectively. Their small droplet size ensures better penetration and absorption without clogging pores. They are ideal for UV protection, hydration, and improved skin texture.	Combine with liposomes in hydrating and brightening products or nanocrystals for improving skin tone and texture. Work well in sunscreens with metallic nanoparticles for enhanced UV protection.
Nanocrystals	Clients with pigmentation issues, uneven skin tone, advanced signs of aging, or those seeking powerful antioxidant	Nanocrystals enhance solubility and bioavailability of potent but poorly soluble ingredients like vitamin C or retinol. They allow for	Synergize with nanoemulsions and liposomes in brightening and anti-aging serums. Enhance the effects of metallic nanoparticles like gold in skin-brightening and

Nanoparticle Technology	Who It's For	Why It Works	Combination Recommendations
	protection and brighter, even skin.	deeper penetration and better efficacy, promoting skin renewal and consistent results.	rejuvenating treatments.
Metallic Nanoparticles	Silver nanoparticles: Acne-prone, irritated, or sensitive skin. Gold nanoparticles: Anti-aging and brightening treatments for dull or mature skin.	Silver nanoparticles provide antimicrobial and anti-inflammatory effects, combating acne-causing bacteria and reducing redness. Gold nanoparticles improve active ingredient delivery, brighten complexion, and protect against free radicals, offering powerful antioxidant and anti-aging benefits.	Silver nanoparticles pair with nanoemulsions or SLNs in acne treatments for hydration and healing. Gold nanoparticles combine well with liposomes and nanocrystals in anti-aging and brightening routines.

Tailored combinations of advanced skincare technologies are designed to address common skin concerns by leveraging the strengths of nanoparticles like liposomes, solid lipid nanoparticles (SLNs), nanoemulsions, nanocrystals, and metallic nanoparticles. Each combination targets specific issues, ensuring optimal outcomes while maintaining skin health and comfort.

For anti-aging concerns such as wrinkles, fine lines, and loss of elasticity, a combination of liposomes and metallic nanoparticles, particularly gold, can enhance collagen production and improve skin elasticity. Liposomes efficiently deliver peptides and antioxidants deep into the skin, while gold nanoparticles amplify their effects by promoting better absorption and providing antioxidant protection. Adding SLNs to this regimen ensures sustained delivery of anti-aging ingredients like retinol and peptides, offering long-term benefits while minimizing irritation.

To address hydration and barrier repair, pairing liposomes with SLNs provides a powerful solution. Liposomes facilitate deep penetration of hydrating agents like hyaluronic acid, while SLNs create a protective matrix that locks in moisture and repairs the skin barrier. For clients who prefer lightweight, non-greasy formulations, nanoemulsions can be included to provide hydration without a heavy or oily feel, making this combination suitable for various skin types, including oily or combination skin.

For brightening and treating pigmentation issues, combining nanocrystals with liposomes maximizes the delivery of brightening agents such as vitamin C. Nanocrystals enhance the solubility and bioavailability of these actives, ensuring they penetrate deeply and act effectively. Adding nanoemulsions to this combination further improves the absorption and distribution of these ingredients, leaving the skin radiant and evenly toned.

For acne-prone or inflamed skin, silver nanoparticles are an excellent choice due to their antimicrobial and anti-inflammatory properties. Combined with nanoemulsions, these particles can effectively target acne-causing bacteria and reduce redness while maintaining a lightweight and breathable finish. Incorporating liposomes into the routine allows for the delivery of calming and repairing ingredients, such as ceramides or niacinamide, to soothe irritation and support skin healing.

Sensitive or irritated skin benefits from a gentle approach using liposomes to deliver soothing botanical extracts that reduce redness and discomfort. Adding nanoemulsions and SLNs ensures hydration and skin repair without overwhelming sensitive skin. These formulations are designed to provide lasting comfort and nourishment, making them ideal for clients prone to irritation or redness.

For UV protection and defense against environmental damage, combining metallic nanoparticles such as gold and silver with nanoemulsions in sunscreen formulations provides robust protection. Gold nanoparticles help reflect harmful UV rays and enhance the absorption of active sunscreen ingredients, while silver nanoparticles offer soothing and antimicrobial benefits. Adding liposomes loaded with antioxidants further combats free radicals, ensuring comprehensive defence against environmental stressors. This combination not only protects but also nourishes the skin, keeping it healthy and resilient.

Chapter 4

Clean Beauty Revolution

Traditional Cosmetic Products

Cosmetics are complex formulations made from a blend of natural, synthetic, and semi-synthetic ingredients. The choice of ingredients and their proportions vary depending on the type of product, such as skincare, makeup, or haircare, and their intended purposes, which may include moisturizing, cleansing, enhancing appearance, or protecting the skin. These products are designed to deliver specific benefits while ensuring safety, stability, and a pleasant sensory experience.

Active ingredients form the cornerstone of cosmetic formulations as they provide targeted benefits, such as hydrating the skin, reducing wrinkles, or protecting against environmental damage. Common examples include hyaluronic acid, used for its excellent hydration and skin-plumping properties, and retinol, a powerful anti-aging and acne treatment agent. Niacinamide is prized for its brightening and anti-inflammatory properties, while salicylic acid is frequently used in acne treatments for exfoliation and oil control. Ingredients like zinc oxide and titanium dioxide are essential in sunscreens, offering physical protection against harmful UV rays. These active compounds can be sourced from both natural origins, such as microbial fermentation or plant extraction, or synthesized in laboratories for enhanced stability and effectiveness.

Emollients play a crucial role in cosmetics by softening and moisturizing the skin while creating a protective barrier to prevent water loss. Natural oils such as coconut, shea butter, and almond oil are extracted through methods like cold pressing, offering hydration and nourishment. Synthetic emollients like dimethicone and mineral oil are derived from petroleum and provide a smooth texture and long-lasting hydration. Plant-based waxes, such as carnauba or candelilla wax, are sustainable options that are often used in solid formulations like lip balms, where they contribute to texture and stability.

Humectants are vital in keeping the skin hydrated by attracting water from the environment or deeper skin layers. Ingredients like glycerin and sorbitol can be derived from natural sources, such as plant or animal fats, or synthesized. Sodium PCA and urea, which also act as humectants, help maintain skin hydration and elasticity, with sodium PCA being derived from amino acids and urea produced through synthetic or natural pathways.

Surfactants are indispensable in cleansing products like shampoos and facial cleansers. These ingredients, including sodium lauryl sulfate (SLS) and cocamidopropyl betaine, reduce surface tension, allowing water to mix with dirt and oil for effective cleaning. SLS and sodium laureth sulfate (SLES) are chemically processed from coconut oil or petroleum, while cocamidopropyl betaine is a milder alternative derived from coconut oil.

Preservatives ensure the safety and longevity of cosmetic products by preventing microbial growth. Synthetic options like parabens and phenoxyethanol are widely used, while natural preservatives such as grapefruit seed extract and rosemary extract offer antimicrobial benefits. Sorbic acid, another natural preservative, is often used in formulations that aim to balance safety with eco-friendliness.

Stabilizers and thickeners improve the consistency and texture of cosmetics, ensuring even application and preventing ingredient separation. Xanthan gum, a natural thickener produced through microbial fermentation, is commonly used in gels and creams. Synthetic carbomers provide a gel-like texture, while fatty alcohols like cetyl and stearyl alcohol, derived from plant oils or synthetic processes, stabilize emulsions. Beeswax, along with its plant-based alternatives, contributes to the texture and solid structure of lip balms and creams.

Fragrances and essential oils enhance the sensory appeal of cosmetics, with synthetic fragrances mimicking natural scents and essential oils like lavender and eucalyptus providing both aromatic and therapeutic benefits. While fragrance-free formulations are popular for sensitive skin, essential oils are often extracted through steam distillation or cold pressing for natural benefits.

Colorants add aesthetic appeal to products like lipsticks and eyeshadows. Mineral pigments such as mica and titanium dioxide are refined from natural sources, while synthetic dyes like FD&C colours provide vibrant shades. Natural colorants, including beetroot powder and turmeric, are derived from plants using grinding or extraction techniques.

Antioxidants like vitamin C, vitamin E, and green tea extract protect the skin from free radical damage caused by environmental stressors. These ingredients also prevent the oxidation of other product components, extending shelf life. Vitamin C can be derived from citrus fruits or synthesized in labs, while green tea extract is obtained through aqueous or alcoholic extraction.

Sunscreen agents protect the skin from harmful UV rays. Physical sunscreens, such as zinc oxide and titanium dioxide, are derived from naturally occurring minerals and refined for cosmetic use. Chemical sunscreens like avobenzone and octinoxate are synthesized for optimal UV-blocking efficacy.

Botanicals and plant extracts are increasingly popular for their soothing and rejuvenating properties. Aloe vera, chamomile, green tea, and cucumber extracts are derived from plants through methods like maceration and steam distillation, offering hydration, antioxidant benefits, and anti-inflammatory effects.

Advanced delivery systems, including liposomes, solid lipid nanoparticles (SLNs), and nanoemulsions, enhance ingredient penetration and effectiveness. Liposomes are made from phospholipids and mimic cell membranes, while SLNs use biodegradable lipids for sustained release. Nanoemulsions improve the absorption of oil-soluble actives, ensuring deeper skin penetration.

Cosmetic formulations vary widely depending on their purpose, with moisturizers typically including humectants, emollients, and stabilizers, while cleansers focus on surfactants and hydrating agents. Serums often feature high concentrations of active ingredients stabilized by antioxidants and preservatives. Makeup formulations incorporate pigments, emollients, and sometimes SPF agents for additional protection.

Modern cosmetics prioritize not only functionality but also sustainability and safety. The growing demand for eco-friendly and health-conscious products has driven the adoption of biodegradable, sustainable, and clean ingredients, ensuring cosmetics meet consumer expectations for efficacy, transparency, and environmental responsibility.

The use of controversial chemicals in cosmetics has raised significant concerns regarding their potential health and environmental impacts. Many of these chemicals serve specific functional purposes, such as preservation, texture improvement, or enhancing product performance. For instance, the inclusion of parabens, which are widely used as preservatives, has been scrutinized due to their association with allergic reactions and potential endocrine disruption [360, 361]. Despite their long-standing presence in cosmetic formulations, the safety of parabens remains contentious, with some studies suggesting they may pose risks to human health, particularly in sensitive populations such as pregnant women [362].

The environmental implications of these chemicals cannot be overlooked. Many cosmetic ingredients, such as triclosan and microplastics, are known for their bioaccumulation potential and persistence in ecosystems, leading to adverse effects on both human health and the environment [363, 364]. The indiscriminate use of cosmetics containing these substances contributes to pollution, as they are often released into water systems during usage and disposal [365]. This highlights the need for stricter regulations and consumer awareness regarding the ingredients in cosmetic products.

Additionally, the cosmetic industry has seen a shift towards the use of biotechnology-derived ingredients and natural alternatives, driven by consumer demand for safer and more environmentally friendly products [247, 366]. However, the transition to greener formulations is complicated by the need for regulatory frameworks that can adequately evaluate the safety and efficacy of these new ingredients [367]. As consumers become more informed about the potential risks associated with traditional cosmetic ingredients, there is an increasing trend towards the adoption of natural and organic products, which are perceived as safer alternatives [368].

Parabens: Parabens, including methylparaben, ethylparaben, and propylparaben, are widely utilized as preservatives in cosmetics due to their effectiveness in preventing the growth of bacteria, mold, and fungi. Their low cost and broad-spectrum antimicrobial properties make them a popular choice in the formulation of various cosmetic products, such as lotions, creams, and makeup, thereby extending their shelf life and ensuring product safety [369-371]. The ability of parabens to maintain microbiological purity is crucial for the cosmetic industry, as it helps prevent product spoilage and degradation [370, 371].

Despite their widespread use, parabens have become a subject of controversy due to their classification as potential endocrine disruptors. Research indicates that parabens can mimic estrogen, leading to concerns about their role in breast cancer and reproductive health issues [372-374]. Studies have shown that parabens can interfere with hormone function, raising alarms about their safety, particularly in products used by women [372, 375]. Regulatory bodies, including the FDA and the European Union's Scientific Committee on Consumer Safety (SCCS), have assessed the safety of parabens, concluding that they are safe at low concentrations—specifically, up to 0.4% for individual parabens and 0.8% for mixtures [376, 377]. However, the ongoing debate about their potential health risks continues to spur research and public concern [374, 375].

In addition to their potential endocrine-disrupting effects, parabens have been linked to allergic reactions, such as contact dermatitis, although these occurrences are relatively rare [360]. The systematic review of allergic responses to parabens indicates that while sensitization can occur, it is not common in the general population [360]. Furthermore, studies have highlighted the presence of parabens in human tissues, including breast tissue, which has fuelled discussions regarding their safety and potential links to cancer [373, 378]. Nevertheless, the consensus among regulatory authorities remains that parabens, when used within established safety limits, do not pose a significant risk to human health [376, 377].

Parabens, including methylparaben, ethylparaben, and propylparaben, can be identified in cosmetic products by carefully reading the ingredient list on product labels. These compounds are typically listed by their specific names, such as "methylparaben" or "propylparaben." In some cases, the ingredient label may group several parabens together under a broader term like "parabens," but most regulations require individual naming for transparency.

Parabens are commonly found in products like moisturizers, foundations, shampoos, conditioners, sunscreens, and deodorants due to their role as preservatives. Their primary function is to inhibit the growth of bacteria, mold, and fungi, which can spoil products and pose a health risk to users. Parabens are particularly effective at preventing microbial contamination in water-based formulations, where bacteria and mold are more likely to grow.

Their widespread use stems from their cost-effectiveness and efficiency in small concentrations, typically less than 1%. They extend the shelf life of cosmetic products, ensuring their stability and safety over time. Despite their benefits, parabens have sparked controversy due to potential health concerns. They are classified as suspected endocrine disruptors, meaning they can mimic estrogen, potentially affecting hormone function. This has raised concerns about their possible links to breast cancer, reproductive issues, and other hormone-related conditions.

Although the scientific community has conducted extensive research on parabens, their safety remains a debated topic. Regulatory agencies, including the U.S. Food and Drug Administration (FDA) and the European Union's Scientific Committee on Consumer Safety (SCCS), have concluded that certain parabens are safe for use in cosmetics when present at low concentrations (up to 0.8% for individual parabens or 1.0% for mixtures). However, the EU has restricted the use of longer-chain parabens, such as isobutylparaben and isopropylparaben, due to insufficient safety data.

For consumers concerned about parabens, many brands now offer "paraben-free" products, clearly labelled as such. These products often use alternative preservatives like phenoxyethanol, potassium sorbate, or natural options like grapefruit seed extract or rosemary extract. While "paraben-free" products are marketed as safer, it's essential to note that the safety of any preservative depends on its concentration, formulation, and individual skin sensitivity.

Phthalates: Phthalates, particularly diethyl phthalate (DEP), are widely utilized in various consumer products, especially in cosmetics, where they serve as plasticizers and solvents. Their primary function in cosmetics includes enhancing the flexibility of products such as nail polishes and hair sprays, as well as acting as fixatives in fragrances to prolong scent longevity [379-381]. The extensive use of phthalates in personal care products is attributed to their ability to improve product performance and stability, making them a common ingredient in formulations ranging from perfumes to lotions [382, 383].

Despite their functional benefits, phthalates have become a focal point of controversy due to their classification as suspected endocrine disruptors. Research has linked phthalates to various health concerns, including developmental and reproductive toxicity [383, 384]. The potential for cumulative exposure is particularly alarming, as individuals may encounter phthalates from multiple sources, including cosmetics, food packaging, and household products [385, 386]. This widespread exposure has prompted regulatory actions in several regions, notably the European Union, which has implemented restrictions on specific phthalates in cosmetic products due to their associated health risks [387].

The concerns surrounding phthalates are underscored by studies indicating their pervasive presence in indoor environments and consumer products. For instance, phthalates are frequently detected in indoor dust, highlighting the potential for non-dietary human exposure [388]. Moreover, the ability of phthalates to leach from products into the environment raises additional questions about their safety and long-term effects on human health [389]. As a result, there is a growing call for increased awareness and regulation regarding the use of phthalates in consumer goods, particularly in cosmetics, where the potential for direct skin absorption and inhalation is significant [385, 390].

Phthalates, such as diethyl phthalate (DEP), can be identified in cosmetic products by examining the ingredient list, where they may appear under specific names such as "diethyl phthalate," "dibutyl phthalate" (DBP), or simply "phthalates." However, they are often more challenging to detect in some formulations, particularly fragrances, as manufacturers are not always required to disclose all individual components of a fragrance blend, which can include phthalates.

Phthalates are widely used in cosmetics for their functional benefits. In nail polishes, phthalates like DBP act as plasticizers, preventing cracking or chipping and enhancing durability. In hair sprays, they improve flexibility and help the product maintain its hold without becoming overly stiff. Additionally, DEP is commonly used in fragrances to stabilize and prolong the scent, making it last longer on the skin.

The controversy surrounding phthalates stems from their classification as suspected endocrine disruptors. These chemicals may interfere with the hormonal system, mimicking or blocking hormones such as estrogen. Studies have raised concerns about their potential links to developmental and reproductive toxicity, including reduced fertility and birth defects in animal studies. While research in humans has not reached definitive conclusions, the potential for cumulative exposure to phthalates from multiple products has amplified concerns.

In response to these risks, regulatory actions have been taken in some regions. For example, the European Union (EU) has banned or restricted certain phthalates, such as DBP and diethylhexyl phthalate (DEHP), in cosmetics due to their potential health risks. The U.S. Food and Drug Administration (FDA) does not currently ban phthalates in cosmetics but continues to monitor scientific evidence related to their safety.

For consumers wishing to avoid phthalates, many brands now label their products as "phthalate-free." These formulations often use alternative solvents or stabilizers that provide similar benefits without the associated risks. It is especially important for individuals sensitive to hormonal imbalances, pregnant women, and parents selecting products for children to carefully check labels or opt for products explicitly free of phthalates. Fragrance-free or "natural fragrance" options may also reduce exposure, as fragrances are a common source of hidden phthalates.

Sodium Lauryl Sulphate (SLS) and Sodium Laureth Sulphate (SLES): Sodium Lauryl Sulphate (SLS) and Sodium Laureth Sulphate (SLES) are widely utilized surfactants and foaming agents in various personal care products, including shampoos, body washes, and cleansers. Their primary function is to create a rich lather, which consumers often associate with effective cleaning. SLS, an anionic surfactant, is known for its ability to reduce surface tension, thereby facilitating the removal of dirt and oils from surfaces, including skin and hair [391]. Similarly, SLES, which is an ethoxylated derivative of SLS, is favoured for its mildness and high foaming ability, making it a common ingredient in many formulations [392].

However, the use of SLS and SLES is not without controversy. Both compounds can be harsh on the skin, stripping natural oils and potentially causing irritation, particularly in individuals with sensitive skin or pre-existing conditions such as eczema [393, 394]. Research indicates that SLS can damage the mucin layer of the skin, which is crucial for maintaining its protective barrier [395]. This denaturing effect can lead to increased skin sensitivity and irritation [396]. In contrast, SLES is generally considered milder than SLS but can still cause irritation in some users [392]. Furthermore, SLES is often processed with ethylene oxide, which raises concerns about the presence of 1,4-dioxane, a potential carcinogen. Regulatory agencies impose limits on the allowable levels of 1,4-dioxane in consumer products, yet its presence continues to be a significant concern for consumers and health professionals alike [393, 394].

The cytotoxic effects of these surfactants have been documented in various studies. For instance, a study found that SLS exhibited high cytotoxicity towards human gingival fibroblasts, indicating that even at low concentrations, it can be harmful to skin cells [397]. Additionally, SLS has been implicated in irritant contact dermatitis, with evidence suggesting that its effects are independent of atopic diathesis, meaning that even individuals without a history of skin conditions can experience adverse reactions [396]. The concentration of SLES in personal care products typically ranges from 5% to 15%, which can still pose risks of irritation and sensitization [398].

Sodium Lauryl Sulphate (SLS) and Sodium Laureth Sulfate (SLES) can be identified in cosmetic products by reading the ingredient list, where they are explicitly labelled as "Sodium Lauryl Sulfate" or "Sodium Laureth Sulfate." These ingredients are most commonly found in products like shampoos, body washes, facial cleansers, toothpaste, and household cleaning items, as they are highly effective surfactants and foaming agents.

SLS and SLES are used to create the rich lather and cleansing action that many consumers associate with cleanliness and efficacy. SLS is a strong detergent that breaks down oils and removes dirt from the skin and hair, making it effective in products that aim to thoroughly cleanse. SLES, a milder derivative of SLS, is often preferred in formulations where reduced skin irritation is a priority, but it is still valued for its ability to create a luxurious foaming texture.

The controversy surrounding these sulphates arises from their potential effects on skin health and safety concerns during their production. Both SLS and SLES are known to strip the skin and hair of natural oils, which can lead to dryness, irritation, and discomfort, particularly for individuals with sensitive or dry skin, or those with conditions such as eczema or dermatitis. SLES, in particular, undergoes a process called ethoxylation, during which it is treated with ethylene oxide to make it less harsh. However, this process can result in contamination with 1,4-dioxane, a byproduct classified as a potential carcinogen by agencies like the U.S. Environmental Protection Agency (EPA).

Regulatory bodies, including the U.S. Food and Drug Administration (FDA) and the European Union, have set limits on the permissible levels of 1,4-dioxane in cosmetic products to ensure consumer safety. Manufacturers are also encouraged to purify products to remove this contaminant. However, its presence in trace amounts has led to ongoing consumer concerns, particularly for those prioritizing non-toxic and clean beauty products.

For individuals seeking to avoid SLS and SLES, many brands now offer sulphate-free alternatives that rely on gentler surfactants derived from coconut oil or other natural sources, such as cocamidopropyl betaine or decyl glucoside. These options are especially appealing to those with sensitive skin, colour-treated hair, or a preference for clean and eco-friendly formulations. To ensure sulphate-free choices, consumers should look for labels that specifically state "sulfate-free" or examine the ingredient list to confirm the absence of these compounds.

Formaldehyde and Formaldehyde-Releasing Agents: Formaldehyde and formaldehyde-releasing agents are widely utilized in personal care products, including shampoos, nail polishes, and hair straighteners, primarily as preservatives. These compounds, such as quaternium-15, DMDM hydantoin, and imidazolidinyl urea, are effective in preventing microbial growth and extending the shelf life of these products, which is crucial given the water-based nature of many cosmetics that can support microbial proliferation [399, 400]. The use of preservatives is essential for maintaining product safety and efficacy, as microbial contamination can lead to product recalls and health risks [400, 401].

However, the use of formaldehyde is not without controversy. Formaldehyde has been classified as a known human carcinogen by several health organizations, including the International Agency for Research on Cancer (IARC) and the National Toxicology Program (NTP) [402, 403]. Exposure to formaldehyde can lead to various health issues, including skin irritation, allergic reactions, and respiratory problems [404, 405]. Regulatory bodies, particularly in the European Union, have responded to these health concerns by banning or heavily restricting the use of formaldehyde and its releasing agents in cosmetics [402, 404]. This regulatory landscape reflects growing public awareness and concern regarding the safety of cosmetic ingredients, particularly those associated with carcinogenic risks [405, 406].

The health risks associated with formaldehyde exposure are particularly significant in occupational settings, where workers may be exposed to higher concentrations of this chemical [404, 406]. Studies have shown that even low-level exposure can pose significant health risks, leading to increased cancer probabilities among exposed populations [406, 407]. As a result, there is a pressing need for the cosmetics industry to explore alternative preservatives that can ensure product safety without the associated health risks posed by formaldehyde and its derivatives [401, 405].

Formaldehyde and its releasing agents can be identified by carefully reading the ingredient list on product labels. While formaldehyde itself is rarely listed outright due to strict regulations and consumer awareness, formaldehyde-releasing compounds are often included as preservatives. Common examples include quaternium-15, DMDM hydantoin, imidazolidinyl urea, diazolidinyl urea, sodium hydroxymethylglycinate, and 2-bromo-2-nitropropane-1,3-diol (bronopol). These ingredients are designed to slowly release small amounts of formaldehyde over time to prevent microbial growth and extend the shelf life of products.

Formaldehyde is a highly effective preservative, preventing the growth of bacteria, mold, and fungi in water-based cosmetics. This makes it particularly useful in products like shampoos, conditioners, hair gels, nail polishes, liquid foundations, and hair straightening treatments. Formaldehyde-releasing agents are often preferred by manufacturers as they offer a steady and controlled release of the compound, ensuring long-lasting preservation without the need to list formaldehyde itself as an ingredient.

Formaldehyde is classified as a known human carcinogen by agencies such as the International Agency for Research on Cancer (IARC). Prolonged or excessive exposure to formaldehyde has been linked to an increased risk of certain cancers, particularly nasopharyngeal cancer. Beyond its carcinogenic potential, formaldehyde is a known irritant, capable of causing skin sensitization, allergic contact dermatitis, and respiratory issues. For people with sensitive skin, even low levels of formaldehyde released from preservatives can trigger redness, irritation, or allergic reactions. In professional settings, such as salons where hair treatments with formaldehyde are used, workers and clients may be exposed to higher concentrations, leading to eye, nose, and throat irritation.

Due to its health risks, many regulatory bodies have restricted or banned the use of formaldehyde and its releasers in cosmetics. The European Union prohibits the use of formaldehyde outright and strictly regulates formaldehyde-releasing agents in personal care products. In the United States, the Food and Drug Administration (FDA) has not banned formaldehyde but requires manufacturers to disclose its presence. Similarly, several countries have issued warnings or bans on the use of formaldehyde in high-risk products like hair straighteners.

Consumers seeking to avoid formaldehyde and its releasing agents should:

- **Check the Ingredient List**: Look for names like quaternium-15, DMDM hydantoin, imidazolidinyl urea, diazolidinyl urea, and bronopol.

- **Choose Formaldehyde-Free or Clean Beauty Products**: Many brands now label their products as "formaldehyde-free" to cater to safety-conscious consumers.

- **Prioritize Certification**: Look for certifications like USDA Organic, COSMOS, or EWG Verified, which often indicate safer formulations without formaldehyde or its derivatives.

By opting for products with safer preservative systems, such as phenoxyethanol, potassium sorbate, or plant-based alternatives, consumers can reduce their exposure to potentially harmful chemicals while still benefiting from effective and stable cosmetic formulations.

Talc: Talc, a hydrous magnesium silicate, is widely utilized in the cosmetic industry for its unique properties that enhance product performance. Its primary functions in cosmetics, such as powders, blushes, eyeshadows, and foundations, include moisture absorption, shine reduction, and texture improvement. Talc's ability to absorb moisture and oils makes it an ideal ingredient in various cosmetic formulations, contributing to a smooth and soft feel on the skin [408, 409]. The mineral's physical characteristics, such as its softness, lamellar structure, and chemical inertness, further support its extensive use in cosmetics [410, 411].

However, the use of talc is not without controversy, primarily due to concerns regarding its potential contamination with asbestos during mining processes. Asbestos, a known carcinogen, has been linked to serious health issues, including ovarian cancer and mesothelioma. Studies have documented cases where individuals developed mesothelioma after exposure to asbestos-contaminated talc, highlighting the risks associated with talc use in cosmetics [412, 413]. Notably, a review of epidemiological studies indicated that while many cosmetic talc products have been asbestos-free since 1976, the historical presence of asbestos in talc raises ongoing public health concerns [414, 415]. Furthermore, recent findings suggest that even talc that is not visibly contaminated can still pose risks, as inhalation of talc particles has been associated with pulmonary diseases and potential carcinogenic effects [416, 417].

Richard Skiba

The cosmetic industry has made strides to ensure the safety of talc used in products, with many companies now sourcing asbestos-free talc. Nevertheless, the possibility of contamination remains a significant public concern, as evidenced by reports linking talc exposure to various forms of cancer [418, 419]. Regulatory bodies and researchers continue to investigate the implications of talc use, emphasizing the importance of stringent quality control measures in the mining and processing of talc to mitigate health risks [414, 420].

Talc can be identified in cosmetic products by looking for the word "talc" or "magnesium silicate" in the ingredient list. Talc is commonly found in products like pressed and loose powders, blushes, eyeshadows, foundations, baby powders, and some body powders. It may also appear in deodorants and certain skincare formulations designed to absorb moisture or reduce shine.

Talc is a naturally occurring mineral that is widely used in cosmetics for its absorbent and smooth texture. Its moisture-absorbing properties make it effective in keeping skin dry and reducing shine, while its soft, fine consistency enhances the spreadability and blendability of powdered makeup products. Talc also prevents caking and provides a silky feel, which is especially desirable in products like foundation and eyeshadow. Its ability to act as a filler and stabilizer in formulations further contributes to its popularity in cosmetics.

The primary concern with talc stems from its potential contamination with asbestos, a fibrous mineral that naturally occurs near talc deposits. Asbestos is a known carcinogen, and its presence in talc has been linked to serious health conditions, including ovarian cancer and mesothelioma. Studies have suggested that talc-based products contaminated with asbestos can pose a risk when inhaled or applied to areas of the body. While many cosmetic manufacturers source asbestos-free talc and conduct rigorous testing to ensure purity, the lack of universal regulations and oversight in some regions has raised public concerns.

Litigation and consumer advocacy have further fueled the controversy. Several high-profile lawsuits have claimed that long-term use of talc-based products contributed to cancer diagnoses, drawing attention to the importance of transparency and safety testing in the industry. Even when talc is asbestos-free, its fine particles may pose a respiratory hazard when inhaled, particularly for people with pre-existing lung conditions.

Different regions have implemented varying levels of regulation regarding talc use in cosmetics. The U.S. Food and Drug Administration (FDA) has issued guidelines encouraging cosmetic manufacturers to test for asbestos contamination but does not mandate testing. In contrast, the European Union has stricter standards for cosmetic talc, prohibiting its use in products if there is any risk of asbestos contamination. Many companies have transitioned to alternatives like cornstarch or rice powder to address consumer concerns and ensure product safety.

Consumers who wish to avoid talc due to safety concerns can:

- **Check Labels**: Look for "talc" or "magnesium silicate" in the ingredient list and avoid products containing these.

- **Choose Talc-Free Products**: Many brands now label their products as "talc-free" to appeal to safety-conscious consumers. Look for alternatives made with cornstarch, rice powder, arrowroot powder, or silica.

- **Prioritize Certifications**: Look for third-party certifications or brands that adhere to strict safety testing, ensuring their talc is asbestos-free.

Triclosan: Triclosan, a synthetic antimicrobial agent, is widely utilized in various consumer products, including antibacterial soaps, toothpaste, and deodorants, primarily for its ability to kill bacteria and reduce odour [421, 422]. Its efficacy as an antibacterial agent has led to its incorporation in numerous personal care products, making it a common household chemical [421, 422]. However, the widespread use of triclosan has raised significant health and environmental concerns, particularly regarding its potential to disrupt endocrine functions and contribute to antibiotic resistance [423].

The controversy surrounding triclosan stems from its classification as an endocrine-disrupting chemical (EDC). Research indicates that triclosan can interfere with thyroid hormone levels, potentially leading to adverse reproductive health outcomes [424, 425]. For instance, studies have shown that exposure to triclosan may impair reproductive functions in various species, including humans, by affecting hormone production and regulation [426, 427]. Furthermore, evidence suggests that triclosan exposure is linked to increased allergic responses and sensitization, raising concerns about its impact on immune health [428].

The FDA has responded to these concerns by banning triclosan in over-the-counter hand soaps, although it remains permissible in other cosmetic products [422]. Environmental implications of triclosan are also significant. Triclosan is known to persist in aquatic ecosystems, where it can accumulate and disrupt the endocrine systems of aquatic organisms [429, 430]. Studies have documented the presence of triclosan in surface waters, primarily due to effluent from wastewater treatment plants, leading to concerns about its ecological impact [429, 431]. The compound has been shown to alter the composition of bacterial communities in aquatic environments, potentially leading to increased resistance among bacterial populations [429]. Additionally, the bioaccumulation of triclosan in marine sediments poses risks to aquatic life and raises questions about the long-term effects on biodiversity [431].

Triclosan can be identified in cosmetic products by checking the ingredient label for the name "triclosan." It is most commonly found in products marketed as antibacterial or antimicrobial, including soaps, hand sanitizers, toothpaste, deodorants, and some skincare products. Triclosan is not typically labelled with alternate names, making it relatively straightforward to spot on ingredient lists.

Triclosan is an antimicrobial and antibacterial agent widely used in personal care products to kill or inhibit the growth of bacteria. Its inclusion in formulations is intended to prevent bacterial contamination and reduce odours caused by bacteria, particularly in products like deodorants and toothpaste. For example, in toothpaste, triclosan can help control gingivitis and plaque buildup by reducing harmful oral bacteria. Similarly, in deodorants, it reduces bacterial growth that causes unpleasant body odour.

Triclosan has come under scrutiny for its potential health and environmental risks. One of the primary concerns is its role in contributing to antibiotic resistance. Overuse of antibacterial agents like triclosan in consumer products may promote the development of resistant bacterial strains, undermining the effectiveness of antibiotics used to treat infections.

Additionally, triclosan is suspected of being an endocrine disruptor, meaning it may interfere with hormone regulation. Some studies suggest that triclosan can alter thyroid hormone levels and impact reproductive health, though more research is needed to establish these effects conclusively.

From an environmental perspective, triclosan poses a significant risk to aquatic ecosystems. When washed into waterways, triclosan can accumulate and negatively affect aquatic organisms, disrupting ecosystems and potentially entering the food chain.

Due to these concerns, triclosan has faced regulatory restrictions in various regions. In 2016, the U.S. Food and Drug Administration (FDA) banned the use of triclosan in over-the-counter hand soaps and body washes, citing insufficient evidence of its safety and effectiveness compared to plain soap and water. However, triclosan remains permitted in other products, such as toothpaste and some deodorants, where its benefits, like reducing oral bacteria, are supported by research.

The European Union has stricter regulations, limiting the concentration of triclosan in cosmetic products to ensure consumer safety. Other countries and regions are also reconsidering its use, with many manufacturers voluntarily phasing it out and replacing it with safer alternatives.

Consumers concerned about triclosan can take the following steps to minimize exposure:

- **Check Labels**: Look specifically for "triclosan" in the ingredient list, particularly in antibacterial or antimicrobial products like toothpaste, deodorants, and cleansers.

- **Choose Triclosan-Free Products**: Many brands now market products as "triclosan-free" to appeal to health-conscious consumers.

- **Opt for Natural Alternatives**: Select products with natural antibacterial agents, such as tea tree oil, eucalyptus oil, or neem oil, which are less likely to contribute to antibiotic resistance or environmental harm.

- **Prioritize Transparency**: Choose brands that provide clear ingredient labelling and adhere to clean beauty standards.

Synthetic Fragrances: Synthetic fragrances are widely utilized in cosmetics and personal care products primarily due to their ability to create pleasant scents at a lower cost compared to natural alternatives. These synthetic compounds are often more stable, allowing for a longer shelf life and consistent scent profiles in products. The use of synthetic fragrances has surged since the late 19th century, becoming a staple in various consumer goods, including perfumes, lotions, and cleaning products [432]. Their prevalence is attributed to the economic advantages they offer manufacturers, as well as their versatility in formulation [366].

However, the use of synthetic fragrances is not without controversy. Many synthetic fragrances contain undisclosed chemicals, including phthalates, which are known endocrine disruptors. These compounds can interfere with hormonal functions and have been linked to various health concerns [433, 434]. The lack of transparency in fragrance formulations raises significant consumer safety issues, as individuals may unknowingly expose themselves to harmful substances. For instance, studies have shown that synthetic fragrances can trigger allergic reactions, skin irritations, and respiratory issues in sensitive individuals [435, 436]. The prevalence of allergens like linalool and limonene, which are commonly found in fragrance formulations, highlights the potential for adverse reactions among consumers [435, 436].

Moreover, the complexity of fragrance mixtures complicates safety assessments. Fragrance formulations can consist of numerous ingredients, often exceeding 300 components, making it challenging to evaluate their overall safety [437]. The regulatory landscape surrounding synthetic fragrances is also evolving, with increasing scrutiny on the use of phthalates and other harmful chemicals in consumer products [438]. This has led to a push for more eco-friendly and transparent alternatives, although the transition to "green" products has not always eliminated exposure to potentially harmful synthetic compounds [439].

Synthetic fragrances can be identified in cosmetic products by looking for terms such as "fragrance," "parfum," or "perfume" on the ingredient label. These terms are umbrella labels for a complex mixture of chemicals used to create a scent and do not disclose the individual components. Unlike natural fragrances, synthetic fragrances are not labelled with specific ingredient breakdowns, making it challenging to determine their exact composition.

Synthetic fragrances are widely used in cosmetics and personal care products to create appealing and long-lasting scents. These fragrances are often more affordable, stable, and versatile than natural alternatives, allowing manufacturers to produce a wide range of unique and consistent scents. In addition to enhancing the sensory experience of using a product, synthetic fragrances mask the base odours of raw ingredients, improving the overall appeal of cosmetics such as shampoos, lotions, and makeup.

Their ability to remain stable over time also ensures that the scent persists throughout the product's shelf life, making them particularly desirable for products like perfumes, deodorants, and body washes. Synthetic fragrances also allow for greater creative freedom in formulating unique scents that are difficult or impossible to achieve with natural ingredients alone.

Synthetic fragrances have sparked controversy due to their potential health and safety concerns. One primary issue is the lack of transparency in fragrance formulations. Manufacturers are not required to disclose the individual chemicals within a fragrance mixture, as they are often considered proprietary or trade secrets. This lack of disclosure makes it difficult for consumers to identify potentially harmful ingredients.

A significant concern with synthetic fragrances is their inclusion of chemicals like phthalates, which are often used to make the scent last longer. Phthalates are suspected endocrine disruptors, meaning they may interfere with the body's hormone systems and potentially contribute to health issues such as reproductive problems and developmental disorders. While not all synthetic fragrances contain phthalates, their presence in some formulations has led to increased scrutiny.

Synthetic fragrances are also a leading cause of allergic reactions and skin sensitivities. They can cause irritation, redness, or itching in individuals with sensitive skin, and in some cases, prolonged exposure may exacerbate conditions such as eczema or dermatitis. For people with respiratory conditions like asthma, strong synthetic scents can trigger symptoms or breathing difficulties.

Environmental concerns have also been raised regarding synthetic fragrances. Many fragrance chemicals, when washed down the drain, persist in the environment and may harm aquatic life or contribute to water pollution.

Consumers concerned about synthetic fragrances can take the following steps to minimize exposure:

1. **Check Labels Carefully**: Look for products labelled as "fragrance-free" or "unscented." However, it is essential to note that some "unscented" products may still contain masking fragrances to neutralize odours, so scrutinize the ingredient list.

2. **Choose Natural or Essential Oil-Based Products**: Opt for products that use natural fragrances derived from essential oils or botanical extracts, such as lavender, rose, or eucalyptus, rather than synthetic alternatives.

3. **Seek Certifications**: Look for certifications such as "Clean at Sephora," "EWG Verified," or "USDA Organic," which ensure that products are free from harmful synthetic chemicals, including certain synthetic fragrances.

4. **Be Aware of Marketing Claims**: Terms like "natural fragrance" can sometimes be misleading, as they may still contain synthetic components. Always verify the ingredient list to ensure transparency.

5. **Prioritize Transparent Brands**: Choose brands that disclose all fragrance components or specifically market their products as phthalate-free and hypoallergenic.

Oxybenzone and Octinoxate: Oxybenzone and octinoxate are widely used chemical sunscreen agents that serve the primary function of absorbing ultraviolet (UV) rays, thereby protecting the skin from sunburn and damage. These compounds are prevalent in various cosmetic products, including sunscreens, moisturizers, and makeup with SPF, due to their effectiveness in filtering UV radiation [440, 441]. Specifically, oxybenzone and octinoxate belong to a class of synthetic organic UV filters that absorb UV radiation, making them essential components in many formulations designed to prevent skin damage from sun exposure [441, 442].

The use of these chemicals has sparked considerable controversy due to their potential health and environmental impacts. Research has indicated that both oxybenzone and octinoxate can act as endocrine disruptors, mimicking or interfering with hormone function in the body [443-445]. Studies have shown that these compounds can penetrate the skin and enter the bloodstream, raising concerns about their long-term effects on human health, including potential links to hormone-related disorders and allergic reactions [446, 447]. For instance, oxybenzone has been linked to alterations in mammary gland development in animal studies, suggesting that it may disrupt normal hormonal signaling [448].

Environmental concerns are equally significant, as oxybenzone and octinoxate have been implicated in coral reef bleaching and other ecological disturbances. When these chemicals are washed off into marine environments, they can contribute to coral degradation, which has prompted legislative actions in places like Hawaii and Palau, where the sale of sunscreens containing these ingredients has been banned [449, 450]. The ecological risks associated with these compounds have led to increased scrutiny and calls for the development of safer, more environmentally friendly alternatives in sunscreen formulations [451, 452].

Oxybenzone and octinoxate can be identified in cosmetic products by examining the ingredient list for their chemical names. Oxybenzone, also known as benzophenone-3 (BP-3), will be explicitly listed as such on product labels. Octinoxate is often identified as ethylhexyl methoxycinnamate or octyl methoxycinnamate (OMC). These ingredients are commonly found in sunscreens, moisturizers with SPF, and makeup products containing SPF, such as foundations, BB creams, and lip balms. Checking the ingredient list is crucial for those looking to avoid these compounds due to health or environmental concerns.

Both oxybenzone and octinoxate are widely used as chemical sunscreen agents that absorb harmful UV rays, protecting the skin from sunburn and long-term damage, including photoaging and skin cancer. They are particularly effective at filtering both UVA and UVB rays, making them key components in broad-spectrum sunscreen formulations. Compared to physical sunscreen agents like zinc oxide or titanium dioxide, oxybenzone and octinoxate are lightweight and invisible on the skin. This makes them highly desirable in cosmetics and sunscreens where a non-greasy, water-resistant, and cosmetically elegant finish is prioritized. Their ability to blend seamlessly into formulations enhances the sensory appeal of products.

Despite their effectiveness as UV filters, these chemicals have raised significant health and environmental concerns. Both are suspected endocrine disruptors, which means they may interfere with hormone function. Oxybenzone, in particular, has been associated with potential effects on hormones such as estrogen and testosterone, raising concerns about fertility and developmental health. Some studies have also linked these chemicals to allergic skin reactions and irritation, especially for individuals with sensitive skin. While regulatory bodies such as the FDA and EU have deemed these ingredients safe at specific concentrations, ongoing research and consumer advocacy have heightened scepticism regarding their use.

Environmental concerns also surround oxybenzone and octinoxate, as they contribute to coral reef bleaching and broader marine ecosystem damage. These chemicals can harm coral DNA, disrupt growth, and increase corals' vulnerability to climate change. When sunscreens containing these agents are washed off into the ocean, they accumulate in the water, adversely affecting marine environments. This has led regions like Hawaii, Palau, and parts of the Caribbean to ban sunscreens containing oxybenzone and octinoxate, encouraging the development of reef-safe alternatives.

In light of these concerns, some governments and regulatory bodies have implemented restrictions or required warnings on products containing these chemicals. This shift has driven many manufacturers to reformulate their products using safer alternatives and to adopt certifications highlighting environmentally friendly and health-conscious formulations.

Consumers looking to avoid oxybenzone and octinoxate can opt for products containing mineral-based sunscreens such as zinc oxide or titanium dioxide. These physical sunscreens provide broad-spectrum UV protection without the risks associated with chemical filters. Products labelled as "reef-safe" or "oxybenzone- and octinoxate-free" are also widely available and are formulated to minimize environmental impact. To avoid these chemicals, consumers should carefully read labels for terms like benzophenone-3 or ethylhexyl methoxycinnamate. Mineral-based or physical sunscreens, often labelled explicitly as such, are excellent alternatives for those seeking safer options.

Certifications such as "reef-safe" or "coral-safe" can provide further assurance, as these labels typically indicate that the product excludes harmful chemical filters. Finally, it is essential to verify that any sunscreen provides broad-spectrum protection to ensure effective shielding against both UVA and UVB rays. By being informed and selecting products with safer and environmentally responsible ingredients, consumers can make choices that protect both their skin and the planet.

Petrolatum (Petroleum Jelly): Petrolatum, commonly known as petroleum jelly, is widely recognized for its moisturizing properties and its role as a barrier to lock in hydration. This occlusive agent is frequently incorporated into various cosmetic products such as lotions, lip balms, and ointments due to its ability to form a protective layer on the skin, thereby preventing transepidermal water loss (TEWL) and enhancing skin hydration [453-455]. The mechanism by which petrolatum operates involves creating a hydrophobic barrier that reduces moisture evaporation, which is particularly beneficial for individuals suffering from dry skin conditions [456-458]. Moreover, petrolatum is often combined with other ingredients in formulations to optimize skin hydration and improve the overall efficacy of moisturizers [453, 458].

Despite its widespread use and effectiveness, petrolatum has been the subject of controversy, particularly concerning its safety profile. If not properly refined, petrolatum can contain polycyclic aromatic hydrocarbons (PAHs), which are known to have carcinogenic potential [459]. This concern has led to regulatory measures in various regions, particularly in the European Union, where only highly refined petrolatum is permitted in cosmetic products [459]. However, in areas with less stringent regulations, the presence of PAHs in petrolatum remains a significant concern, prompting ongoing debates about the safety of using petrolatum in personal care products [459]. The potential health risks associated with poorly refined petrolatum highlight the importance of stringent quality control measures in the cosmetic industry to ensure consumer safety [459].

Petrolatum, also known as petroleum jelly, can be identified in cosmetic products by looking for its chemical name, "petrolatum," "petroleum jelly," or "white petrolatum," on the ingredient list. It is commonly found in products such as moisturizers, lotions, lip balms, ointments, and even some makeup formulations. In products marketed as "mineral oil-free" or "petroleum-free," petrolatum is typically excluded.

Petrolatum is widely used in cosmetics for its excellent moisturizing properties and ability to form a protective barrier on the skin. This barrier locks in hydration, making it an effective ingredient in products designed for dry or cracked skin. It is also valued for its ability to soothe irritation, protect the skin from environmental aggressors, and enhance the texture and spreadability of cosmetic formulations. Its versatility and cost-effectiveness make it a staple in both high-end and budget-friendly products.

However, petrolatum is not without controversy. If not properly refined, it may contain impurities known as polycyclic aromatic hydrocarbons (PAHs), which are associated with potential carcinogenic risks. This concern has led to stricter regulations in regions like the European Union, where only highly refined petrolatum meeting specific safety standards is allowed in cosmetic products. In contrast, regions with less stringent regulations may not enforce similar requirements, raising concerns about the potential presence of harmful contaminants in some products.

To ensure safety, consumers can check for certifications or assurances that the petrolatum used in a product is "USP-grade" or "highly refined." These labels indicate that the ingredient meets pharmaceutical-grade purity standards and is free of harmful impurities like PAHs. Opting for products made by reputable brands or sold in regions with rigorous safety standards, such as the EU, can further minimize risks.

For consumers concerned about using petrolatum-based products, alternatives such as plant-derived oils and waxes (e.g., shea butter, cocoa butter, or jojoba oil) can provide similar moisturizing and barrier-forming benefits. Products labelled as "petroleum-free" or "natural" often replace petrolatum with these ingredients to cater to environmentally conscious and health-focused consumers.

Synthetic Dyes (FD&C and D&C colours): Synthetic dyes, particularly FD&C (Food, Drug, and Cosmetic) and D&C (Drug and Cosmetic) colours, are widely utilized in various personal care products, including makeup, shampoos, and skincare items. Their primary appeal lies in their ability to impart vibrant colours that enhance the aesthetic quality of these products. The global production of synthetic dyes is substantial, with estimates suggesting that over 800,000 tons are produced annually, reflecting their extensive use across industries such as textiles, cosmetics, and food [460, 461]. The versatility and stability of synthetic dyes make them preferable over natural alternatives, as they offer a broader spectrum of colours and are often more cost-effective [462, 463].

The use of synthetic dyes is not without controversy. Many of these dyes are derived from petroleum or coal tar, raising concerns about their safety and potential health impacts. For instance, specific synthetic dyes like Red 40 and Yellow 5 have been scrutinized for their links to hyperactivity in children and allergic reactions [464]. Additionally, certain dyes, such as Rhodamine B, have been classified as carcinogenic, further complicating the safety profile of synthetic colorants used in cosmetics and personal care products [465, 466]. The presence of impurities in these dyes can also pose significant health risks, leading to calls for stricter regulations and greater transparency in their use [467, 468].

The environmental implications of synthetic dyes are another area of concern. The production and disposal of synthetic dyes can result in considerable pollution, as these compounds are often resistant to biodegradation due to their complex chemical structures [469, 470]. This stability can lead to their accumulation in water systems, contributing to ecological damage and posing risks to human health [471]. As a result, there is a growing interest in natural dyes as safer and more environmentally friendly alternatives, although they may not always provide the same level of vibrancy or stability as synthetic options [472, 473].

Synthetic dyes, often listed as FD&C (Food, Drug, and Cosmetic) and D&C (Drug and Cosmetic) colors, can be identified in cosmetic products by their specific names and numbers. They are typically labeled on ingredient lists with terms like "FD&C Red No. 40," "D&C Yellow No. 5," or simply "Red 40 Lake" or "Yellow 5." These dyes are commonly found in brightly colored makeup, nail polishes, shampoos, soaps, and even some skincare products to enhance their aesthetic appeal.

Synthetic dyes are used in cosmetics to provide vivid and consistent coloring, making products more visually attractive and engaging for consumers. Their stability and broad color spectrum allow manufacturers to create a wide range of shades that are not always achievable with natural pigments. For instance, bold lipsticks, vibrant eyeshadows, and colorful nail polishes often rely on synthetic dyes for their striking hues. In skincare and haircare products, synthetic dyes are used to make products more visually appealing and to reinforce branding through color.

Despite their popularity, synthetic dyes are surrounded by controversy due to health and environmental concerns. Many of these dyes are derived from petroleum or coal tar, which raises questions about their sustainability and safety. Impurities in these dyes, such as heavy metals or byproducts from their manufacturing process, have been linked to potential health risks, including cancer and allergic reactions. For example, dyes like Red 40 and Yellow 5 have been scrutinized for their possible role in hyperactivity in children and for causing skin sensitivity in some individuals.

In regions with stringent regulations, such as the European Union, synthetic dyes must meet safety standards, and their use is restricted or banned in certain cases. In the United States, the Food and Drug Administration (FDA) requires cosmetic manufacturers to use only approved synthetic dyes and to clearly list them on product labels. However, the regulations for monitoring impurities or the long-term effects of these dyes remain a topic of debate.

Consumers who wish to avoid synthetic dyes can look for products labelled "dye-free" or "colorant-free." Additionally, they can choose products that use natural colorants, such as beetroot powder, turmeric, or annatto, instead of synthetic alternatives. These natural pigments are typically labelled with their botanical or mineral names and are increasingly found in products marketed as "clean," "natural," or "organic." For those with sensitive skin or concerns about synthetic dyes, these alternatives may provide a safer and more environmentally friendly option.

Mineral Oil: Mineral oil, a byproduct of petroleum refining, is widely utilized in cosmetic formulations due to its effectiveness as an emollient. It is particularly valued for its ability to lock in moisture and soften the skin, making it a common ingredient in creams, lotions, and makeup removers. The properties of mineral oil, such as its stability and dermatological compatibility, allow it to serve as an excellent moisturizer and non-allergenic component in various cosmetic products [474, 475]. The versatility of mineral oil enables it to be incorporated into a range of formulations, from skin creams to sunscreens, where it helps in viscosity regulation and provides protective and lubricating effects [474, 475].

Despite its widespread use and recognized benefits, mineral oil is not without controversy. One significant concern revolves around the potential contamination of mineral oil with polycyclic aromatic hydrocarbons (PAHs), which are known environmental pollutants and potential carcinogens [476, 477]. While highly refined mineral oils are generally considered safe for cosmetic use, the risk of contamination with PAHs, particularly from less refined sources, raises questions about their long-term safety [476, 478]. The presence of PAHs in mineral oil can occur due to environmental factors or during the refining process, leading to concerns about the health implications of prolonged exposure through cosmetic products [476, 477].

Moreover, the environmental sustainability of mineral oil, being a petroleum-derived ingredient, has sparked discussions regarding its ecological impact. The extraction and refining processes associated with mineral oil production contribute to environmental degradation, raising ethical questions about its continued use in cosmetics and personal care products [474, 475]. As consumers become increasingly aware of the environmental implications of their choices, the demand for sustainable alternatives to mineral oil is likely to grow, prompting the cosmetic industry to explore more eco-friendly options [474, 475].

Mineral oil can be identified in cosmetic products by looking for terms like "mineral oil," "paraffinum liquidum," "petrolatum liquid," or "liquid paraffin" on the ingredient label. It is commonly found in moisturizers, lotions, creams, ointments, makeup removers, and some hair care products due to its ability to lock in moisture, soften the skin, and provide a smooth texture.

Mineral oil is widely used in cosmetics because it is inexpensive, effective, and non-reactive. It acts as a barrier on the skin's surface, preventing water loss and creating a protective layer that helps keep the skin hydrated. Its non-comedogenic nature also makes it suitable for use in products designed for dry and sensitive skin. In makeup removers, mineral oil is particularly effective at dissolving oil-based cosmetics, including waterproof makeup, while remaining gentle on the skin.

Despite its benefits, mineral oil has faced controversy, primarily due to its origin as a petroleum-derived ingredient. While highly refined mineral oil used in cosmetics is considered safe by regulatory bodies such as the FDA and the European Medicines Agency (EMA), concerns about contamination with polycyclic aromatic hydrocarbons (PAHs) remain. PAHs are potentially carcinogenic compounds that can be present in improperly refined mineral oil. In the European Union, only highly refined and purified mineral oil is permitted in cosmetics to minimize this risk.

Another point of concern is the environmental impact of mineral oil, as it is a byproduct of petroleum production. Its non-renewable nature raises questions about its sustainability, leading some environmentally conscious consumers to seek plant-based alternatives such as coconut oil, jojoba oil, or shea butter. These natural emollients offer similar moisturizing benefits while aligning with eco-friendly practices.

For consumers who wish to avoid mineral oil, products labeled "mineral oil-free" or marketed as "natural" or "clean beauty" often exclude this ingredient. Additionally, scanning the ingredient list for alternative emollients like plant-derived oils, glycerin, or squalane can help identify mineral oil-free options. As awareness of sustainability and safety grows, many brands are transitioning to renewable, plant-based ingredients as alternatives to mineral oil.

While controversial chemicals in cosmetics serve specific functional roles, their safety and environmental impact remain under scrutiny. Many companies are responding to consumer demand by reformulating products to exclude such ingredients, opting for safer, more sustainable alternatives. However, regulatory bodies often differ in their stance on acceptable levels, leading to varying standards worldwide. Transparency, ongoing research, and informed decision-making are essential to addressing these concerns.

The Rise of Organic and Natural Products

The rise of organic and natural products in cosmetology reflects a growing consumer demand for safer, sustainable, and environmentally friendly skincare, haircare, and beauty solutions. This trend is driven by increased awareness of the potential long-term effects of synthetic chemicals, a desire for transparency in product formulations, and a shift toward holistic wellness and eco-conscious lifestyles. As a result, the beauty industry has witnessed significant growth in organic and natural product lines, transforming the landscape of cosmetology.

Organic and natural products are increasingly formulated with ingredients derived from plants, minerals, and other naturally occurring substances, reflecting a growing consumer demand for sustainable and health-conscious options. These formulations typically avoid synthetic chemicals, parabens, sulphates, and artificial fragrances, focusing instead on clean, nutrient-rich ingredients that cater to diverse skin types and concerns. Research indicates that the cosmetic industry is shifting towards botanical formulations to meet the demands for sustainability and effectiveness, emphasizing the importance of using natural ingredients that are perceived as safer and more beneficial for skin health [479].

The appeal of organic and natural products lies significantly in their perceived safety and efficacy. Consumers are increasingly inclined to choose products that are gentle on the skin and devoid of harsh chemicals that may lead to irritation or long-term harm. Ingredients such as aloe vera, shea butter, coconut oil, and green tea have gained popularity due to their moisturizing, anti-inflammatory, and antioxidant properties [479]. Furthermore, the incorporation of natural actives like botanical extracts and plant-derived peptides addresses specific concerns such as anti-aging and hydration, aligning with consumer preferences for effective skincare solutions [479].

Sustainability is a pivotal factor driving the rise of organic and natural cosmetology products. Consumers are actively seeking brands that prioritize eco-friendly practices, including sustainable sourcing, cruelty-free testing, and environmentally responsible packaging. Many organic beauty brands emphasize the use of biodegradable materials and recyclable containers, which resonate with environmentally conscious consumers [479]. This commitment to sustainability not only enhances brand loyalty but also aligns with broader consumer values regarding environmental stewardship [479].

The role of social media and influencer marketing cannot be overlooked in the promotion of organic and natural products. The rise of beauty bloggers and wellness influencers has significantly increased consumer awareness regarding the benefits of natural ingredients and the potential risks associated with synthetic additives. This visibility has made organic alternatives more accessible and appealing to a wider audience [69]. Influencers often highlight the efficacy of natural products, thereby shaping consumer perceptions and purchasing decisions [69].

However, the organic and natural product sector faces challenges, particularly concerning regulatory standards for labelling, which can vary significantly across regions. This inconsistency can lead to consumer scepticism and confusion regarding what constitutes a genuinely organic product. Additionally, the phenomenon of greenwashing, where brands falsely claim to be natural or sustainable, further complicates the landscape and undermines consumer trust [480]. Moreover, some natural ingredients may trigger allergic reactions in sensitive individuals, underscoring the need for rigorous testing and transparent labelling practices [479].

In response to these challenges, many brands are adopting transparency as a key strategy. Providing detailed ingredient lists, obtaining certifications from reputable organizations, and engaging in third-party testing are becoming standard practices to foster consumer trust [480]. Education about the benefits and limitations of organic and natural products is also crucial, enabling consumers to make informed choices [479].

Formulating with Biodegradable and Sustainable Ingredients

Formulating cosmetic products with biodegradable and sustainable ingredients has become a pivotal focus in the beauty and personal care industry as brands and consumers increasingly prioritize environmental responsibility and ethical practices. This approach involves the careful selection of ingredients and production methods that not only ensure product efficacy but also minimize harm to the environment, promote sustainability, and align with consumer demands for greener alternatives.

The use of biodegradable and sustainable ingredients significantly reduces the environmental footprint of cosmetic products. Biodegradable components prevent the accumulation of microplastics and harmful chemicals in waterways, protecting marine life and ensuring cleaner ecosystems. Sustainable sourcing supports reforestation, reduces greenhouse gas emissions, and ensures the long-term availability of raw materials.

For consumers, these products provide a safer alternative to conventional cosmetics, as they are often free from harsh chemicals and allergens. This makes them suitable for sensitive skin and promotes overall health and well-being. Additionally, consumers increasingly value brands that align with their environmental and ethical values, creating a strong market for sustainable beauty products.

To fully embrace sustainability, brands often pair biodegradable formulations with eco-friendly packaging. Recyclable, refillable, or compostable materials, such as glass, aluminium, or plant-based plastics, complement the sustainable ethos of the products. Minimalistic and waterless formulations, such as solid shampoos or concentrated serums, also reduce the need for excess packaging and conserve resources during production and transportation.

Biodegradable Ingredients

Biodegradable ingredients are substances that can naturally decompose into harmless compounds, such as water, carbon dioxide, and biomass, through the action of microorganisms. These ingredients are essential for reducing the environmental impact of cosmetics, as they break down quickly without leaving persistent residues in ecosystems. Common biodegradable components include plant-based oils, extracts, and surfactants, such as coconut oil derivatives, shea butter, and aloe vera. Biodegradable alternatives to synthetic polymers, such as xanthan gum or cellulose, are often used as thickeners and stabilizers in formulations. These choices ensure that once the product is washed off the skin or hair, it will not contribute to water pollution or harm aquatic life.

Plant-based oils and butters, including coconut oil, argan oil, shea butter, and cocoa butter, are celebrated for their moisturizing and nourishing properties. These ingredients are biodegradable and serve as sustainable alternatives to synthetic emollients, which can be harmful to the environment. For instance, L'Occitane's Shea Butter Hand Cream utilizes sustainably sourced shea butter, while Kiehl's Midnight Recovery Concentrate features evening primrose oil and lavender essential oil, both of which are biodegradable and derived from natural sources [481]. The Body Shop's Argan Oil Range exemplifies the use of Community Fair Trade argan oil, further emphasizing the commitment to sustainability in cosmetic formulations [481].

Natural surfactants such as coco-glucoside, decyl glucoside, and sodium cocoyl isethionate are derived from plant sources like coconut oil and sugar. These biodegradable surfactants are commonly found in cleansers and shampoos, providing gentle foaming effects without harming the environment. Dr. Bronner's Pure-Castile Liquid Soap is formulated with coconut oil and other plant-based surfactants, while Ethique Shampoo Bars incorporate sodium cocoyl isethionate, a biodegradable surfactant [482, 483]. Aveda's Shampure Nurturing Shampoo also utilizes plant-derived surfactants, showcasing the trend towards eco-friendly cleansing products [482].

Botanical extracts such as aloe vera, chamomile, green tea, and calendula are valued for their antioxidant and soothing properties. These extracts are biodegradable and contribute therapeutic benefits to cosmetic formulations while minimizing environmental impact. Herbivore Botanicals' After Sun Soothing Aloe Mist includes biodegradable aloe vera and lavender extract, while Burt's Bees Radiance Day Cream features royal jelly and other plant-derived ingredients [481, 484]. Fresh's Rose Deep Hydration Toner incorporates biodegradable rosewater, further highlighting the use of natural extracts in skincare [481].

Natural polymers like xanthan gum, guar gum, and cellulose serve as thickeners and stabilizers in cosmetics, replacing synthetic polymers that are less eco-friendly. Tata Harper's Resurfacing Mask contains xanthan gum, while Weleda's Skin Food uses cellulose for texture and stability [481]. REN's Evercalm Ultra Comforting Rescue Mask is formulated with guar gum, showcasing the versatility of biodegradable polymers in cosmetic formulations [481].

Essential oils such as tea tree oil, lavender oil, and eucalyptus oil are biodegradable and often included for their antibacterial and calming properties. Neal's Yard Remedies Lavender Essential Oil offers pure lavender oil for soothing effects, while Aesop's Tacit Eau de Parfum features biodegradable essential oils like basil and citrus [485, 486]. Origins' Clear Improvement Active Charcoal Mask incorporates tea tree oil, demonstrating the multifunctional benefits of essential oils in cosmetics [485].

Biodegradable alcohols like sorbitol and erythritol, derived from sugar or corn, are used as humectants in skincare products. Biossance's Squalane + Probiotic Gel Moisturizer utilizes sorbitol for hydration, while Drunk Elephant's B-Hydra Intensive Hydration Serum contains biodegradable humectants such as glycerin and propanediol [481]. Simple's Water Boost Hydrating Gel Cream is another example that incorporates sugar-derived hydrating agents [481].

Algae and seaweed extracts, such as spirulina and kelp, are rich in nutrients and biodegradable. They are used in various skincare products for their anti-aging and hydrating properties. La Mer's Crème de la Mer includes marine algae extracts for hydration, while Elemis's Pro-Collagen Marine Cream utilizes sustainable seaweed extracts to promote collagen production [481]. The Seaweed Bath Co.'s Hydrating Body Wash features sustainably harvested seaweed, emphasizing the environmental benefits of these ingredients [481].

Mineral-based sunscreen ingredients like zinc oxide and titanium dioxide, particularly in non-nano forms, are biodegradable and safe for marine life. Coola's Mineral Face Matte Tint SPF 30 uses non-nano zinc oxide for reef-safe sun protection, while Badger's Broad Spectrum SPF 30 Sunscreen contains biodegradable zinc oxide [481]. Raw Elements' Face + Body SPF 30 is formulated with sustainable, biodegradable minerals, highlighting the shift towards eco-friendly sun protection [481].

Naturally derived acids such as glycolic acid, lactic acid, and citric acid are biodegradable and serve as effective exfoliants in skincare products. Pixi's

Glow Tonic contains biodegradable glycolic acid for gentle exfoliation, while Sunday Riley's Good Genes All-in-One Lactic Acid Treatment uses lactic acid to enhance skin texture [481]. The Ordinary's AHA 30% + BHA 2% Peeling Solution combines fruit-derived acids for effective exfoliation [481].

Coconut-derived emollients like caprylic/capric triglyceride are biodegradable and commonly used for their lightweight moisturizing properties. Kopari's Coconut Melt offers pure, biodegradable coconut oil for hydration, while First Aid Beauty's Ultra Repair Cream includes coconut-derived emollients [481]. Youth To The People's Superberry Hydrate + Glow Oil utilizes caprylic/capric triglyceride for effective hydration [481].

Sustainable Ingredients

Sustainable ingredients are sourced in ways that protect natural resources, biodiversity, and local communities. This means selecting raw materials that are renewable, cultivated through sustainable farming practices, or responsibly harvested from natural ecosystems. For example, sustainably sourced palm oil, which adheres to the Roundtable on Sustainable Palm Oil (RSPO) standards, ensures minimal deforestation and ethical labour practices. Ingredients like argan oil, moringa oil, and jojoba oil are often sourced from fair-trade cooperatives, supporting local economies while promoting environmental conservation.

Sustainable ingredients in cosmetics are increasingly recognized for their role in minimizing environmental impact, supporting biodiversity, and promoting fair trade practices. These ingredients are typically renewable, biodegradable, and harvested from natural sources in a manner that ensures ecological balance and longevity. The following discussion highlights specific sustainable ingredients commonly used in cosmetics, along with examples of products that feature them.

Sustainable plant-based oils, such as argan oil, coconut oil, jojoba oil, and shea butter, are often sourced through fair trade and sustainable farming practices. These oils provide essential hydration and nourishment to the skin while supporting ethical sourcing communities. For instance, The Body Shop's Shea Body Butter is made with Community Fair Trade shea butter, which not only hydrates the skin but also supports local communities in Africa [487]. Similarly, Josie Maran's 100% Pure Argan Oil features sustainably harvested argan oil from Morocco, emphasizing both quality and ethical sourcing [487]. Kopari's Organic Coconut Melt, containing sustainably sourced organic coconut oil, further exemplifies the commitment to sustainable ingredients in cosmetic formulations [487].

Bamboo is a rapidly renewable resource that grows without the need for pesticides or fertilizers, making it an environmentally friendly choice for cosmetics. Its high silica content is beneficial for skin and hair health. Products like Herbivore's Bamboo Charcoal Cleansing Bar Soap utilize bamboo charcoal for deep cleansing, while Love Beauty and Planet's Bamboo & Green Tea Conditioner incorporates sustainably sourced bamboo extract for hair nourishment [487]. Origins' Zero Oil™ Pore Purifying Toner also employs bamboo extract to purify and mattify the skin, showcasing the versatility of this sustainable ingredient [487].

Algae and seaweed are sustainable marine ingredients rich in minerals, vitamins, and antioxidants, making them ideal for hydrating and anti-aging products. La Mer's Crème de la Mer contains sustainably harvested marine algae extracts, which contribute to its renowned moisturizing properties [487]. The Seaweed Bath Co.'s Hydrating Body Wash features bladderwrack seaweed sourced sustainably from the Atlantic Ocean, while Elemis' Pro-Collagen Marine Cream utilizes sustainably sourced seaweed for its collagen-boosting effects [487]. These examples illustrate the efficacy and sustainability of marine-derived ingredients in cosmetics.

Recycling coffee grounds into cosmetics not only minimizes waste but also promotes circular economy practices. Frank Body's Original Coffee Scrub uses recycled coffee grounds for exfoliation, while UpCircle's Coffee Face Scrub is made with repurposed coffee grounds sourced from London cafes [487]. Lush's Cup O' Coffee Face and Body Mask also incorporates ground coffee beans, demonstrating the innovative use of a waste product in skincare formulations [487].

Ethanol derived from sugarcane serves as a sustainable alternative to synthetic alcohol in cosmetics. It is often produced through renewable farming practices, enhancing its eco-friendliness. Biossance's 100% Squalane Oil features sugarcane-derived squalane for hydration, while Drunk Elephant's D-Bronzi Anti-Pollution Sunshine Drops contains sugarcane-derived ethanol for formulation stability [487]. Caudalie's Vinoperfect Radiance Serum also utilizes sustainable ethanol sourced from sugarcane, highlighting the ingredient's versatility [487].

Mica, commonly used for its shimmering properties in cosmetics, poses significant ethical and environmental challenges due to its traditional mining practices. However, sustainable mica is sourced through transparent supply chains that prioritize safe labour practices. RMS Beauty's Living Luminizer uses sustainably sourced mica, while Ilia Beauty's True Skin Serum Foundation features ethically sourced mica for a luminous finish [487]. Kosas' 10-Second Eye Gel Watercolor Eyeshadow also incorporates sustainable mica, showcasing the industry's shift towards ethical sourcing [487].

Botanical extracts from plants such as chamomile, lavender, aloe vera, and calendula are often sustainably grown and harvested without pesticides, promoting soil health and biodiversity. Weleda's Skin Food contains sustainably grown calendula and chamomile extracts, while Dr. Hauschka's Rose Day Cream features sustainably sourced rose extracts for hydration and calming effects [487]. Neal's Yard Remedies' Wild Rose Beauty Balm utilizes certified organic and sustainably sourced wild rosehip oil, emphasizing the importance of sustainable practices in botanical sourcing [487].

Plant-based surfactants derived from coconut oil, palm oil (certified sustainable), or sugar serve as eco-friendly alternatives to harsh synthetic surfactants in cleansers and shampoos. Ethique's Shampoo Bars use coconut-derived surfactants for gentle cleansing, while Aveda's Shampure™ Nurturing Shampoo contains sustainably sourced plant-based surfactants [487]. L'Occitane's Almond Shower Oil also employs biodegradable surfactants, underscoring the industry's commitment to sustainability [487].

Traditionally derived from shark liver oil, squalane is now sustainably sourced from sugarcane, ensuring eco-friendly and cruelty-free production. Biossance's Squalane + Omega Repair Cream features sugarcane-derived squalane for deep hydration, while Indie Lee's Squalane Facial Oil uses 100% plant-derived squalane [487]. Kiehl's Ultra Facial Cream incorporates sustainable squalane as a key hydrating ingredient, reflecting a broader trend towards sustainable sourcing in the cosmetics industry [487].

Biopolymers such as xanthan gum, carrageenan, and alginate are derived from natural sources like seaweed and fermentation processes. They are biodegradable and serve as thickeners and stabilizers in cosmetics. Tata Harper's Resurfacing Mask uses xanthan gum for a smooth application, while REN Clean Skincare's Evercalm Global Protection Day Cream contains carrageenan as a natural thickener [487]. The Ordinary's Multi-Peptide Lash and Brow Serum features alginate for its stabilizing properties, highlighting the functional benefits of biopolymers [487].

Sustainable packaging is integral to the eco-friendly nature of cosmetic products. Brands increasingly utilize recycled or biodegradable materials to house their formulations. Lush's Naked Solid Shampoo Bars eliminate plastic packaging entirely, while Herbivore's Emerald Glow Oil is packaged in glass bottles with minimal waste [487]. Fenty Skin's Hydro Vizor SPF features refillable packaging to reduce plastic waste, demonstrating innovative approaches to sustainable packaging solutions [487].

The integration of sustainable ingredients in cosmetics represents a significant shift towards environmentally conscious beauty practices. By incorporating ingredients such as plant-based oils, algae extracts, recycled coffee, and sugarcane-derived ethanol, brands are not only providing high-performance products but also supporting biodiversity, ethical sourcing, and waste reduction. These choices empower consumers to care for their skin without compromising the planet, fostering a more sustainable future for the cosmetics industry.

Challenges in Formulation

The formulation of cosmetics using biodegradable and sustainable ingredients presents a multitude of challenges that necessitate innovative approaches and extensive research. One of the primary concerns is ensuring the stability and efficacy of products when substituting synthetic ingredients with natural alternatives. For instance, natural preservatives such as rosemary extract and potassium sorbate often do not provide the same shelf life as their synthetic counterparts, which can lead to product degradation over time [488, 489]. This necessitates the exploration of advanced stabilization methods, including the use of bioferments, which have shown promise in enhancing the biocompatibility and efficacy of cosmetic formulations [488, 490].

Moreover, the replacement of synthetic surfactants with plant-derived alternatives can significantly alter the product's performance, particularly in terms of foam quality and cleansing ability. Studies indicate that formulations incorporating sophorolipids and essential oils can effectively combat acne-causing bacteria while maintaining a self-preserving nature, showcasing the potential of natural ingredients in achieving desired cosmetic effects [489, 491]. However, the challenge remains in balancing the functional properties of these natural ingredients with consumer expectations regarding performance [485, 492].

Cost considerations also play a crucial role in the formulation of sustainable cosmetics. Biodegradable and sustainably sourced materials are frequently more expensive than synthetic options, which can deter manufacturers from adopting these alternatives [493]. To mitigate these costs, brands are increasingly investing in sustainable technologies, such as bioengineered ingredients derived from fermentation processes. These innovations not only enhance product performance but also reduce the environmental impact associated with traditional sourcing methods [488, 494]. The use of fermentation in cosmetic formulations is gaining traction, as it allows for the production of high-quality ingredients that are both effective and environmentally friendly [490, 494].

Efficacy of Biodegradable and Sustainable Cosmetic Formulations

Biodegradable and sustainable cosmetic formulations often incorporate natural, plant-derived, or marine-based ingredients that have been utilized for their beneficial properties for centuries. Ingredients such as aloe vera, chamomile, shea butter, and algae extracts are well-documented for their hydrating, soothing, anti-inflammatory, and antioxidant properties [479, 495]. For instance, sustainably harvested algae and seaweed extracts are rich in minerals and amino acids that promote skin rejuvenation and hydration, while ethically sourced shea butter provides deep nourishment and protection [479]. The efficacy of these ingredients is enhanced through sustainable sourcing practices, which ensure that they retain their natural potency while minimizing environmental impact [496].

The exclusion of synthetic chemicals and harsh additives in biodegradable formulations contributes to their gentleness and compatibility with various skin types, including sensitive skin. The use of mild, plant-based surfactants and biodegradable emulsifiers significantly reduces the risk of irritation and allergic reactions [497]. For example, squalane derived from sugarcane mimics the skin's natural lipids, providing effective hydration without greasiness [498]. Additionally, natural biopolymers such as xanthan gum and carrageenan enhance the texture and stability of formulations, further improving user experience [495].

Sustainable cosmetic formulations often employ advanced delivery systems to enhance the bioavailability of active ingredients. Techniques such as liposomal encapsulation and solid lipid nanoparticles improve the stability and absorption of sensitive compounds like vitamin C and retinol [499, 500]. These innovative approaches ensure that the active ingredients remain effective over time, bridging the gap between eco-conscious formulations and cutting-edge skincare science [496].

Many sustainable formulations include potent antioxidants derived from natural sources, such as green tea, vitamin E, and pomegranate, which protect the skin from oxidative stress caused by environmental factors [495]. Ingredients like sustainably sourced argan oil and jojoba oil are rich in fatty acids and antioxidants, supporting skin barrier repair and rejuvenation [499]. This makes biodegradable formulations particularly appealing for consumers seeking effective anti-aging solutions without synthetic additives [479, 495].

Biodegradable formulations frequently utilize plant-based humectants such as glycerin and hyaluronic acid, alongside emollients like coconut oil and cocoa butter, to provide deep hydration and support the skin barrier [479, 495]. The use of biodegradable surfactants derived from renewable sources is less stripping than conventional detergents, helping to preserve the skin's natural oils and maintain hydration (Guzmán et al., 2022).

Sustainable and biodegradable formulations are adept at addressing specific skin concerns. For instance, eco-conscious formulations may include tea tree oil for acne-prone skin, while vitamin C from sustainable sources effectively targets hyperpigmentation [479, 495]. Ingredients like calendula and chamomile are ideal for sensitive skin, offering calming and soothing effects [495].

The ethical production practices associated with sustainable cosmetics contribute to their efficacy. Ingredients harvested at their peak ensure maximum potency, while the absence of harmful synthetic chemicals leads to cleaner formulations that prioritize skin health [496]. This alignment with ethical standards enhances the overall appeal of biodegradable products [479].

The efficacy of biodegradable and sustainable cosmetics is further enhanced by advancements in formulation techniques. Technologies such as nanoemulsions improve the absorption of hydrophobic ingredients, while cold-processing methods preserve the integrity of botanical extracts [496, 500]. Upcycling ingredients from byproducts, such as coffee grounds, enriches formulations with antioxidants and exfoliants, showcasing the innovative potential within sustainable cosmetics [496].

Despite their numerous benefits, biodegradable and sustainable formulations face challenges, including shorter shelf lives due to natural preservatives and the complexity of achieving stability without synthetic additives [479]. These challenges necessitate advanced expertise and research, potentially increasing production costs [496].

Certifications and Standards for Clean Beauty

Global clean beauty standards play a vital role in shaping the cosmetics industry by ensuring safety, transparency, sustainability, and ethical practices. These standards not only guide brands in creating responsible products but also empower consumers to make informed choices about their skincare and beauty routines. As the demand for clean beauty continues to rise, certifications have become essential for maintaining trust and accountability between brands and their customers.

Advances in Cosmetology

One of the primary benefits of clean beauty standards is the trust they instil in consumers. Certifications provide assurance that products meet stringent safety and ethical requirements, which can be especially important in a market where terms like "clean," "natural," or "organic" are often used without regulation. By adhering to established standards, brands demonstrate their commitment to quality, safety, and ethical responsibility, empowering consumers to choose products confidently and without fear of harmful ingredients or deceptive marketing claims.

Transparency is another key pillar of global clean beauty standards. Certifications require clear ingredient labelling and full disclosure, helping consumers avoid harmful chemicals, allergens, or synthetic compounds that may pose health risks. This transparency not only enables consumers to understand exactly what they are applying to their skin but also promotes accountability within the industry. When brands commit to transparency, they contribute to a culture of trust and allow consumers to make choices that align with their personal health and wellness goals.

Sustainability is a central focus of many clean beauty certifications, reflecting a broader shift toward eco-conscious consumerism. Standards often promote sustainable sourcing of raw materials, the use of biodegradable ingredients, and the adoption of environmentally friendly packaging. These practices help reduce the environmental impact of cosmetic production and contribute to a healthier planet. By prioritizing sustainability, certifications ensure that beauty products align with the values of eco-conscious consumers, fostering a shared responsibility for protecting the environment.

Health benefits are another crucial aspect of clean beauty standards. By minimizing exposure to toxic ingredients such as parabens, sulphates, phthalates, and synthetic fragrances, these standards ensure that products are safer for all skin types, including those with sensitive or allergy-prone skin. This focus on non-toxic formulations reduces the risk of irritation, long-term health issues, and other adverse effects associated with conventional cosmetics. As consumers become increasingly aware of the potential hazards of certain ingredients, clean beauty standards offer a pathway to safer, more skin-friendly alternatives.

Ethical practices are also deeply embedded in clean beauty certifications. Standards such as Fair Trade and Leaping Bunny emphasize cruelty-free production, fair wages for workers, and the ethical sourcing of ingredients. These practices ensure that beauty products are not only safe for consumers but also respectful of the environment, animals, and people involved in their production. Ethical certifications help combat exploitative practices and promote a more just and equitable industry, which is a significant factor for consumers seeking to align their purchases with their values.

The clean beauty movement has emerged as a significant trend in the global cosmetics industry, emphasizing safety, transparency, and sustainability in cosmetic formulations. This movement has led to the establishment of various certifications and standards that vary by region, ensuring that products meet strict ethical, environmental, and health-related criteria. A comprehensive overview of major clean beauty certifications and standards across different parts of the world reveals a growing commitment to these principles.

Global Certifications: Several certifications have gained international recognition, providing a consistent framework for clean beauty standards across various regions. The COSMOS (Cosmetic Organic and Natural Standard) is one of the most prominent certifications, recognized globally and utilized by certifying bodies such as Ecocert (France), Soil Association (UK), and BDIH (Germany). COSMOS sets stringent criteria for natural and organic ingredients, prohibiting synthetic fragrances, parabens, and GMOs, while also mandating sustainable sourcing and environmentally friendly packaging practices [492].

The Leaping Bunny certification, administered by the Coalition for Consumer Information on Cosmetics (CCIC), guarantees that no animal testing occurs at any stage of product development. This certification is recognized across North America, Europe, and parts of Asia, reflecting a growing consumer demand for cruelty-free products [501]. Similarly, PETA's Beauty Without Bunnies certification assures consumers that products are cruelty-free, with an additional vegan designation for those free from animal-derived ingredients, further enhancing transparency in the beauty market [501].

Another significant certification is the Cradle to Cradle Certified®, which evaluates products based on their sustainability and environmental impact. This certification assesses various factors, including material health, renewable energy use, water stewardship, and product circularity, aligning with the clean beauty ethos of minimizing ecological footprints [492].

North America: In North America, several certifications specifically cater to the clean beauty movement. The USDA Organic seal is applied to cosmetics that meet organic agricultural standards, requiring at least 95% of a product's ingredients to be organically produced, with no synthetic pesticides, fertilizers, or GMOs [492]. The EWG Verified™ certification from the Environmental Working Group ensures that products meet strict safety standards, avoiding harmful chemicals and requiring full ingredient transparency [492].

The NSF/ANSI 305 certification applies to personal care products containing organic ingredients, mandating that at least 70% of the content be organic [492]. Additionally, the Clean at Sephora label, while not an official certification, identifies products free from over 50 harmful chemicals, becoming a significant marker for clean beauty in the U.S. market [492]. In Canada, CertClean focuses on non-toxic cosmetics, banning over 1,400 harmful ingredients, thus ensuring safety for consumers and the environment [492].

Europe: In Europe, certifications such as the Soil Association and NaTrue play crucial roles in the clean beauty movement. The Soil Association, a founding member of COSMOS, certifies organic and natural beauty products with strict rules about organic ingredient percentages and the prohibition of synthetic chemicals [492]. NaTrue offers three levels of certification for natural and organic cosmetics, ensuring that products avoid synthetic preservatives and harmful chemicals [492].

EcoCert, one of the oldest organic certification organizations, requires that at least 95% of a product's ingredients come from natural origins, with a significant portion being organic [492]. The FairWild certification focuses on sustainable sourcing practices for wild-harvested ingredients, ensuring fair wages for harvesters and biodiversity preservation [492].

Asia: In Asia, the Japan Organic Cosmetic Association (JOCA) certifies organic cosmetics, emphasizing natural ingredients and environmentally friendly production processes [492]. Although animal testing is mandated for some imported cosmetics in China, the Leaping Bunny Partnership is gaining traction as domestic brands and new products in pilot zones can avoid animal testing if they meet certain regulatory standards [501]. South Korea has established strict standards for eco-friendly cosmetics, focusing on safety and sustainability [492].

Oceania: In Oceania, the Australian Certified Organic (ACO) certifies cosmetics that meet stringent organic standards, requiring at least 95% organic ingredients and prohibiting harmful chemicals [492]. Safe Cosmetics Australia (SCA) awards various certifications, including cruelty-free and non-toxic labels, promoting safer formulations free from harsh chemicals [492].

Latin America: In Latin America, BioVidaSana certification focuses on ecological and sustainable cosmetics, ensuring the use of natural ingredients and prohibiting harmful substances [492]. In Brazil, the **IBD Organic seal** applies to cosmetics made with organically farmed ingredients, enforcing sustainability practices in sourcing and production [492].

Chapter 5

Customization and DIY Innovations

Personalized Beauty Products: From DNA to AI

Personalized beauty products represent a transformative trend in the cosmetics and skincare industry, focusing on creating customized solutions tailored to an individual's unique needs, preferences, and goals. This approach diverges from traditional one-size-fits-all formulations, addressing the diversity in skin types, tones, concerns, and even lifestyle factors. With advancements in technology, data collection, and ingredient science, personalized beauty is becoming increasingly accessible and effective.

Personalized beauty revolves around the creation of skincare, makeup, and haircare products tailored specifically to an individual's unique characteristics and needs. This innovative approach moves beyond the traditional one-size-fits-all model, acknowledging that each person's skin, lifestyle, and preferences are distinct. The idea is to develop formulations that cater to an individual's unique biological, environmental, and personal factors, ensuring more effective results and a superior consumer experience.

One key factor in personalization is addressing skin type, which can vary widely among individuals. Products are designed to suit dry, oily, combination, or sensitive skin types. For instance, a person with oily skin may benefit from lightweight, mattifying products with ingredients like salicylic acid or niacinamide, while someone with dry skin may require richer, hydrating formulations featuring hyaluronic acid or ceramides.

Another critical aspect is addressing specific skin concerns, such as wrinkles, acne, pigmentation, redness, or uneven texture. Personalization allows active ingredients to be precisely targeted to these issues. For example, a person concerned with hyperpigmentation might receive a product containing vitamin C and kojic acid, while someone dealing with acne might benefit from a formula with benzoyl peroxide or retinol. This focus on individual concerns enhances the product's effectiveness compared to generalized formulations.

Lifestyle factors also play a significant role in personalized beauty. Exposure to environmental aggressors like pollution, UV radiation, or extreme weather can greatly influence skin health. Individuals living in urban areas might need products fortified with antioxidants like green tea extract or vitamin E to combat free radicals, while those exposed to high UV levels may benefit from added SPF protection or soothing agents like aloe vera.

Genetics further personalizes beauty routines, as hereditary traits can influence predispositions to certain skin conditions, such as premature aging, sensitivity, or acne. By incorporating insights from genetic testing or family history, products can be formulated to address these inherent tendencies. For example, someone predisposed to fine lines might be offered products rich in collagen-boosting peptides and antioxidants.

Consumer preferences add another layer to personalization, allowing individuals to choose products based on their ethical values, sensory experiences, or specific ingredient desires. Vegan and cruelty-free options cater to ethical preferences, while customizable fragrances, textures, or ingredient lists ensure that products align with personal tastes. For instance, a consumer seeking eco-conscious solutions might opt for products with biodegradable packaging and sustainably sourced ingredients.

By gathering detailed information through tools like online quizzes, diagnostic devices, or consultations with experts, brands can craft formulations that are not only highly effective but also resonate with the consumer's unique lifestyle and values. This tailored approach enhances product efficacy, fosters brand loyalty, and empowers individuals to make informed decisions about their skincare, makeup, and haircare needs. The result is a highly personalized beauty experience that reflects the individuality of each consumer.

The creation of personalized beauty products is a meticulous process that revolves around understanding the unique characteristics of each individual and tailoring formulations to meet their specific needs. This approach ensures that consumers receive highly effective and satisfying products that address their personal skin concerns, preferences, and lifestyle factors. The process typically involves several key steps:

Assessment: The first step in creating personalized beauty products is a thorough assessment of the individual's skin, preferences, and lifestyle. Consumers often fill out detailed questionnaires or take online quizzes that inquire about their skin type, concerns (such as acne, wrinkles, or pigmentation), sensitivities, lifestyle habits, and environmental exposure. Advanced tools, including AI-powered apps and in-store diagnostic devices, take the assessment to the next level by analysing the skin's condition in real time. These devices can measure hydration levels, pore size, elasticity, and even the presence of fine lines or redness. Some brands offer even more in-depth analyses by requesting genetic or microbiome samples. This level of personalization ensures that the product is designed not only for the skin's current state but also for its biological tendencies.

Formulation: Once the assessment is complete, the collected data is used to craft a bespoke formula tailored specifically to the individual's needs. For example, a product designed for oily skin might include ingredients like salicylic acid to manage excess oil and niacinamide to reduce pore size and inflammation. On the other hand, a formulation for dry skin could focus on intense hydration with ingredients like hyaluronic acid and ceramides. Additionally, skin conditions such as hyperpigmentation may prompt the inclusion of brightening agents like vitamin C and licorice root extract. Each ingredient is selected to address the consumer's unique combination of concerns, ensuring maximum efficacy.

Production: After the formulation is finalized, the product is created in small batches to ensure its quality and alignment with the individual's profile. This process often involves advanced manufacturing techniques to ensure the stability and potency of the active ingredients. Many personalized beauty brands go a step further by adding personal touches, such as the customer's name or a unique identifier on the packaging. This not only enhances the sense of personalization but also creates an emotional connection between the consumer and the product.

Feedback and Adjustment: One of the key features of personalized beauty is its adaptability. Many brands encourage consumers to provide feedback on how their skin responds to the product over time. Changes in seasons, lifestyle, or even the individual's skin condition may necessitate adjustments to the formulation. Brands often offer ongoing consultations or subscriptions that allow customers to tweak their formulas periodically. This dynamic approach ensures that the product evolves alongside the consumer's needs, maintaining its effectiveness and relevance.

The creation of personalized beauty products combines technology, science, and consumer insights to deliver a truly tailored skincare experience. By focusing on assessment, precise formulation, small-batch production, and ongoing adjustments, this approach not only addresses specific skin concerns but also fosters trust and loyalty by making each consumer feel uniquely understood and valued.

The landscape of personalized beauty is increasingly shaped by technological advancements, particularly in artificial intelligence (AI), machine learning, skin diagnostics, genomic analysis, and 3D printing. Each of these technologies contributes to a more tailored approach to beauty and skincare, enhancing precision and accessibility for consumers.

AI and machine learning are pivotal in analysing vast datasets collected from various sources, such as quizzes and diagnostic tools, to recommend personalized skincare products and formulations. These technologies enable brands to create highly targeted marketing strategies that resonate with individual consumer preferences, thereby enhancing customer engagement [502]. For instance, AI algorithms can analyse user data to predict the most suitable ingredients for specific skin types, effectively personalizing the customer experience [503]. The integration of AI in the beauty industry not only streamlines product recommendations but also fosters a deeper connection between consumers and brands, as they receive tailored solutions based on their unique needs [504].

The advent of skin scanners and diagnostic tools has revolutionized how consumers assess their skin health. These devices measure critical parameters such as hydration, oiliness, elasticity, and pigmentation, providing users with a comprehensive understanding of their skin's condition [504]. This data-driven approach allows for more informed decisions regarding skincare routines and product choices, ultimately leading to improved skin health outcomes. The ability to personalize skincare based on real-time data enhances the efficacy of products and aligns with the growing consumer demand for customized beauty solutions [503].

Genomic and microbiome analyses are emerging as significant contributors to personalized beauty. Genetic testing can reveal predispositions to certain skin conditions or sensitivities, while microbiome sampling provides insights into the skin's unique ecosystem [504]. This molecular-level understanding enables brands to formulate products that cater specifically to the genetic and microbial makeup of an individual's skin, thereby enhancing product effectiveness and reducing adverse reactions. The integration of these advanced analyses into skincare regimens represents a significant leap toward truly personalized beauty solutions [503].

3D printing technology is increasingly being explored in the beauty industry to create customized products, such as masks and makeup that match the user's skin tone and facial contours precisely. This technology allows for mass customization, enabling brands to produce personalized items at scale without the limitations of traditional manufacturing methods [505]. The ability to tailor products to individual specifications not only enhances user satisfaction but also positions brands at the forefront of innovation in the beauty sector [506]. As 3D printing continues to evolve, its applications in personalized beauty are expected to expand, offering consumers unprecedented levels of customization [507].

Personalized beauty offers a range of benefits that cater specifically to the individual needs of consumers, making it a transformative trend in the cosmetics industry. One of the most significant advantages is the ability to provide targeted solutions. Unlike generic formulations that aim to meet the needs of a broad audience, customized products address specific concerns such as acne, wrinkles, hyperpigmentation, or dryness with precision. This ensures that each product is uniquely tailored to solve the individual's primary skincare challenges.

Improved efficacy is another key benefit of personalized beauty. Ingredients are carefully selected and optimized based on an individual's unique skin type, condition, and environmental factors. This targeted approach enhances the effectiveness of the product, leading to noticeable results and higher satisfaction. For instance, a person with oily, acne-prone skin may receive a product with niacinamide and salicylic acid, while someone with dry skin may benefit from hyaluronic acid and ceramides.

Personalization also minimizes risks, particularly for individuals with sensitive skin or allergies. By customizing formulations, allergens or irritants can be avoided, ensuring a safer experience. This level of care is especially important for those prone to reactions from common cosmetic ingredients. Furthermore, personalized beauty aligns with sustainability goals. By producing only what is needed, it reduces waste in packaging and overproduction, making it an eco-friendly option in an industry often criticized for its environmental impact.

The enhanced user experience is another cornerstone of personalized beauty. Consumers feel valued and understood when brands take the time to tailor products to their specific needs. This emotional connection fosters deeper loyalty to the brand and creates a sense of ownership and pride in using products that are uniquely theirs.

Several brands have successfully capitalized on the demand for personalized beauty, offering tailored solutions across various categories. Prose, for example, provides customizable haircare products based on a detailed online consultation. Customers answer questions about their hair type, goals, and lifestyle, and the brand creates a bespoke shampoo, conditioner, or treatment to meet their needs.

Function of Beauty is another leading brand that specializes in tailored shampoos, conditioners, and skincare products. Customers can select their desired benefits, scents, and even colours, ensuring a truly customized experience. For those with specific skincare concerns, Curology offers customized prescription solutions. By evaluating photos of the customer's skin and completing an online quiz, Curology dermatology providers create bespoke formulations to target issues like acne, dark spots, and fine lines.

SkinCeuticals Custom D.O.S.E. takes personalization a step further by offering in-store skin analysis to create customized serums. This service combines advanced diagnostic technology with professional recommendations, ensuring highly effective treatments. Clinique iD allows users to mix a base (such as a hydrating gel or mattifying lotion) with a targeted active ingredient to create a personalized moisturizer that suits their skin's needs.

Despite its many advantages, personalized beauty faces challenges that must be addressed as the trend continues to grow. Producing small, customized batches can be costly and resource-intensive, posing a challenge for scalability and profitability. Brands must balance the high cost of customization with affordable pricing to attract a wider audience. Additionally, ensuring the privacy and security of consumer data is critical. As personalization relies on collecting detailed information, from skin type to lifestyle habits, protecting this sensitive data is essential to maintaining consumer trust.

Another challenge lies in educating consumers about the science and benefits of personalization. Many people are unaware of how tailored formulations can improve their skincare outcomes. Brands must invest in transparent communication and marketing to highlight the value of their products and the technology behind them.

Looking to the future, personalized beauty holds immense promise. Advancements in biotechnology may enable even more precise formulations based on genetic or microbiome data. Wearable devices could provide real-time skin monitoring, offering dynamic updates to formulations as the skin's needs change. Furthermore, deeper integration of sustainability practices, such as refillable packaging and eco-friendly ingredients, could make personalized beauty even more appealing to environmentally conscious consumers.

As personalized beauty evolves, it is poised to redefine self-care and skincare. By addressing the unique needs of each individual, this trend not only enhances results but also fosters a stronger connection between consumers and their beauty routines, paving the way for a more innovative, effective, and inclusive future in the cosmetics industry.

DNA in Personalized Beauty Products

The integration of DNA analysis into personalized beauty products represents a significant advancement in the cosmetics industry, allowing for the development of tailored solutions based on individual genetic profiles. This approach leverages genetic insights to enhance the efficacy of beauty products, addressing specific skin and hair characteristics that vary among individuals.

The process of utilizing DNA in beauty begins with the collection of a DNA sample, typically through a non-invasive method such as a cheek swab or saliva kit. This sample is then sent to a laboratory for analysis, where specific genetic markers associated with skin and hair health are identified. Research indicates that these markers can provide critical insights into various aspects of skin health, including genetic predispositions to skin aging, pigmentation issues, and hydration levels [508, 509]. For instance, variations in genes related to collagen production can inform how quickly an individual may develop signs of aging, such as wrinkles and fine lines [508]. Similarly, genetic markers like MC1R can indicate susceptibility to sunburn and hyperpigmentation, which can guide recommendations for sun protection and skin brightening treatments [508, 509].

Furthermore, DNA analysis can reveal an individual's antioxidant capacity, which is crucial for understanding their vulnerability to oxidative stress from environmental factors [508]. This information can lead to the formulation of products rich in antioxidants for those with lower natural defences. Additionally, genetic insights into skin hydration can help brands recommend specific ingredients, such as hyaluronic acid or ceramides, to enhance moisture retention [508, 509]. The analysis can also uncover predispositions to skin inflammation or sensitivity, allowing for the creation of gentler formulations tailored to individual needs [508, 509].

Once genetic data is analysed, beauty brands can create bespoke products tailored to the unique genetic makeup of each consumer. For example, individuals identified as having a predisposition to dry skin may receive customized moisturizers enriched with hydrating ingredients, while those prone to pigmentation issues might be recommended serums containing vitamin C and niacinamide [508, 509]. Some companies offer comprehensive reports based on DNA analysis, outlining specific skincare or haircare concerns and suggesting a range of products tailored to address these issues [508, 509]. This personalized approach not only enhances customer satisfaction but also optimizes product efficacy, as formulations are designed to meet the unique biological needs of each individual.

Moreover, the ongoing evolution of DNA analysis in beauty allows for continuous adaptation of products as environmental and lifestyle factors change. This dynamic approach ensures that consumers receive the most relevant and effective solutions for their beauty needs over time [508, 509].

Geneu, a UK-based company, exemplifies this trend by providing DNA-analyzed serums that specifically target skin aging concerns. Their approach is rooted in the understanding that genetic factors significantly influence skin health and aging processes. By analysing an individual's DNA, Geneu can formulate serums that address unique skin needs, thereby optimizing the effectiveness of their products [510]. This personalized approach is supported by research indicating that genetic insights can lead to more informed skincare choices, ultimately improving skin health outcomes [511].

Similarly, Skinshift utilizes DNA insights to recommend personalized skincare regimens based on individual factors such as collagen production and antioxidant needs. This brand's methodology highlights the importance of understanding genetic variations in skin biology, which can inform product selection and application strategies [510]. The ability to tailor skincare routines based on genetic predispositions not only enhances product efficacy but also fosters a deeper connection between consumers and their skincare choices [511].

EpigenCare takes a slightly different approach by focusing on epigenetic factors, which consider both genetic data and environmental influences. This dual focus allows for a more comprehensive understanding of how lifestyle and environmental factors interact with genetic predispositions to affect skin health. By combining these insights, EpigenCare can suggest customized products that address the unique challenges faced by individuals in different environments [510].

Omy Laboratories further exemplifies the trend of personalized skincare by combining DNA analysis with consultations to create bespoke formulations tailored to genetic predispositions. This holistic approach not only emphasizes the significance of genetic factors in skincare but also incorporates professional guidance to ensure that consumers receive products that are optimally suited to their skin's needs [510]. The integration of expert consultations with genetic analysis represents a significant advancement in the personalization of skincare, aligning with the growing consumer demand for tailored beauty solutions [511].

DNA-based personalization in beauty has several advantages. By tailoring products to genetic predispositions, this approach can enhance efficacy, providing visible and long-lasting results. It also helps consumers avoid ingredients that may not align with their unique genetic makeup, reducing the risk of irritation or ineffectiveness. Additionally, DNA-based products often feel more exclusive, enhancing the user's experience and sense of value.

Despite its promise, DNA-based beauty also raises some challenges. The cost of DNA analysis and bespoke formulation can make these products expensive, limiting their accessibility. Privacy concerns are also significant, as genetic data is sensitive and must be handled with strict confidentiality. Ethical questions around the long-term storage and use of genetic information remain a topic of debate, necessitating transparent policies from brands using this technology.

As technology advances, the integration of DNA analysis with other data, such as microbiome analysis and lifestyle factors, may create even more precise and effective beauty solutions. Wearable devices and real-time genetic monitoring could further enhance personalization. Combined with increasing consumer demand for tailored and effective products, DNA-based beauty is poised to become a major trend, redefining how individuals approach skincare, haircare, and self-care.

Cosmetologists play a pivotal role in the emerging field of DNA-based beauty personalization by serving as advisors, facilitators, and practitioners who deliver tailored beauty solutions. With proper training and access to advanced tools, cosmetologists bridge the gap between clients and genetic-based beauty technologies, offering unique and customized services aligned with each client's genetic profile. This personalized approach allows cosmetologists to elevate their practice and meet the growing demand for individualized beauty care.

To participate in DNA-based beauty personalization, cosmetologists can assist clients in collecting DNA samples using specialized kits provided by beauty brands. These samples, such as cheek swabs or saliva, are analysed in laboratories to provide insights into the client's genetic makeup. Cosmetologists are responsible for ensuring accurate and proper sample collection while building trust with clients by explaining the process and its benefits. Additionally, they can collaborate with companies specializing in DNA analysis to interpret genetic reports. These reports reveal markers associated with skin aging, hydration, pigmentation, and inflammation, empowering cosmetologists to recommend targeted treatments and products based on scientific data.

Cosmetologists can provide in-depth consultations tailored to clients' genetic findings. For example, they can help clients understand their predispositions, such as tendencies for dryness, sensitivity, or premature aging. Using this information, cosmetologists recommend tailored products designed to address the client's unique needs, such as serums with antioxidants for those prone to oxidative stress or gentle cleansers for sensitive skin. Furthermore, they can develop personalized skincare or haircare regimens, specifying the right ingredients, application techniques, and frequency of use. By incorporating DNA-based insights into their consultations, cosmetologists deliver a highly personalized and premium experience, enhancing client satisfaction and differentiating their services in a competitive industry.

Collaboration with DNA-based beauty brands offers another avenue for cosmetologists to expand their offerings. By partnering with these companies, cosmetologists gain access to bespoke products and cutting-edge technologies. These partnerships often provide training, marketing materials, and diagnostic tools, enabling cosmetologists to offer co-branded or exclusive packages that combine their expertise with genetic insights. This collaboration not only increases revenue opportunities but also strengthens client loyalty by offering tailored, science-backed solutions.

Cosmetologists can further integrate DNA-based personalization into their practice by incorporating advanced technologies. AI-powered skin scanners, for example, can complement genetic data by analysing real-time skin conditions, providing a more comprehensive understanding of a client's needs. Customized treatment protocols can be developed based on DNA results, including spa or salon treatments featuring specific actives or scalp therapies targeting hair loss. Educational initiatives, such as workshops or events, can also position cosmetologists as leaders in innovative beauty practices by informing clients about the benefits of DNA-based beauty.

To effectively deliver DNA-based services, cosmetologists may need additional training and certification in genetic science and its applications in beauty. Certification programs, online courses, and workshops offered by beauty brands or specialized institutes can provide the necessary knowledge and skills. These programs often cover topics such as understanding genetic markers, interpreting DNA analysis reports, selecting suitable products, and communicating findings in an accessible way. By obtaining these credentials, cosmetologists enhance their credibility and attract clients seeking cutting-edge personalized solutions.

Ethical considerations are paramount in DNA-based personalization. Clients entrust cosmetologists with sensitive genetic data, so it is essential to prioritize data security and confidentiality. Cosmetologists should work with brands that adhere to stringent privacy standards and educate clients about how their data will be used and stored. Transparency in these processes fosters trust and reassures clients about the safety of engaging in DNA-based beauty services.

As DNA-based personalization continues to gain traction, cosmetologists who embrace this innovation will remain at the forefront of the beauty industry. Integrating genetic insights into their practice allows them to offer unique, science-backed services that enhance client results and experiences. Additionally, by combining DNA analysis with emerging trends such as microbiome research or AI diagnostics, cosmetologists can further elevate their offerings and solidify their role as leaders in personalized beauty care. This forward-thinking approach ensures that cosmetologists meet evolving consumer demands while driving the future of the beauty industry.

At-Home Beauty Gadgets and Kits

Innovation in at-home beauty gadgets and kits has significantly transformed personal care routines, enabling consumers to achieve professional-grade results from the comfort of their homes. These advanced tools leverage cutting-edge technologies, including LED therapy, microcurrent stimulation, and ultrasonic waves, to provide convenience, cost-effectiveness, and personalized solutions. The proliferation of these devices has democratized access to beauty treatments, allowing users to tailor their skincare and haircare regimens according to their specific needs and preferences [512].

LED light therapy devices exemplify a major innovation in this sector. These devices utilize specific wavelengths of light to address various skin concerns, such as acne, wrinkles, and redness. For instance, red light is known to stimulate collagen production, thereby reducing fine lines and enhancing skin elasticity, while blue light effectively targets acne-causing bacteria. The market now offers a variety of LED devices, including face masks, handheld wands, and therapy panels, designed for user-friendliness with features like built-in timers and pre-set settings to ensure safe and effective treatments [512]. The effectiveness of these devices has been supported by studies demonstrating their ability to improve skin conditions, thus validating their growing popularity among consumers [512].

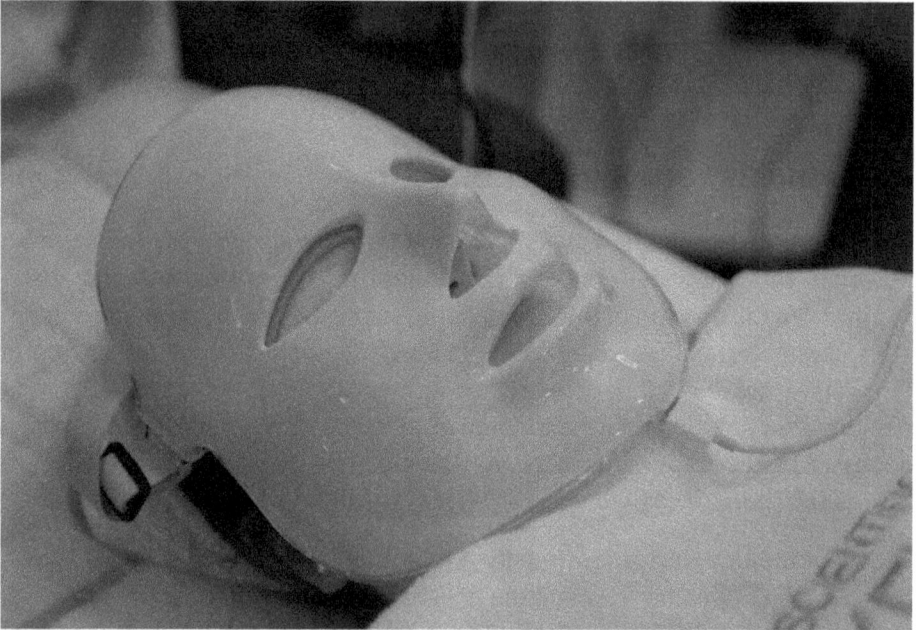

Figure 16: Close-up of a Person with an LED Face Mask On. Dinç Tapa, CC0, via Pexels.

LED light therapy devices, such as the Dr. Dennis Gross DRx SpectraLite FaceWare Pro and the CurrentBody Skin LED Light Therapy Mask, have been shown to effectively target skin issues like acne and signs of aging. The combination of red and blue light therapy in these devices is particularly noted for its efficacy in promoting collagen production and reducing inflammation [512]. Research indicates that these devices can enhance skin rejuvenation by improving skin elasticity and texture, making them popular among consumers seeking non-invasive beauty treatments [512]. Additionally, the Foreo UFO 2 integrates LED therapy with T-Sonic pulsations, which further enhances the absorption of skincare products, demonstrating the trend towards multifunctional beauty gadgets [512].

Microcurrent devices represent another significant advancement in at-home beauty technology. These gadgets employ low-level electrical currents to tone facial muscles and enhance skin firmness, mimicking the body's natural currents to stimulate ATP production, which is crucial for cellular repair and collagen synthesis. Such devices are particularly appealing to consumers seeking non-invasive alternatives to surgical procedures. Recent developments have also introduced app connectivity in microcurrent wands and rollers, allowing users to customize their treatments and monitor their progress over time [512, 513]. The integration of microcurrent technology into home beauty routines is supported by research highlighting its efficacy in improving skin tone and elasticity [513].

Microcurrent technology is another innovative approach in at-home beauty devices, exemplified by products like the NuFACE Trinity Advanced Facial Toning Device and the Foreo Bear. These devices utilize low-level electrical currents to stimulate facial muscles, thereby improving skin tone and reducing the appearance of fine lines [513]. Studies have highlighted the effectiveness of microcurrent therapy in enhancing skin firmness and elasticity, which supports the claims made by manufacturers regarding their benefits for facial rejuvenation [513]. The ZIIP GX Series Nano Current Device takes this a step further by combining microcurrent with nanocurrent technology, offering personalized treatment plans through app connectivity, which reflects the increasing integration of technology in beauty care [513].

Ultrasonic devices further illustrate the innovation in at-home beauty tools. Ultrasonic devices utilize high-frequency vibrations to cleanse pores deeply, exfoliate dead skin, and enhance serum absorption. These technologies, previously confined to professional settings, are now accessible in compact, user-friendly formats for home use. Many of these devices offer adjustable intensity levels, catering to diverse skin sensitivities and conditions [512]. The effectiveness of these technologies in promoting skin rejuvenation has been documented, reinforcing the value of these at-home devices [512].

Ultrasonic and radiofrequency devices, such as the PMD Clean Pro and Tripollar Stop Vx, are designed for deep cleansing and skin tightening. These devices utilize ultrasonic waves to enhance serum absorption and stimulate collagen production, which is crucial for maintaining youthful skin. The efficacy of these treatments has been supported by clinical evaluations that demonstrate significant improvements in skin texture and elasticity following regular use [512]. Furthermore, the Dermaflash Luxe employs ultrasonic technology for exfoliation, indicating a trend towards devices that combine multiple functionalities to address various skin concerns [512].

In the realm of haircare, advancements in at-home beauty gadgets have also made significant strides. Laser hair removal devices utilizing intense pulsed light (IPL) technology have become popular for targeting hair follicles and reducing regrowth. These devices often come equipped with skin tone sensors and precision attachments, ensuring safe and effective treatments across various body areas. Additionally, scalp care gadgets that combine LED light therapy, microcurrent stimulation, and massage functions are gaining traction for their ability to promote hair growth and improve scalp health [512]. The integration of these technologies into home beauty routines reflects a broader trend towards personalized and effective beauty solutions.

The market for at-home laser hair removal devices has also expanded, with products like the Philips Lumea Prestige IPL and Braun Silk-Expert Pro 5 IPL leading the way. These devices utilize intense pulsed light technology, which has been shown to be effective for various skin tones and hair types, providing a safe and convenient alternative to professional treatments. Clinical studies have validated the safety and effectiveness of these devices, reinforcing consumer confidence in their use for long-term hair reduction [512].

Scalp care gadgets, such as the iGrow Laser Hair Growth System and HairMax LaserBand 82, utilize laser therapy to promote hair growth and improve scalp health. These devices are designed to stimulate hair follicles, which is essential for individuals experiencing hair thinning or loss. Research supports the use of laser therapy as a viable option for enhancing hair regrowth, further solidifying the role of technology in personal care [512].

The incorporation of AI and smart technology has further enhanced the personalization and effectiveness of at-home beauty gadgets. AI-driven skin analysers and diagnostic tools can assess various skin conditions, providing users with tailored recommendations for products and treatments. Furthermore, app-connected devices facilitate real-time feedback, guided tutorials, and progress tracking, creating a more engaging and educational experience for consumers [514]. This technological integration not only empowers users but also fosters a deeper understanding of their skincare needs.

The rise of DIY beauty kits, such as the Starpil Wax Kit and GloPRO Microneedling Regeneration Tool, allows consumers to perform professional-grade treatments at home. These kits are designed to be user-friendly while delivering effective results, appealing to a broad audience. Additionally, sustainable beauty gadgets like the Foreo Luna 4 and EcoTools Bioblender highlight the industry's move towards environmentally conscious products, addressing consumer concerns about sustainability in beauty practices.

Sustainability is also becoming a focal point in the development of at-home beauty gadgets and kits. Many brands are now prioritizing eco-friendly practices by incorporating rechargeable batteries, durable materials, and refillable components to minimize waste. This shift towards sustainability resonates with environmentally conscious consumers who seek innovative yet responsible beauty solutions [514].

Hybrid Beauty: Combining Therapy with Wellness

Hybrid beauty is an approach that merges traditional beauty treatments with wellness therapies, recognizing that skincare and personal care extend beyond surface-level aesthetics. This trend reflects the growing consumer demand for holistic self-care solutions that not only enhance physical appearance but also promote overall well-being. By integrating elements of skincare, therapeutic treatments, relaxation techniques, and wellness practices, hybrid beauty provides a more comprehensive, results-driven experience.

The intersection of beauty and wellness has gained significant attention in recent years, particularly as consumers increasingly recognize the holistic nature of beauty that encompasses not only physical appearance but also mental and emotional well-being. Hybrid beauty, which integrates traditional beauty treatments with wellness practices, reflects this evolving perspective. This approach acknowledges that skin health and overall appearance are influenced by a myriad of factors, including lifestyle choices, stress levels, nutrition, and mental health [158, 166].

Research indicates that traditional beauty treatments, such as facials and body treatments, are increasingly incorporating therapeutic techniques. For instance, practices like aromatherapy, mindfulness, LED therapy, and acupuncture are being integrated into skincare regimens to address deeper concerns beyond surface-level aesthetics [166]. This integration is not merely cosmetic; it aims to enhance both the skin's health and the individual's emotional and mental well-being. The Mindfulness-to-Meaning Theory posits that mindfulness practices can broaden awareness and facilitate positive emotion regulation, leading to improved mental health outcomes [515, 516]. This theory supports the idea that incorporating mindfulness into beauty routines can enhance the overall experience and effectiveness of beauty treatments.

One of the notable innovations in hybrid beauty is the incorporation of stress-relief therapies into skincare routines. Many skincare brands are now formulating products infused with adaptogens, CBD, and essential oils, which not only nourish the skin but also help alleviate stress and promote relaxation [517]. The use of such ingredients reflects a growing understanding of the connection between mental health and skin health. Furthermore, spa treatments are increasingly adopting elements such as sound therapy, guided meditation, and herbal medicine to create a more holistic experience that nurtures both body and mind [517]. This trend highlights the importance of a comprehensive approach to beauty that prioritizes wellness.

The role of nutrition in this intersection cannot be overlooked. Studies have shown that healthy eating habits significantly influence physical and mental health, which in turn affects skin health and overall appearance [518]. The integration of nutritional considerations into beauty and wellness practices underscores the importance of a balanced lifestyle in achieving desired beauty outcomes. As such, the hybrid beauty movement is not just about external treatments but also emphasizes the importance of internal health and well-being.

Hybrid Beauty in Skincare and Facial Treatments

In the evolving landscape of skincare, the concept of hybrid beauty is increasingly becoming prominent, particularly through the rise of multi-functional products that blend cosmetic and therapeutic benefits. A significant illustration of this trend is the incorporation of cannabidiol (CBD) in skincare formulations. CBD has garnered attention for its anti-inflammatory properties, which can effectively reduce skin irritation and promote relaxation, thereby enhancing overall skin health and well-being [519, 520]. The therapeutic potential of CBD is underscored by its interaction with cannabinoid receptors, which mediates various physiological responses, including inflammation reduction [521]. This aligns with the growing consumer interest in functional cosmetics that not only enhance appearance but also provide health benefits, reflecting a broader trend towards cosmeceuticals—products that merge cosmetic and pharmaceutical qualities [522].

Cosmeceuticals are defined as cosmetic-pharmaceutical hybrids designed to improve skin health while offering aesthetic benefits [523]. These products are formulated with bioactive ingredients that possess therapeutic properties, thereby addressing various skin concerns such as aging, acne, and inflammation [524, 525]. The market for cosmeceuticals has expanded significantly, with consumers increasingly seeking products that deliver both beauty and health benefits [526, 527]. The integration of active ingredients, such as CBD, into skincare products exemplifies this trend, as these ingredients are not merely for cosmetic enhancement but are intended to provide additional health-related functions [523]. The rise of such products indicates a shift in consumer preferences towards formulations that prioritize skin health alongside aesthetic appeal, marking a significant evolution in the skincare industry [522, 527].

Moreover, the concept of hybrid beauty is further supported by the scientific community's recognition of the efficacy of cosmeceuticals. Research indicates that these products can effectively target specific skin conditions while also enhancing the overall appearance of the skin [522, 524]. For instance, the anti-inflammatory effects of CBD not only help in soothing irritated skin but also contribute to a more radiant complexion by reducing redness and promoting an even skin tone [519, 520]. This dual functionality of cosmeceuticals, particularly those infused with CBD, illustrates the potential for innovative skincare solutions that cater to the modern consumer's desire for products that are both effective and health-conscious [523, 527].

Cosmeceuticals are advanced skincare and personal care products that combine the benefits of cosmetics with pharmaceutical-grade active ingredients. Unlike conventional cosmetics, which primarily focus on enhancing appearance, cosmeceuticals contain bioactive compounds designed to improve skin health at a cellular level. These products address specific concerns such as aging, hyperpigmentation, acne, and inflammation while delivering scientifically validated results. While cosmeceuticals do not require FDA approval like pharmaceutical drugs, they often contain clinically tested ingredients with proven therapeutic benefits.

Advancements in dermatology, biotechnology, and nanotechnology have contributed to the rapid evolution of cosmeceuticals. Many modern formulations incorporate bioengineered peptides, stem cell extracts, probiotics, neurocosmetics, and DNA repair enzymes to deliver targeted and long-lasting skin benefits. These innovations have transformed skincare into a science-backed field where products not only improve the skin's appearance but also enhance its function and resilience.

Cosmeceuticals stand out from traditional skincare products due to their advanced formulation and scientifically backed efficacy. One of their defining characteristics is the inclusion of medical-grade active ingredients, such as retinoids, peptides, antioxidants, and growth factors, which deliver measurable results. Unlike standard cosmetics, many cosmeceuticals are supported by clinical research, proving their ability to improve skin conditions and restore skin health over time. These products are also designed for targeted treatment, addressing specific concerns such as fine lines, hyperpigmentation, acne, or rosacea.

Another major innovation in cosmeceuticals is the use of advanced delivery systems. Technologies like liposomal encapsulation, nanocarriers, and slow-release formulas enhance ingredient stability and absorption, allowing active compounds to penetrate deeper into the skin without causing irritation. This ensures optimal effectiveness while maintaining skin compatibility, even for sensitive individuals.

With the rapid advancements in skincare science, several new and highly innovative cosmeceuticals have emerged. These cutting-edge formulations use breakthrough ingredients and sophisticated technologies to deliver superior skin benefits.

DNA Repair Enzyme Serums: DNA repair enzymes help reverse skin damage caused by UV exposure, pollution, and oxidative stress. These enzymes work by detecting and repairing damaged DNA strands, preventing premature aging and reducing the risk of long-term skin damage.

A leading example is Eryfotona Actinica by ISDIN, a DNA repair enzyme sunscreen containing photolyase, which not only protects the skin from harmful UV rays but also helps repair sun-induced DNA damage. This innovative approach to sun protection provides both prevention and active skin restoration.

Neurocosmetics for Stress-Resistant Skin: Neurocosmetics focus on the connection between the skin and the nervous system by using ingredients that interact with neurotransmitters. These formulations help reduce stress-induced inflammation, slow down skin aging, and promote an overall healthier complexion.

An example is Biologique Recherche Sérum de Teint, a tinted serum enriched with neuropeptides and antioxidants to combat stress-related skin damage while delivering a radiant and even skin tone.

Stem Cell-Based Cosmeceuticals: Stem cell extracts from plants and human sources are now widely used in skincare to stimulate cellular regeneration and repair damaged tissues. These cosmeceuticals enhance collagen production, making them ideal for anti-aging treatments.

Lifeline ProPlus Advanced Molecular Serum is a pioneering product in this field, utilizing human stem cell-derived peptides to accelerate skin renewal, improve elasticity, and minimize the appearance of wrinkles.

Probiotic and Postbiotic Skincare: Probiotic skincare introduces beneficial bacteria to balance the skin microbiome, while postbiotics (the byproducts of probiotic activity) enhance skin resilience and repair. These ingredients help reduce inflammation, strengthen the skin barrier, and prevent breakouts.

A well-known example is TULA 24-7 Moisture Hydrating Day & Night Cream, which incorporates probiotics and prebiotics to restore balance, boost hydration, and enhance skin vitality.

Encapsulated Retinol and Peptides: Encapsulation technology has revolutionized retinol and peptide-based skincare by delivering active ingredients in a more stable and controlled manner. This minimizes irritation while ensuring maximum effectiveness.

SkinMedica Retinol Complex 1.0 features encapsulated retinol for gradual release, which reduces the risk of irritation while improving skin texture, tone, and elasticity.

Smart Hydrogels & Bioengineered Peptides: Advanced hydrogels and bioengineered peptides mimic the skin's natural repair mechanisms to enhance hydration, wound healing, and collagen production. These cosmeceuticals provide long-lasting benefits by delivering active ingredients in a time-controlled manner.

An example is Dr. Dennis Gross DRx SpectraLite EyeCare Pro, an LED-powered eye mask infused with bioactive peptides to target fine lines, wrinkles, and dark circles around the eyes.

Exosome Therapy in Skincare: Exosomes are nano-sized vesicles derived from stem cells that contain growth factors, proteins, and RNA, which help accelerate skin healing, repair damaged cells, and stimulate collagen production.

Benev Exosome Regenerative Complex is a groundbreaking formulation that utilizes exosome technology to rejuvenate the skin, reduce wrinkles, and improve elasticity at a cellular level.

Copper Peptide-Infused Cosmeceuticals: Copper peptides are potent skin-repairing agents that help tighten the skin, reduce inflammation, and improve tone. These peptides stimulate fibroblast activity, promoting faster collagen and elastin production.

Advances in Cosmetology

NIOD Copper Amino Isolate Serum 3.1 is a leading example, using highly concentrated copper peptides to restore skin barrier function, reduce signs of aging, and improve overall skin texture.

Advanced Sunscreens with Pollution Protection: Modern sunscreens now go beyond UV protection by shielding the skin from pollution, blue light, and infrared radiation. These advanced formulations help neutralize environmental stressors while keeping the skin healthy and protected.

Supergoop! Unseen Sunscreen SPF 40 is a standout product that combines broad-spectrum UV protection with antioxidants that block blue light and pollution-induced oxidative stress.

Personalized Cosmeceuticals and AI-Powered Skincare: With the integration of AI and personalized skin diagnostics, cosmeceuticals are becoming increasingly customized to individual needs. AI-driven formulations provide tailor-made solutions based on real-time skin analysis.

A prime example is SkinCeuticals Custom D.O.S.E., which uses AI-powered dermatological assessments to create personalized skincare serums tailored to an individual's specific skin concerns.

The future of cosmeceuticals is being shaped by advancements in biotechnology, nanoscience, and dermatological research. Emerging trends such as epigenetic skincare, regenerative medicine, and wearable skin tech are set to redefine personalized beauty solutions. As science continues to evolve, consumers can expect even more targeted, clinically validated, and results-driven skincare.

Consumers today seek products that offer both immediate and long-term benefits, and cosmeceuticals meet this demand by combining cutting-edge science with medical-grade formulations. With DNA-based skincare, regenerative exosome therapy, and neurocosmetic innovations, the next generation of cosmeceuticals is poised to revolutionize how people approach skincare and beauty, offering science-backed solutions tailored to every individual's unique skin needs.

Advanced facial treatments have also increasingly integrated techniques such as lymphatic drainage, acupuncture, and Gua Sha massage, which are recognized for their multifaceted benefits. These methods not only enhance circulation and facilitate skin detoxification but also contribute significantly to relaxation and stress relief. Lymphatic drainage, in particular, is noted for its ability to improve lymphatic flow, which can reduce swelling and promote a clearer complexion, thereby enhancing overall skin health [528]. Similarly, Gua Sha massage, a traditional Chinese technique, has been shown to stimulate blood flow and lymphatic drainage, further supporting skin rejuvenation and relaxation.

Lymphatic drainage is a gentle massage technique designed to stimulate the lymphatic system, which is responsible for removing toxins, excess fluids, and waste from the body. Unlike the circulatory system, which has the heart to pump blood, the lymphatic system relies on muscle movement and manual stimulation to move lymph fluid through the body. When the lymphatic system becomes sluggish due to stress, poor diet, or lack of physical activity, it can result in puffiness, fluid retention, and a buildup of toxins that may affect skin health.

Lymphatic drainage helps reduce swelling, improve circulation, and boost the immune system by removing excess fluid and toxins from tissues. In beauty and skincare, it is particularly beneficial for reducing facial puffiness, improving skin tone, and promoting a sculpted appearance. The technique can also help reduce dark circles, minimize breakouts, and enhance the skin's natural glow by increasing oxygen and nutrient delivery to skin cells.

Lymphatic drainage massage is often used in post-surgical care to help reduce swelling and speed up recovery. It is also popular among individuals experiencing bloating, fatigue, or fluid retention due to hormonal changes or lifestyle factors.

Lymphatic drainage involves light, rhythmic, and directional strokes applied in a specific pattern that follows the natural flow of lymphatic vessels. The goal is to encourage the movement of lymph fluid toward the lymph nodes, where toxins are filtered and eliminated. Techniques include:

- **Manual Lymphatic Drainage (MLD)**: A trained therapist performs a gentle, hands-on massage to stimulate the lymph nodes and encourage detoxification.

- **Facial Lymphatic Drainage**: A technique used to reduce puffiness, contour the face, and improve skin clarity. This is commonly performed using hands, jade rollers, or specialized massage tools.

- **Dry Brushing and Body Gua Sha**: Tools such as dry brushes or Gua Sha stones can be used to enhance lymphatic flow and stimulate circulation.

Many facial and body treatments incorporate lymphatic drainage techniques to reduce inflammation, sculpt facial contours, and improve skin health without invasive procedures.

Acupuncture is a traditional Chinese medicine (TCM) practice that involves the insertion of fine needles into specific points on the body to balance the flow of Qi, or life energy. It is based on the belief that energy circulates through pathways called meridians, and blockages or imbalances in these pathways can lead to various health concerns, including skin problems, stress, and chronic pain. By stimulating these specific points, acupuncture aims to restore harmony within the body, leading to improved overall well-being.

Modern research supports the idea that acupuncture has a tangible impact on the body's physiological functions. It has been shown to stimulate the nervous system, increase blood circulation, and promote the release of natural pain-relieving and anti-inflammatory compounds. This not only helps alleviate pain and tension but also contributes to skin health, as improved circulation ensures that oxygen and nutrients are effectively delivered to skin cells.

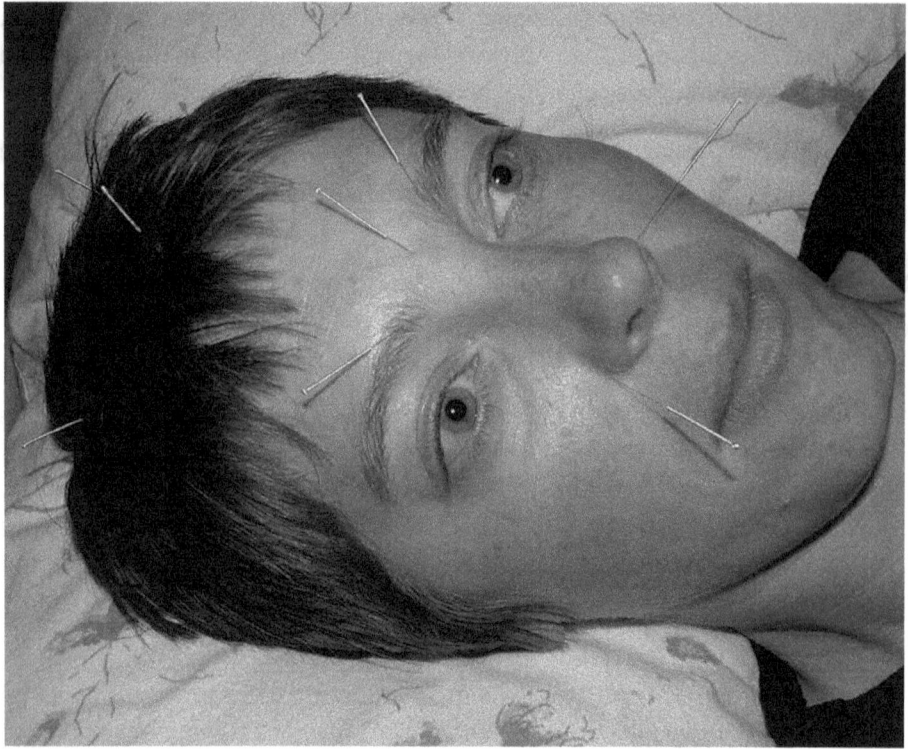

Figure 17: Facial acupuncture. mscaprikell, CC BY-SA 2.0, via Wikimedia Commons.

Acupuncture is widely recognized for its ability to reduce inflammation, enhance circulation, and support the body's natural healing processes. When applied to beauty and skincare, it offers several significant benefits. Facial acupuncture is known for its ability to improve skin elasticity, reduce wrinkles, and stimulate collagen production, leading to firmer and more youthful-looking skin. For individuals dealing with acne and redness, acupuncture helps regulate hormones, reduce inflammation, and soothe skin sensitivity, making it beneficial for conditions like breakouts and rosacea.

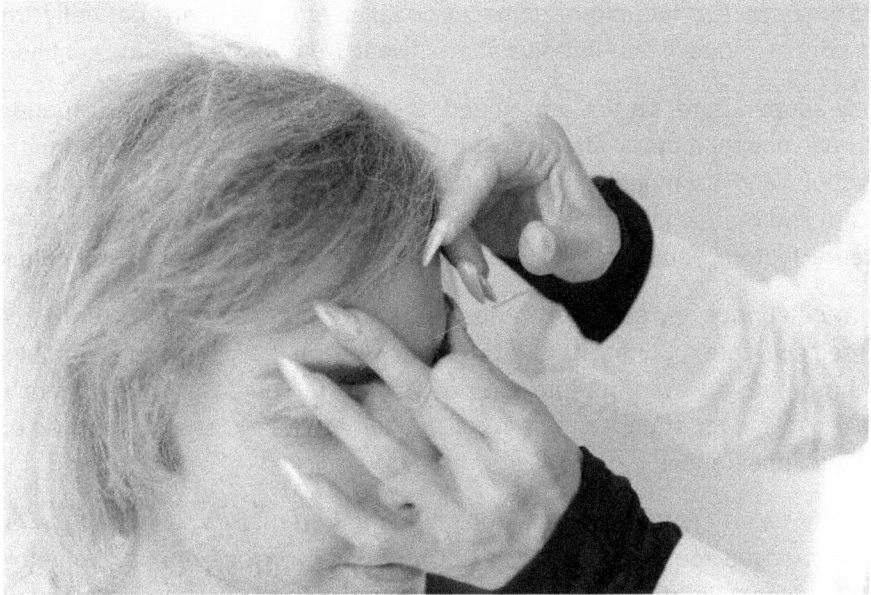

Figure 18: Male receiving facial acupuncture. RDNE Stock project, CC0, via Pexels.

One of the key benefits of acupuncture is its ability to enhance circulation, which results in increased oxygen and nutrient flow to the skin. This leads to a brighter, more even complexion, often referred to as the "acupuncture glow." Additionally, acupuncture helps manage stress, which is a major contributor to premature aging and skin issues. By calming the nervous system and reducing cortisol levels, acupuncture indirectly improves skin clarity and minimizes inflammation caused by stress-related breakouts.

During an acupuncture session, a licensed practitioner carefully inserts ultra-thin needles into specific points on the body, depending on the individual's needs. These needles work by stimulating the nervous system, increasing blood flow, and triggering the body's natural healing response. Facial acupuncture, also known as cosmetic acupuncture, involves placing small needles in targeted areas of the face to address concerns such as wrinkles, sagging skin, and dullness. This technique increases collagen production and naturally firms the skin, providing a non-invasive alternative to treatments like Botox or fillers.

Body acupuncture, on the other hand, focuses on points that correspond to internal health factors affecting the skin. Areas related to digestion, liver function, and hormonal balance are often targeted to support overall skin health and reduce inflammation from within. By addressing both external and internal factors, acupuncture offers a holistic approach to beauty and wellness.

Many celebrities and skincare enthusiasts have embraced acupuncture as part of their self-care routines. Its ability to naturally firm the skin, reduce puffiness, and promote an even complexion has made it a sought-after treatment for those looking for effective, non-invasive solutions to maintain a youthful and radiant appearance.

Gua Sha is an ancient Chinese healing technique that involves the use of a smooth-edged tool, traditionally made from jade or rose quartz, to perform gentle scraping motions along the face and body. Originally used in traditional Chinese medicine for body treatments to relieve pain and stagnation, Gua Sha has gained widespread popularity as a facial massage technique in modern skincare routines. The primary purpose of Gua Sha is to increase circulation, promote lymphatic drainage, release muscle tension, and sculpt the skin, providing both therapeutic and cosmetic benefits.

The benefits of Gua Sha extend beyond relaxation, as it is highly regarded for its ability to enhance skin health and overall well-being. One of its most notable advantages is facial contouring and lifting. Regular use of Gua Sha helps sculpt and define facial features by draining excess fluid and reducing puffiness, giving the skin a more lifted and toned appearance. Additionally, the gentle scraping motion stimulates blood flow, which enhances radiance and reduces dullness by delivering oxygen and essential nutrients to the skin.

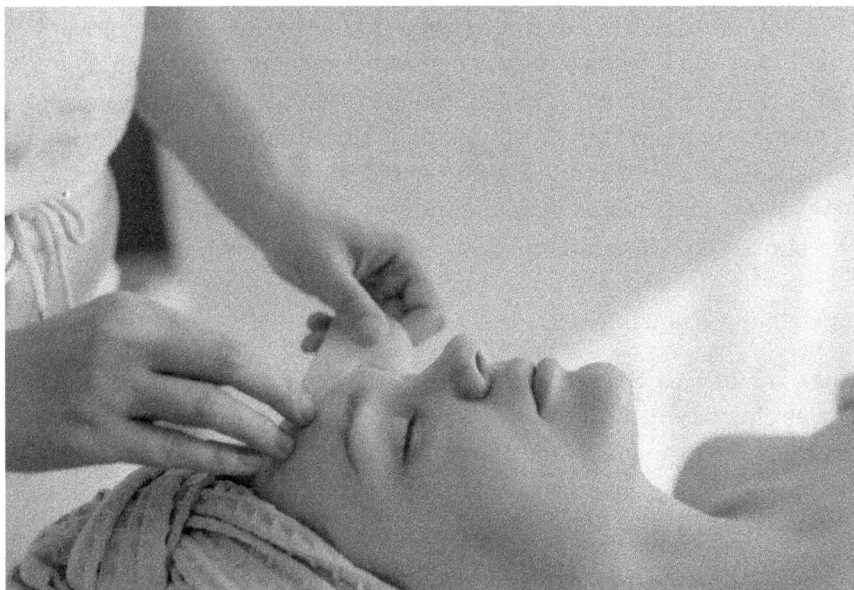

Figure 19: Gua Sha massage. Arina Krasnikova, CC0, via Pexels.

Lymphatic drainage is another significant benefit of Gua Sha. By promoting the removal of excess fluids and toxins, the technique helps diminish dark circles, under-eye bags, and facial bloating, resulting in a more refreshed and revitalized look. Furthermore, Gua Sha is highly effective for muscle relaxation and tension release, particularly in areas like the jaw and forehead where stress tends to accumulate. This makes it an excellent tool for individuals experiencing tension headaches or jaw clenching due to stress.

With consistent use, Gua Sha can also contribute to reducing fine lines and wrinkles. By stimulating circulation and collagen production, it improves skin elasticity, softens fine lines, and supports long-term skin rejuvenation. Many skincare professionals and enthusiasts incorporate Gua Sha into their routines as a natural, non-invasive way to prevent premature aging and promote a youthful complexion.

The process of performing Gua Sha involves using a curved, smooth-edged tool to glide over the face and neck in upward and outward motions, following the natural contours of the face. To ensure a smooth glide and prevent skin irritation, Gua Sha is typically performed with a facial oil or serum that provides hydration and nourishment. A basic routine often begins with massaging the neck and jawline to stimulate lymphatic drainage and reduce puffiness. The tool is then used on the cheeks and cheekbones with lifting and sculpting motions to enhance definition and improve tone. On the forehead and brows, gentle strokes help smooth fine lines and release tension from the forehead muscles. The under-eye area is treated with light, feathery movements to reduce puffiness and brighten the eyes.

Regular use of Gua Sha enhances skin texture, reduces inflammation, and improves circulation, making it a valuable addition to both professional and at-home skincare regimens. Many dermatologists and aestheticians recommend integrating Gua Sha into self-care routines to maximize skin benefits and promote relaxation.

As holistic beauty techniques gain more recognition, practices like lymphatic drainage, acupuncture, and Gua Sha massage continue to rise in popularity. These methods not only promote detoxification and circulation but also support skin rejuvenation in a natural and non-invasive way. Whether used individually or in combination, they offer effective alternatives for those seeking healthier skin, reduced inflammation, and a sculpted, youthful appearance. Their growing acceptance in modern beauty and wellness highlights a shift toward integrative skincare that prioritizes both external beauty and overall well-being.

Hybrid facials often incorporate oxygen therapy, which is touted for its rejuvenating effects on the skin. Oxygen therapy can enhance cellular metabolism and promote skin healing, leading to improved mental clarity and overall energy levels. The combination of these advanced techniques not only addresses aesthetic concerns but also emphasizes holistic well-being, aligning with contemporary trends in skincare that prioritize both physical and mental health benefits.

Oxygen therapy in facials involves infusing the skin with highly concentrated oxygen, often in combination with vitamins, antioxidants, and botanical extracts. The goal of this treatment is to improve oxygenation at the cellular level, enhancing circulation, hydration, and nutrient absorption. Oxygen is essential for cellular regeneration, and as the skin ages or becomes exposed to environmental pollutants, its ability to absorb and utilize oxygen efficiently declines. By replenishing oxygen levels, this treatment helps revitalize the skin, leaving it refreshed and glowing.

One of the primary benefits of oxygen therapy is its ability to deeply hydrate and plump the skin. Oxygen infusion delivers moisture directly to skin cells, making it particularly beneficial for individuals with dry, dehydrated, or sensitive skin. This immediate boost in hydration gives the skin a smoother, more youthful appearance, making it a popular choice before special events.

Another significant advantage of oxygen therapy is its ability to stimulate collagen production. Collagen is a crucial protein responsible for skin elasticity and firmness, and as its production declines with age, fine lines and wrinkles begin to appear. By increasing oxygen levels in the skin, this therapy promotes collagen synthesis, leading to firmer and more resilient skin over time.

Oxygen therapy also plays a role in detoxification and skin repair. Environmental pollutants, toxins, and oxidative stress can contribute to premature aging and skin dullness. By delivering purified oxygen, this treatment supports the skin's natural detoxification process, helping to flush out impurities and enhance cellular repair. This makes it especially effective for individuals living in urban areas exposed to high pollution levels.

In addition to its rejuvenating effects, oxygen therapy has anti-inflammatory and antibacterial properties. This makes it an excellent option for individuals with acne-prone or sensitive skin. Oxygen helps to kill acne-causing bacteria while reducing redness and inflammation. Unlike harsh acne treatments, oxygen therapy provides a gentle yet effective approach to calming the skin without excessive dryness or irritation.

Hybrid facials use oxygen therapy in conjunction with other treatments to maximize results. One common combination is oxygen therapy with microdermabrasion. Microdermabrasion first exfoliates the outer layer of dead skin cells, creating a clean and receptive surface for oxygen infusion. This enhances the penetration of oxygen and accompanying serums, allowing for deeper hydration and nourishment.

Another popular pairing is oxygen therapy with LED light therapy. After the skin is infused with oxygen, LED therapy is applied to further stimulate collagen production, calm inflammation, and promote overall skin healing. This combination is especially beneficial for individuals looking to improve skin texture, reduce redness, and achieve a more even complexion.

For individuals seeking intense hydration and anti-aging benefits, oxygen therapy is often combined with hyaluronic acid or vitamin-infused serums. These serums, delivered through oxygen infusion, penetrate deeply into the skin, locking in moisture and providing antioxidants that protect against environmental damage. Hyaluronic acid, in particular, binds water molecules to the skin, ensuring long-lasting hydration and plumpness.

Additionally, oxygen therapy can be integrated into cryotherapy-based facials, where cold air is applied after oxygen infusion to further tighten pores, reduce puffiness, and boost circulation. This combination is highly effective for individuals with inflamed or reactive skin, as it helps soothe irritation while enhancing skin clarity.

Oxygen therapy is suitable for all skin types, including sensitive and acne-prone skin. It is particularly beneficial for those experiencing dryness, dullness, or signs of aging, as well as individuals with environmentally stressed or tired skin. It is also a great choice for event-ready facials, as it provides instant hydration and a radiant glow without downtime.

For those dealing with acne or inflammation, oxygen therapy helps calm redness and prevents bacterial growth, making it a gentle alternative to harsher acne treatments. Similarly, individuals with rosacea or sensitive skin conditions may find oxygen facials soothing due to their anti-inflammatory properties.

The integration of these modalities reflects a growing understanding of the interconnectedness of physical treatments and mental health. For instance, the relaxation achieved through acupuncture and massage can lead to reduced stress levels, which is crucial for maintaining healthy skin. The cumulative effect of these treatments can significantly enhance patient satisfaction and perceived quality of life, as evidenced by studies showing improvements in self-esteem and reduced anxiety following such interventions [529].

Advances in Cosmetology

Hair and Scalp Wellness in Hybrid Beauty

The concept of hybrid beauty in haircare is increasingly recognized for its integration of scalp health treatments with relaxation techniques, reflecting a holistic approach to hair wellness. This trend encompasses various therapeutic practices, including scalp massages with essential oils, infrared therapy, and microcurrent treatments, which combine traditional relaxation methods with scientific advancements in hair health.

Scalp massages, often enhanced with essential oils, have been shown to improve blood circulation and promote relaxation, which can be beneficial for scalp health. Essential oils such as rosemary and peppermint are noted for their potential to stimulate hair growth and improve scalp conditions [530]. Furthermore, infrared therapy has gained traction as a method to enhance hair growth by increasing blood flow to hair follicles, thereby facilitating nutrient delivery essential for hair regeneration [531, 532]. Microcurrent treatments, which utilize low-level electrical currents, are also employed to stimulate hair follicles and improve scalp health, merging modern technology with age-old relaxation practices [532, 533].

The emergence of adaptogenic haircare products signifies a shift towards addressing both external hair concerns and internal stress levels. Adaptogens are natural substances that help the body adapt to stress and exert a normalizing effect on bodily processes. This is particularly relevant as conditions like hair thinning and dandruff have been linked to hormonal imbalances, particularly cortisol, and nutritional deficiencies [534]. Research indicates that stress can exacerbate scalp conditions, leading to issues such as seborrheic dermatitis, which is characterized by dandruff and inflammation [534]. Therefore, products that incorporate adaptogenic ingredients aim to balance cortisol levels while simultaneously addressing the physical aspects of hair health.

Adaptogens are known for their ability to help the body manage stress, balance hormones, and improve overall resilience, which translates into benefits for hair health as well. These ingredients are particularly useful in combating hair thinning, scalp irritation, dryness, and damage caused by environmental aggressors or internal imbalances.

Richard Skiba

Adaptogens are bioactive compounds found in plants and fungi that help the body adapt to stress and restore equilibrium. In traditional medicine systems like Ayurveda and Traditional Chinese Medicine (TCM), adaptogens have been used for centuries to support immunity, energy levels, and stress resistance. When applied to haircare, adaptogens work by reducing oxidative stress, improving scalp circulation, and balancing oil production to create an optimal environment for healthy hair growth.

Stress is one of the leading causes of hair thinning, breakage, and scalp conditions such as dandruff or sensitivity. Adaptogens mitigate these effects by lowering cortisol levels, regulating the nervous system, and improving blood flow to hair follicles, ensuring they receive the nutrients needed for strong, resilient hair.

Adaptogens, known for their ability to help the body adapt to stress, can play a significant role in mitigating stress-related hair issues, balancing oil production, and promoting overall scalp health. For instance, ashwagandha is recognized for its capacity to lower cortisol levels, a hormone linked to hair loss and premature graying. By reducing cortisol, ashwagandha protects hair follicles from stress-induced shedding and stimulates keratin production, enhancing hair strength and vitality [535].

Rhodiola Rosea is another adaptogen that has shown promise in haircare. It enhances cellular oxygenation and improves blood circulation to the scalp, which is crucial for delivering nutrients to hair follicles. This increased nutrient delivery not only promotes stronger hair growth but also possesses anti-inflammatory properties that can alleviate scalp irritation and inflammation, making it particularly beneficial for individuals experiencing hair thinning or scalp sensitivity [536]. The adaptogenic properties of Rhodiola Rosea thus contribute to a healthier scalp environment conducive to hair growth.

Reishi mushroom is widely utilized in adaptogenic haircare formulations due to its ability to inhibit DHT (dihydrotestosterone), a hormone that contributes to hair loss. Its antioxidant and anti-inflammatory properties further support scalp health and hair density by reducing oxidative stress and inflammation, which are critical factors in maintaining healthy hair follicles and preventing premature shedding [537]. The inclusion of Reishi mushroom in haircare

242

products can thus be seen as a strategic approach to combat hair loss effectively.

Schisandra berry is particularly noted for its detoxifying properties and its ability to regulate oil production on the scalp. By improving scalp elasticity and reducing excess sebum, Schisandra berry is ideal for individuals with oily scalps or dandruff. This regulation helps maintain a balanced scalp environment, preventing buildup and irritation, which are detrimental to hair growth [538]. Moreover, the adaptogenic nature of Schisandra berry aligns with the growing trend of holistic beauty, emphasizing the importance of natural ingredients in personal care products.

Tulsi, or holy basil, is another adaptogen that offers significant benefits for scalp health. Its antimicrobial and soothing properties are beneficial for individuals suffering from itchy scalps, dandruff, or conditions like psoriasis. Tulsi helps regulate sebum production, preventing both excessive dryness and oiliness, and promotes a balanced scalp microbiome. Its natural antibacterial effects make it an excellent choice for addressing scalp inflammation and irritation [539].

Ginseng is a well-established adaptogen that enhances hair follicle strength by improving blood circulation and stimulating the scalp. It is frequently included in anti-hair loss treatments due to its ability to extend the anagen (growth) phase of the hair cycle. By increasing nutrient supply to the follicles, ginseng promotes thicker, healthier hair while reducing hair shedding [540]. The multifaceted benefits of ginseng make it a valuable ingredient in adaptogenic haircare formulations.

Adaptogenic haircare formulations target the root causes of hair and scalp concerns rather than simply masking symptoms. By addressing underlying stressors, hormonal imbalances, and environmental damage, adaptogens help restore balance and promote long-term hair health.

One of the primary benefits of adaptogens in haircare is their ability to regulate oil production. Many individuals struggle with an overly dry or excessively oily scalp due to imbalances in sebaceous gland activity. Adaptogens work by stabilizing these glands, ensuring that the scalp remains hydrated without becoming greasy. This balance is crucial in maintaining a healthy scalp environment, preventing clogged follicles and scalp irritation.

Another significant advantage of adaptogenic haircare is its role in reducing hair loss. Stress and hormonal fluctuations are major contributors to excessive shedding, particularly through the overproduction of cortisol and the presence of DHT (dihydrotestosterone), a hormone linked to hair thinning. Adaptogens such as ashwagandha and reishi mushroom help lower cortisol levels and block DHT, reducing the impact of stress-related and hormonal hair loss. By targeting these internal factors, adaptogens offer a proactive solution to hair thinning and shedding.

Hair strength and resilience also benefit from adaptogenic ingredients. Adaptogens like ashwagandha and ginseng enhance keratin synthesis, which is essential for fortifying hair strands and reducing breakage. This leads to stronger, healthier hair that is less prone to split ends and damage. Additionally, these ingredients help repair the hair's natural structure, improving texture and elasticity over time.

A detoxified scalp is another key component of healthy hair, and adaptogens contribute by removing toxins, pollutants, and excess buildup. Botanical extracts such as schisandra berry and tulsi (holy basil) have natural detoxifying and antimicrobial properties that cleanse the scalp, reduce inflammation, and restore its natural protective barrier. This cleansing action helps prevent scalp conditions such as dandruff, itching, and irritation while promoting an optimal environment for hair growth.

Boosting blood circulation is crucial for delivering oxygen and nutrients to hair follicles, and adaptogens play a vital role in this process. Improved circulation ensures that hair follicles receive the nourishment they need to remain strong and productive, ultimately supporting thicker and healthier hair growth. Adaptogens like rhodiola and ginseng stimulate blood flow, revitalizing the scalp and encouraging the growth phase of the hair cycle.

Several haircare brands have recognized the power of adaptogens and incorporated them into their products to enhance scalp health and hair vitality. Briogeo's *Destined for Density™ MegaStrength+ Caffeine + Biotin Peptide Density Serum* includes ashwagandha, caffeine, and biotin to boost hair thickness and support scalp health. Act+Acre's *Cold Processed Scalp Detox* features adaptogenic mushrooms and basil leaf extract to rebalance the scalp and remove buildup. RANAVAT's *Mighty Majesty Fortifying Hair Serum* combines amla and ashwagandha to nourish the scalp and prevent hair fall. Vegamour's *GRO+ Advanced Hair Serum* is infused with cannabidiol (CBD) and turmeric, reducing inflammation and supporting follicle growth. Dr. Barbara Sturm's *Super Anti-Aging Scalp Serum* includes ginseng extract to improve circulation and protect against oxidative stress on the scalp.

As adaptogenic haircare continues to gain popularity, these innovative formulations provide consumers with natural and effective solutions for scalp balance, hair growth, and overall hair vitality. By integrating adaptogens into daily haircare routines, individuals can experience stronger, healthier hair while benefiting from the holistic, stress-reducing properties of these powerful botanicals.

The scientific community has increasingly recognized the connection between nutrition and hair health. For instance, deficiencies in essential nutrients such as vitamins A, B complex, and zinc can lead to hair issues, including brittleness and thinning [530, 541]. This understanding has prompted brands to formulate products that not only target the scalp and hair directly but also consider the internal factors influencing hair health, thereby embodying the principles of hybrid beauty.

Body Care and Holistic Wellness

Hybrid beauty has significantly influenced the body care sector, particularly through the integration of advanced treatments such as cryotherapy and lymphatic drainage massages. Cryotherapy-infused body treatments are recognized for their ability to aid muscle recovery while simultaneously tightening and firming the skin. Research indicates that whole-body cryotherapy can reduce inflammation and improve muscle strength and endurance, particularly in patients with conditions like osteoarthritis [542, 543]. However, some studies suggest a lack of quantitative evidence supporting cryotherapy's efficacy in muscle recovery [544]. Other research highlights its potential benefits, including the release of endorphins and a reduction in pain, which may enhance overall physical performance [545].

Lymphatic drainage massages complement these treatments by detoxifying the body and sculpting the physique. Such massages are known to improve lymphatic flow, which can alleviate lymphedema and enhance recovery post-surgery, particularly in breast cancer patients [546]. The systematic review by Ezzo et al. [546] emphasizes the effectiveness of manual lymphatic drainage in managing lymphedema, suggesting that these massages not only provide aesthetic benefits but also contribute to health improvements). Furthermore, the integration of these therapies into wellness routines reflects a growing trend where beauty and health are intertwined, promoting holistic well-being.

In addition to cryotherapy and lymphatic drainage, wellness-infused body treatments have gained traction. Magnesium-infused body lotions are particularly noted for their relaxing properties and ability to aid muscle recovery [547]. These lotions leverage the therapeutic benefits of magnesium, which is essential for muscle function and relaxation. Similarly, essential oil-infused body butters provide nourishment to the skin while offering aromatherapeutic benefits, enhancing both physical and emotional well-being [547]. The combination of these treatments illustrates a comprehensive approach to body care, where the focus is not solely on aesthetics but also on overall health and wellness.

Makeup and Mental Well-being

The evolution of makeup into a hybrid beauty category reflects a significant shift in consumer preferences towards products that not only enhance appearance but also provide skincare benefits. Many contemporary makeup formulations now incorporate skincare ingredients such as hyaluronic acid, niacinamide, and antioxidants. These components are known for their hydrating and nourishing properties, which contribute to healthier skin while simultaneously enhancing one's aesthetic appeal [548]. This trend is indicative of a broader movement within the beauty industry, where the lines between makeup and skincare are increasingly blurred, allowing consumers to achieve both beauty and skin health in a single application [549].

In addition to the integration of skincare ingredients, brands are increasingly focusing on the sensory experiences associated with makeup products. This includes the development of formulations that feature soothing textures and calming scents, which can significantly enhance the user experience and promote a positive self-image [550]. The sensory attributes of cosmetic products, such as texture and fragrance, play a crucial role in consumer satisfaction and emotional well-being, as they can evoke pleasant memories and feelings, thereby reducing stress [551]. The emphasis on sensory experiences aligns with the growing recognition of the psychological impact of beauty rituals, where the act of applying makeup is seen as a form of self-care rather than merely a means to achieve aesthetic perfection [552].

Furthermore, the introduction of breathable and probiotic-infused foundations represents a significant advancement in makeup technology. These products are designed to support the skin's microbiome, promoting overall skin health rather than simply masking imperfections [549]. This approach reflects a shift towards more mindful makeup application, where the focus is on enhancing natural beauty and supporting skin health as part of a holistic self-care routine. The trend towards mindful application underscores the importance of consumer education regarding the benefits of such products, encouraging a more informed and health-conscious approach to beauty [552].

The Future of Hybrid Beauty

The integration of technology into the beauty industry has led to the emergence of hybrid beauty, which combines skincare with mindfulness practices. AI-powered skincare devices are at the forefront of this trend, as they analyse various skin parameters, including hydration and inflammation markers, to assess stress levels. These devices offer personalized recommendations for skincare routines and mindfulness techniques, thereby creating a tailored self-care experience that addresses both physical and mental well-being [553]. The use of neurocosmetics, which aim to influence brain activity and mood through sensory interactions, further exemplifies this trend, as these products are designed to enhance emotional satisfaction and overall wellness [298].

Neurocosmetics is an innovative field that merges principles from neuroscience and dermatology to enhance skincare products, focusing on the intricate mind-skin connection. Unlike conventional cosmetics that primarily address superficial skin issues, neurocosmetics target the skin's neuroreceptors and sensory pathways, thereby influencing overall skin health and emotional well-being. This approach is grounded in the understanding that the skin is not merely a barrier but a complex organ with its own nervous system, capable of responding to various stimuli. Research indicates that neurocosmetic formulations, which often include bioactive ingredients, can modulate neurochemical signals to promote skin regeneration, reduce inflammation, and enhance mood-related responses [554].

The skin's interaction with the nervous system is crucial for understanding how neurocosmetics function. The presence of a network of nerve endings, neurotransmitters, and sensory receptors allows the skin to communicate with the brain, influencing its behaviour and health. Neurocosmetic products aim to mitigate the adverse effects of stress on the skin, which is particularly significant given that chronic stress can lead to the release of cortisol. This hormone is known to accelerate skin aging and exacerbate conditions such as acne and eczema [554]. By regulating stress responses, neurocosmetic ingredients can help maintain skin resilience and promote a more youthful appearance [555].

One of the primary objectives of neurocosmetics is to counteract stress-induced skin damage. Studies have shown that specific neuro-relaxing ingredients derived from plant extracts can effectively combat the inflammatory responses associated with skin stress [554]. Furthermore, the physiological benefits of skincare routines extend beyond mere aesthetics; they can also enhance emotional well-being.

Neurocosmetics offer a range of benefits that go beyond traditional skincare by addressing both physical and emotional aspects of skin health. By targeting the skin's nervous system and biochemical pathways, these products help improve overall skin function while enhancing emotional well-being.

One of the primary benefits of neurocosmetics is stress reduction and skin soothing. Many of the active ingredients used in these formulations have calming effects on the nervous system, which helps reduce redness, irritation, and inflammation triggered by stress. By modulating neurotransmitters such as serotonin and dopamine, neurocosmetics create a soothing effect that minimizes stress-induced skin reactions, making them particularly beneficial for individuals with sensitive or reactive skin.

Neurocosmetics also play a crucial role in enhancing skin repair and regeneration. By stimulating the production of essential proteins like collagen and elastin, these products help improve skin elasticity and firmness. This leads to a visible reduction in wrinkles and fine lines, giving the skin a more youthful and rejuvenated appearance. The ability of neurocosmetics to accelerate cellular renewal makes them a valuable tool in anti-aging skincare.

A strong skin barrier is essential for retaining moisture and protecting against environmental aggressors. Neurocosmetic ingredients help reinforce the skin's natural defense mechanisms, ensuring better hydration and resilience. This enhanced skin barrier function protects against pollutants, UV radiation, and oxidative stress, which are all factors that contribute to premature aging and skin sensitivity.

Another unique advantage of neurocosmetics is their mood-boosting effects. Some formulations incorporate aromatherapy principles by using specific scents that stimulate the brain's pleasure centers. Fragrances such as lavender, sandalwood, and rose not only provide a sensory experience but also have a calming, uplifting, or energizing impact on the user's mood. This integration of neuroscience and skincare creates a more holistic approach to beauty and self-care.

Several innovative bioactive compounds are commonly used in neurocosmetics to optimize both skin function and emotional wellness. Neuropeptides are one such ingredient, as they influence communication between skin cells and nerve endings. By relaxing facial muscles and reducing dynamic wrinkle formation, neuropeptides like Acetyl Hexapeptide-8 (also known as Argireline) provide a non-invasive alternative to Botox.

Cannabidiol (CBD) is another key ingredient in neurocosmetic formulations. Known for its anti-inflammatory and calming properties, CBD interacts with the skin's endocannabinoid system to regulate oil production, soothe irritation, and promote balance. Adaptogens such as ashwagandha and rhodiola also play an important role by helping the nervous system regulate cortisol levels. By minimizing the effects of stress on the skin, these botanical extracts enhance skin resilience and prevent premature aging.

Certain natural plant extracts, such as algae and monk's pepper (Vitex agnus-castus), stimulate the release of beta-endorphins, the body's natural "feel-good" molecules. These beta-endorphin-boosting ingredients create a relaxing and uplifting effect, benefiting both the skin and emotional well-being. Amino acids like glutamine and tryptophan are also commonly used in neurocosmetics to support collagen synthesis, maintain skin hydration, and aid in cellular repair.

The beauty industry has increasingly embraced neurocosmetics, incorporating advanced neuroscience into skincare formulations. Several leading brands have launched products that integrate neurocosmetic principles to provide both skin-enhancing and mood-lifting benefits. Filorga's NCEF-Shot Supreme Polyrevitalizing Concentrate uses neuropeptides and amino acids to stimulate skin regeneration and reduce fatigue. L'Oréal Revitalift Filler Eye Serum with Caffeine combines caffeine and hyaluronic acid to improve circulation, reduce puffiness, and refresh the under-eye area.

Biologique Recherche's Sérum de Teint is a tinted serum infused with neurocosmetic ingredients that help reduce stress-related skin inflammation and promote a more even complexion. Augustinus Bader The Rich Cream features TFC8 (Trigger Factor Complex) technology to enhance skin renewal and boost resilience. EviDenS de Beauté The Serum incorporates bioengineered neuropeptides to improve skin elasticity and reduce the appearance of wrinkles.

Dermalogica's Stress Positive Eye Lift is an advanced neurocosmetic eye treatment designed to combat stress-induced aging, using cooling botanicals and peptides to rejuvenate the delicate eye area. These products demonstrate the growing influence of neurocosmetics in the beauty industry, offering consumers a science-backed approach to skincare that enhances both physical appearance and emotional well-being.

As research into the skin-brain connection continues to evolve, neurocosmetics are expected to play an even greater role in the future of beauty. By combining cutting-edge neuroscience with dermatological innovation, these products offer a revolutionary approach to skincare that not only enhances the skin's health and appearance but also improves overall emotional well-being.

At-home beauty gadgets, such as microcurrent facial devices and LED therapy masks, have also evolved to include guided meditation features. This merging of beauty treatments with mindfulness exercises allows consumers to engage in a more immersive self-care routine, promoting relaxation and enhancing the effectiveness of the beauty treatments. The incorporation of mindfulness into beauty practices reflects a broader understanding of self-care that recognizes the importance of mental health alongside physical appearance.

As hybrid beauty continues to evolve, the emphasis on personalized wellness-driven solutions is expected to strengthen. Future innovations may include biometric scanning tools that assess both skin conditions and stress levels, as well as AI-driven beauty coaching that integrates insights from mental health research. This holistic approach acknowledges that true beauty is not solely about external appearance but also involves a balance of physical care, mental well-being, and inner confidence. By combining therapeutic wellness practices with advanced skincare routines, hybrid beauty is redefining consumer approaches to beauty, making it more functional and mindful.

Technology also plays a role in hybrid beauty, with AI-powered skincare devices that analyse stress levels through skin hydration and inflammation markers. These devices provide tailored recommendations for both skincare and mindfulness techniques, creating a truly personalized self-care experience.

At-home beauty gadgets such as microcurrent facial devices and LED therapy masks now come with guided meditation features, merging beauty treatments with mindfulness exercises for a more immersive self-care routine.

As hybrid beauty continues to evolve, the focus on personalized wellness-driven beauty solutions will only grow stronger. Future innovations may include biometric scanning tools that assess both skin and stress levels, AI-driven beauty coaching that integrates mental health insights, and further advancements in neurocosmetics—products designed to impact brain activity and mood through skin and scent interactions.

Hybrid beauty represents a significant shift in the beauty industry, acknowledging that true beauty comes from a balance of physical care, mental well-being, and inner confidence. By merging therapeutic wellness practices with advanced skincare and self-care routines, hybrid beauty is redefining the way consumers approach beauty, making it more holistic, functional, and mindful.

Chapter 6

Holistic Beauty and Wellness

Integrating Aromatherapy, Acupuncture, and Ayurveda

The integration of aromatherapy, acupuncture, and Ayurveda in beauty therapy represents a holistic approach that enhances both physical appearance and overall well-being. This approach is rooted in the understanding that beauty is not merely a superficial concern but is deeply connected to the internal state of the body and mind. Aromatherapy utilizes essential oils to promote relaxation and emotional well-being, which can significantly impact skin health and appearance [556, 557]. Studies have shown that aromatherapy can influence neurotransmitter secretion, thereby contributing to stress reduction and improved skin conditions [558]. Furthermore, the use of essential oils in aromatherapy has been linked to enhanced circulation, which is essential for skin regeneration and overall vitality [558].

Acupuncture, another key component of this integrative approach, focuses on restoring balance within the body by stimulating specific points that correspond to various bodily functions. This practice has been shown to improve circulation and promote relaxation, which are critical for maintaining healthy skin and reducing stress [559, 560]. The combination of acupuncture with aromatherapy can amplify these benefits, creating a synergistic effect that enhances the overall therapeutic experience [556, 557]. Moreover, acupuncture has been recognized for its ability to alleviate various skin conditions, further supporting its role in beauty therapy [561].

Ayurveda, with its ancient wisdom, emphasizes the importance of internal balance and holistic health. Ayurvedic practices advocate for the use of natural ingredients and treatments that not only enhance external beauty but also promote internal well-being [39, 562]. The principles of Ayurveda suggest that beauty treatments should address the root causes of skin issues, which often lie in dietary and lifestyle choices [39]. Ayurvedic cosmeceuticals, for instance, utilize natural formulations that are free from harmful chemicals, thereby supporting long-term skin health [562, 563]. The integration of Ayurvedic principles with aromatherapy and acupuncture creates a comprehensive beauty therapy regimen that nurtures both the body and mind, fostering a deeper connection to one's overall health and appearance [39].

Aromatherapy involves the use of essential oils extracted from plants, flowers, and herbs to promote relaxation, enhance skin health, and improve emotional balance. Essential oils have therapeutic properties that can benefit the skin, scalp, and hair while also influencing mood and mental well-being.

In beauty therapy, essential oils such as lavender, chamomile, and rose are commonly used in facial treatments, massage oils, and skincare products to calm the skin and reduce inflammation. Tea tree and eucalyptus oils are valued for their antibacterial and purifying properties, making them beneficial for acne-prone or congested skin. Essential oils like frankincense and geranium are often used in anti-aging treatments due to their ability to promote collagen production and skin elasticity.

Aromatherapy is integrated into beauty therapy through facial steam treatments, diffusers, infused massage oils, and customized skincare formulations. When inhaled, essential oils stimulate the limbic system, the part of the brain responsible for emotions and memory, reducing stress and enhancing relaxation. When applied topically, they penetrate the skin, providing nourishment and therapeutic effects. Combining aromatherapy with facial massages, scalp treatments, and body therapies creates a multi-sensory experience that improves circulation, relieves tension, and enhances skin radiance.

Advances in Cosmetology

Acupuncture, a key component of Traditional Chinese Medicine (TCM), involves inserting fine needles into specific points along the body's meridians to restore balance and stimulate natural healing. In beauty therapy, acupuncture is used to promote skin health, improve circulation, and reduce signs of aging.

Facial acupuncture, also known as cosmetic acupuncture, targets key areas of the face to stimulate collagen production, reduce wrinkles, and enhance skin elasticity. By increasing blood flow and oxygenation, acupuncture revitalizes the skin, resulting in a firmer and more youthful appearance. It also helps to reduce puffiness by promoting lymphatic drainage, effectively eliminating toxins and excess fluid retention.

Beyond facial treatments, acupuncture addresses internal imbalances that contribute to skin issues such as acne, rosacea, and eczema. By targeting meridian points associated with digestion, hormonal balance, and stress relief, acupuncture promotes overall well-being, which in turn reflects in a healthier complexion. Acupuncture is often combined with herbal medicine, facial gua sha, or LED light therapy to enhance its effects in beauty therapy.

Ayurveda, the ancient healing system from India, focuses on balancing the body's energies, or doshas—Vata, Pitta, and Kapha—to maintain health and beauty. Ayurvedic beauty therapy emphasizes personalized skincare and self-care rituals tailored to an individual's dosha type.

Ayurvedic beauty treatments often incorporate herbal ingredients like turmeric, neem, and sandalwood, which have antibacterial, anti-inflammatory, and skin-brightening properties. Ubtans (herbal pastes), Ayurvedic oils, and botanical extracts are used in facial treatments, body scrubs, and scalp therapies to detoxify and nourish the skin.

Abhyanga, the Ayurvedic practice of self-massage using warm oils, is commonly integrated into beauty therapy to improve skin texture, stimulate lymphatic flow, and promote deep relaxation. Shirodhara, where warm oil is poured over the forehead, is another Ayurvedic treatment that reduces stress, improves hair health, and enhances overall well-being.

Ayurveda also highlights the importance of diet and lifestyle in maintaining beauty. According to Ayurvedic principles, incorporating nutrient-rich foods, herbal teas, and detoxifying practices can help address underlying imbalances that manifest as dull skin, hair loss, or premature aging.

Integrating these three holistic practices in beauty therapy creates a comprehensive approach to skin health and wellness. While aromatherapy enhances relaxation and provides therapeutic skin benefits, acupuncture stimulates the body's natural healing mechanisms, and Ayurveda offers personalized care based on an individual's constitution.

For example, a holistic facial treatment may begin with an Ayurvedic herbal mask, followed by a lymphatic massage using essential oils selected based on the client's dosha. Facial acupuncture can then be incorporated to stimulate collagen production and improve circulation. This combination helps to address both external and internal beauty concerns, ensuring long-term skin health and emotional well-being.

By integrating aromatherapy, acupuncture, and Ayurveda into beauty therapy, practitioners can provide treatments that not only enhance beauty but also restore balance, reduce stress, and improve overall health. This holistic approach aligns with the growing consumer demand for natural, personalized, and wellness-driven beauty treatments, making it a valuable addition to modern skincare and spa practices.

Cosmetologists can incorporate aromatherapy, acupuncture, and Ayurveda into beauty therapy to create a holistic approach that nurtures both external beauty and internal well-being. By blending these traditional healing techniques with modern beauty treatments, practitioners can enhance their services, offering personalized experiences that promote relaxation, skin health, and emotional balance.

By combining aromatherapy, acupuncture, and Ayurveda in beauty therapy, cosmetologists can offer clients a more comprehensive and transformative experience. These holistic approaches address both external and internal beauty concerns, ensuring long-term skin health and emotional well-being.

A typical holistic beauty session could begin with an Ayurvedic consultation to determine the client's dosha and skincare needs. This could be followed by a customized facial using essential oils and herbal masks suited to their skin type. Acupuncture or acupressure massage could then be applied to enhance circulation and reduce fine lines, while a scalp massage with Ayurvedic oils could promote relaxation and hair growth.

Cosmetologists can also create signature spa packages that blend these practices, such as a "Detox & Glow Facial" combining Ayurvedic herbal treatments, essential oils, and facial acupuncture. Another example is a "Rejuvenation Ritual," incorporating aromatherapy massage, stress-relieving acupuncture, and a hydrating Ayurvedic facial.

Modern consumers are increasingly seeking beauty treatments that align with their health and wellness goals. The integration of holistic therapies into beauty services offers a unique and personalized approach that appeals to those looking for natural, non-invasive solutions. Cosmetologists who embrace these practices can set themselves apart in the industry, attracting a clientele that values self-care and sustainability.

Stress Management and Its Impact on Skin Health

Stress management is increasingly recognized as a critical factor in maintaining skin health. The relationship between stress and skin conditions is complex, involving physiological responses that can exacerbate various dermatological issues. When the body is under stress, it releases cortisol, a hormone that can lead to increased inflammation and disruption of skin barrier functions. Elevated cortisol levels can stimulate sebaceous glands to produce excess oil, contributing to acne and other skin disorders [564, 565]. Furthermore, chronic stress can compromise the immune system, making the skin more vulnerable to infections and delaying healing processes [565, 566].

Research indicates that stress can lead to a deterioration of the skin's moisture retention capabilities, resulting in dryness and a lacklustre complexion. This is partly due to the breakdown of collagen and elastin, which are essential for maintaining skin elasticity and firmness [567, 568]. The psychological aspects of stress can also manifest in behaviours that negatively impact skin health, such as poor sleep, unhealthy dietary choices, and inadequate hydration, all of which can accelerate the aging process and contribute to skin imbalances [569, 570].

Moreover, stress is closely linked to inflammatory skin conditions such as eczema, psoriasis, and rosacea. Stress can trigger the release of pro-inflammatory cytokines, exacerbating symptoms like redness and itching in individuals with sensitive skin [571, 572]. Studies have shown that individuals with pre-existing skin conditions often experience heightened symptoms during periods of emotional or physical stress, indicating that effective stress management could alleviate these issues [565, 566, 573].

Implementing stress management techniques can significantly enhance skin health and overall well-being. Techniques such as mindfulness meditation, yoga, and other relaxation methods have been shown to lower cortisol levels and reduce inflammation, thereby supporting the skin's natural repair processes [572, 574]. By managing stress effectively, individuals can help regulate their skin's response to environmental and psychological stressors, promoting a healthier, more radiant complexion [572, 575].

Developing a consistent stress management routine can lead to noticeable improvements in skin condition and overall wellness. Several techniques are particularly beneficial for reducing stress and enhancing skin health. Cosmetologists can integrate these techniques into their services, providing holistic treatments that address both emotional and physical well-being.

Practicing mindfulness through meditation, deep breathing, or yoga can reduce cortisol levels and promote relaxation. These techniques improve blood circulation, allowing more oxygen and nutrients to reach skin cells, enhancing their function and appearance. Cosmetologists can incorporate guided breathing exercises at the beginning of facials or spa treatments to help clients relax and improve treatment effectiveness. Offering calming music, dim lighting, and a peaceful atmosphere in the treatment room can further enhance mindfulness and create a stress-relieving experience.

Physical activity helps release endorphins, which counteract stress hormones and promote overall relaxation. Sweating during exercise also aids in detoxifying the skin, clearing out impurities, and improving circulation for a healthy glow. Cosmetologists can educate clients about the benefits of movement for skin health, suggesting facial yoga or simple stretching exercises that improve circulation and prevent tension buildup in the facial muscles. Recommending lymphatic drainage massage techniques can also support detoxification, especially for clients with dull or congested skin.

Quality sleep is essential for skin repair and regeneration. During deep sleep, the body produces growth hormones that help repair damaged skin and rebuild collagen. Poor sleep disrupts this process, leading to dark circles, puffiness, and a lacklustre complexion. Cosmetologists can offer nighttime skincare routines tailored to support skin recovery, including hydrating masks, anti-aging serums, and melatonin-infused skincare products. Providing advice on relaxation techniques, such as aromatherapy or silk pillowcases, can further help clients achieve better sleep and improved skin health.

Consuming a nutrient-rich diet with antioxidants, vitamins, and essential fatty acids supports skin resilience against stress. Hydrating the body with sufficient water intake helps maintain skin elasticity and flush out toxins that can contribute to breakouts. Cosmetologists can recommend skincare products enriched with antioxidants like vitamin C, green tea extract, or niacinamide, which combat oxidative stress. They can also offer personalized consultations that discuss the impact of diet on skin health, suggesting anti-inflammatory foods and hydration strategies for optimal skin hydration and glow.

Essential oils such as lavender, chamomile, and frankincense have calming effects that help reduce stress and promote a sense of well-being. Incorporating aromatherapy into skincare routines through facial mists, massage oils, or diffusers can enhance relaxation and improve skin conditions. Cosmetologists can use aromatherapy diffusers in treatment rooms to create a soothing ambiance, apply essential oils during facial massages, or offer personalized aromatherapy blends based on the client's needs. This not only enhances relaxation but also provides therapeutic benefits for the skin.

Establishing a consistent skincare routine can be a form of self-care, providing a moment of relaxation and stress relief. Massaging the face with facial oils, using Gua Sha tools, or applying hydrating masks can stimulate circulation, reduce tension, and enhance skin radiance. Cosmetologists can educate clients on facial massage techniques that boost circulation and encourage relaxation at home. They can also incorporate mindfulness practices into treatments by encouraging slow, intentional application of skincare products to deepen the self-care experience.

Stress-relief therapies such as acupuncture, lymphatic drainage massages, and Ayurvedic treatments can improve overall well-being and address stress-related skin issues. These treatments enhance circulation, reduce inflammation, and promote detoxification. Cosmetologists can collaborate with wellness practitioners, such as acupuncturists or Ayurvedic specialists, to offer integrated treatment plans that target stress-induced skin concerns. Adding stress-relief facials that combine facial acupuncture, lymphatic drainage, and aromatherapy can further elevate the client experience and provide long-lasting benefits.

By incorporating these stress management techniques into beauty therapy services, cosmetologists can offer a holistic approach to skincare that goes beyond aesthetics. Addressing the root causes of stress-related skin concerns allows for more effective treatments and deeper client satisfaction, making holistic beauty therapy a valuable and sought-after practice.

Mindfulness Practices in Beauty Therapy

Mindfulness in beauty therapy represents a transformative approach that integrates relaxation, self-awareness, and intentionality into skincare and wellness treatments. This practice emphasizes being fully present during beauty rituals, fostering a deeper connection between the mind, body, and skin health. Research indicates that mindfulness techniques can significantly enhance the efficacy of beauty treatments by promoting relaxation and reducing stress, which are critical for maintaining healthy skin. The relationship between stress perception and body image, noting that stress can negatively impact skin health, can lead to issues such as breakouts and premature aging [8]. Furthermore, the incorporation of mindfulness practices in beauty therapy not only aids in achieving radiant skin but also contributes to emotional well-being, as clients often report feeling more balanced and rejuvenated after sessions [576].

The connection between mindfulness and skin health is particularly relevant in the context of stress-related skin conditions. Stress and anxiety can elevate cortisol levels, which adversely affect skin health by impairing circulation and cellular repair processes. Mindfulness-based beauty therapy can counteract these effects by fostering relaxation, which has been shown to lower cortisol levels and enhance skin barrier function [577]. By creating a calming environment and guiding clients through relaxation techniques, beauty professionals can facilitate a more positive skin response during treatments, allowing for better absorption of active ingredients and improved overall skin appearance [576].

To effectively integrate mindfulness into beauty therapy, cosmetologists can adopt several strategies. First, creating a relaxing environment is essential. This includes utilizing soft lighting, calming scents, and soothing music to establish a tranquil atmosphere. Such environments have been shown to significantly enhance the relaxation response in clients, thereby improving their overall experience [576]. Additionally, guided breathing techniques can be employed to help clients centre themselves before treatments, which further promotes relaxation and prepares the body to absorb the benefits of the treatment [576].

The practice of mindful touch and slow movements during treatments can deepen the client's sensory experience. By applying skincare products with intentional, rhythmic motions, cosmetologists can encourage clients to focus on the sensations of touch and texture, enhancing their mindfulness practice [576]. Engaging the senses through the use of natural fragrances and tactile elements can also heighten awareness and promote relaxation, making the beauty treatment a more holistic experience [576].

Encouraging gratitude and positive affirmations during beauty rituals can further enhance the mindfulness experience. By inviting clients to set intentions or repeat affirmations, beauty professionals can help shift the focus from external appearance to self-care and self-acceptance, fostering a more positive relationship with their skin [576]. Incorporating meditation and visualization exercises during treatments can also deepen the relaxation response, allowing clients to visualize stress leaving their bodies and healing energy being absorbed by their skin [576].

The benefits of mindfulness-based beauty therapy extend beyond immediate skin improvements. Clients often report reduced stress and anxiety, enhanced absorption of skincare products, improved skin elasticity, and a greater sense of self-care and self-love [576]. As the demand for holistic beauty and wellness solutions continues to rise, integrating mindfulness into beauty therapy offers a unique opportunity for cosmetologists to provide transformative experiences that promote both physical and emotional well-being [576].

Chapter 7

Digital Transformation in Beauty

Beauty Tech Startups and Apps

The beauty industry has experienced a significant digital transformation, primarily driven by the emergence of beauty tech startups and innovative applications that revolutionize consumer engagement with skincare, makeup, and personal care. These advancements leverage technologies such as artificial intelligence (AI), augmented reality (AR), machine learning, and data analytics to provide personalized experiences, virtual try-ons, and AI-driven recommendations, thereby making beauty products more accessible, convenient, and customized than ever before [578].

Beauty tech startups are at the forefront of this transformation, integrating cutting-edge technology into product development and shopping experiences. For instance, companies like Proven Skincare utilize AI and machine learning to create customized skincare formulations based on user data and scientific research [578]. Similarly, HiMirror employs facial recognition technology to analyse skin conditions, offering users tailored skincare advice [578]. The use of big data and machine learning allows these startups to predict consumer preferences and optimize product formulations, leading to hyper-personalized beauty experiences that cater to individual needs [578].

Many startups are focusing on sustainability and ethical sourcing, utilizing blockchain technology to ensure ingredient transparency [579]. The subscription-based model is also gaining traction, with companies offering AI-curated beauty boxes that are tailored to individual skin concerns and preferences [578]. This shift towards personalization and sustainability reflects a broader trend in the beauty industry, where consumer expectations are increasingly centred on customized and responsible beauty solutions [579].

Prominent examples of beauty tech innovations include L'Oréal's Modiface, which provides AR-powered virtual try-on technology, allowing consumers to experiment with makeup and hair colours in real-time [578]. Atolla and Curology are also noteworthy, as they offer personalized skincare solutions through AI-driven skin analysis and dermatologist consultations [578]. These technologies not only enhance the consumer experience but also empower brands to leverage data analytics for improved customer engagement and satisfaction [578, 579].

Beauty apps have become a major part of digital beauty transformation, offering services that range from virtual makeup application to AI-powered skin diagnostics. These apps leverage AR, AI, and deep learning to provide tailored beauty solutions, improve product discovery, and elevate the online shopping experience.

One of the most impactful innovations in beauty apps is AR-based virtual try-ons. Consumers can see how makeup, hair colours, and skincare products will look on their faces before making a purchase, reducing uncertainty and increasing confidence in buying decisions. Apps like Sephora Virtual Artist and YouCam Makeup allow users to experiment with different looks using their smartphone cameras.

AI-powered skin analysis apps have also gained popularity, enabling users to scan their faces and receive detailed reports on their skin health. These apps use deep learning algorithms to detect issues such as fine lines, wrinkles, dark spots, and hydration levels, then suggest appropriate products and treatments. Neutrogena's Skin360 and L'Oréal's Skin Genius are leading apps in this space.

Some beauty apps focus on personalized product recommendations, leveraging AI to suggest the best skincare and makeup options based on user input, skin type, and environmental factors. Apps like Think Dirty also help consumers make informed choices by analysing product ingredients and identifying potential toxins.

In the wellness and holistic beauty sector, meditation and skincare tracking apps like TroveSkin combine mindfulness and skincare by helping users track their routines, stress levels, and diet to see how they impact their skin over time.

Beauty professionals, cosmetologists, and brands are leveraging these tech advancements to enhance their services and reach a broader audience. Salons and dermatologists use AI-powered consultation tools to offer remote skincare analysis and virtual consultations. Brands integrate AR into their e-commerce platforms, allowing customers to test and buy products seamlessly. Influencers and beauty professionals also use these apps to engage with their audiences, offering live tutorials and AI-enhanced beauty advice.

With the rise of smart beauty devices, such as AI-powered hairdryers, personalized skincare dispensers, and at-home microcurrent devices, beauty tech is extending beyond virtual experiences into tangible, real-world applications. Devices like the Foreo Luna 4 and NIRA Skincare Laser bring professional-grade beauty treatments into homes, blending AI, IoT (Internet of Things), and personalized algorithms to deliver optimal results.

The future of beauty tech lies in hyper-personalization, AI-driven diagnostics, and sustainability-focused innovations. Advancements in 3D printing for custom cosmetics, voice-activated beauty assistants, and blockchain for ingredient transparency will shape the next phase of digital beauty transformation. Additionally, the metaverse and virtual beauty experiences will redefine how consumers engage with beauty brands, with digital avatars trying on products in immersive, interactive environments.

The Role of Social Media and Influencers

The influence of social media and influencers on the cosmetology industry has been profound, fundamentally reshaping how beauty trends emerge, products are marketed, and services are delivered. Platforms such as Instagram, TikTok, YouTube, and Pinterest have become essential tools for cosmetologists, beauty brands, and independent professionals to engage with consumers in a direct and visually compelling manner. The vast user base consuming beauty-related content daily underscores the critical role social media plays in educating, inspiring, and influencing purchasing decisions [580, 581].

Social media has significantly accelerated the spread of beauty trends, allowing new techniques, products, and treatments to gain rapid popularity. Viral trends such as "glass skin," "soap brows," and "clean beauty" often originate from influencers or professional cosmetologists sharing their expertise online. The short-form content enabled by platforms like TikTok and Instagram Reels facilitates quick dissemination of these trends, capturing attention almost instantaneously [581]. Furthermore, social media fosters innovation by providing real-time consumer feedback, enabling beauty brands and professionals to monitor engagement metrics and customer reviews. This feedback loop allows for the refinement of techniques and the development of new offerings that align with consumer preferences, exemplifying a shift towards community-driven beauty [580].

Influencers have emerged as pivotal figures in beauty marketing, acting as modern-day beauty advisors who shape consumer preferences and purchasing decisions. Unlike traditional celebrity endorsements, influencers engage with their audiences on a personal level, making their recommendations feel more authentic and trustworthy [581]. Collaborations with macro-, micro-, and nano-influencers allow beauty brands to promote their products through sponsored posts, product reviews, and brand ambassadorships. The authenticity of influencer marketing is particularly valuable in the cosmetology industry, where consumer trust is crucial for trying new products or services [580]. For professional cosmetologists, partnering with influencers can enhance brand awareness, increase clientele, and establish credibility, as local influencers often share their experiences with beauty services, attracting new clients through social media exposure [581].

Social media platforms have democratized beauty education, enabling aspiring cosmetologists and beauty enthusiasts to access professional knowledge without formal training. Influencers, dermatologists, and professional cosmetologists share tutorials and product recommendations in an easily digestible format. YouTube serves as a hub for in-depth educational content, while TikTok and Instagram provide quick beauty tips [580]. The rise of virtual beauty training, facilitated by social media, allows licensed cosmetologists to offer online courses and live masterclasses, expanding their reach beyond physical locations. This trend not only enables beauty professionals to build their personal brands but also creates multiple revenue streams and connects them with a global audience [580].

Social media has made beauty more accessible and inclusive, empowering consumers to make informed decisions about the products and services they use. Many consumers rely on user-generated content, such as reviews and product demonstrations, before purchasing beauty products. Platforms like TikTok and Instagram have revolutionized product discovery, with viral beauty products often selling out rapidly due to social media hype [580]. Cosmetologists can leverage this shift by using social media to educate their audience about their expertise and the science behind beauty treatments, thereby establishing credibility and building a loyal client base [580].

The integration of live streaming and interactive consultations on platforms like Instagram Live and TikTok Live has transformed how beauty professionals engage with their audience. Cosmetologists can host live Q&A sessions, product demonstrations, and virtual consultations, providing real-time advice to consumers. This direct engagement builds trust and enhances brand loyalty, offering an additional revenue stream through online consultations and product sales [580].

As technology advances, the role of social media in cosmetology is expected to evolve further. The rise of augmented reality (AR) filters and AI skin analysis will enhance the digital beauty experience, allowing users to experiment with beauty looks before purchasing [580]. Additionally, as consumers prioritize sustainability and ethical beauty, social media will play a crucial role in promoting eco-conscious beauty brands. Cosmetologists who align with these values and integrate them into their online presence will likely attract a growing audience of conscious consumers [580].

Richard Skiba

E-commerce Trends in Beauty Product Distribution

The beauty industry has experienced a significant digital revolution, with e-commerce emerging as the predominant channel for product distribution. This shift has led to the decline of traditional brick-and-mortar retail, as consumers increasingly favour online marketplaces and direct-to-consumer (DTC) brands for their convenience and accessibility. The rise of DTC brands such as Glossier and Fenty Beauty exemplifies this trend, as these companies leverage their online presence to bypass traditional retail channels, thereby enhancing customer engagement and brand loyalty through personalized experiences and direct interactions [582]. This model allows brands to collect valuable first-party data, which can be utilized to refine product offerings and marketing strategies, ultimately creating hyper-personalized shopping experiences that resonate with consumers [583].

In addition to the DTC model, advancements in artificial intelligence (AI) and augmented reality (AR) have revolutionized the beauty shopping experience. Brands like L'Oréal and Sephora have integrated AR technologies that enable virtual try-ons, allowing consumers to test products digitally before making a purchase. This innovation not only enhances consumer confidence but also significantly increases conversion rates [584]. Furthermore, AI-driven skin diagnostics tools, such as those offered by Proven Skincare, provide tailored product recommendations based on individual skin concerns, mimicking the personalized service typically found in physical stores [585].

The integration of social commerce and influencer marketing has further transformed the beauty industry's e-commerce landscape. Social media platforms like Instagram and TikTok have introduced shoppable posts and livestream shopping features, facilitating direct purchases without leaving the app [586]. Influencers play a crucial role in this ecosystem, as their endorsements can significantly enhance product visibility and consumer trust. Collaborations between brands and influencers, such as Morphe x James Charles, exemplify how influencer-driven e-commerce can drive sales and foster brand loyalty [587].

Moreover, the popularity of subscription beauty services has surged, providing consumers with curated experiences that allow them to discover new products conveniently. Companies like Birchbox and Ipsy have capitalized on this trend by offering personalized beauty boxes that cater to individual preferences, thereby enhancing customer engagement and ensuring recurring revenue for brands [588]. This subscription model aligns well with the growing consumer demand for customization and convenience in beauty shopping.

Sustainability has also become a pivotal concern in the beauty industry, prompting brands to adopt eco-friendly practices. Many companies are now offering refillable packaging and carbon-neutral shipping options to meet the increasing consumer demand for sustainable products [582]. Brands like Fenty Beauty and Kjaer Weis are leading the charge in this area, demonstrating that eco-conscious practices can coexist with profitability in the e-commerce landscape.

As the beauty industry continues to evolve, the growth of online marketplaces such as Sephora and Amazon highlights the importance of providing a comprehensive shopping experience. These platforms not only offer a wide range of products but also leverage customer reviews and fast shipping to enhance consumer satisfaction [582]. The emergence of niche marketplaces catering to specific consumer demands further illustrates the dynamic nature of beauty e-commerce, allowing smaller brands to reach targeted audiences effectively [584].

As metaverse shopping, blockchain authentication, and 3D-printed cosmetics become more mainstream, the beauty industry will evolve to provide even more immersive and personalized online shopping experiences.

Metaverse shopping is transforming the beauty industry by blending virtual reality (VR), augmented reality (AR), artificial intelligence (AI), and blockchain technology to create an immersive and interactive shopping experience. Unlike traditional e-commerce, which relies on static images and product descriptions, the metaverse allows consumers to engage with beauty brands in a dynamic virtual environment. Through digital storefronts, users can explore product offerings, interact with AI-powered advisors, and test beauty products in real time, making online shopping more experiential and engaging.

Metaverse shopping takes place within virtual worlds and 3D environments where users can create personalized avatars, visit digital stores, and try on beauty products before making a purchase. Transactions can be completed using digital payments, including cryptocurrency and blockchain-based tokens, offering seamless and secure transactions.

Consumers access metaverse beauty stores through VR headsets, AR apps, or browser-based platforms, allowing them to walk through virtual boutiques, interact with beauty consultants, and attend live masterclasses hosted by top influencers and industry experts. Major beauty brands such as Charlotte Tilbury, Gucci Beauty, and Estée Lauder have already launched metaverse experiences that provide personalized recommendations and allow customers to purchase both physical and digital beauty products via blockchain authentication.

One of the primary innovations in metaverse shopping is the creation of virtual beauty stores and showrooms that replicate the in-store shopping experience. Beauty brands now design 3D flagship boutiques where customers can browse products, watch tutorials, and receive AI-driven beauty consultations. This technology enhances personalization, ensuring each user receives recommendations tailored to their individual beauty needs.

A major advancement in metaverse beauty is augmented reality (AR) virtual try-ons, which allow consumers to test makeup, hairstyles, and skincare effects in real time using their device's camera. This feature eliminates the need for in-store testers and helps customers visualize how products will look on their skin before making a purchase. Brands such as L'Oréal's ModiFace, MAC Cosmetics, and Maybelline have integrated AR technology into their shopping apps, making virtual try-ons a seamless part of the buying process.

Metaverse shopping also introduces NFT beauty and digital collectibles, allowing brands to offer exclusive virtual beauty products, avatar accessories, and branded NFTs. These digital assets can be used for gaming, virtual events, and online brand engagement. For example, Clinique launched NFT beauty rewards that grant customers access to exclusive digital experiences, while Estée Lauder released limited-edition NFT beauty items designed specifically for metaverse users.

Another revolutionary feature is live shopping events and virtual beauty consultations. The metaverse allows brands to host interactive masterclasses, real-time Q&A sessions, and influencer-led shopping experiences, where users can receive personalized recommendations and purchase products instantly. Companies such as Sephora and NYX Cosmetics have explored live-stream shopping in virtual spaces, creating an engaging and immersive online retail experience.

The integration of blockchain and secure digital transactions further enhances the metaverse shopping experience by allowing cryptocurrency payments and NFT-based product authentication. Some beauty brands, including Lush and KIKO Milano, now accept crypto payments for beauty products, while others are using blockchain verification to authenticate high-end and sustainable beauty items.

Cryptocurrency payments are becoming increasingly popular among various sectors, including retail. The decentralized nature of cryptocurrencies allows for streamlined transactions without the need for intermediaries, which can enhance the efficiency of payment processes in beauty brands. This shift towards digital currencies aligns with the broader trend of adopting blockchain technologies across industries, as it provides a secure and transparent method for transactions [589]. The use of blockchain can also facilitate better customer experiences by offering faster and more reliable payment options, which is particularly appealing in the fast-paced beauty market.

In addition to payment systems, blockchain technology is being utilized for product authentication, which is crucial in combating counterfeiting—a significant issue in the luxury beauty sector. Blockchain enables the creation of unique digital identities for products, which can be verified at every stage of the supply chain. This process not only ensures the authenticity of high-end beauty products but also enhances consumer trust [590, 591]. By employing smart contracts and digital tokens, brands can provide customers with a means to verify the legitimacy of their purchases, thereby reducing the risk of counterfeit products entering the market [590, 591].

The metaverse offers a highly personalized shopping experience by using AI and machine learning to analyse user preferences and recommend products based on individual beauty needs. Global accessibility is another advantage, as consumers can visit luxury virtual beauty stores, engage with top makeup artists, and attend exclusive events from anywhere in the world.

Metaverse shopping is also eco-friendly and sustainable, as digital beauty products and virtual experiences reduce waste from physical testers, excess packaging, and product returns. This approach aligns with the growing demand for sustainable and cruelty-free beauty solutions.

Additionally, the metaverse enhances consumer engagement through gamification, such as virtual beauty challenges, brand loyalty-based NFT rewards, and interactive product experiences. These elements encourage deeper brand interaction and foster a strong community of beauty enthusiasts.

Despite its many advantages, metaverse shopping still faces challenges related to technology adoption, accessibility, and consumer familiarity with digital currencies. Many consumers are still adapting to VR and AR interfaces, while others are hesitant about using cryptocurrency and blockchain-based transactions for beauty purchases.

As metaverse technology continues to evolve, the future of beauty shopping will likely include AI-powered skincare consultations, biometric scanning for hyper-personalized formulations, and real-time skin condition tracking. Brands will also explore hyper-realistic digital avatars that reflect users' actual skin and hair conditions, allowing for even more precise beauty recommendations.

With more beauty brands embracing virtual retail experiences, metaverse shopping is set to redefine the future of cosmetics and self-care by offering an innovative, immersive, and interactive way to shop for beauty products.

Blockchain authentication is a decentralized verification system that ensures the authenticity, security, and traceability of digital and physical assets. It leverages blockchain technology—a distributed ledger that records transactions in an immutable and transparent way—to verify the legitimacy of products, documents, and ownership records. Unlike traditional authentication methods that rely on centralized databases, blockchain authentication creates a tamper-proof and publicly verifiable record, making it particularly valuable for industries such as beauty, luxury goods, supply chain management, digital identity, and intellectual property protection.

Blockchain authentication operates by assigning a unique cryptographic signature, such as a token, hash, or QR code, to an asset or transaction. Once recorded on the blockchain, this information cannot be altered or erased, ensuring that every product, document, or transaction has a permanent and verifiable history.

When a user scans a blockchain-registered QR code or checks a digital certificate, the system cross-verifies the data with the blockchain ledger to confirm whether the product is genuine, who owns it, and whether any modifications have been made. The process eliminates reliance on third-party verification services, making it more secure and efficient.

Blockchain authentication is widely used in cryptocurrency transactions, luxury goods verification, supply chain tracking, and NFT ownership validation. It is also gaining momentum in the beauty and fashion industries to authenticate sustainable products, verify ingredient sourcing, and prevent counterfeit goods.

Counterfeit beauty and luxury products pose significant risks to consumers, including health hazards and financial losses. Blockchain authentication ensures that luxury skincare, fragrances, and designer cosmetics are genuine and ethically sourced. Brands like LVMH (Louis Vuitton Moët Hennessy) use blockchain-based systems such as the Aura Blockchain Consortium, which allows consumers to verify product authenticity by scanning a QR code on the packaging, linking directly to the item's blockchain history.

Consumers are increasingly demanding transparency in ingredient sourcing, ethical manufacturing, and sustainability claims. Blockchain authentication provides real-time tracking of raw materials, ensuring that brands meet ethical and environmental standards. Companies like Provenance and Lush Cosmetics use blockchain to track ethically sourced ingredients, allowing consumers to verify that their products are free from harmful chemicals and sourced responsibly.

In the metaverse and digital beauty industry, blockchain authentication is used to verify NFT beauty products, digital avatars, and virtual fashion assets. These blockchain-backed digital items ensure exclusive ownership and prevent unauthorized duplication. Brands such as Clinique and Estée Lauder have introduced NFT-based beauty rewards, allowing customers to own limited-edition digital beauty products that are securely stored on the blockchain.

Blockchain authentication is also used for verifying credentials, certifications, and professional licenses in industries like cosmetology and dermatology.

Instead of relying on paper certificates, professionals can have blockchain-registered credentials that clients and employers can verify instantly. IBM's Blockchain for Digital Credentials allows beauty professionals and skincare specialists to store their certifications securely on the blockchain, preventing fraud and misrepresentation.

Blockchain authentication prevents counterfeiting by ensuring that products, documents, and transactions cannot be tampered with once recorded on the blockchain. It increases transparency by allowing consumers and businesses to trace the entire history of a product, from raw materials to final sale. The decentralized nature of blockchain enhances security, as transactions and records are encrypted and protected against fraud or hacking.

Empowering consumers is another key benefit, as shoppers can independently verify product authenticity, ethical sourcing, and brand sustainability claims. Additionally, blockchain authentication reduces intermediary costs by eliminating the need for third-party verification services, lowering expenses while improving efficiency for brands.

Despite its advantages, blockchain authentication faces challenges such as high implementation costs, slow adoption by mainstream businesses, and regulatory uncertainties. Scaling blockchain systems for mass-market adoption requires more efficient and environmentally friendly solutions, as traditional blockchain networks like Bitcoin and Ethereum consume significant amounts of energy.

As technology advances, new blockchain models like Proof-of-Stake (PoS) and Layer 2 scaling solutions are making blockchain authentication more sustainable and accessible. In the future, more industries will integrate blockchain verification systems, making it a standard for secure product authentication, digital identity management, and ethical supply chain tracking.

Blockchain authentication is revolutionizing how brands, consumers, and businesses verify authenticity, creating a trust-based digital economy where ownership, ethical sourcing, and transparency are permanently recorded and accessible to all.

3D-printed cosmetics represent a revolutionary advancement in the beauty industry, leveraging additive manufacturing technology to create customized makeup, skincare, and even hair products with precision and efficiency. This innovation allows consumers to personalize their beauty routines by printing products on demand, reducing waste, and expanding the possibilities of beauty customization.

3D printing in cosmetics utilizes specialized printers that deposit layers of pigments, skincare ingredients, or other active compounds in precise patterns to create beauty products. These printers work similarly to traditional 3D printing but are adapted for cosmetic formulations. Depending on the type of beauty product, different printing technologies such as inkjet, stereolithography (SLA), or fused deposition modelling (FDM) are used.

For makeup applications, a 3D printer can mix and layer different pigments to create custom foundation, lipstick, eyeshadow, or blush shades that match an individual's unique skin tone. Skincare formulations, such as face masks or serums, can also be printed with active ingredients tailored to the user's needs, ensuring a completely personalized product.

One of the most exciting applications of 3D-printed cosmetics is the ability to create customized makeup on demand. Brands like Mink and Perso (by L'Oréal) have developed portable 3D makeup printers that allow users to choose and print their preferred shade of foundation, lipstick, or eyeshadow instantly. Consumers can use an app or scan their skin tone to generate a perfect colour match, eliminating the need for mass production of multiple shades.

3D printing is also transforming skincare formulations by enabling personalized serums, face masks, and even skincare patches. By analysing an individual's skin condition, AI-driven technology can determine the exact combination of active ingredients needed and print a fresh product accordingly. This level of customization ensures that consumers receive skincare solutions specifically tailored to their skin type, environmental conditions, and personal concerns.

The technology is also being explored in medical and dermatological applications. Researchers are developing 3D-printed skin patches infused with active compounds that deliver targeted treatment for conditions like acne, hyperpigmentation, or wound healing. These skincare solutions enhance precision and efficiency in dermatological treatments.

One of the most significant advantages of 3D-printed cosmetics is personalization. Consumers no longer need to rely on mass-produced beauty products that may not perfectly match their skin tone, texture, or specific needs. The ability to print custom formulations ensures a perfect fit for each user.

Another key benefit is sustainability. Traditional beauty manufacturing often leads to excess waste from packaging, unsold inventory, and excess raw materials. With 3D printing, products can be created on demand, reducing waste and the environmental impact of overproduction. Additionally, some companies are developing refillable and biodegradable 3D-printed packaging to further enhance sustainability.

3D printing also enhances efficiency and accessibility. Instead of waiting for a brand to release new shades or formulations, users can create their desired product instantly at home or at beauty retailers. This not only speeds up the beauty customization process but also allows individuals with specific skin conditions or sensitivities to access specialized products without the need for expensive, custom-made formulations.

Despite its promise, 3D-printed cosmetics face several challenges. The initial cost of 3D beauty printers and cartridges remains high, limiting accessibility to a broader market. Additionally, regulatory approval for printed skincare and cosmetic products must ensure safety, stability, and effectiveness before widespread adoption.

As technology advances, the future of 3D-printed cosmetics will likely involve even greater integration with AI-driven beauty analysis, offering hyper-personalized formulations based on genetic data, skin microbiome assessments, and real-time skin diagnostics. More beauty brands are expected to invest in 3D printing technology to create innovative solutions that blend science, sustainability, and self-expression.

3D-printed cosmetics are set to redefine beauty by offering consumers an unprecedented level of customization, convenience, and sustainability. As the industry continues to develop, this technology will play an integral role in the evolution of personalized and on-demand beauty solutions.

Chapter 8

Advances in Trichology

Trichology, the scientific study of hair and scalp health, has seen remarkable advancements in recent years. Innovations in diagnostic tools, regenerative treatments, and biotechnology are transforming how hair loss, scalp conditions, and hair restoration are approached. With a growing demand for non-invasive and effective solutions, modern trichology now integrates genetics, AI, and regenerative medicine to enhance hair and scalp health.

The trichology industry, which focuses on the study and treatment of hair and scalp disorders, has evolved significantly over the years, becoming a vital component of dermatological practice worldwide. This industry encompasses various aspects, including clinical practices, cosmetic applications, and emerging technologies, reflecting a diverse and growing field.

Trichology has its roots in ancient practices but has developed into a specialized field within dermatology. The discipline addresses various hair disorders, with androgenetic alopecia (AGA) being the most prevalent condition treated in trichology clinics globally [592, 593]. The treatment landscape for AGA includes a range of options such as topical minoxidil, oral finasteride, and innovative therapies like platelet-rich plasma (PRP) treatments [594, 595]. The effectiveness of these treatments is often assessed through advanced diagnostic tools like trichoscopy, which facilitates the identification of hair and scalp conditions [596]. Moreover, the integration of telemedicine in trichology has emerged as a promising avenue for patient follow-up, enhancing accessibility and patient engagement [597].

The cosmetic aspect of trichology cannot be overlooked, as hair care products and treatments are widely marketed and utilized. The industry has seen a rise in the popularity of hair cosmetics, which are often used in conjunction with medical treatments to improve hair health and aesthetics [598]. Cultural practices, such as hair oiling prevalent in South Asia and Africa, also play a significant role in the trichological landscape, highlighting the intersection of traditional practices and modern dermatological care [599]. Despite the lack of extensive clinical evidence supporting some of these practices, they remain integral to many individuals' hair care routines.

The trichology industry operates within a complex economic framework influenced by capitalism, where profit motives can sometimes overshadow patient care [600]. This has led to concerns regarding the marketing of ineffective treatments and the potential for malpractice within the field [601]. As the industry continues to grow, it faces challenges related to ethical practices and the need for evidence-based treatment protocols to ensure patient safety and satisfaction.

Globally, the practice of trichology varies, with different regions adopting unique approaches based on cultural, economic, and medical factors. For instance, the prevalence of cicatricial alopecia and its management strategies differ across populations, reflecting the need for tailored treatment approaches [602, 603]. Additionally, the rise of artificial intelligence in dermatology presents new opportunities for improving diagnostic accuracy and treatment efficacy in trichology [604]. As the field evolves, ongoing research and collaboration among professionals will be crucial in addressing the complexities of hair disorders and enhancing patient outcomes.

The global expenditure on trichological services, encompassing hair loss treatments, hair transplant procedures, and related therapeutic interventions, is substantial and has been experiencing significant growth. While precise figures for the entire trichological services market are challenging to ascertain due to its broad scope, specific segments provide insight into the overall spending.

In 2020, the global hair transplant market was valued at approximately USD 6 billion and is projected to reach USD 27.9 billion by 2027, reflecting a compound annual growth rate (CAGR) of 24.55% [605]. Similarly, the market for hair loss treatment products was valued at USD 1.98 billion in 2023 and is expected to grow to USD 2.86 billion by 2032, with a CAGR of 4.2% [606]. Additionally, the global alopecia treatment market, which addresses various forms of hair loss, was valued at USD 8.89 billion in 2019 and is projected to reach USD 16.1 billion by 2032 [607]. These figures indicate that annual global spending on trichological services and related products is in the tens of billions of dollars, with a strong upward trend driven by increasing awareness, advancements in treatment options, and a growing emphasis on aesthetic appearance.

AI and Digital Scalp Diagnostics

The integration of artificial intelligence (AI) and digital scalp analysis represents a transformative advancement in the field of trichology, enhancing the diagnosis, monitoring, and treatment of various hair and scalp conditions. AI-powered tools facilitate precise, data-driven assessments by analysing critical factors such as hair density, follicular health, and scalp conditions, thereby enabling early identification of issues and personalized treatment plans for optimal outcomes [608, 609].

AI-based scalp analysis employs high-resolution imaging, machine learning algorithms, and predictive analytics to assess hair and scalp health in real-time. High-resolution imaging techniques, such as dermatoscopic or microscopic imaging, allow for the detection of conditions like follicular miniaturization and seborrheic dermatitis [610, 611]. Machine learning algorithms are utilized to compare scalp images against extensive datasets of known hair and scalp conditions, enabling the identification of abnormalities and the prediction of hair loss trends [611]. These systems can effectively differentiate between various types of hair loss, including androgenetic alopecia and telogen effluvium, by analysing changes over time [608, 611]. Predictive analytics further enhances the capability of AI tools by forecasting hair loss progression and treatment effectiveness based on genetic predispositions and lifestyle factors, allowing for tailored haircare regimens [608, 609].

AI-driven scalp analysis is revolutionizing trichology through various applications. Professional AI scalp scanners, such as TrichoScope and HairMetrix, are now commonplace in clinics and salons, providing non-invasive, detailed assessments of scalp conditions [608, 609]. These devices utilize AI-powered image recognition to deliver precise measurements of hair density and follicular health. Additionally, AI-powered mobile applications, like L'Oréal's HairCoach and Miiskin Hair Health App, empower consumers to conduct at-home scalp analyses using smartphone cameras, offering instant insights and product recommendations [608, 609]. Furthermore, AI facilitates personalized hair treatments by matching individuals with the most effective products based on their unique scalp profiles, as seen in systems like P&G's Opté Precision System and Shiseido's AI Hair Diagnostics [608, 609].

Table 7: AI-Driven Scalp Analysis Applications.

Application	Description	Examples
AI Scalp Scanners in Clinics and Salons	Professional AI scalp analysis devices used in trichology clinics, dermatology offices, and salons for instant, in-depth hair assessments.	TrichoScope & TrichoLab AI Systems analyse scalp conditions with AI-powered image recognition; HairMetrix by Canfield Scientific uses 3D scalp mapping and AI diagnostics.
AI-Powered Mobile Apps for At-Home Hair Analysis	AI-driven mobile apps allow users to scan their scalp using smartphone cameras to receive real-time scalp health insights and product recommendations.	L'Oréal's HairCoach monitors hair quality, detects breakage, and recommends personalized haircare; Miiskin Hair Health App tracks hair thinning and regrowth.

Advances in Cosmetology

Application	Description	Examples
AI-Powered Personalized Hair Treatments	AI scalp analysis matches individuals with the best haircare treatments based on unique scalp profiles, providing customized recommendations for shampoos, serums, and supplements.	P&G's Opté Precision System delivers personalized hair loss treatments using micro-serum dispensers; Shiseido's AI Hair Diagnostics suggests customized haircare regimens.
AI for Monitoring Hair Transplant Success	AI revolutionizes hair transplantation by optimizing hair graft placement, tracking follicle survival rates, and assessing scalp healing.	ARTAS Robotic Hair Transplant System analyzes donor hair density and performs robotic follicle extraction and implantation with precision.

The benefits of AI and digital scalp analysis in trichology are manifold. Early detection of hair loss and scalp conditions is paramount, as AI tools can identify issues before they escalate, enabling proactive treatment [608, 609]. Personalized treatment plans generated by AI ensure that individuals receive tailored recommendations suited to their specific scalp and hair types [608, 609]. Moreover, AI allows for accurate progress tracking, enabling users to monitor hair regrowth and treatment efficacy over time [608]. The non-invasive nature of AI scalp analysis presents a cost-effective alternative to traditional diagnostic methods, while the scalability of mobile applications enhances accessibility to trichology insights for consumers worldwide [608, 609].

The adoption of AI-driven scalp analysis, hair diagnosis, and treatment solutions represents a significant investment for clinics and salons. However, these technologies provide a strong return on investment by enhancing diagnostic accuracy, increasing client retention, and enabling high-value treatment recommendations. By integrating AI in trichology and dermatology practices, clinics can differentiate themselves from competitors while improving overall treatment outcomes and patient satisfaction.

AI scalp scanners in clinics and salons offer instant, in-depth hair assessments without requiring invasive procedures. The cost of implementing these systems varies depending on the device and software used. TrichoScope and TrichoLab AI Systems typically range from $5,000 to $15,000 as a one-time purchase, with software licensing fees between $1,000 and $5,000 annually. HairMetrix by Canfield Scientific is another widely used system, costing between $10,000 and $30,000 for hardware and AI software, with optional cloud-based subscriptions that range from $500 to $3,000 per year. Additional training for staff may cost between $500 and $2,000 per technician. The expected returns from AI scalp scanners are substantial, as they allow clinics to justify premium consultation fees, typically adding $50 to $200 per session. AI-based analysis also facilitates personalized treatment plans, leading to increased sales of serums, topical treatments, and hair regrowth therapies. Additionally, these tools enhance client retention by fostering repeat visits and long-term treatment adherence. Clinics using AI technology can market themselves as offering advanced, science-backed solutions, attracting high-end clientele. The potential return on investment for AI scalp scanners can range from an additional $20,000 to $100,000 annually, depending on patient volume and service pricing.

AI-powered mobile apps for at-home hair analysis are also becoming a valuable tool for clinics. These applications enable users to scan their scalp using their smartphone cameras, receiving instant insights into their scalp health and personalized product recommendations. Clinics can integrate existing AI-powered apps such as L'Oréal's HairCoach and Miiskin Hair Health App, which operate on subscription-based models ranging from $1,000 to $5,000 annually for professional partnerships. Alternatively, developing a branded AI-powered app in-house can cost between $10,000 and $50,000. The expected returns from mobile app integration include increased client engagement, as users can track their scalp conditions and are more likely to book follow-up treatments. AI-driven recommendations also lead to higher product sales, increasing the average order value. Additionally, digital scalp monitoring encourages clients to adhere to treatment regimens, improving long-term efficacy. Clinics integrating AI-powered apps can expect an additional $15,000 to $75,000 in annual revenue through product sales and online consultation fees.

Advances in Cosmetology

AI-powered personalized hair treatments further enhance the value of AI-driven trichology services. AI scalp analysis helps match individuals with the best haircare treatments based on their unique scalp profile. AI-generated reports provide customized recommendations for shampoos, serums, supplements, and professional treatments based on factors like sebum levels, follicle density, and scalp sensitivity. The cost of AI-powered diagnostic tools such as P&G's Opté Precision System or Shiseido AI Hair Diagnostics ranges from $5,000 to $20,000 per system, plus treatment formulation costs. The production of customized products can range from $10 to $100 per unit, with bulk production lowering costs. The expected returns from these treatments include higher product margins, as clinics can charge premium prices of $100 to $300 per treatment. AI-driven recommendations also encourage commitment to multi-session plans, typically lasting three to six months, ensuring consistent revenue. Additionally, bundling AI-based treatments with other services like platelet-rich plasma (PRP) therapy or microneedling can further increase revenue. Clinics introducing personalized AI-driven treatments can generate an additional $30,000 to $150,000 in revenue.

AI for monitoring hair transplant success is another revolutionary development in trichology. AI-based monitoring systems provide pre- and post-surgery tracking, ensuring successful hair graft retention. AI tools optimize hair transplant placement, track follicle survival rates, and assess scalp healing over time. The ARTAS Robotic Hair Transplant System, a leading AI-driven hair transplant solution, costs between $200,000 and $350,000 as a one-time investment, with maintenance and software updates adding $10,000 to $50,000 per year. AI-based pre- and post-surgical monitoring software costs between $5,000 and $20,000 annually for digital tracking platforms. The expected returns for AI in hair transplantation include higher client confidence, as AI-based monitoring provides precise tracking of graft survival, leading to increased patient satisfaction and referrals. AI-assisted precision also reduces errors, improving outcomes and enhancing the clinic's reputation. Clinics offering AI-monitored hair restoration treatments can charge a premium of $5,000 to $20,000 per procedure. Depending on patient volume and pricing, clinics performing regular transplants can see an additional $100,000 to $500,000 in annual revenue.

Table 8: Overall Investment vs. Return Projection for AI-Integrated Clinics.

AI Service	Estimated Cost (Annual/One-Time)	Potential Annual ROI
AI Scalp Scanners	$10,000 – $30,000	$20,000 – $100,000
AI-Powered Mobile Apps	$1,000 – $50,000	$15,000 – $75,000
AI Personalized Hair Treatments	$5,000 – $20,000	$30,000 – $150,000
AI Hair Transplant Monitoring	$200,000 – $400,000	$100,000 – $500,000
Total Potential ROI		**$216,000 – $500,000+ annually**

The overall investment in AI-powered trichology services varies, but the potential return is significant. AI scalp scanners, mobile apps, personalized hair treatments, and AI-monitored hair transplants all contribute to increasing clinic revenue and enhancing patient experience. Clinics adopting these technologies can expect substantial growth, improved patient satisfaction, and a competitive advantage in the haircare industry.

AI-driven trichology solutions require an initial investment but offer significant financial returns by improving diagnostic precision, increasing client retention, and enhancing treatment outcomes. Clinics that integrate AI scalp analysis, mobile-based monitoring, personalized treatments, and AI-supported hair transplant procedures can position themselves as premium providers, attracting high-end clientele willing to pay for cutting-edge services. With increasing consumer demand for personalized hair restoration and hair loss prevention, AI-powered trichology clinics stand to see substantial growth and profitability in the coming years.

3D-Printed Hair Follicles for Hair Regeneration

Regenerative medicine has made significant strides in hair follicle bioengineering, particularly through the application of 3D printing technology. This innovative approach aims to create 3D-printed hair follicles that can be implanted into the scalp, potentially stimulating natural hair growth. Traditional hair restoration techniques often face limitations due to the scarcity of donor hair; however, the development of lab-grown hair follicles presents a solution by providing an unlimited source of hair follicles, thus addressing a critical challenge in hair restoration practices [612, 613].

The success of 3D-printed hair follicles hinges on the ability to replicate the intricate microenvironment of natural hair follicles, which are essential for hair production and growth cycles. Researchers employ bioprinting techniques that utilize biocompatible materials, such as hydrogels or collagen, to create scaffolds for hair follicle cells. These scaffolds not only support the structural integrity of the follicles but also deliver the necessary biochemical and mechanical signals that facilitate the organization and functionality of hair follicle cells, mimicking their natural counterparts [614, 615].

Notably, groundbreaking research from Columbia University Irving Medical Center has demonstrated the potential of this technology. Scientists successfully engineered 3D microenvironments that replicate the structure of natural hair follicles, incorporating dermal papilla cells—key regulators of hair follicle growth. When these cells were placed within the engineered environments, they effectively stimulated hair follicle formation, underscoring the feasibility of using bioengineered follicles for hair regeneration [612, 616].

The implications of 3D-printed hair follicles extend beyond merely increasing the availability of donor hair. This technology allows for customization based on individual genetic and scalp conditions. By utilizing a patient's own stem cells, researchers can create hair follicles that closely match the patient's natural hair characteristics, thereby enhancing compatibility and reducing the risk of rejection. This personalized approach aligns with broader trends in medicine towards individualized treatments tailored to the unique biological profiles of patients [613].

Richard Skiba

Despite the promising advancements, the technology remains in the experimental phase, with ongoing research focused on improving the survival and functionality of bioengineered follicles. Key challenges include ensuring the long-term viability of the printed follicles, enhancing their integration into the scalp, and optimizing the bioengineered environment to sustain hair growth cycles over time [616, 617]. As research progresses, the potential commercialization of 3D-printed hair follicle transplantation could revolutionize hair restoration, offering a scalable and permanent solution for individuals experiencing hair loss due to various factors, including genetics and medical conditions [613, 618].

Exosome Therapy for Hair Loss

Exosome therapy is gaining recognition as a transformative approach in hair restoration, primarily due to its ability to stimulate hair regrowth and enhance scalp health through non-invasive means. Exosomes, which are nanoscale extracellular vesicles, function as vital mediators of intercellular communication by transporting a variety of bioactive molecules, including growth factors, proteins, lipids, and RNA. These components are crucial for cellular regeneration and communication, particularly in the context of hair follicle activation and scalp rejuvenation [619, 620].

In comparison to traditional treatments like Platelet-Rich Plasma (PRP) therapy, exosome therapy offers several advantages. PRP therapy requires blood extraction and processing, which can lead to variability in the concentration and quality of growth factors based on individual patient factors. In contrast, exosome therapy utilizes a standardized and concentrated formulation derived from mesenchymal stem cells (MSCs), ensuring a consistent delivery of regenerative factors that can enhance hair thickness and density [619, 621]. Research has shown that exosome therapy can significantly improve hair thickness and density, with clinical studies reporting increases in hair thickness from 57.5 mm to 64.0 mm and hair density from 105.4 to 122.7 counts/cm [619].

The regenerative potential of exosomes is attributed to their rich content of over 300 growth factors and signalling molecules that promote the transition of hair follicles from the telogen (resting) phase to the anagen (growth) phase. This transition is critical for effective hair regeneration, as it stimulates vascularization and reduces inflammation, which are essential for combating conditions like androgenetic alopecia [620, 622]. Additionally, exosomes derived from MSCs have been shown to activate dermal papilla cells, which play a pivotal role in hair follicle cycling and regeneration [620].

Exosome therapy can be integrated with other hair restoration techniques, such as microneedling or laser therapy, to enhance overall treatment outcomes. This combination approach not only accelerates healing but also optimizes graft survival in hair transplant procedures, thereby improving the efficacy of the overall hair restoration strategy [619, 623]. The minimally invasive nature of exosome injections, coupled with their low risk of side effects, positions them as an appealing option for patients seeking effective hair restoration solutions without the complications associated with more invasive procedures [622].

While exosome therapy is still under investigation, preliminary clinical trials and patient outcomes indicate promising results in terms of hair regrowth and improved scalp health. As research progresses and more data become available, exosome-based treatments are poised to redefine the standard of care for hair loss, offering a biologically-driven alternative to conventional methods [619, 623]. The future of hair restoration may very well hinge on the continued development and application of exosome therapy, making it a cutting-edge solution for individuals experiencing hair thinning or loss.

While the initial investment required for clinics can be significant, the potential for high profit margins and long-term returns makes it an attractive addition to hair restoration services. Clinics that incorporate exosome therapy can benefit from increased revenue, premium pricing, and enhanced patient satisfaction.

Implementing exosome therapy requires investments in product procurement, equipment, staff training, and marketing. The primary cost factor is the exosome product itself, as well as the necessary tools for administration.

Exosome vials typically range from $1,000 to $3,000 per vial, with most treatments requiring one to two vials per session, depending on the patient's needs. Leading suppliers such as ExoCoBio, Benev, Kimera Labs, Direct Biologics, and XoFlo provide high-quality exosome products, often offering bulk discounts to clinics that purchase in larger quantities.

Additional costs include microneedling pens and injectors, which are required if the treatment is combined with PRP or microneedling procedures. These devices range from $500 to $2,000 as a one-time purchase. Consumables such as sterile needles, syringes, and scalp preparation kits add another $50 to $100 per patient to operational costs.

Training is another essential investment for clinics offering exosome therapy. Clinics typically spend between $1,000 and $5,000 on training courses for exosome injection techniques, with ongoing professional development costing $500 to $2,000 annually to stay updated on best practices and advanced applications.

Marketing and patient acquisition are critical components for clinics aiming to attract clients for exosome therapy. Digital advertising through Google Ads, social media campaigns, and targeted email marketing can cost between $2,000 and $10,000 per month, depending on the scale of outreach. Additional marketing efforts such as website enhancements, digital content, and patient testimonials typically require a one-time investment of around $5,000. Referral programs and promotional discounts can further increase client retention and attract new patients.

Exosome therapy is marketed as a premium hair restoration treatment, allowing clinics to set higher pricing per session compared to PRP therapy or traditional scalp injections. On average, clinics charge $3,500 to $7,500 per session, depending on the brand of exosomes used and the complexity of the treatment. When combined with PRP therapy or microneedling, the price per session can increase to $4,500 to $8,000, offering a compelling upselling opportunity.

Many clinics offer multi-session treatment packages, which provide an additional revenue stream and encourage patient commitment to long-term hair restoration plans. A three-session treatment plan is typically priced between $10,000 and $20,000, while a six-month comprehensive package, which may include PRP, laser therapy, or pre-hair transplant preparation, can range from $15,000 to $30,000.

Additional revenue is generated through upselling complementary services such as scalp health serums, supplements, and LED light therapy sessions. Clinics offering customized exosome scalp treatments can charge an additional $1,000 to $3,000 per patient, while LED light therapy or Low-Level Laser Therapy (LLLT) sessions as post-treatment enhancements are priced at $100 to $500 per session.

The financial success of exosome therapy depends on patient volume, effective marketing, and bundling strategies. A clinic that treats five patients per month at an average session price of $5,000 can expect a monthly revenue of $25,000. Clinics that attract ten or more patients per month with multi-session packages priced at $15,000 per patient can generate $150,000 per month.

Annually, a low-volume clinic treating 50 patients per year can earn between $250,000 and $500,000, while a mid-sized clinic treating 100 patients annually can generate $500,000 to $1,000,000 in revenue. High-end clinics that cater to 200 or more patients per year can reach revenue figures exceeding $1,500,000.

Profit margins for exosome therapy are highly favourable. The cost per vial is typically $1,500 to $3,000, while operational expenses, including staff, equipment, and marketing, add $500 to $1,000 per treatment. This results in a gross profit of $3,000 to $6,000 per session, with an average profit margin of 60 to 80 percent per patient.

Hair Cloning and Stem Cell Therapy

Hair cloning, also referred to as hair follicle multiplication, represents a significant advancement in the field of regenerative medicine and trichology, aiming to address hair loss through innovative techniques that surpass traditional hair transplantation methods. Unlike conventional approaches that rely on a finite number of donor follicles, hair cloning seeks to generate an unlimited supply of hair follicles from a patient's own cells, thereby offering a potentially revolutionary solution for individuals experiencing baldness or severe hair loss [624, 625].

The process of hair cloning involves several critical steps. Initially, dermal papilla cells, which are essential for hair follicle development, are harvested from a small sample of the patient's scalp. These cells are then cultured in a laboratory setting using advanced tissue engineering techniques to multiply and differentiate into new hair follicle structures [624, 625]. The final step involves the implantation of these lab-grown follicles back into the scalp, where they are expected to integrate with the surrounding tissue and begin producing hair in a natural cycle [624, 625]. Recent research has explored the use of induced pluripotent stem cells (iPSCs) in this process, which can be reprogrammed to develop into hair follicle cells, thereby enhancing the potential for successful hair regeneration [624].

The benefits of hair cloning are manifold. One of the most significant advantages is the ability to produce an unlimited supply of hair follicles, which is particularly beneficial for patients with advanced baldness or those who lack sufficient donor hair for traditional transplants [624, 625]. Additionally, since the follicles are generated in a laboratory, patients can avoid the scarring associated with donor site extraction, a common issue in traditional hair transplants [624, 625]. Furthermore, because the cloned follicles originate from the patient's own cells, the risk of immune rejection is minimized, leading to more personalized and effective treatment outcomes [624, 625]. The cloned follicles are designed to function similarly to natural hair follicles, cycling through growth phases and producing hair that closely resembles the patient's original hair [624, 625].

Despite the promising nature of hair cloning, several challenges remain before it can be widely adopted as a treatment option. Regulatory approvals are necessary, as hair cloning is a new form of regenerative therapy that must undergo rigorous clinical trials to ensure its safety and efficacy [624, 625]. Additionally, the scalability of the technology and the associated costs present significant hurdles; the specialized techniques required for lab-grown hair follicles can be expensive, potentially limiting accessibility for many patients [624, 625]. Researchers also need to ensure that the longevity and growth cycles of cloned follicles mirror those of natural hair, which is crucial for long-term success [624, 625].

Several leading organizations are at the forefront of hair cloning research. Stemson Therapeutics, for instance, is developing techniques utilizing iPSCs to create new hair follicles that can be implanted into areas of baldness [624]. The Tsuji Lab in Japan is pioneering organ germ technology to regenerate hair follicles, while HairClone in the UK focuses on dermal papilla cell banking and multiplication, aiming to bring hair cloning to clinical applications [624, 625].

As research progresses, the potential for hair cloning to revolutionize hair restoration becomes increasingly tangible, promising a future where effective, permanent solutions for hair loss are readily available [624, 625].

Personalized Hair Growth Treatments Using Genetics

The integration of genetic testing into the field of trichology has ushered in a new era of personalized hair growth treatments. By analysing specific genetic markers associated with hair loss, specialists can tailor interventions that address the unique genetic predispositions of each individual. This personalized approach not only enhances the effectiveness of treatments but also allows for a more proactive stance in managing hair loss.

Genetic hair loss tests focus on analysing genes that influence various aspects of hair health, including follicle function and hormonal sensitivity, particularly to dihydrotestosterone (DHT), which is a significant factor in androgenetic alopecia. The testing process typically involves DNA collection through saliva or cheek swabs, followed by genetic sequencing to identify variants that affect hair growth cycles and follicular sensitivity [626]. A large genome-wide association study (GWAS) identified 287 genetic signals linked to male pattern baldness, highlighting the genetic complexity underlying hair loss [626]. Following genetic analysis, specialists can develop personalized treatment plans that may include topical and oral solutions tailored to the individual's genetic makeup, thereby optimizing treatment efficacy and minimizing side effects [627].

The advantages of genetic testing for hair loss are manifold. Early detection of genetic predispositions allows for timely intervention, potentially preventing significant hair loss before it occurs. This precision medicine approach contrasts sharply with traditional treatments, which often rely on a trial-and-error methodology that can be both time-consuming and ineffective. By leveraging genetic insights, healthcare providers can recommend specific combinations of treatments, such as minoxidil and finasteride, that are more likely to yield positive results based on the patient's genetic profile [627].

Genetic testing can inform dietary and supplementation strategies by identifying markers related to nutrient absorption, which can further support hair health. For example, understanding an individual's genetic predisposition to vitamin deficiencies can lead to customized supplement regimens that bolster hair growth. This tailored approach not only enhances treatment outcomes but also reduces the likelihood of adverse reactions to standard therapies, as treatments can be selected based on how an individual's body metabolizes certain medications.

One prominent example of genetic testing in hair restoration is the TrichoTest by Fagron Genomics, which analyses genetic markers associated with hair thinning and scalp health. This test aids trichologists in identifying hormonal, nutritional, and inflammatory factors contributing to hair loss, allowing for the formulation of customized treatment plans that include both topical and oral therapies [627]. The ability to create long-term prevention and regrowth strategies based on genetic data represents a significant advancement in the field of hair restoration.

The future of personalized hair growth treatments is poised for further innovation, particularly with the integration of artificial intelligence and advanced genetic research. As the understanding of genetic influences on hair loss deepens, the development of customized hair care products—such as DNA-tailored shampoos and serums—will likely become more prevalent [627]. Companies are increasingly investing in precision trichology, which emphasizes data-driven treatments that are tailored to individual genetic profiles, thereby promising sustainable solutions for hair restoration and scalp health.

The integration of genetic testing in trichology and hair restoration offers clinics the ability to provide highly personalized, evidence-based treatments for patients experiencing hair thinning or scalp conditions. This approach allows clinics to move beyond conventional, one-size-fits-all treatments and offer tailored solutions based on an individual's genetic makeup. While the initial investment in genetic testing kits, laboratory partnerships, and staff training may be substantial, clinics can expect a strong return on investment through premium pricing, increased patient engagement, and the sale of customized treatment plans.

Advances in Cosmetology

Offering personalized hair growth treatments using genetic testing requires investments in testing kits, laboratory services, staff training, and marketing efforts. The wholesale cost of DNA test kits ranges from $100 to $300 per kit, with bulk pricing available to clinics that order in large quantities. The laboratory processing and analysis of genetic data cost between $200 and $500 per test. Some of the leading providers of genetic testing for hair loss include Fagron Genomics (TrichoTest), 23andMe (Hair Loss Risk Reports), DNAfit, and Gene Blueprint. In addition to purchasing test kits, clinics may need to invest in training and certification for their staff. Trichology or genetic testing certification programs range from $1,500 to $5,000 as a one-time cost, with ongoing education in advanced genetic interpretation costing between $500 and $2,000 per year.

To enhance the patient experience and improve diagnostic capabilities, clinics may also need to purchase scalp imaging devices for pre- and post-treatment comparisons, which range from $3,000 to $10,000. Additionally, clinics may subscribe to cloud-based AI or data storage platforms to manage patient genetic reports, with annual costs ranging from $1,000 to $5,000. Marketing and patient acquisition costs also play a significant role in the success of genetic hair growth treatments. Digital advertising and social media campaigns can range from $2,000 to $10,000 per month, while website integration for online genetic test booking may require a one-time investment of $3,000 to $7,000. Referral programs and partnerships with other healthcare providers can help drive patient traffic but vary in cost depending on the business model.

Genetic hair loss testing is a premium service, allowing clinics to charge higher consultation fees while encouraging personalized treatment sales. A standalone genetic hair loss test typically costs between $500 and $1,500 per patient, while a combined genetic test and consultation package is priced between $800 and $2,000. Subscription-based genetic monitoring for hair health, which provides ongoing insights and personalized treatment recommendations, can generate an additional $250 to $500 per patient annually. Beyond the genetic test itself, clinics can offer personalized treatment plans based on genetic results. Custom-formulated serums and topicals cost patients between $100 and $500 per month, while personalized oral supplements and prescription plans range from $50 to $300 per month. Multi-

293

session therapy packages, which may include PRP therapy, microneedling, or laser treatments, range from $3,000 to $15,000 per patient.

Additional revenue can be generated through the sale of complementary services and upselling opportunities. For example, clinics that combine scalp PRP therapy with genetic testing can charge between $2,000 and $5,000 per session. Exosome therapy, when combined with personalized genetic haircare, can cost between $5,000 and $8,000 per package. AI-driven hair and scalp monitoring services, offered as a digital subscription, provide another revenue stream at $500 to $1,500 per year.

The financial viability of genetic hair loss testing depends on patient volume, consultation pricing, and bundled services. Clinics that see just five patients per month for standalone genetic testing at $1,000 per test can generate $5,000 in monthly revenue. Clinics that offer a combination of genetic testing and personalized treatments, priced at $3,000 per patient, can generate $30,000 per month with just ten patients. High-volume clinics that offer multi-session treatment plans at $10,000 per patient can generate up to $200,000 per month if they treat twenty patients.

On an annual basis, low-volume clinics treating fifty patients per year can generate between $250,000 and $500,000 in revenue. Mid-sized clinics treating one hundred patients annually can see revenues between $500,000 and $1,000,000. High-end clinics catering to two hundred or more patients per year can generate over $1.5 million in annual revenue.

The profit margins for genetic hair growth treatments are significant, with genetic test kits and lab processing costs ranging from $300 to $800 per patient. Additional operational costs, including staff wages, equipment, and marketing, add another $500 to $1,500 per patient. This results in a gross profit per patient of $500 to $3,000 or higher for bundled services. With profit margins ranging between 60 and 80 percent, genetic testing for hair loss represents a lucrative opportunity for clinics.

Genetic-based hair loss treatments align with the growing trend of precision medicine and trichology, positioning clinics at the forefront of advanced hair restoration services. By incorporating genetic diagnostics, clinics can differentiate themselves in a competitive market, attract high-paying clients, and create long-term revenue streams through personalized haircare plans. The ability to bundle genetic testing with customized treatment solutions allows clinics to maximize revenue while providing data-driven, highly effective hair restoration solutions. This shift toward personalized trichology not only enhances patient outcomes but also solidifies a clinic's reputation as a leader in modern hair and scalp health solutions.

Scalp Microbiome Research and Probiotic Scalp Care

The scalp microbiome represents a complex ecosystem composed of various microorganisms, including bacteria and fungi, which play a vital role in maintaining scalp health. Similar to the gut microbiome, the balance between beneficial and harmful microbes on the scalp significantly influences overall well-being, with imbalances linked to conditions such as dandruff, seborrheic dermatitis, and scalp inflammation. Research indicates that a disrupted scalp microbiome, often due to factors such as harsh hair products, pollution, and stress, can lead to excessive oil production, irritation, flaking, and even hair thinning [628-630].

Traditional treatments for scalp conditions have primarily involved the use of antifungal shampoos, medicated lotions, and corticosteroids. While these approaches may provide temporary relief, they often fail to address the underlying microbial imbalance [631, 632]. Emerging research is now shifting towards strategies that aim to restore the scalp's microbiome through the application of probiotics, prebiotics, and postbiotics. Probiotics, which are live beneficial bacteria, have shown promise in rebalancing the scalp microbiome by inhibiting the growth of pathogenic microorganisms such as Malassezia, a common contributor to dandruff [628, 632, 633]. Prebiotics, such as inulin and fructooligosaccharides, serve as nourishment for these beneficial bacteria, promoting their growth and enhancing their ability to outcompete harmful microbes [634].

The integration of probiotic scalp care into haircare products is revolutionizing the treatment of scalp disorders by focusing on nurturing the scalp's natural defences rather than merely alleviating symptoms. Products containing strains like Lactobacillus and Bifidobacterium have been shown to regulate oil production, soothe inflammation, and strengthen the skin barrier [631, 633, 635]. Brands such as Aurelia London and Gallinée are at the forefront of this trend, offering probiotic and prebiotic scalp treatments designed to enhance scalp health and alleviate symptoms like dryness and flaking [630, 636].

Moreover, the significance of diet and lifestyle in maintaining a healthy scalp microbiome has gained attention. A diet rich in fermented foods, probiotics, and essential fatty acids can support the scalp microbiome from within, while stress management and gentle cleansing routines can help preserve microbial balance [637, 638]. As consumer demand for science-backed, natural solutions in haircare continues to rise, the focus on probiotic scalp care is expected to expand, making scalp health an integral aspect of holistic beauty and wellness [630, 634].

Low-Level Laser Therapy (LLLT) & LED Hair Growth Devices

Low-Level Laser Therapy (LLLT) has emerged as a non-invasive treatment modality for promoting hair regrowth, particularly beneficial for individuals suffering from androgenetic alopecia, thinning hair, or those recovering from hair transplants. This therapy employs red and near-infrared light to stimulate hair follicles at the cellular level, enhancing blood circulation in the scalp and improving follicular metabolism. The mechanism of action involves the penetration of laser light into the scalp, energizing weakened hair follicles by interacting with mitochondria, which boosts adenosine triphosphate (ATP) synthesis, thereby promoting cellular energy production and repair [639-641].

Clinical studies have demonstrated the effectiveness of LLLT in increasing hair density and thickness. For instance, a multicentre, randomized, sham-controlled study confirmed that LLLT significantly increased terminal hair counts in both male and female subjects with pattern hair loss [642]. Furthermore, a systematic review indicated that LLLT is one of the FDA-approved devices for treating androgenetic alopecia, underscoring its safety and efficacy [643]. The wavelengths typically utilized in LLLT, particularly around 650 nm, have been shown to effectively stimulate hair growth by prolonging the anagen phase of the hair cycle and minimizing premature follicle shrinkage [641, 644].

One of the significant advantages of LLLT is its accessibility compared to traditional hair restoration treatments, such as Platelet-Rich Plasma (PRP) therapy or hair transplants. LLLT devices, such as the Capillus Laser Cap and the iRestore Laser Hair Growth System, provide a convenient, at-home solution for hair loss management. These devices are designed for hands-free use, allowing individuals to incorporate therapy into their daily routines without discomfort [645]. Research indicates that consistent use of LLLT devices can lead to visible results within 4 to 6 months, with significant reductions in hair shedding and improvements in overall scalp health [639, 645].

Despite its benefits, LLLT is most effective for individuals in the early to moderate stages of hair loss. It may not yield significant results for those with extensive baldness where hair follicles have completely miniaturized [639, 640]. Moreover, while LLLT is generally safe, adherence to usage guidelines is crucial for achieving optimal results. The future of LLLT in hair restoration appears promising, with advancements in wearable technology and personalized light therapy settings expected to enhance treatment efficacy further [644, 645].

The introduction of Low-Level Laser Therapy (LLLT) into clinical practice offers a high-margin, non-invasive solution for hair regrowth. While the initial investment in LLLT devices, staff training, and marketing is necessary, the long-term revenue potential and profitability make it an attractive option for clinics specializing in trichology, dermatology, and hair restoration. Clinics that implement LLLT treatments can expect increased patient retention, higher service pricing, and improved overall revenue.

Clinics must invest in high-quality LLLT machines, which vary in price based on their features, number of laser diodes, and treatment coverage. In-clinic LLLT devices, which include high-power laser machines, range from $10,000 to $50,000 per unit. Portable LLLT devices, such as caps, helmets, or handheld systems for rental or retail, cost between $500 and $3,500 per unit. Leading LLLT device suppliers include Capillus, Theradome, iRestore, HairMax, LaserCap, and Revian Red. Maintenance and replacement parts for these devices can cost between $500 and $3,000 annually.

Clinics also need to allocate funds for staff training and certification. The cost of LLLT therapy training for clinic staff is approximately $1,500 to $5,000 as a one-time investment. Ongoing education and certification renewals range from $500 to $2,000 per year to keep professionals updated with the latest advancements in laser therapy and hair restoration.

To enhance the patient experience and monitor treatment outcomes, clinics may invest in consultation technology and scalp analysis tools. Patient management and progress tracking software cost between $2,000 and $5,000 per year, while scalp analysis tools for pre- and post-treatment assessments range from $3,000 to $10,000. These tools help document improvements, guide treatment recommendations, and ensure optimal results for patients undergoing LLLT therapy.

Marketing and patient acquisition strategies are essential to attract and retain clients. Digital advertising and social media promotions typically require an investment of $2,000 to $10,000 per month, depending on the clinic's target audience and reach. Website integration for online appointment booking and treatment plans costs between $3,000 and $7,000 as a one-time investment. Clinics may also implement referral programs and influencer partnerships to boost credibility and increase patient bookings.

LLLT is positioned as a premium hair restoration therapy, allowing clinics to charge competitive rates while increasing patient retention. A single LLLT session costs between $100 and $300 per treatment, while multi-session LLLT treatment plans, typically consisting of 12 to 24 sessions over three to six months, range from $2,000 to $5,000 per patient. Clinics that bundle LLLT with PRP or microneedling treatments can charge between $4,000 and $8,000 per package.

In addition to in-clinic treatments, clinics can generate revenue through LLLT device rental and retail sales. Monthly LLLT device rentals range from $300 to $600 per patient, while retail purchase prices for at-home LLLT devices range from $1,500 to $3,500 per unit. Clinics earn a 30% to 50% profit margin on device sales, further enhancing revenue potential.

Additional services and upselling opportunities allow clinics to increase per-patient spending. Clinics can offer topical hair growth serums and supplements for $100 to $500 per patient. Personalized hair loss treatment plans, which include LLLT combined with PRP and AI-driven scalp monitoring, can generate $5,000 to $10,000 per package. AI-based scalp health monitoring subscriptions add another revenue stream, ranging from $500 to $1,500 annually.

The financial viability of LLLT depends on patient volume, session pricing, and bundled treatment offerings. Clinics treating five LLLT patients per month, each paying $2,500, generate $12,500 in monthly revenue. Clinics treating ten patients per month with a multi-therapy package priced at $5,000 each can expect $50,000 in monthly revenue. High-end clinics treating 20 patients per month with an $8,000 package can generate $160,000 per month.

Annual revenue potential varies depending on patient volume. Low-volume clinics treating 50 patients per year can earn between $250,000 and $500,000. Mid-sized clinics treating 100 patients annually can generate $500,000 to $1,000,000. High-end clinics treating over 200 patients per year can achieve revenue exceeding $1,500,000.

Profit margins for LLLT treatments are substantial. The operational costs per LLLT session, including device depreciation, staff expenses, and marketing, range from $50 to $150 per session. Clinics offering multi-session packages can achieve gross profits of $1,500 to $6,000 per patient. Profit margins per patient range from 60% to 80%, making LLLT a highly lucrative service for clinics.

LLLT represents a lucrative, non-invasive hair restoration solution with high patient demand and excellent ROI potential. Clinics that invest in high-quality LLLT systems and bundle treatments with complementary therapies such as PRP, exosome therapy, or genetic-based treatments can maximize revenue while providing cutting-edge solutions for hair loss.

By integrating LLLT into their practice, clinics can position themselves as leaders in innovative trichology services, attract premium clientele, and generate consistent long-term revenue. With a strong combination of in-clinic treatments, device sales, and additional scalp health services, LLLT provides a sustainable business model for clinics looking to expand their hair restoration offerings.

Nanoencapsulation Technology for Hair Growth Serums

Nanoencapsulation represents a significant advancement in the field of drug delivery, particularly in hair growth treatments. This technology involves the entrapment of bioactive compounds within nano-sized carriers, such as liposomes or polymeric nanoparticles, which enhances the stability, absorption, and penetration of these compounds into the scalp and hair follicles. By reducing the size of active ingredients to the nanometre scale, nanoencapsulation facilitates more efficient bypassing of surface barriers, leading to deeper penetration and prolonged release of therapeutic agents [646].

One of the primary benefits of nanoencapsulation in hair restoration is its ability to deliver active ingredients directly to hair follicles, thereby improving bioavailability and minimizing side effects associated with traditional treatments. For instance, conventional topical treatments like Minoxidil often suffer from poor skin absorption, resulting in inconsistent efficacy and potential adverse reactions such as scalp irritation [647]. Nanoencapsulated formulations can overcome these limitations by ensuring targeted delivery, which enhances the therapeutic effects while reducing unwanted reactions [646].

A notable example of nanoencapsulation in hair growth treatment is Nanoxidil, developed by DS Laboratories. This formulation utilizes nanoencapsulation technology to transport hair growth-stimulating compounds more effectively into the scalp, promoting follicular activity without the common side effects associated with Minoxidil, such as itching and dryness [647]. The innovative approach of Nanoxidil makes it particularly appealing for individuals who experience sensitivity to traditional Minoxidil treatments, thereby expanding the options available for hair restoration therapies [647].

Nanoencapsulation is not limited to hair regrowth; it is also transforming scalp health treatments by enabling the controlled release of anti-inflammatory, antioxidant, and antimicrobial agents. This targeted delivery is especially beneficial for individuals suffering from scalp conditions like seborrheic dermatitis or folliculitis, where encapsulated botanicals and vitamins can improve nutrient retention and prolong efficacy while minimizing degradation due to environmental factors [646]. The ability to deliver these compounds effectively can lead to improved scalp health, which is crucial for optimal hair growth.

In addition to enhancing efficacy, nanoencapsulation contributes to the development of non-greasy, lightweight formulations that are more user-friendly. Unlike traditional creams or serums, nano-formulated treatments absorb quickly and leave minimal residue on the scalp, which is a significant consideration in the consumer market where ease of application can influence adherence to hair growth regimens [646]. This improvement in formulation texture not only enhances user experience but also encourages consistent use of hair growth products.

As research in nanotechnology progresses, the potential for customized nanoencapsulation formulations tailored to individual hair loss conditions is becoming increasingly feasible. The integration of AI diagnostics and genetic testing in trichology may allow for the development of personalized hair growth treatments that consider a patient's unique scalp microbiome and genetic predispositions [646]. This personalized approach could revolutionize hair restoration therapies, making them more effective and better tolerated by patients.

Integrating nanoencapsulation-based hair growth treatments into clinical practice presents a significant opportunity for clinics specializing in trichology and dermatology. With its ability to enhance the effectiveness of hair growth solutions, nanoencapsulation technology allows for deeper penetration of active ingredients, ensuring better results for patients. While the initial investment in acquiring nanoencapsulated formulations, specialized equipment, staff training, and marketing is necessary, the potential revenue from premium pricing and repeat client engagement makes this technology a valuable addition to a clinic's offerings.

Clinics need to source high-quality nanoencapsulated hair growth solutions from reputable manufacturers or formulate their own using specialized nanoencapsulation equipment. Wholesale nanoencapsulated serums and lotions typically range between $50 to $150 per unit, with bulk pricing discounts available for large orders. Custom-formulated nanoencapsulation solutions, including research and small-batch production, can cost between $1,000 and

$5,000. Leading suppliers and brands in this space include DS Laboratories (Nanoxidil), Fagron TrichoConcept, RevivHair Max, and Nanotech Cosmetics.

For clinics aiming to produce or enhance nanoencapsulated treatments in-house, investment in nano-formulation equipment and delivery systems is required. The cost of a nanoencapsulation machine can range from $10,000 to $50,000, depending on capacity and advanced features. Additionally, clinics may invest in microneedling and scalp infusion devices to improve the delivery of nanoencapsulated formulas, which cost between $1,500 and $5,000. Cold storage units, essential for maintaining the stability of active ingredients, typically range from $2,000 to $5,000.

Proper training is necessary to ensure staff can administer nanoencapsulation-based treatments effectively. Trichology or nanoencapsulation training courses range from $1,500 to $5,000 as a one-time investment. To stay updated on advancements in hair loss treatments, clinics may also allocate $500 to $2,000 per year for ongoing education and professional development in scalp and hair loss therapies.

Nanoencapsulation-based treatments require education-driven marketing strategies to attract high-value clients seeking innovative hair loss solutions. Digital advertising and social media promotions can cost between $2,000 and $10,000 per month, depending on campaign scope and target audience. Website integration for online booking systems and patient education may require a one-time investment of $3,000 to $7,000. Clinics may also collaborate with influencers or medical professionals to build trust and attract new patients, with costs varying depending on the partnership.

Nanoencapsulation-based hair growth treatments are positioned as premium services, allowing clinics to charge higher prices while increasing patient retention through multi-session packages and personalized treatment plans.

Nanoencapsulated solutions can be offered as standalone treatments or in combination with other hair restoration techniques such as microneedling, PRP therapy, or exosome therapy. A single nanoencapsulation scalp treatment typically costs between $300 and $800 per session. Combining nanoencapsulation with microneedling for enhanced delivery can increase pricing to $500 to $1,200 per session. Clinics offering bundled nanoencapsulation and PRP therapy packages can charge between $2,500 and $5,000 for multi-session plans.

Clinics can boost revenue by offering customized nanoencapsulation hair regrowth kits for at-home use. Personalized nanoencapsulated serums and scalp treatments can be priced between $200 and $600 per unit, depending on formulation complexity. Subscription-based nanoencapsulation hair growth programs, lasting three to six months, can generate between $1,500 and $4,000 per patient. Additional services such as scalp health supplements or AI-driven hair analysis reports can range from $100 to $500 per patient.

Nanoencapsulation technology allows clinics to expand their product offerings through retail sales. Clinics can sell retail nanoencapsulated hair growth serums for $100 to $300 per bottle. Nanoencapsulation-based shampoo and scalp care kits, formulated for long-term hair health, can be priced between $200 and $500 per package. With profit margins ranging between 40% and 60%, retail sales provide a steady revenue stream while complementing in-clinic treatments.

Nanoencapsulation technology represents a high-margin, scientifically advanced solution for hair restoration clinics. With its enhanced absorption, prolonged ingredient release, and reduced side effects, nanoencapsulated formulations offer superior results compared to traditional topical treatments. Clinics that integrate nanoencapsulation into personalized treatment plans can maximize revenue, attract premium clientele, and create long-term patient engagement through subscription-based haircare programs and in-clinic therapies.

By investing in nanoencapsulation technology, clinics can differentiate themselves from competitors, offer next-generation hair regrowth solutions, and achieve sustainable growth in the rapidly evolving field of trichology and hair loss treatment.

Advanced Hair Transplantation Techniques

Modern hair transplantation has evolved significantly from traditional methods such as Follicular Unit Extraction (FUE) and Follicular Unit Transplantation

(FUT). These advancements have resulted in higher precision, improved graft survival rates, faster recovery times, and more natural-looking results. The introduction of innovative technologies like Robotic Hair Transplantation (ARTAS) and Direct Hair Implantation (DHI) has redefined the landscape of surgical hair restoration, enhancing both efficiency and aesthetic outcomes.

The ARTAS Robotic Hair Transplant System represents a significant leap in hair transplantation technology. This system automates the follicular unit extraction and implantation processes, utilizing artificial intelligence (AI) to analyse the scalp and select the healthiest donor follicles for extraction. Unlike traditional manual FUE techniques, which heavily depend on the surgeon's skill, ARTAS minimizes human error and enhances accuracy, thereby reducing trauma to the scalp [648, 649]. The automation of graft extraction not only accelerates the process but also ensures consistent follicle quality, leading to improved graft survival rates and less post-procedure discomfort for patients [649]. Furthermore, the minimally invasive nature of ARTAS allows for quicker recovery, enabling patients to resume normal activities sooner [648, 649]. The system also optimizes hairline design and follicle placement, contributing to more natural-looking results [648].

In contrast, Direct Hair Implantation (DHI) is another cutting-edge technique that eliminates the need for pre-made incisions, which can enhance graft survival rates and improve hair density. DHI employs a specialized tool known as the DHI Implanter Pen, allowing for immediate implantation of extracted follicles without prior storage in a solution [648]. This method minimizes handling of the follicles, preserving their viability and increasing the likelihood of successful implantation [648]. Each follicle is implanted at a specific angle, depth, and direction, resulting in a more natural appearance compared to traditional methods [648]. Additionally, DHI's lack of incisions reduces post-procedure inflammation and discomfort, making it a favourable option for patients who prefer a less invasive approach [648].

When comparing ARTAS and DHI, both techniques offer distinct advantages over traditional methods. ARTAS is particularly suitable for patients requiring large-scale hair restoration due to its automated process, which ensures consistent extraction and placement of follicles [649]. On the other hand, DHI is ideal for high-density transplants in localized areas, such as the hairline or temples, and is favoured by patients seeking minimal scarring and quicker healing times [648].

The introduction of Robotic Hair Transplantation (ARTAS) and Direct Hair Implantation (DHI) provides clinics with a high-revenue, high-demand service that attracts patients seeking precision hair restoration. While the initial investment in technology, training, and facility setup is substantial, the high per-procedure pricing, repeat patient demand, and strong word-of-mouth referrals ensure long-term profitability. Investing in these advanced procedures allows clinics to differentiate themselves in a competitive market, offering state-of-the-art hair restoration solutions that yield natural and lasting results.

The ARTAS robotic system acquisition represents a major investment, with costs ranging between $200,000 and $350,000 for the initial purchase. Additional expenses include software and AI algorithm updates ranging from $10,000 to $50,000 per year, as well as maintenance and calibration costs of $5,000 to $20,000 annually. Staff training for ARTAS procedures requires an initial one-time investment of $5,000 to $15,000, ensuring that the surgical team is well-equipped to handle robotic-assisted hair transplantation. Consumables such as needles, punch tools, and extraction cartridges add an additional per-patient cost of $50 to $150.

DHI procedures require a different set of investments, including specialized DHI implanter pens and tools costing between $5,000 and $20,000. Training and certification for surgeons and technicians range from $3,000 to $10,000 per specialist, ensuring that procedures are conducted with precision. Establishing a sterile operating room and securing medical supplies requires an investment between $10,000 and $50,000, while graft handling and scalp preparation equipment add another $5,000 to $15,000 in costs.

Marketing and patient acquisition efforts are crucial for ensuring a steady flow of clients. Digital advertising and social media campaigns typically require an investment of $5,000 to $20,000 per month, while website development, SEO optimization, and online booking systems range from $10,000 to $30,000. Clinics may also engage in referral programs and influencer collaborations to drive brand awareness and credibility. Consultation software and scalp analysis tools further enhance patient experience and diagnostic accuracy, costing between $3,000 and $10,000.

Hair transplantation is a premium service that commands high per-procedure pricing. ARTAS hair transplant procedures range from $6,000 to $10,000 for small sessions involving 1,000 to 1,500 grafts. Medium-sized procedures, covering 2,000 to 3,000 grafts, are priced between $12,000 and $18,000. Large procedures requiring 4,000 grafts or more can cost between $20,000 and $30,000. DHI pricing follows a similar structure, with hairline and temple restoration procedures ranging from $7,000 to $12,000, crown restoration procedures priced at $15,000 to $20,000, and full scalp transplants exceeding 3,500 grafts costing between $25,000 and $35,000.

Beyond transplantation, clinics can generate additional revenue through complementary treatments. Exosome therapy for post-transplant healing is priced between $2,000 and $5,000 per session, while low-level laser therapy (LLLT) for hair growth acceleration costs between $1,000 and $3,000 per treatment package. PRP therapy, which enhances graft survival and hair regrowth, ranges from $2,000 to $4,500 per session. Scalp micropigmentation (SMP) offers a non-surgical solution for adding density, with prices varying between $1,500 and $5,000.

The financial viability of ARTAS and DHI hair transplants depends on patient volume and pricing strategies. Clinics treating five patients per month at an average procedure price of $12,000 can generate $60,000 in monthly revenue. Clinics with ten patients per month at an average price of $15,000 can achieve $150,000 in monthly revenue, while those handling twenty patients at $18,000 per procedure can reach $360,000 in revenue per month. Annually, low-volume clinics handling fifty patients can generate between $500,000 and $1,000,000, while mid-sized clinics treating one hundred patients can achieve between $1,000,000 and $2,000,000. High-end clinics with two hundred or more patients per year can generate between $3,500,000 and $5,000,000 in revenue.

Profit margins in hair transplantation remain substantial. ARTAS procedures, including depreciation and consumables, cost between $2,500 and $5,000 per patient. DHI procedures, including training and tools, cost between $3,000 and $6,000 per patient. Gross profit per patient can range from $6,000 to $25,000, depending on procedure size, with clinics achieving profit margins of 60% to 80%.

Hair transplantation using ARTAS and DHI presents one of the most lucrative opportunities for clinics specializing in trichology and aesthetic medicine. ARTAS requires a significant upfront investment but offers automation, efficiency, and accuracy that improve patient outcomes. DHI, on the other hand, has lower capital investment requirements but relies more on specialized training and manual skill for achieving high-density, natural-looking results.

With strong market demand, high per-procedure pricing, and the ability to bundle services with complementary treatments such as PRP, exosome therapy, and laser therapy, clinics can quickly recover their investment and establish substantial annual revenue. The future of hair restoration continues to evolve with advancements in AI-assisted follicle selection, regenerative medicine, and personalized transplant techniques, positioning this sector as a promising and highly profitable field for clinic expansion.

Bioengineered Hair Growth Ingredients

Bioengineered hair growth ingredients represent a significant advancement in the field of hair restoration, providing alternatives to traditional pharmaceutical treatments such as Minoxidil and Finasteride. These bioengineered compounds, which include plant-based extracts and synthetic peptides, have been developed to stimulate hair growth, strengthen hair follicles, and reduce hair loss while minimizing the side effects commonly associated with conventional medications. Traditional treatments like Minoxidil and Finasteride have been effective but are often accompanied by adverse effects such as scalp irritation, unwanted hair growth in unintended areas, hormonal imbalances, and sexual dysfunction [650, 651].

To address these limitations, researchers have focused on bioengineered ingredients that target multiple pathways involved in hair follicle stimulation. For instance, compounds derived from plant extracts and synthetic peptides can enhance blood circulation, reduce inflammation, inhibit dihydrotestosterone (DHT), and promote the anagen (growth) phase of the hair cycle [652]. This multifaceted approach not only improves the efficacy of hair restoration treatments but also reduces the risk of side effects associated with systemic medications like Finasteride, which can lead to hormonal imbalances [653].

One of the most notable bioengineered ingredients is Redensyl, a plant-based compound that activates stem cells within hair follicles, promoting regrowth and reducing shedding. Clinical studies have shown that Redensyl increases the expression of genes responsible for hair follicle regeneration, leading to improved hair density and thickness over time. Results indicate that noticeable improvements can be observed within three months of use, making it a popular alternative for individuals seeking non-prescription treatments [652]. Similarly, Procapil combines biotinyl-GHK, apigenin, and oleanolic acid to strengthen hair follicles and improve scalp circulation while acting locally to mitigate DHT-related hair loss, thus minimizing systemic side effects [652].

Capixyl, another innovative bioengineered ingredient, is derived from a combination of peptides and red clover extract. It is known for its ability to inhibit DHT production while stimulating follicular activity. Capixyl enhances the extracellular matrix surrounding hair follicles, thereby strengthening their anchorage and reducing hair fall. Its application in high-performance hair care products underscores the growing trend towards integrating bioengineered ingredients into everyday hair care routines [652].

These bioengineered ingredients are not only effective in promoting hair regrowth but also exhibit anti-inflammatory and scalp-balancing properties. Many hair loss conditions, including androgenetic alopecia and telogen effluvium, are exacerbated by inflammation and oxidative stress. By incorporating bioengineered peptides, antioxidants, and plant extracts into topical treatments, researchers are developing multifunctional hair care solutions that not only promote hair growth but also improve overall scalp health [652].

As the field of biotechnology and trichology advances, future hair growth treatments are expected to feature personalized, AI-driven formulations that cater to individual scalp microbiomes, genetic predispositions, and lifestyle factors. Ongoing research into stem cell-derived peptides, exosome therapy, and AI-optimized regimens indicates that bioengineered hair growth ingredients will play a crucial role in the evolution of non-invasive, effective hair restoration therapies [652].

Treatment Options and the Future of Trichology

The best hair restoration treatments depend on factors such as hair loss severity, underlying causes, budget, and personal preferences. Treatments that offer high efficacy, minimal side effects, and accessibility tend to be the most beneficial to consumers.

AI-powered scalp analysis is highly beneficial for early detection and personalized treatment planning. It helps consumers understand their scalp condition and hair loss progression, making it particularly useful for those in the early stages of hair thinning or looking for preventative care. Digital scalp scanning apps allow consumers to assess their scalp health remotely and receive AI-driven product recommendations, making hair care more personalized and data-driven.

3D-printed hair follicles are still in research but could revolutionize hair transplantation by eliminating donor hair limitations. This would be ideal for individuals with advanced baldness who currently do not qualify for traditional hair transplants due to poor donor supply. Once commercially available, this technology will offer a permanent, natural-looking hair restoration solution.

Exosome therapy is a non-invasive regenerative treatment that enhances follicle activity, increases hair thickness, and improves scalp health. It is particularly beneficial for those experiencing thinning hair, early-stage androgenetic alopecia, or post-hair transplant patients seeking faster recovery and improved graft survival. Unlike PRP therapy, it does not require blood extraction, making it a convenient and highly effective alternative for consumers.

Hair cloning is still in clinical trials but could offer an unlimited supply of hair follicles, making it a potential cure for baldness. This treatment would be ideal for individuals with severe hair loss who are not good candidates for traditional transplants. If successful, it could replace hair transplants as the gold standard for long-term hair restoration.

Genetic testing enables customized hair loss treatments by analysing an individual's DNA markers related to scalp health and hair follicle function. It is best suited for those with a family history of hair loss or individuals who have tried standard treatments with limited success. By understanding genetic predispositions, consumers can receive precise and effective treatments, avoiding the trial-and-error approach of traditional hair growth solutions.

Balancing the scalp microbiome is crucial for preventing dandruff, scalp inflammation, and hair thinning. Probiotic-based scalp treatments are highly effective for individuals with sensitive scalps, seborrheic dermatitis, or conditions aggravated by fungal overgrowth and inflammation. Unlike medicated shampoos that may cause scalp dryness, prebiotic and probiotic formulations offer long-term scalp health benefits.

Low-Level Laser Therapy devices are non-invasive and FDA-approved for stimulating hair follicles and increasing blood circulation. These at-home or in-clinic treatments work well for individuals in the early to moderate stages of hair loss. They are particularly useful for those who prefer a drug-free approach to hair restoration. While effective, LLLT requires consistent use for visible results, making it best for patients committed to long-term treatment regimens.

Nanoencapsulation enhances the penetration and absorption of active ingredients, making topical hair loss treatments more effective. This technology benefits those who want stronger alternatives to Minoxidil without irritation or unwanted side effects. Products like Nanoxidil are ideal for consumers who experience sensitivity to traditional topical hair regrowth formulas.

Modern robotic hair transplants provide higher precision, faster healing, and natural-looking results. ARTAS is best suited for patients seeking large-scale hair restoration with minimal scarring, while DHI is ideal for high-density transplants in specific areas such as the hairline or crown. These methods provide a permanent solution for baldness, making them a worthwhile investment for individuals with sufficient donor hair and budget.

Bioengineered compounds like Redensyl, Procapil, and Capixyl are natural alternatives to Minoxidil and Finasteride, offering DHT-blocking and follicle-stimulating benefits without harsh side effects. These are suitable for consumers seeking over-the-counter, non-prescription solutions for hair regrowth. They are particularly effective for early-stage hair loss prevention and maintenance.

Advances in Cosmetology

For early-stage hair loss and prevention, combining AI scalp diagnostics with personalized genetic testing and bioengineered hair growth serums such as Redensyl, Procapil, and Capixyl can offer a highly effective preventative approach. Adding probiotic scalp care and LLLT therapy can improve scalp health and maintain strong follicles.

For moderate hair thinning, exosome therapy combined with nanoencapsulation-based serums and LLLT therapy can enhance follicle stimulation and regrowth. If hairline recession is noticeable, DHI transplants can be supplemented with post-transplant exosome therapy to improve density and healing.

For severe hair loss and balding, advanced hair transplantation using ARTAS or DHI combined with exosome therapy can accelerate healing and improve results. In the future, 3D-printed hair follicles or hair cloning could provide an unlimited donor supply, revolutionizing hair restoration for those with extensive hair loss.

For consumers, selecting the best hair loss treatment depends on the stage of hair loss, personal preference, and budget. Non-invasive options like AI scalp diagnostics, probiotic scalp care, bioengineered ingredients, and LLLT therapy work best for preventative care and mild hair thinning. Exosome therapy and nanoencapsulation-based products are highly effective for moderate hair loss, while advanced transplantation techniques like ARTAS and DHI provide permanent solutions for severe baldness.

As hair cloning and 3D-printed follicle technology advance, consumers may soon have access to truly permanent and natural-looking hair restoration solutions. In the meantime, a combination of precision diagnostics, regenerative therapies, and scientifically backed topical treatments offers the most effective approach to hair restoration today.

The future of trichology is set to be defined by advancements in gene therapy, bioengineered follicle regeneration, and AI-powered diagnostics. Researchers are exploring CRISPR gene editing to modify genetic factors contributing to hair loss, while new discoveries in exosome therapy and regenerative medicine promise even more effective hair restoration treatments.

Richard Skiba

With technology playing a more significant role in hair health, AI-driven scalp analysis, personalized genetic testing, and lab-grown hair follicles will soon become mainstream solutions in trichology. As these innovations continue to evolve, individuals experiencing hair loss or scalp conditions will have access to more effective, non-invasive, and customized treatments tailored to their unique biological and genetic needs.

Chapter 9

Advances in Nail Technology

The nail technology industry is a thriving segment of the beauty and personal care market, encompassing nail care products, services, and technological advancements. Valued at approximately $10-15 billion USD globally, the industry continues to grow due to increasing consumer interest in personal grooming, rising disposable incomes, and the influence of social media and beauty trends.

The global nail salon market was valued at USD 11.00 billion in 2022 and is projected to grow at a compound annual growth rate (CAGR) of 8.0% from 2023 to 2030 [654]. This growth is driven by an increasing emphasis on personal grooming and appearance, as consumers become more conscious of maintaining well-manicured nails. Nail salons provide specialized services that cater to this demand, offering convenience and expertise that many individuals seek for both aesthetic and self-care purposes [654].

The COVID-19 pandemic had a significant impact on the nail salon industry, introducing new trends and operational changes. Salons implemented strict hygiene measures, including mandatory mask-wearing, frequent sanitization of tools and surfaces, hand sanitizing stations, and social distancing within salon spaces. These protocols reassured customers and helped rebuild confidence in visiting nail salons. Many establishments transitioned to an appointment-only model to manage customer flow efficiently and minimize wait times. Online booking platforms and mobile apps became increasingly popular, allowing customers to schedule appointments conveniently and enabling salons to optimize their capacity [654].

The millennial demographic has played a crucial role in shaping the nail industry, particularly through their emphasis on self-expression and individuality. Nail salons provide a creative outlet through unique nail designs, vibrant colours, and intricate embellishments. Millennials seek out nail technicians who can create customized, trend-driven designs, often inspired by social media influencers and celebrity nail trends. High-profile figures such as Kylie Jenner, Nicki Minaj, Billie Eilish, and Cardi B have further popularized elaborate acrylic nails, leading to increased demand for professional nail services [654].

Social media platforms, particularly Instagram and TikTok, have transformed the nail industry by driving trends and increasing customer engagement. TikTok's short-form videos have made nail art tutorials and salon experiences more accessible to a global audience, fostering a trend-driven culture around nail care. Additionally, advancements in technology have enhanced the quality of services offered by salons. New nail care products, tools, and equipment have expanded treatment options, improving the precision and durability of nail services. Digital marketing, enhanced online presence, and customer engagement strategies have also contributed to market growth by helping salons reach a wider audience [654].

Manicure services dominated the market in 2022, accounting for approximately 32% of the market share. Many customers view manicures as a form of relaxation and self-care, creating ongoing demand for these services. The UV gel overlays and extensions segment is expected to register a CAGR of 9.5% from 2023 to 2030, as more consumers seek long-lasting, low-maintenance manicures [654]. The professional expertise required for gel polish application and removal has driven demand for salon services, as customers prefer precise application and safe removal by trained professionals.

Women remain the dominant consumer group in the nail salon industry, making up approximately 69% of the market share in 2022. For many women, visiting a nail salon extends beyond beauty maintenance and serves as a ritualistic self-care practice, allowing them to relax and unwind. This emphasis on wellness-oriented experiences has increased customer satisfaction and long-term loyalty. The male segment is also experiencing notable growth, with a projected CAGR of 8.7% from 2023 to 2030 [654]. Well-groomed nails are increasingly seen as an extension of personal style, and more men are visiting nail salons for manicures, pedicures, and overall nail maintenance. In India, for example, the ratio of female-to-male customers in nail salons has shifted significantly, with men now making up a larger percentage of clientele compared to pre-pandemic years [654].

The age group of 19 to 40 years dominated the market in 2022, accounting for over 46% of the industry's revenue. Individuals in this demographic frequently attend social events, weddings, and parties, making nail salon visits an integral part of their beauty routine. Millennials and Gen Z consumers are the biggest spenders on nail services, prioritizing nail aesthetics and regularly trying new trends. The segment for individuals below 18 years old is projected to grow at the fastest CAGR of 10.2% during the forecast period [654]. Nail salons catering to teenagers have adapted to their preferences by offering age-appropriate designs, trendy decor, and a welcoming atmosphere. Some salons provide dedicated children's manicure and pedicure services at affordable price points, making nail care more accessible to younger consumers.

Regionally, North America led the global market with over 33% of the market share in 2022. The expansion of nail salon franchises, particularly in the United States, has significantly contributed to market growth. Many salon brands are focusing on franchise expansion while maintaining high hygiene standards and offering chemical-free nail processes. An example is Prose Nails, which recently opened its 27th location in Sandy Springs, Georgia. The Asia-Pacific region is expected to grow at a CAGR of 9.4% from 2023 to 2030, driven by a rising number of male customers visiting nail salons [654]. Grooming culture among men has gained traction in this region, with an increasing number of men seeking professional nail care services. In India, post-pandemic shifts have led to more frequent visits by male clients for manicures and pedicures, reducing the gender gap in salon clientele [654].

The nail salon industry is evolving rapidly, with technological advancements, changing consumer preferences, and increased social media influence shaping its growth. As salons continue to adopt new innovations in nail care and hygiene, the market is poised for significant expansion, offering consumers a broader range of high-quality, personalized, and wellness-focused services.

Nail care products form a significant part of the industry, including nail polishes, gels, acrylics, nail strengtheners, cuticle care products, and removers. The demand for non-toxic, long-lasting, and fast-drying formulas has led to innovations such as gel polishes, breathable polishes, and vegan, cruelty-free options. Major players in this segment include OPI, Essie, Sally Hansen, CND, and Revlon.

The service sector within the nail industry is equally expansive, with salons offering a variety of treatments, including manicures, pedicures, gel applications, acrylic extensions, and nail art. The rise of specialized nail bars and mobile nail services has made professional nail care more accessible. Popular services also include nail extensions, 3D nail art, and intricate designs, often showcased on social media platforms like Instagram and TikTok.

Nail tools and equipment play a crucial role in both professional and at-home nail care. This category includes LED/UV lamps for curing gel nails, electric nail drills, cuticle pushers, nail files, and brushes. The professional salon market heavily relies on durable, efficient, and versatile tools, while home-use devices, such as portable LED lamps and electric files, have gained popularity among DIY consumers.

The North American market, led by the United States, is a major player in the global nail industry. The popularity of nail salons, DIY kits, and the growing demand for organic and non-toxic nail products drive this market. The rise of nail art and customization trends has further fuelled its growth. In Europe, with leading markets in Germany, France, and the UK, there is a strong emphasis on luxury and high-quality nail products. European consumers favour eco-friendly, vegan, and 5-free or 7-free formulations, while premium services like spa manicures and pedicures are widely sought after.

Asia-Pacific is one of the fastest-growing regions, with China, Japan, and South Korea leading the way. The market benefits from a strong focus on beauty innovations, K-beauty trends, and a high demand for nail art. Japanese gel nails and Korean press-on nails have gained international appeal and influence global beauty standards. In Latin America and the Middle East, the nail industry is expanding due to rising disposable incomes and a growing beauty consciousness. Brazil is known for its vibrant nail culture, while the Middle East sees an increasing demand for luxury nail care products and services.

Innovations in nail technology are shaping the future of the industry. Gel and hybrid polishes, such as Shellac and Gelish, offer longer-lasting wear without the chipping associated with traditional polishes. The development of breathable and non-toxic formulations allows oxygen and moisture to pass through, promoting nail health. Many new polishes are now labeled "10-free" or "12-free," excluding harmful chemicals like formaldehyde, toluene, and DBP.

At-home gel kits with LED/UV lamps and easy-to-apply formulas have democratized professional-grade manicures. Brands like Sensationail and Le Mini Macaron cater to the DIY market, making high-quality nail care accessible to consumers. Digital nail art printers and stamping kits have revolutionized intricate nail designs, allowing for quick and precise applications.

Smart nail technology is an emerging trend, with innovations such as LED nails, NFC-enabled nails, and smart nail art merging beauty with digital technology to create interactive and customizable designs. Sustainability is another driving force in the industry, with brands moving towards eco-friendly solutions such as sustainable packaging, biodegradable glitters, and plant-based ingredients to meet consumer demand for environmentally responsible beauty products.

Despite these advancements, the industry faces challenges, including concerns about the health impact of nail product chemicals and the environmental effects of plastic packaging, non-biodegradable glitters, and chemical disposal. However, there are significant opportunities for growth, particularly in personalization through AI and digital diagnostics, which enable customized nail care recommendations. E-commerce and social media continue to be powerful tools for marketing, showcasing trends, and reaching global audiences. Additionally, wellness integration within the industry is growing, with salons offering spa-like experiences, organic treatments, and mindful self-care approaches.

The nail technology industry is expected to continue its growth trajectory, driven by innovation, consumer demand for safe and sustainable products, and the influence of social media trends. With emerging technologies such as AI diagnostics, 3D printing, and bio-engineered nail treatments, the industry is poised to offer personalized, efficient, and eco-friendly solutions to consumers worldwide.

Traditional Nail Products

Nail products, including polishes, gels, acrylics, and removers, are formulated with various chemical ingredients that enhance their durability, shine, and adhesion. However, the safety of these chemicals has become a significant concern due to potential health risks associated with prolonged exposure. This response will detail common ingredients found in nail products, their functions, and associated safety considerations.

Nail polish typically comprises film-forming agents, solvents, plasticizers, pigments, and resins. Nitrocellulose serves as a primary film-forming agent, providing a smooth and glossy finish upon drying [655]. Solvents like toluene are crucial for maintaining consistency but are linked to respiratory and neurological effects with prolonged exposure [655]. Formaldehyde, used as a hardening agent, is classified as a carcinogen when inhaled in significant amounts [655]. Additionally, dibutyl phthalate (DBP) acts as a plasticizer to prevent chipping but has been associated with endocrine disruption and reproductive toxicity (Jia, 2024). Camphor, another ingredient, enhances gloss but can cause dizziness and nausea when inhaled in large quantities [655]. In response to health concerns, many brands have adopted "3-free," "5-free," "7-free," and "10-free" formulas that exclude harmful chemicals like formaldehyde, DBP, and toluene, thereby reducing potential health risks [655].

Gel polishes share many ingredients with traditional nail polishes but include photoinitiators that harden under UV or LED light. Methacrylate monomers provide flexibility and durability but can lead to allergic reactions and skin irritation [656]. UV filters such as benzophenone-1 and -3 prevent yellowing but are linked to hormonal disruptions [656]. Furthermore, excessive exposure to UV light from curing lamps raises concerns about skin damage and an increased risk of premature aging or skin cancer, prompting recommendations for protective measures such as gloves or SPF during gel applications [656].

Figure 20: Traditional nail salon environnement. Jenny Bui Nail Salon, Valereee, CC BY-SA 4.0, via Wikimedia Commons.

Acrylic nails are created by mixing liquid monomers and powder polymers that harden into a durable coating. Ethyl methacrylate (EMA) and methyl methacrylate (MMA) are bonding agents that create strong artificial nails, with MMA being banned in many countries due to its extreme hardness and potential to cause allergic reactions and nail damage [656]. Benzoyl peroxide serves as a catalyst for curing acrylics but can irritate the skin in sensitive individuals [656]. Long-term use of acrylic nails can weaken natural nails, leading to brittleness, thinning, and infections if not properly applied or removed [656].

Nail polish removers typically contain strong solvents to dissolve nail coatings. Acetone is the most common solvent, effectively removing polish and gel but can dry out nails and skin, leading to brittleness and irritation [655]. Ethyl acetate and butyl acetate are gentler alternatives but still produce fumes that may irritate the eyes and respiratory system [655]. While acetone-free removers are available, they tend to be less effective in removing long-wear polishes and gels [655].

Many chemicals in nail products pose risks with prolonged exposure, poor ventilation, or improper use. Key concerns include respiratory issues from inhaling fumes of solvents like toluene and formaldehyde, which may cause headaches, dizziness, and breathing difficulties [656]. Frequent exposure to methacrylates can lead to contact dermatitis or allergic reactions [656]. Hormonal disruption and reproductive effects have been linked to chemicals such as DBP and benzophenones [656]. Additionally, formaldehyde's classification as a known carcinogen raises concerns about increased cancer risks with frequent exposure to high levels over time [656].

With increased awareness of chemical safety, many brands are shifting toward natural, breathable, and non-toxic formulations. Water-based nail polishes, plant-derived bio-engineered resins, and biodegradable formulas are becoming more popular, making nail care safer and more eco-friendly.

As nail technology advances, the industry is focusing on health-conscious alternatives, ensuring that consumers can enjoy beautiful nails without compromising their health.

Innovations and Advancements in Nail Technology

The evolution of nail technology in recent years has been marked by significant advancements in materials, digital tools, and sustainable practices. These innovations have transformed the nail care industry, providing consumers with options that are not only aesthetically pleasing but also healthier and more environmentally friendly.

Artificial intelligence (AI) and digital tools are at the forefront of this transformation. AI-powered nail scanners and robotic manicure systems are enhancing precision and customization in nail care. For instance, brands like Nimble and Clockwork have developed robotic manicure machines that deliver salon-quality results in a fraction of the time, minimizing human error and reducing wait times for consumers [657]. These advancements are indicative of a broader trend towards automation in beauty services, which is making high-quality nail care more accessible [658]. Furthermore, AI-driven nail printers enable intricate nail art designs, allowing for a level of customization that was previously unattainable [659].

Sustainability has become a central theme in the beauty industry, including nail technology. Traditional nail products often contain harmful chemicals that pose risks to both health and the environment. In response, many brands are now offering biodegradable and plant-based nail polishes that decompose naturally, thus reducing environmental impact [660]. Water-based and non-toxic formulations are gaining popularity as safer alternatives to conventional polishes, which often contain toxic substances such as formaldehyde and toluene [661]. This shift towards eco-friendly products is not only beneficial for the environment but also aligns with consumer demand for safer beauty options [662].

While gel manicures have been favoured for their durability, they often involve harsh UV curing processes and acetone removal, which can weaken nails over time [663]. New hybrid formulas, such as powder-based and air-drying gel alternatives, provide similar longevity without the associated damage [664]. Brands like DipWell and Revel Nail have pioneered dip powder systems that offer strength and durability while eliminating the need for UV exposure [665].

These innovations reflect a growing awareness of nail health and the desire for products that enhance rather than compromise nail integrity.

Breathable nail polishes, which allow oxygen and moisture to penetrate the nail plate, are becoming increasingly popular. These formulations help maintain nail health while providing vibrant colour and chip resistance [666]. Notably, halal-certified breathable polishes are also emerging, catering to consumers who seek products that align with their ethical and religious standards [667]. Brands such as Orly and Inglot have introduced lines that emphasize these qualities, further expanding the market for health-conscious nail care products [668].

The integration of 3D printing technology into the nail industry has opened new avenues for creativity and personalization. High-tech 3D printers can create customized nail embellishments and extensions with precision, allowing for intricate designs that were previously difficult to achieve [669]. This technology not only enhances the aesthetic possibilities of nail art but also streamlines the application process, making it more efficient and accessible for consumers [670].

Light therapy is being incorporated into nail care routines to promote nail health. LED-based treatments utilize low-level red light therapy to stimulate keratin production, enhancing nail strength and resilience [671]. These treatments are particularly beneficial for individuals with brittle or damaged nails, offering a non-invasive method to improve nail health [672].

The traditional practice of soaking nails in water during manicures can weaken nail adhesion. Waterless manicures, which utilize hydrating sprays and steam treatments, are becoming more prevalent as they enhance nail longevity and improve hygiene by reducing the risk of bacterial and fungal infections [673]. Many high-end salons are adopting this method, reflecting a shift towards more hygienic and efficient nail care practices [674].

Innovative self-healing nail polishes are formulated with polymers that can repair minor chips and scratches autonomously. These smart formulas react to heat or pressure, restoring a smooth finish without the need for touch-ups, thereby extending the lifespan of nail applications [675]. This technology represents a significant advancement in nail care, making maintenance easier and less time-consuming for consumers [676].

Modern press-on nails have evolved significantly from their early iterations. Today's press-ons are made from flexible materials that closely mimic the appearance and feel of salon-quality acrylics. Advanced adhesive systems, including gel-based tabs, allow for strong yet damage-free applications, making these products reusable and environmentally friendly [677]. This innovation caters to consumers seeking convenient and cost-effective nail enhancement options [677].

AI-powered beauty applications are now capable of analysing nail health and providing personalized care recommendations. By scanning nails and cuticles, these tools can suggest targeted treatments and hydration levels, ensuring that consumers receive tailored nail care routines [678]. This level of customization optimizes nail health and enhances the overall consumer experience [679].

AI-Powered Nail Scanners and Robotic Manicure Systems

The integration of AI-powered nail scanners and robotic manicure systems is significantly transforming the nail care industry, enhancing service delivery through automation, precision, and personalization. These technologies are designed to improve efficiency, accuracy, and hygiene in nail care, appealing to both salons and consumers seeking high-quality treatments.

AI-powered nail scanners utilize advanced imaging technology and artificial intelligence to evaluate nail conditions, identifying imperfections and recommending appropriate treatments. These systems assess various factors, including nail health, moisture levels, ridges, discoloration, and cuticle conditions, thereby enabling personalized product recommendations tailored to individual needs. For instance, the OPTE Precision System and Perfect Corp's AI Nail Scanner exemplify how AI can provide real-time diagnostic insights and virtual try-on features for nail polish colours, enhancing the customer experience by allowing them to visualize potential outcomes before application [680]. Furthermore, the hygienic nature of these scanners minimizes direct contact, which is particularly beneficial in maintaining cleanliness in nail salons [681].

Robotic manicure systems complement these scanners by automating the nail painting and shaping processes. These systems leverage computer vision and AI algorithms to ensure precise application of nail polish, significantly reducing service time and eliminating common human errors such as streaks or uneven coverage. Innovations like Clockwork's "Minicure" Robot and the Nimble Nail Robot demonstrate the potential for these systems to deliver professional-quality manicures in a fraction of the time traditionally required [681]. The touchless nature of robotic systems further enhances hygiene standards, making them a desirable option in the post-pandemic beauty landscape [681].

The benefits of these technologies extend beyond mere convenience. They offer significant time savings, consistent results, and a high level of customization, which are increasingly important to consumers. AI systems can tailor nail care routines based on individual assessments, suggesting treatments that address specific nail health issues [680]. Moreover, the reduction in cross-contamination risks associated with contactless services aligns with growing consumer concerns regarding hygiene and safety in beauty treatments [681].

Despite the promising advancements, challenges remain in the widespread adoption of AI and robotic technologies in nail care. High initial costs and maintenance requirements can deter salons from investing in these systems. Additionally, some consumers may still prefer the personal touch of human technicians, suggesting that hybrid models combining AI automation with traditional services might be more appealing [681]. The future of AI in nail technology looks bright, with potential developments in smart nail coatings and fully automated nail salons on the horizon [681].

Integrating AI-powered nail scanners and robotic manicure systems into nail salons requires an initial investment in technology, training, and maintenance. However, these innovations present a lucrative opportunity by increasing efficiency, reducing service times, and attracting tech-savvy clients who seek precision, customization, and hygiene in their nail care experience. The ability to offer faster, consistent, and high-quality services allows salons to charge premium prices while increasing customer retention.

Advances in Cosmetology

Salons investing in AI nail scanners need to consider equipment costs, software subscriptions, and staff training. The purchase of an AI nail scanner typically ranges from $5,000 to $30,000 as a one-time cost, while software licensing and AI updates require an annual investment of $1,000 to $5,000. Training salon staff to operate these advanced diagnostic systems costs between $500 and $2,000 as a one-time expense. Additionally, ongoing maintenance and calibration fees range from $500 to $1,500 per year to ensure accurate nail health assessments and smooth system functionality.

Robotic manicure machines require a higher initial investment but can handle multiple clients per day, reducing reliance on manual labour and increasing overall service speed. The cost of purchasing a robotic manicure system varies between $50,000 and $150,000, depending on the complexity of the device. Software and AI algorithm updates cost an additional $2,000 to $10,000 annually. Maintenance and repair expenses typically range from $3,000 to $10,000 per year. Training salon staff to operate and troubleshoot the system requires an upfront investment of $1,000 to $5,000.

Promoting AI-driven services and integrating them into existing salon management systems requires additional investment. Digital marketing and social media campaigns cost between $2,000 and $10,000 per month to increase visibility and attract high-value clients. Website development and online booking integration can cost between $5,000 and $15,000 as a one-time investment, ensuring a seamless digital experience for customers. Implementing customer loyalty programs and AI-driven personalized recommendations costs between $1,000 and $5,000 per year, helping salons increase repeat business and improve customer satisfaction.

AI-powered nail technology allows salons to charge premium prices for high-tech nail diagnostics and robotic manicures. Faster service times and reduced technician involvement also increase overall customer throughput. AI nail scanner services generate revenue through nail health assessments and personalized recommendations, with pricing ranging from $25 to $100 per session. Virtual nail colour matching consultations range from $15 to $50, while custom AI-recommended nail treatments cost between $50 and $200 per package. A salon performing 10 AI nail scanner sessions per day at an average price of $50 per session can generate up to $15,000 per month or $180,000 per year.

Robotic manicures provide an additional revenue stream, with express robotic manicures priced between $20 and $50 per session. Advanced robotic nail art and gel polish applications range from $50 to $150 per session, while AI-assisted custom nail designs cost between $75 and $250 per session. With a robotic manicure machine servicing 20 clients per day at an average price of $80 per service, the potential monthly revenue from robotic manicures could reach $48,000 per month or $576,000 per year.

The ROI for AI-powered nail scanners and robotic manicure systems depends on pricing, service volume, and efficiency gains. AI nail scanner services yield profit margins of approximately 60% to 80%, while robotic manicure services generate profit margins of 70% to 85%. The break-even period for these technologies typically ranges from six months to two years, depending on service pricing and customer volume.

The benefits of AI-powered nail scanners and robotic manicure systems extend beyond revenue generation. These innovations increase service efficiency by reducing manual labour and service time while maintaining high precision. Higher revenue per client is achievable as AI-powered and robotic services allow for premium pricing. The contactless nature of these services enhances hygiene and safety, attracting health-conscious customers. Additionally, offering cutting-edge, technology-driven services positions a salon as an industry leader, differentiating it from competitors.

Despite the numerous advantages, there are challenges to consider. The high initial investment may be prohibitive for smaller salons, requiring a long-term financial strategy to justify the expense. Some customers may prefer traditional nail services over automated solutions, meaning salons must educate clients about the benefits of AI-driven treatments. Maintenance costs for robotic systems can add up over time, requiring regular servicing to maintain efficiency and precision.

AI-powered nail scanners and robotic manicure systems represent the future of the nail industry, offering precision, customization, and increased profitability for salons. While the initial investment may be substantial, the ability to attract premium clients, reduce labour costs, and scale operations makes it a financially viable long-term investment. Salons that integrate these innovations effectively will be well-positioned for sustained growth and industry leadership.

Chapter 10

Advances in Intimate Area Aesthetic Therapies

Innovative and advanced cosmetology treatments for the genital area have gained significant traction in recent years, driven by a growing demand for aesthetic enhancement, rejuvenation, and overall intimate health. These procedures cater to both men and women, addressing various concerns such as skin laxity, pigmentation, hair removal, rejuvenation, and functional improvements. The expansion of genital cosmetic procedures is closely linked to advancements in laser technology, regenerative medicine, and non-invasive aesthetic solutions, which have transformed the landscape of intimate health treatments [682, 683].

Laser and energy-based treatments have emerged as prominent modalities for genital rejuvenation, offering both aesthetic and functional benefits. These treatments are designed to improve skin tone, stimulate collagen production, and enhance sexual well-being. For instance, fractional CO_2 laser resurfacing is widely utilized for vaginal and penile rejuvenation, effectively stimulating collagen and elastin production. This process not only improves tightness and hydration but also reduces signs of aging, making it a valuable option for addressing conditions such as vaginal atrophy, dryness, and urinary incontinence [684-686]. Additionally, radiofrequency (RF) therapy, exemplified by treatments like ThermiVa and Morpheus8 V, employs controlled heat to stimulate collagen production and tighten vaginal or scrotal skin. These non-invasive procedures enhance laxity, increase blood flow, and improve sexual sensation without the need for surgical intervention [687, 688].

High-Intensity Focused Ultrasound (HIFU) is another innovative approach that has transitioned from facial aesthetics to genital rejuvenation. HIFU penetrates deeper layers of tissue, promoting tightening and elasticity over time, thereby offering a non-invasive alternative for individuals seeking genital enhancement [689]. The integration of these advanced technologies into genital cosmetic procedures reflects a broader trend towards non-invasive solutions that prioritize patient comfort and satisfaction [690].

The psychological and physical comfort of patients undergoing these procedures is noteworthy. Studies indicate that many individuals seeking genital cosmetic treatments report increased self-confidence and reduced discomfort, particularly among women dissatisfied with the appearance of their genitalia [691, 692]. This growing awareness of aesthetic concerns has led to a rise in demand for cosmetic gynecology, which focuses on enhancing sexual satisfaction and attractiveness [683, 693]. Furthermore, the aesthetic outcomes of gender-affirming surgeries underscore the importance of aesthetics in patient satisfaction, highlighting the role of genital aesthetics in overall well-being [691, 694].

Regenerative and Injectable Therapies

Advancements in regenerative medicine have significantly transformed the landscape of intimate wellness by introducing innovative, minimally invasive treatments that leverage the body's natural healing processes. These procedures, including platelet-rich plasma (PRP) therapy, stem cell therapy, and exosome therapy, provide non-surgical alternatives to traditional cosmetic and reconstructive genital treatments. They address various concerns such as sensitivity, hydration, tissue firmness, and structural enhancement, ultimately improving genital aesthetics and function [695-697].

PRP therapy, often referred to as the O-Shot for women and the P-Shot for men, utilizes the patient's own blood-derived growth factors to stimulate tissue repair and cellular regeneration in intimate areas. The procedure involves drawing a small amount of blood, processing it to isolate platelet-rich plasma, and injecting it into targeted areas of the vaginal or penile tissue. For women, the O-Shot has been shown to enhance sensitivity, increase natural lubrication, and improve orgasmic function, particularly for those experiencing vaginal dryness or reduced sensation [695]. In men, the P-Shot enhances penile sensitivity, promotes stronger erections, and increases penile girth, making it an effective treatment for erectile dysfunction (ED) and Peyronie's disease [695, 696].

Stem cell therapy is another cutting-edge approach in regenerative medicine, utilizing mesenchymal stem cells (MSCs) to regenerate damaged or aging tissue. These stem cells can be sourced from adipose tissue or bone marrow and are injected into the vaginal or penile tissue to stimulate natural repair processes. Research indicates that MSCs can improve hydration and restore elasticity in the genital area, addressing age-related concerns such as vaginal laxity or atrophic vaginitis in women and enhancing penile tissue function in men [698, 699]. Furthermore, exosome therapy, which involves the use of exosomes derived from stem cells, enhances cellular communication and accelerates tissue repair, thus supporting collagen production and increased blood circulation [697, 700]. This therapy is gaining traction as a non-surgical option for rejuvenating intimate areas without the need for invasive procedures [696, 697].

In addition to PRP and stem cell therapies, hyaluronic acid-based dermal fillers are increasingly being utilized to enhance the appearance and comfort of the genital area. Fillers such as Voluma, Restylane, and Juvederm are used for labial puffing, restoring lost volume due to aging or childbirth, and improving comfort by reducing irritation caused by excess skin laxity [695]. For men, treatments like Scrotox, which involves the use of botulinum toxin to relax scrotal muscles, can enhance aesthetic appearance and alleviate discomfort related to excessive scrotal tightness [695].

Overall, the integration of these advanced regenerative techniques into intimate wellness practices not only enhances aesthetic outcomes but also addresses functional concerns, significantly improving the quality of life for individuals seeking such treatments [695-697].

Integrating regenerative and injectable therapies for intimate wellness into a salon or medical spa requires specialized equipment, trained professionals, and adherence to strict hygiene and safety protocols. While the initial investment may be substantial, the high demand for these treatments and their premium pricing ensure strong profitability and long-term returns.

PRP therapy, commonly referred to as the O-Shot for women and the P-Shot for men, requires essential medical-grade equipment for blood extraction, plasma separation, and injection. A high-quality PRP centrifuge machine is necessary, with costs ranging from $3,000 to $10,000. PRP collection kits for blood draw and processing typically cost between $50 and $200 per patient. Some salons also incorporate microneedling devices for enhanced PRP absorption, which adds another $2,000 to $5,000 to the initial investment. Medical-grade syringes, needles, and anaesthetics such as lidocaine contribute to an annual expense of $500 to $1,500. Hygiene and disinfection supplies, including sterile gloves, alcohol wipes, and cleaning solutions, require an additional $1,000 to $3,000 per year to maintain compliance with safety standards. Staff training and certification for PRP therapy is a one-time investment that ranges from $3,000 to $10,000, while compliance and licensing costs vary by region and can range from $1,500 to $5,000.

Stem cell and exosome therapy require advanced medical equipment, laboratory partnerships, and specialized training. If performed in-house, stem cell processing and storage equipment can cost between $50,000 and $200,000. Exosome therapy vials for each treatment session range from $1,500 to $5,000, while stem cell harvesting kits for adipose-derived cells cost between $1,000 and $3,000 per procedure. Injection syringes and other medical disposables add an annual cost of $1,000 to $3,000. Regulatory compliance, including FDA-approved stem cell sourcing fees, requires an investment of $5,000 to $15,000 annually. Advanced training and certification in regenerative medicine is also necessary, with one-time costs ranging from $5,000 to $20,000.

Dermal fillers for labia and scrotal enhancement require aesthetic filler injectables and expertise in dermal filler techniques. Hyaluronic acid fillers such as Voluma, Restylane, and Juvederm cost between $300 and $900 per syringe, while botulinum toxin for Scrotox, such as Botox or Dysport, ranges from $400 to $1,000 per vial. Sterile needles and injection tools contribute an additional $500 to $2,000 per year. To ensure safe and effective procedures, dermal filler injection training costs between $3,000 and $7,000 per specialist. Post-treatment skincare and soothing products add another $500 to $2,000 annually.

Genital rejuvenation treatments are high-value services, allowing clinics to generate substantial revenue per session. PRP-based treatments such as the O-Shot for women are priced between $1,200 and $2,500 per session, while the P-Shot for men ranges from $1,500 to $3,000 per session. Exosome therapy for genital rejuvenation commands a price range of $3,000 to $6,000 per session, while stem cell therapy can cost between $5,000 and $10,000 per treatment. Labial puffing, a procedure that enhances the appearance and comfort of the labia majora, typically costs between $1,500 and $4,000 per session. Scrotox, which relaxes the scrotal muscles for a smoother and fuller appearance, is priced between $1,200 and $3,500 per session. Scrotal filler enhancement treatments range from $2,000 to $5,000 per session.

Revenue potential depends on patient volume and service pricing. Clinics that perform five genital rejuvenation treatments per week at an average cost of $2,000 per session can generate $40,000 per month, translating to an annual revenue of $480,000. With ten patients per week, including high-end treatments such as stem cell and exosome therapy, monthly revenue can reach $100,000, or $1.2 million annually. A full-service intimate rejuvenation clinic treating twenty patients per week can generate over $200,000 per month, or more than $2.5 million per year.

Profit margins for these treatments are significant. PRP therapy has a profit margin of 60% to 85%, given its low material costs and high treatment pricing. Exosome and stem cell therapy yield profit margins of 50% to 75%, as they involve higher material costs but also command premium pricing. Dermal filler and Scrotox treatments have a profit margin of 55% to 80%, depending on the cost of injectables and service pricing. Most salons and clinics can expect to break even within six months to two years, depending on service volume and pricing.

Advances in Cosmetology

There are several key benefits to integrating genital rejuvenation treatments into a salon or medical spa. These services are in high demand, with many clients willing to pay premium prices for intimate health and aesthetic enhancement. The procedures are non-surgical, requiring minimal downtime for clients, making them attractive to busy professionals. Many of these treatments require maintenance sessions, ensuring long-term client retention and recurring revenue. Additionally, offering cutting-edge regenerative therapies differentiates a clinic from competitors, positioning it as an advanced aesthetic centre that attracts a high-end clientele.

Despite the lucrative potential, clinics must navigate certain challenges. Regulatory and legal compliance is essential, as clinics must adhere to medical guidelines, FDA approvals, and local regulations concerning stem cell and injectable treatments. Specialist training and certification are also critical, requiring professionals to undergo advanced education in regenerative medicine, PRP therapy, and aesthetic injectables. Since intimate rejuvenation is a sensitive topic, client education and targeted marketing strategies are crucial for attracting the right demographic. Finally, the initial investment costs for equipment and training can be substantial, requiring financial planning and strategic business positioning.

Genital rejuvenation therapies represent a cutting-edge, high-profit niche within the aesthetics industry. Salons and medical spas that integrate PRP, stem cell therapy, exosome injections, and dermal fillers into their services can expect significant returns due to the rising demand for intimate health and aesthetic procedures. While the initial investment is considerable, the ability to offer premium-priced, non-surgical solutions ensures long-term financial success. As technology advances, the market for intimate aesthetic treatments will continue to expand, making this a lucrative and future-focused opportunity for aesthetic businesses.

As advancements in regenerative and injectable therapies continue to evolve, non-surgical genital rejuvenation is becoming more accessible and effective for individuals seeking aesthetic enhancement and improved intimate wellness. With ongoing research in stem cell applications, biomaterial advancements, and precision-based injectables, the future of genital cosmetology promises even more personalized, safe, and minimally invasive treatment options for both men and women.

Pigmentation Correction and Skin Brightening

Hyperpigmentation in the genital region is a prevalent concern that can significantly affect individuals' self-esteem and quality of life. Advanced cosmetology offers various safe and effective solutions for skin lightening, including chemical peels, laser treatments, and topical brightening agents.

Mild chemical peels, particularly those containing ingredients such as kojic acid, lactic acid, and arbutin, have been shown to effectively lighten darkened skin in sensitive areas, including the genital and perianal regions. These agents work by exfoliating the outer layer of the skin, thereby removing dead skin cells and promoting collagen renewal, which improves skin texture and appearance [701]. For instance, studies have demonstrated that formulations with alpha-arbutin can significantly reduce hyperpigmentation by inhibiting melanin transfer and production [702]. Furthermore, the combination of chemical peels with topical treatments can enhance the overall efficacy of pigmentation correction [703].

Laser treatments, particularly Q-switched Nd:YAG and picosecond lasers, are increasingly utilized for their ability to target excess melanin effectively. These laser technologies provide a permanent solution for skin lightening with minimal downtime, making them suitable for delicate areas [704]. Research indicates that these lasers can selectively destroy melanin without damaging surrounding tissues, thus offering a safe option for individuals seeking to reduce hyperpigmentation in intimate areas [704]. The precision of these lasers allows for tailored treatments that can address specific pigmentation concerns while minimizing the risk of adverse effects [704].

Topical formulations containing active ingredients such as glutathione, niacinamide, and tranexamic acid have gained popularity for their skin-brightening properties. Niacinamide, in particular, has been shown to decrease hyperpigmentation by inhibiting melanosome transfer and providing anti-inflammatory benefits [705, 706]. Studies have reported that consistent use of niacinamide can lead to a significant reduction in skin discoloration, making it an effective option for treating hyperpigmentation in sensitive areas [706]. Additionally, glutathione has been recognized for its antioxidant properties, which contribute to skin lightening by reducing oxidative stress and melanin production [701]. Tranexamic acid has also emerged as a promising agent in the treatment of melasma and other forms of hyperpigmentation, demonstrating efficacy in clinical trials [701, 704].

Salons and aesthetic clinics incorporating these treatments can expect strong demand, particularly among clients looking for non-invasive solutions for intimate skin concerns. While initial equipment and training costs are required, these treatments offer high profit margins and recurring revenue from maintenance sessions and skincare product sales.

Chemical peels designed for intimate skin lightening require specialized formulations with mild acids and active ingredients that safely target pigmentation without causing irritation. Essential equipment includes: A selection of chemical peels containing kojic acid, lactic acid, mandelic acid, and arbutin costs between $50 and $300 per bottle, depending on the brand and formulation. Application tools such as brushes, fan applicators, and peel neutralizers cost approximately $200 to $500 for a complete set. Disposable gloves, cotton pads, and protective gear are necessary for safety and cost around $500 to $1,500 annually. A cooling or soothing post-treatment serum with ingredients like aloe vera and hyaluronic acid is essential, costing between $200 and $1,000 per year. Professional training in intimate-area chemical peels is required for safe and effective application, with certification courses ranging from $1,500 to $5,000.

Laser technology is a highly effective method for treating hyperpigmentation in intimate areas, offering long-lasting results by breaking down excess melanin. Clinics providing laser skin brightening treatments must invest in high-quality laser equipment.

A Q-switched Nd:YAG laser system, suitable for targeting melanin and correcting pigmentation in sensitive areas, costs between $50,000 and $120,000. Picosecond laser systems, which offer faster and more precise pigment removal with minimal downtime, range from $80,000 to $150,000. Laser handpieces and consumables, including protective eyewear and cooling gel, add an additional annual expense of $2,000 to $5,000. Maintenance and calibration of laser equipment are crucial for ensuring optimal performance and cost between $3,000 and $10,000 per year. Certified laser training for professionals performing intimate-area pigmentation treatments is necessary and typically costs $3,000 to $10,000 per provider.

Professional-grade topical brightening products can be used as standalone treatments or in conjunction with peels and laser therapy for optimal results. Salons and clinics offering pigmentation correction often retail medical-grade skincare products for at-home maintenance.

Brightening serums and creams containing glutathione, niacinamide, tranexamic acid, and alpha-arbutin cost between $50 and $200 per unit. Bulk purchasing of professional skincare lines for in-clinic use and retail purposes requires an initial investment of $2,000 to $10,000. Skincare product storage and display units add another $500 to $2,000.

Pigmentation correction treatments offer high revenue potential, with clients often requiring multiple sessions for optimal results.

Chemical peels for intimate areas typically cost between $150 and $400 per session. A complete treatment package of three to six sessions is priced at $600 to $2,000. Laser pigmentation removal is a premium service, with individual sessions costing between $300 and $800, depending on the laser type and treatment area. Full treatment packages with three to five sessions can range from $1,500 to $4,000. Custom topical brightening regimens for at-home use can generate additional revenue, with product bundles ranging from $150 to $500 per client.

Revenue potential depends on patient volume and treatment offerings. A salon performing ten chemical peel sessions per week at an average price of $250 per session can generate $10,000 per month, translating to $120,000 annually. Offering laser pigmentation treatments to five clients per week at an average session price of $600 can result in $12,000 in monthly revenue, or $144,000 per year. Combining both chemical peels and laser treatments for a full-service intimate brightening program could generate $250,000 to $500,000 in annual revenue.

Advances in Cosmetology

Chemical peel treatments offer a high profit margin of 65% to 85%, given the relatively low cost of products and materials. Laser pigmentation removal has a profit margin of 60% to 80%, factoring in equipment costs and maintenance. The retail sale of topical brightening agents provides an additional revenue stream with a profit margin of 50% to 70%. Most clinics can expect to break even within six months to two years, depending on patient volume and service pricing.

Intimate-area pigmentation correction is a growing market, with increasing awareness and demand for safe and effective treatments. The ability to offer multiple solutions, including chemical peels, laser treatments, and topical brightening products, allows salons to cater to a wider range of clients. These treatments require minimal downtime, making them attractive to clients who prefer non-invasive solutions. Many clients seek maintenance treatments, ensuring long-term retention and repeat business.

Regulatory compliance for laser treatments and chemical peels is essential, requiring clinics to obtain proper certifications and adhere to safety guidelines. Professional training is necessary to ensure effective and safe treatment application, particularly for intimate-area procedures. Targeted marketing and client education are required to address the sensitivity of these treatments and attract the right demographic. High initial investment costs for laser technology may require financial planning and a strategic approach to pricing and service bundling.

Pigmentation correction and skin brightening treatments for intimate areas represent a lucrative and rapidly growing niche in the aesthetics industry. Salons and clinics that invest in chemical peels, laser pigmentation removal, and professional-grade skincare products can expect strong demand and high profit margins. While the initial costs for equipment and training are considerable, the ability to offer premium-priced services ensures long-term financial success. As client awareness and demand for safe, effective solutions continue to grow, salons that integrate these treatments into their service offerings will be well-positioned for sustained profitability and industry leadership.

Hair Removal and Grooming Innovations

Advancements in hair removal and grooming technology have introduced more effective, long-lasting, and non-invasive methods to enhance aesthetics and hygiene in the intimate areas. Traditional hair removal techniques such as shaving and waxing can cause irritation, ingrown hairs, and discomfort. Newer technologies, including laser hair removal, electrolysis, and intimate hair transplants, offer improved solutions that cater to different needs and preferences. These treatments are particularly beneficial for individuals seeking permanent hair reduction, gender-affirming procedures, or restoration of pubic hair due to aging or medical conditions.

Laser hair removal is one of the most advanced and widely used methods for permanent hair reduction in intimate areas. It uses laser energy to target melanin in hair follicles, destroying them at the root while preventing future growth. Diode and Alexandrite laser technologies are among the most effective for treating the sensitive genital region, providing long-lasting results with minimal discomfort.

Diode lasers operate at a wavelength of 810nm, allowing deeper penetration into the skin while minimizing damage to surrounding tissues. They are particularly effective for darker skin tones and thick, coarse hair, making them an excellent choice for intimate-area hair removal. Alexandrite lasers use a 755nm wavelength, which is highly effective for individuals with lighter skin tones. This laser provides faster treatment sessions and a higher absorption rate in melanin, making it ideal for fine and lighter-coloured hairs.

Laser hair removal significantly reduces the risk of ingrown hairs, irritation, and razor burns commonly caused by shaving or waxing. Most clients require multiple sessions, typically spaced four to six weeks apart, to achieve optimal results. After six to eight treatments, hair growth is permanently reduced by up to 90%. This method is popular among individuals looking for a smooth, hair-free appearance or those who want to minimize maintenance in intimate grooming.

Electrolysis is the only FDA-approved method for permanent hair removal, making it a preferred choice for individuals seeking complete removal of pubic hair. Unlike laser hair removal, which targets the pigment in hair follicles, electrolysis works by delivering an electrical current directly into each hair follicle, permanently destroying its ability to regrow.

This method is highly effective for all skin tones and hair colours, as it does not rely on melanin absorption. Electrolysis is particularly beneficial for individuals with light, blonde, grey, or red pubic hair, which may not respond well to laser treatments. It is also an essential procedure in gender-affirming treatments, as some transgender individuals opt for complete removal of pubic hair to align with their gender identity.

Because electrolysis treats one hair follicle at a time, the process is more time-consuming than laser hair removal. However, it provides permanent results, ensuring that hair will never grow back once the follicle is fully treated. Patients typically require multiple sessions over several months to achieve full clearance, depending on the density and thickness of the hair.

For individuals experiencing pubic hair thinning due to aging, hormonal changes, or medical conditions, follicular unit extraction (FUE) hair transplants can restore natural-looking hair in the genital area. This procedure involves harvesting healthy hair follicles from a donor site, typically the scalp, and transplanting them into the pubic region.

Pubic hair thinning can occur due to factors such as aging, menopause, excessive laser hair removal, or certain medical conditions like alopecia. FUE hair transplants allow patients to regain a fuller and more youthful appearance in the intimate area. This procedure is also useful for individuals who naturally have sparse or uneven pubic hair and desire a more symmetrical and aesthetically pleasing look.

During the procedure, individual hair follicles are carefully extracted from the donor area and implanted into the recipient site using microsurgical techniques. The newly transplanted hair grows naturally, mimicking the texture and direction of existing pubic hair. Results are permanent, with full hair growth appearing within six to twelve months.

Hair removal and grooming innovations provide more effective and long-term solutions for individuals seeking to enhance the appearance and hygiene of their intimate areas. Laser hair removal offers a semi-permanent and low-maintenance solution for hair reduction, while electrolysis provides a permanent option for complete hair removal. For those experiencing hair loss in the genital area, FUE hair transplants offer a restorative solution that provides natural and lasting results. As technology continues to advance, these treatments will become even more precise, comfortable, and accessible, catering to a diverse range of personal preferences and aesthetic goals.

The integration of laser hair removal, electrolysis, and intimate hair transplants into a salon or medical spa requires specialized equipment, trained professionals, and strict hygiene and safety standards. While the initial investment is substantial, these treatments are high-demand services with strong profitability, particularly in the niche market of intimate grooming and gender-affirming procedures.

Laser Hair Removal for the Genital Area requires medical-grade laser systems capable of targeting coarse and sensitive-area hair with precision. The choice of laser technology, such as Diode or Alexandrite lasers, affects both the efficacy and cost of treatments. A Diode Laser Hair Removal Machine costs between $50,000 and $150,000, while an Alexandrite Laser Hair Removal Machine ranges from $75,000 to $200,000. Protective eyewear and cooling devices add an additional $1,000 to $5,000, with laser handpieces and replacement parts costing $2,000 to $10,000 per year. Professional certification and training for laser technicians require a one-time investment of $3,000 to $7,000, and regulatory compliance and licensing fees vary between $2,000 and $10,000.

Electrolysis for Permanent Hair Removal is a more precise and permanent solution for clients who want complete removal of pubic hair, including those undergoing gender-affirming treatments. This method requires high-quality electrolysis machines and fine probes. A professional-grade FDA-approved electrolysis machine costs between $5,000 and $15,000, while disposable electrolysis probes and needles range from $500 to $3,000 per year. Topical anaesthetics for pain management require an annual budget of $500 to $2,000. Professional electrolysis certification and training cost a one-time fee of $2,000 to $5,000, with sterilization equipment and hygiene supplies adding an annual expense of $1,500 to $5,000.

Intimate Hair Transplants (FUE Technique) require highly specialized equipment and trained professionals with experience in follicular unit extraction (FUE) procedures. While this service requires the highest initial investment, it offers one of the highest returns due to its premium pricing. An FUE Hair Transplant Machine such as ARTAS or Neograft Systems costs between $100,000 and $300,000, while microsurgical tools for follicle extraction and implantation range from $5,000 to $20,000. Local anesthetic and numbing agents add an annual cost of $2,000 to $5,000. Medical-grade operating chairs and magnification loupes cost between $10,000 and $25,000. Advanced training for FUE hair transplant specialists requires a one-time investment of $10,000 to $25,000, while regulatory compliance and medical licensing cost $5,000 to $20,000 annually.

Hair removal and grooming treatments are in high demand, with clients willing to pay a premium for permanent and non-invasive solutions. The revenue per treatment varies depending on the service offered. Laser hair removal for the genital area is priced between $250 and $600 per session. Electrolysis for permanent hair removal costs $75 to $250 per hour. A full FUE intimate hair transplant procedure is priced between $4,000 and $10,000. Maintenance and follow-up treatments for laser or electrolysis touch-ups cost between $150 and $400 per session.

The revenue potential depends on the volume of clients and the pricing structure. A salon offering laser hair removal services to 10 clients per week at an average price of $400 per session can generate $16,000 per month, equating to $192,000 per year. An electrolysis clinic treating five clients per week, with each session lasting three hours at $150 per hour, can generate $9,000 per month or $108,000 per year. A salon offering three intimate hair transplant procedures per month at an average cost of $6,000 per procedure can generate $18,000 per month, totalling $216,000 per year. A comprehensive intimate grooming clinic offering all three services has the potential to generate over $500,000 annually.

The profit margins for these treatments vary based on service type. Laser hair removal has a profit margin of 60% to 85%, given its low consumable costs and high demand. Electrolysis has a profit margin of 50% to 70%, as it is labour-intensive but highly specialized. Intimate hair transplants yield a profit margin of 70% to 90%, given the high revenue per procedure and premium clientele.

The break-even period for these treatments ranges from six months to three years, depending on the size of the clinic and the investment in equipment.

The high demand and niche market for permanent hair removal and grooming services make these treatments a valuable addition to salons and medical spas. Recurring clientele is another major advantage, as laser hair removal and electrolysis require multiple sessions, ensuring repeat business. Premium pricing potential is another benefit, as hair transplants and permanent removal treatments attract high-paying clients. The relatively low competition in this field offers an opportunity for salons to differentiate themselves, as many only offer basic waxing services and do not provide advanced solutions such as electrolysis and intimate hair transplants.

Non-Surgical Genital Lifting and Tightening

As aesthetic medicine continues to evolve, non-surgical options for genital rejuvenation, including thread lifting and Botox injections (Scrotox), have gained traction among individuals seeking to enhance the firmness and appearance of their intimate areas without the need for invasive surgery. These procedures effectively address concerns such as skin laxity, wrinkles, and overall tissue support in both women and men.

Thread lifting, particularly with Polydioxanone (PDO) threads, is a minimally invasive technique that provides immediate lifting effects while promoting collagen production for long-term tissue enhancement. This procedure is particularly beneficial for women experiencing labial laxity due to factors such as childbirth or hormonal changes. The insertion of PDO threads beneath the labia majora restores firmness and improves contour, leading to a more youthful appearance [682, 707]. In men, PDO threads can also be utilized to tighten and lift the scrotal area, addressing concerns of sagging skin and enhancing aesthetic appeal [682]. The procedure is quick, typically lasting between 30 to 60 minutes, and involves minimal downtime, allowing patients to resume normal activities shortly after treatment [682, 707].

Scrotox, or the injection of Botulinum toxin into the scrotal area, has emerged as a popular non-surgical option for enhancing the aesthetic and functional aspects of the male genitalia. Originally developed for medical conditions such as scrotal pain and hyperhidrosis, Scrotox works by relaxing the cremaster muscles, which can reduce wrinkles and create a smoother appearance [707, 708]. This treatment not only enhances the aesthetic appeal of the scrotum but also improves comfort by alleviating excessive tightness and reducing sweating [707, 708]. The procedure is quick, typically taking around 20 minutes, with results visible within a few days and lasting approximately three to six months [707, 708].

While both thread lifting and Scrotox serve the purpose of genital rejuvenation, they target different aspects. Thread lifting is primarily focused on addressing skin laxity and providing long-term collagen benefits, making it ideal for individuals seeking a more permanent solution to sagging tissue [682, 707]. In contrast, Scrotox is best suited for those looking for a quick, temporary solution to improve the smoothness and appearance of the scrotum [707, 708]. Some patients may choose to combine both treatments to achieve comprehensive aesthetic enhancement of the genital area [707, 708].

The rise of non-surgical genital lifting and tightening procedures reflects a growing demand for safe, effective, and minimally invasive alternatives to surgical interventions. Both PDO thread lifting and Scrotox offer unique benefits that cater to the aesthetic needs of individuals seeking rejuvenation in their intimate areas. As these treatments continue to evolve, they provide advanced and personalized solutions for enhancing confidence and comfort without the risks associated with traditional surgery [682, 707, 708].

Expanding a salon or medical spa to include non-surgical genital rejuvenation treatments such as PDO thread lifting for labia and scrotal tightening and Scrotox (Botulinum toxin for scrotal relaxation) requires investment in specialized equipment, certified training, and compliance with aesthetic medical regulations. While the initial costs can be substantial, these services cater to a high-end clientele and generate significant returns due to premium pricing and repeat treatments.

Thread lifting requires biodegradable PDO threads, precision-based injection tools, and sterilized surgical instruments to ensure safe and effective tissue tightening. PDO thread lift kits come in various sizes and types, typically costing between $500 and $3,000 per batch. Sterile cannulas and needles for thread placement range from $500 to $2,000 per year, while local anaesthetics such as lidocaine or numbing creams cost between $300 and $1,500 annually. Medical-grade surgical instruments, including forceps, scissors, and retractors, range from $1,500 to $5,000.

LED or magnification lamps for precision work cost between $500 and $2,000, while sterilization and disinfection equipment such as autoclaves and medical-grade wipes range from $2,000 to $5,000. Certification and advanced training for PDO thread lifting is a one-time investment of $3,000 to $10,000. Regulatory compliance and licensing fees vary by region, typically ranging from $1,500 to $5,000 annually.

Scrotox requires high-quality Botulinum toxin, precision syringes, and medical-grade injection tools to ensure accurate placement and effective results. Each vial of Botulinum toxin (Botox or Dysport) costs between $400 and $1,000 per treatment. Sterile syringes and fine-gauge needles for injection range from $500 to $2,000 per year. Cooling or numbing devices for client comfort cost between $200 and $1,500 annually, while gloves, alcohol wipes, and post-treatment creams range from $1,000 to $3,000 per year.

Professional training in Botox injection techniques is a one-time investment of $2,000 to $7,000. Medical licensing and compliance fees are required annually, costing between $2,000 and $5,000. These investments ensure that practitioners can safely and effectively perform Scrotox injections with minimal risks.

Non-surgical genital lifting and tightening services command premium pricing due to the specialized nature of the procedures. PDO thread lifts for labial tightening range from $2,000 to $5,000 per session, while PDO thread lifts for scrotal tightening range from $1,500 to $4,500 per session. Scrotox injections cost between $1,200 and $3,500 per session, with combination treatments of thread lifting and Scrotox priced between $3,500 and $7,000 per session. Maintenance or follow-up sessions range from $800 to $2,500 per session.

The profitability of these treatments depends on client volume, pricing strategy, and treatment frequency. A clinic treating five thread lift patients per week at an average of $3,500 per session can generate approximately $70,000 per month, equating to $840,000 annually. Five Scrotox patients per week at $2,000 per session can bring in $40,000 per month or $480,000 per year. Clinics offering combination procedures to four clients per week at $5,000 per session can generate an additional $56,000 per month or $672,000 per year. A high-end aesthetic clinic offering a full range of non-surgical genital rejuvenation treatments has the potential to generate over $1 million in annual revenue.

PDO thread lifting has a profit margin of 60% to 85% due to low material costs and high treatment pricing. Scrotox procedures have a profit margin of 50% to 75%, with higher product costs but repeat treatments that boost long-term revenue. Combination treatments yield a profit margin of 65% to 85%, as higher pricing justifies increased profitability. The break-even period for these investments typically ranges from six months to two years, depending on service volume, pricing structure, and clinic marketing efforts.

Legal Aspects of Intimate Area Treatments

Non-surgical genital rejuvenation treatments, including laser and radiofrequency procedures, are increasingly popular but are subject to varying regulations across the globe. In the United States, the Food and Drug Administration (FDA) has raised concerns regarding the marketing of energy-based devices for "vaginal rejuvenation." The FDA has highlighted potential risks associated with these devices, such as burns, scarring, and pain, and has emphasized that these devices have not been approved for such indications [709]. Furthermore, the FDA cautions against their use for these purposes, underscoring the need for regulatory oversight in the realm of cosmetic procedures [709].

In the United Kingdom, the government has acknowledged the fragmented regulatory landscape surrounding non-surgical cosmetic procedures. There are ongoing efforts to establish a licensing scheme aimed at ensuring that practitioners adhere to specific training and hygiene standards. High-risk procedures, particularly those involving the genitalia, are proposed to be restricted to qualified and regulated healthcare professionals, reflecting a growing recognition of the need for stringent regulatory frameworks in this area.

Richard Skiba

The American College of Obstetricians and Gynecologists (ACOG) has also voiced concerns regarding female genital cosmetic surgeries, including non-surgical interventions. ACOG advises that these procedures lack sufficient evidence supporting their safety and efficacy, recommending that patients be thoroughly informed about potential risks and benefits before undergoing such treatments. This caution is echoed by the Royal Australian and New Zealand College of Obstetricians and Gynaecologists (RANZCOG), which has publicly opposed female genital cosmetic surgery, emphasizing the necessity for standardized nomenclature and cautioning against procedures that lack robust evidence of safety and effectiveness.

Given the evolving regulatory landscape and the potential risks associated with non-surgical genital rejuvenation treatments, it is crucial for individuals to consult with qualified healthcare professionals. Patients should consider current guidelines and regulations in their specific regions before proceeding with such procedures, as the lack of standardization and oversight can lead to significant health risks.

Chapter 11

Advances in Makeup Artistry

The makeup industry continues to evolve with advancements and innovations that enhance product performance, sustainability, and customization. Emerging trends focus on smart beauty technology, skincare-infused formulations, and eco-conscious products, shaping the future of cosmetics.

The global makeup industry is a dynamic and multifaceted market, currently valued at approximately $85 billion USD and projected to experience steady growth driven by evolving consumer preferences, technological advancements, and a rising demand for sustainable and personalized beauty products. The industry is significantly influenced by trends in clean beauty, artificial intelligence (AI) for customization, and hybrid formulations that merge skincare with makeup [580, 710]. The integration of social media and influencer marketing has also reshaped consumer engagement, making beauty products more accessible and appealing to a broader audience [580, 711].

The global cosmetics market was valued at approximately $295.95 billion in 2023 and is projected to grow at a Compound Annual Growth Rate (CAGR) of 6.1% from 2024 to 2030 [712]. This steady growth is driven by increasing consumer awareness of personal grooming and self-care, the rising popularity of clean beauty, and the integration of technological innovations into cosmetic products. Millennials, in particular, are fuelling demand for skincare, colour cosmetics, and hair care, incorporating these products into their daily routines. Additionally, the introduction of cosmetics featuring natural, organic, and non-toxic ingredients has further contributed to market expansion.

The cosmetics industry includes a diverse range of personal care products (PCPs) such as skincare, hair care, UV protection creams, facial cleansers, fragrances, and grooming essentials. Reports suggest that nearly 30-40% of dermatological prescriptions include a personal care product, and the average consumer uses at least two personal care products every 24 hours [712].

Skincare dominates the cosmetics market, accounting for 43.3% of total revenue in 2023, as consumers increasingly prioritize skin health and anti-aging solutions. Hair care is another key segment projected to grow at a CAGR of 7.0%, with brands like Drunk Elephant and The Inkey List pioneering innovative hair and scalp treatments [712].

The cosmetics market is highly concentrated, with established brands controlling significant market share due to their strong manufacturing capabilities, extensive distribution networks, and brand loyalty. However, indie and niche brands continue to disrupt the market by launching customized, sustainable, and technology-driven beauty solutions [712].

The shift toward sustainable and eco-friendly beauty has transformed consumer behaviour, with 78% of consumers prioritizing sustainability in 2023 [712]. Approximately 55% of consumers are willing to pay a premium for eco-conscious brands, favouring companies that use natural, ethical, and environmentally safe ingredients [712].

Consumers are also drawn to clean beauty products free from parabens, sulphates, and synthetic chemicals. This shift has encouraged major brands to invest in sustainable packaging, biodegradable ingredients, and refillable cosmetic solutions. Brands incorporating organic components such as green tea, ginseng, aloe vera, and botanical extracts have gained a competitive edge in the market [712].

Women's cosmetics accounted for 62.9% of the global market revenue in 2023. Social media, beauty influencers, and celebrity-backed brands have significantly shaped purchasing decisions. Major celebrity-owned brands such as Fenty Beauty (Rihanna), Rare Beauty (Selena Gomez), and Haus Labs (Lady Gaga) have capitalized on inclusivity and clean beauty trends, further fuelling market growth [712].

Figure 21: Photoshoot makeup application. Unsplash. CC0, via Picryl.

The men's cosmetics segment is experiencing significant growth, driven by increasing awareness of skincare, grooming, and personal hygiene. A 2022 study by the Global Cosmetic Industry found that 27% of men were dissatisfied with their current skincare products, indicating a demand for better formulations tailored to male consumers [712]. Furthermore, 52% of men reported purchasing more colour cosmetics than they did five years ago, reflecting a cultural shift in attitudes toward male grooming [712].

The cosmetics industry continues to evolve in response to changing shopping habits, with both offline and online retail playing significant roles in market expansion [712]. Traditional retail channels, including department stores, specialty beauty stores, and pharmacies, accounted for 72.2% of global cosmetics sales in 2023. Consumers prefer purchasing beauty products in physical stores to test textures, scents, and shades, especially for skincare and fragrance items [712].

The online cosmetics market is expected to grow at a high CAGR, as brands and retailers invest in digital platforms, virtual try-ons, and AI-powered personalization. Sephora, Ulta Beauty, and major brands have launched dedicated sections on their websites to showcase new product releases and enhance the customer shopping experience. Additionally, social commerce on platforms like TikTok, Instagram, and Xiaohongshu (China's Little Red Book) is reshaping how consumers discover and purchase cosmetics [712].

The North American cosmetics market, particularly the United States, accounted for 23.8% of the global market share in 2023. Growth is fuelled by self-enhancement trends, social media influence, and high disposable income. The presence of established beauty giants like L'Oréal, Procter & Gamble, and Estée Lauder further supports market expansion [712].

Europe's cosmetics market benefits from technological advancements in beauty, AI-powered skincare analysis, and virtual makeup try-ons. In 2022, Proven Skincare expanded into the EU and UK, using AI and big data analytics to develop personalized beauty solutions [712].

Asia-Pacific held the largest market share (45%) in 2023, driven by sustainable beauty trends and the influence of K-Beauty and J-Beauty. Countries such as China, South Korea, and Japan emphasize natural ingredients and holistic beauty, leading to innovations in fermented skincare, lightweight makeup, and multi-step beauty routines [712].

Cosmetic companies must adhere to strict safety and efficacy regulations to ensure product quality and consumer safety. Non-compliance can result in legal penalties, product recalls, and damage to brand reputation. The prevalence of counterfeit cosmetics presents a major challenge. Low-cost fake beauty products often contain harmful ingredients, posing health risks to consumers and affecting the sales of legitimate brands [712].

With numerous brands entering the industry, competition remains intense. To stay relevant, companies must focus on product innovation, digital marketing, and customer engagement. The launch of new collections, limited-edition collaborations, and personalized beauty solutions helps brands maintain consumer interest and loyalty [712].

In January 2024, L'Oréal's venture capital division, BOLD (Business Opportunities for L'Oréal Development), invested in Timeline, a consumer health company focused on aging and longevity science. This collaboration aims to integrate skincare supplements and advanced dermatological solutions into L'Oréal's product portfolio [712].

In December 2023, Estée Lauder partnered with Stanford University's Center for Longevity to fund research into aging, wellness, and aesthetic perceptions, reinforcing the industry's commitment to science-backed beauty innovations [712].

The cosmetics market is poised for continuous growth, driven by clean beauty trends, AI-powered personalization, and digital innovations. As sustainability becomes a defining factor in consumer choices, brands that invest in eco-friendly packaging, cruelty-free formulations, and ethical sourcing will gain a competitive edge [712].

With the rise of beauty tech, hybrid skincare-makeup formulations, and inclusive beauty campaigns, the global cosmetics industry is set to evolve into a more personalized, technology-driven, and socially conscious market. The increasing influence of e-commerce, direct-to-consumer brands, and influencer marketing will further reshape how beauty products are developed, marketed, and sold in the years ahead [712].

The makeup market is segmented into various product categories, including foundations, lipsticks, and eyeshadows, with a notable rise in hybrid products that offer skincare benefits alongside cosmetic functions. This trend reflects a consumer shift towards multifunctional beauty solutions, such as tinted moisturizers with SPF and serum-infused foundations [713]. Luxury brands like Chanel and Dior dominate the high-end segment, while mass-market brands such as Maybelline and L'Oréal provide affordable alternatives. Additionally, indie brands like Fenty Beauty and Rare Beauty have disrupted traditional market dynamics by focusing on inclusivity and cruelty-free formulations [714-716].

Regionally, the makeup industry exhibits distinct characteristics. In North America, particularly the United States, there is a strong emphasis on clean beauty and innovative technologies, with brands leveraging AI for personalized beauty solutions. The influence of celebrity endorsements and social media marketing is profound, with brands like Glossier and Fenty Beauty leading the charge in inclusive marketing strategies [710, 711]. In Europe, luxury brands are complemented by a growing focus on sustainability, with strict regulations promoting eco-friendly practices and biodegradable packaging [713, 714]. The Asia-Pacific region, especially South Korea and Japan, is a trendsetter in beauty innovations, with K-Beauty and J-Beauty emphasizing lightweight, skincare-infused products [713, 714].

Latin America showcases vibrant beauty trends characterized by bold colours and high-coverage products, with local brands competing effectively against international giants by tailoring products to regional preferences [714, 715]. The Middle East and Africa are emerging markets for luxury and halal-certified cosmetics, reflecting cultural preferences and the demand for high-performance products [714, 716].

The future outlook for the global makeup industry is optimistic, with sustainability, customization, and technological advancements at the forefront. Emerging trends such as biodegradable glitter and AI-driven skin analysis are set to redefine consumer experiences, while social media continues to play a crucial role in shaping beauty standards and purchasing behaviours [580, 710].

AI and Smart Beauty Technology

The integration of artificial intelligence (AI) and augmented reality (AR) into the beauty industry has significantly transformed consumer experiences, particularly in the selection, customization, and application of makeup products. These technologies have made beauty products more personalized, accessible, and convenient, allowing consumers to experiment with various shades and products virtually, thereby reducing the risk of purchasing unsuitable items and enhancing the overall shopping experience.

Advances in Cosmetology

AI-powered shade matching and customization tools have revolutionized how consumers identify their ideal makeup products. Traditional methods of swatching in-store are increasingly being supplanted by personalized AI recommendations that consider skin tone, undertone, and individual preferences. For instance, L'Oréal's Perso is an innovative device that utilizes AI to analyse a user's skin tone and environmental factors such as humidity and UV exposure to create custom skincare and foundation blends. This technology not only adapts to the user's skin over time but also ensures a tailored makeup experience [717, 718]. Similarly, YSL's Rouge Sur Mesure allows users to mix custom lipstick shades at home, drawing inspiration from fashion trends or personal moods, thus offering a virtually limitless palette of colour options [718, 719]. These innovations exemplify how AI facilitates hyper-personalization, empowering consumers to achieve their desired makeup looks with precision and real-time adjustments [720].

Augmented reality has further enhanced the beauty shopping experience through virtual try-on technologies, which allow consumers to test makeup products without physical application. Major beauty brands like Sephora and MAC have integrated AR tools into their platforms to improve customer engagement and satisfaction. For example, Sephora's Virtual Artist, developed in collaboration with ModiFace, enables users to visualize how different makeup products will appear on their faces using their smartphone cameras. This tool not only mitigates the issue of shade mismatching but also boosts consumer confidence during online shopping [721, 722]. The YouCam Makeup app, powered by Perfect Corp, employs facial recognition technology to provide accurate shade recommendations by analysing skin texture and undertones, thereby enhancing the virtual try-on experience [721, 722]. Such AR applications not only promote hygiene by reducing the need for physical testers but also foster greater interaction between consumers and beauty brands [722, 723].

Beauty salons can integrate AI-powered shade matching and virtual consultations to provide tailored beauty services. AI-driven tools like L'Oréal's Perso and YSL Rouge Sur Mesure can help salons analyse clients' skin tones, undertones, and environmental factors, offering personalized recommendations for foundations, skincare treatments, and lip colors. This level of customization allows salons to provide bespoke makeup applications that adapt to individual needs.

Salons can use AR-powered virtual try-on tools to enhance client experiences. AR technology, such as Sephora's Virtual Artist and YouCam Makeup, enables customers to test different makeup looks in real time without physical application. Salons can implement these features during makeup consultations, allowing clients to preview looks before booking services for weddings, special events, or makeovers. This reduces guesswork and increases client confidence in beauty decisions.

Consumers can use AI-powered shade-matching tools to find the perfect foundation, concealer, and lipstick shades without relying on in-store swatching. Devices like L'Oréal Perso offer real-time shade recommendations by analysing skin tone and environmental factors, ensuring an accurate match for changing skin conditions. This eliminates the frustration of purchasing the wrong shade, making beauty routines more efficient and precise.

With the rise of online beauty shopping, consumers can test makeup products virtually using AR-powered try-on tools like Perfect Corp and Sephora Virtual Artist. These platforms allow users to experiment with different shades and styles before making a purchase, reducing returns and improving the overall shopping experience. Virtual try-ons also encourage users to explore new makeup trends confidently without commitment.

The advent of 3D printing technology in the beauty sector is also noteworthy, as it allows for unprecedented levels of product customization and sustainability. Companies like Mink have pioneered portable 3D makeup printers that enable users to create eyeshadows, lipsticks, and foundations in any desired shade by extracting colours from digital images. This innovation not only minimizes product waste but also offers consumers a wide array of colour choices tailored to their preferences [717, 718]. Other startups are exploring ways to 3D print customizable foundation textures and skincare formulations using non-toxic ingredients, thus promoting environmentally friendly practices in beauty consumption [717, 718]. The integration of 3D printing into the beauty industry signifies a shift towards more sustainable and cost-effective production methods, allowing consumers to generate specific colours and formulations on demand [717, 718].

Advances in Cosmetology

The rise of 3D printing in beauty allows salons to offer custom makeup formulations tailored to individual client needs. Mink's 3D makeup printer enables salons to create unique eyeshadows, lipsticks, and foundations, giving customers a fully personalized experience. By offering 3D-printed makeup, salons can eliminate excess inventory, reduce waste, and provide exclusive, on-demand beauty products. Additionally, customized 3D-printed skincare formulations can enhance spa treatments, offering clients precisely blended serums and face masks.

3D printing allows consumers to create their own custom beauty products at home. Mink's 3D makeup printer lets users print personalized eyeshadows, lipsticks, and foundations based on their unique preferences. This enables full control over color selection, texture, and finish, catering to individualized makeup needs. 3D-printed skincare products also provide customized serums and masks tailored to specific skin concerns.

With growing consumer demand for sustainability, salons can use AI and 3D printing to reduce product waste and adopt eco-friendly beauty solutions. AI-driven formulations optimize product usage, ensuring minimal waste, while 3D printing eliminates excess packaging and overproduction. Salons that promote sustainable, high-tech beauty solutions can attract environmentally conscious clients and differentiate themselves in a competitive market.

AI can analyse customer data to predict beauty trends, optimize product recommendations, and enhance marketing strategies. By integrating AI-powered customer insights, salons can track consumer preferences, skincare needs, and makeup trends to offer highly targeted promotions and personalized beauty experiences. AI-powered chatbots and virtual assistants can also streamline customer service by handling appointment bookings and beauty consultations online.

By adopting AI and 3D-printed beauty solutions, consumers can embrace sustainable and waste-free beauty routines. AI-generated custom formulations reduce the need for excessive product purchases, while 3D printing minimizes packaging waste. Personalized beauty solutions also ensure long-term cost savings, as users no longer need to buy multiple products to find the perfect match.

Beyond makeup, AI-driven tools offer real-time skin and hair analysis to help consumers make informed beauty decisions. Apps like L'Oreal's AI skincare assistant assess skin texture, hydration levels, and aging signs, recommending personalized skincare routines and treatments. AI-driven haircare solutions help users select customized shampoos, conditioners, and treatments based on hair type and scalp conditions.

The integration of artificial intelligence (AI), augmented reality (AR), and 3D printing in the beauty industry has significantly enhanced the level of personalization and customization available to consumers. Salons and beauty professionals investing in these technologies can offer AI-driven shade matching, virtual try-ons, and 3D-printed makeup formulations. However, to implement these innovations, they must acquire the necessary equipment, software, and training while also accounting for ongoing maintenance and compliance costs.

To provide AI-powered skin analysis, custom foundation blends, and virtual consultations, salons require specialized devices and software solutions. L'Oréal Perso, an AI-driven skin analysis and formulation device, costs between $300 and $1,000 per unit. The YSL Rouge Sur Mesure lipstick customization tool is priced between $400 and $1,200 per unit. Professional AI beauty analysis software, such as YouCam Makeup, Perfect Corp, and ModiFace, requires an annual subscription that ranges from $1,500 to $5,000. Advanced AI-enabled skincare and makeup diagnostic devices, such as Foreo Skin Analyzer and HiMirror Pro, can cost between $2,000 and $10,000. Integrating these technologies with salon customer relationship management (CRM) and data analytics software incurs an additional investment of $2,000 to $10,000. To maximize efficiency and expertise, staff must undergo AI and beauty tech training, which costs between $1,000 and $5,000 as a one-time investment.

Salons can enhance client experiences by integrating AR-powered virtual try-on solutions that allow customers to preview makeup looks before physical application. Sephora Virtual Artist and Perfect Corp YouCam Makeup offer professional enterprise subscriptions priced between $5,000 and $20,000 per year. Augmented reality mirrors and smart beauty kiosks, such as ModiFace AR makeup mirrors, cost between $3,000 and $10,000 per unit. A high-resolution camera setup with professional lighting for live AI/AR consultations adds an additional expense ranging from $500 to $3,000. Businesses interested in developing custom AR beauty apps to personalize customer engagement should expect development costs between $10,000 and $50,000 or more, depending on the level of customization. To ensure seamless integration, salons may also invest in tablets or smart displays such as the iPad Pro, Microsoft Surface, or Samsung Galaxy Tab, costing between $800 and $2,500 per device.

3D printing is revolutionizing beauty by allowing professionals and consumers to create custom makeup formulations on demand. Salons can invest in the Mink 3D makeup printer, which costs between $1,200 and $5,000 per unit. For high-end customization, advanced 3D beauty printing systems that produce serums, masks, and scalp treatments range from $10,000 to $50,000. Consumables, including colour ink cartridges and 3D printing pigments, require an annual budget of $500 to $5,000. Additional investments in 3D-printed skincare formulation ingredients and customization software range from $3,000 to $10,000 annually. Training and certification for specialists in 3D-printed makeup customization costs between $2,000 and $7,000.

AI, AR, and 3D printing technologies require continuous software updates, data security measures, and regulatory compliance. The cost of annual software and AI system updates ranges from $2,000 to $10,000. Salons must also adhere to regulatory compliance and licensing fees for AI-powered beauty formulations, costing between $1,500 and $5,000 annually. Device repairs and tech support for AI and 3D beauty equipment require an additional budget of $2,000 to $7,000 per year.

The implementation of AI, AR, and 3D printing in beauty services provides high-profit margins due to their premium pricing and personalized nature. Salons that leverage these technologies can offer exclusive services that differentiate them from traditional beauty businesses.

AI-powered skin and makeup analysis consultations range from $50 to $200 per session. Custom AI-generated foundation or lipstick blends using devices like L'Oréal Perso and YSL Rouge Sur Mesure can generate revenue between $80 and $300 per product. AR virtual makeup try-on and consultation services typically cost between $40 and $150 per session. Personalized 3D-printed makeup and skincare products, such as custom lipsticks, eyeshadows, and foundations, command a price between $100 and $400 per unit. Subscription-based AI and AR beauty consultations, offering exclusive shade-matching and skincare analysis services, can be priced between $50 and $150 per month per customer.

A salon conducting ten AI-powered skin and makeup analysis sessions per week at an average price of $100 each can generate $4,000 per month, leading to an annual revenue of $48,000. Offering five custom 3D-printed makeup creations per week at $250 each can result in $5,000 in monthly revenue, or $60,000 per year. AR virtual try-on and consultation services with fifteen sessions per week, priced at $75 per session, can bring in $4,500 per month, totalling $54,000 annually. AI subscription-based salon memberships with fifty clients at $100 per month can generate $5,000 per month, or $60,000 per year. A comprehensive tech-driven beauty salon offering all of these services has the potential to generate between $250,000 and $750,000 or more in annual revenue.

AI-powered beauty consultations and skin analysis services have a profit margin ranging from 65% to 85%. AR virtual try-on and consultation services generate profit margins between 60% and 80%. Custom 3D-printed makeup and skincare products offer the highest margins, ranging from 70% to 90%. The break-even period for AI and AR beauty tools typically falls between six months and two years, depending on service volume and pricing strategy. For 3D beauty printing equipment, businesses can expect a break-even period between one and three years.

Integrating AI, AR, and 3D printing into beauty salons enables professionals to provide highly customized, technology-driven services that cater to evolving consumer preferences. These innovations not only enhance the client experience but also improve operational efficiency and revenue potential. While the initial investment in equipment, training, and software is significant, the long-term financial benefits, high profit margins, and differentiation in the competitive beauty market make this a worthwhile investment. As the demand for personalized beauty experiences continues to rise, salons that embrace these cutting-edge technologies will position themselves as industry leaders, attracting tech-savvy and high-value clientele.

Skincare-Infused and Hybrid Makeup

The modern cosmetics industry is witnessing a significant transformation characterized by the integration of skincare and makeup into multifunctional products. This trend reflects a growing consumer preference for cosmetics that not only enhance appearance but also provide skin health benefits. Research indicates that consumers are increasingly inclined to choose products that incorporate skincare-grade ingredients such as hyaluronic acid, niacinamide, peptides, and SPF into makeup formulations. These ingredients are recognized for their ability to deliver hydration, anti-aging effects, and sun protection, thereby enhancing the efficacy of cosmetic products and contributing to long-term skin health [724, 725].

One of the most notable innovations in this hybrid beauty category is the emergence of serum foundations and skin tints. These products, such as ILIA Super Serum Skin Tint SPF 40 and Fenty Beauty Eaze Drop Blurring Skin Tint, exemplify the trend by combining lightweight coverage with active skincare benefits. They are designed to provide breathable formulas that are enriched with hydrating and protective ingredients, catering to the increasing demand for makeup that feels weightless while improving the skin's overall texture and appearance [724, 725]. The incorporation of broad-spectrum sunscreens in these formulations further enhances their appeal, as they offer protection against both UV and visible light, which are known contributors to skin damage and pigmentation issues [726-728].

Lip products have evolved significantly, moving away from traditional formulations to include hydrating, treatment-infused options that nourish the lips while providing colour. Products like Dior Addict Lip Glow and Laneige Lip Sleeping Mask are prime examples, as they not only enhance lip colour but also deliver intense moisture through ingredients like shea butter and vitamin C. This evolution illustrates the industry's shift towards bridging the gap between beauty and self-care, enabling consumers to achieve long-lasting hydration without compromising on vibrancy or pigmentation [724, 725].

As this trend continues to gain momentum, more brands are embracing the concept of hybrid beauty, integrating dermatologist-approved ingredients into their formulations. The demand for makeup with skincare benefits is anticipated to rise as consumers prioritize efficiency and health-conscious beauty routines. With advancements in formulation science, the future of cosmetics is likely to witness further innovations that blur the lines between skincare and traditional makeup, making beauty products not only more effective but also more beneficial for everyday use [724, 725].

The rise of hybrid beauty, which combines skincare and makeup, has created new opportunities for cosmetologists to enhance their services. To successfully implement skincare-infused makeup innovations, salons and beauty professionals must invest in specialized equipment, a diverse product inventory, and advanced training. The level of investment required depends on the scope of services provided, ranging from personalized product consultations to professional applications using these advanced formulas.

Cosmetologists offering skincare-infused makeup services must stock high-quality products that cater to various skin types and concerns. This includes serum foundations, skin tints, SPF-infused cosmetics, hydrating lip treatments, and antioxidant-rich primers. A well-rounded product inventory should include serum foundations and skin tints from brands like ILIA, Fenty Beauty, and Kosas, with an initial stock investment ranging from $500 to $5,000. Lip treatments and tinted balms from brands such as Dior and Laneige may require an investment of $300 to $2,500. Multi-functional concealers and primers, along with custom blending pigments for personalized foundation and lipstick formulations, add an additional investment of $1,000 to $5,000.

To provide tailored skincare-infused makeup solutions, salons can integrate AI-powered skin analysis devices that assess hydration levels, skin texture, and other conditions. Devices such as the Foreo Skin Analyzer and HiMirror Pro cost between $2,000 and $10,000, while UV and hydration detection scanners for customized formulations range from $3,000 to $15,000. Handheld skin assessment tools for professional makeup artists add an investment of $500 to $3,000.

Professional-grade application tools and hygiene equipment are essential for maintaining the integrity of skincare-infused makeup. Airbrush foundation kits, which ensure a seamless application of serum foundations, range from $500 to $3,000. LED magnification mirrors with skin tone detection cost between $300 and $2,000. High-quality, hygienic makeup brushes, sponges, and medical-grade UV sterilization equipment require an additional investment of $1,000 to $5,000.

Cosmetologists looking to specialize in skincare-infused makeup should pursue advanced training and certifications to enhance their expertise. Courses in hybrid beauty formulation and application cost between $1,500 and $7,000 per specialist. Training for custom foundation and lipstick mixing techniques to offer personalized beauty services ranges from $1,000 to $5,000.

The revenue potential for skincare-infused makeup services is substantial, as consumers are willing to pay premium prices for personalized beauty solutions. Services such as skincare-infused makeup consultations and skin analysis can generate between $50 and $150 per session. Professional applications of serum foundations and tinted balms for events can bring in $80 to $300 per session. Custom-blended skincare-infused foundations and lipsticks, tailored to individual client needs, can sell for $100 to $400 per unit. Subscription-based beauty memberships, which provide monthly skincare and makeup consultations, can be priced between $50 and $150 per month per client.

A salon offering ten personalized makeup consultations per week at an average rate of $100 can generate $4,000 per month or $48,000 annually. Five custom skincare-infused makeup blends per week at $250 each can bring in $5,000 per month or $60,000 annually. If a salon performs fifteen hybrid makeup application services per week at $150 each, this equates to $9,000 per month or $108,000 annually. Subscription-based beauty memberships with fifty clients at $100 per month contribute an additional $5,000 per month or $60,000 annually. A full-service skincare-infused beauty business offering all of these services can generate an annual revenue of $200,000 to $600,000 or more.

Profit margins for these services are highly favourable, with skincare-infused makeup consultations yielding a profit margin of 65% to 85%. Custom blended skincare-infused makeup products have a profit margin between 70% and 90%, while professional applications of hybrid makeup, including foundations, lipsticks, and tints, range from 60% to 85%. The break-even period for AI-powered beauty tools and training is estimated between six months and two years, while skincare-infused product inventory typically sees a return on investment within the first year.

The increasing demand for hybrid beauty products benefits cosmetologists and salons by creating new revenue streams and enhancing customer retention. Consumers are willing to pay higher prices for personalized skincare-makeup hybrids, making these services a premium offering. Since skincare-infused cosmetics adapt to changes in skin condition over time, clients return for seasonal skin assessments, shade adjustments, and new formulations. Subscription-based beauty memberships further enhance client retention by providing monthly skincare consultations and exclusive product offerings.

Cosmetologists who integrate AI-powered skin analysis, custom blending technologies, and advanced formulations can position themselves as industry leaders. This creates a competitive advantage, attracting eco-conscious, tech-savvy clients seeking tailored beauty solutions. Additionally, sustainability is an essential factor in hybrid beauty, as custom-blended makeup formulations reduce waste and overproduction. This appeals to environmentally conscious clients looking for sustainable beauty solutions.

While the profit potential for skincare-infused makeup services is high, there are some challenges to consider. The initial investment in AI-powered skin analysis devices, custom blending tools, and premium inventory can be substantial, though returns are quick due to premium pricing. Regulatory compliance is also a key consideration, as hybrid beauty products must meet safety standards set by regulatory bodies such as the FDA in the U.S., the EMA in Europe, and the TGA in Australia. Specialized training in hybrid beauty formulations and skin physiology is essential to provide expert recommendations and ensure compliance with industry standards.

The integration of skincare-infused makeup innovations into professional beauty services is a lucrative, future-focused investment for cosmetologists. While initial costs for AI-powered tools, custom blending equipment, and premium product inventory may be high, the ability to offer hyper-personalized, skincare-makeup hybrid services ensures strong client retention, premium pricing, and long-term revenue growth. Salons that embrace this evolution in beauty will establish themselves as leaders in the cosmetics industry, catering to the increasing demand for health-conscious, customizable beauty experiences.

Long-Lasting, Sweat-Proof, and Transfer-Resistant Makeup

Advancements in formulation technology have transformed the cosmetics industry, particularly in enhancing the durability and performance of products. Modern formulations are designed to withstand challenging conditions such as sweat, humidity, and prolonged mask-wearing, which have become increasingly relevant in today's lifestyle. This shift has led to the emergence of high-performance, long-wear cosmetics that maintain their finish and vibrancy throughout the day, catering to consumer expectations for makeup that remains intact despite exposure to heat, moisture, and natural skin oils [729, 730].

One notable innovation in this realm is the development of powder-to-liquid foundation technology. This formulation combines the lightweight feel of powder with the long-lasting coverage of liquid foundations, providing a smooth and even finish that adapts to the skin's natural texture and moisture levels [731]. Additionally, waterproof mascaras have become essential in long-wear beauty, ensuring smudge-proof and flake-free lashes that endure sweat and tears. Similarly, breathable, transfer-resistant lipsticks have gained traction among consumers seeking comfortable yet durable lip colour that retains vibrancy without frequent reapplication [732].

Powder-to-liquid foundation technology is an innovative formulation that transforms from a dry powder into a smooth, liquid-like texture upon application. This advanced cosmetic technology combines the lightweight feel of a powder with the blendability and coverage of a liquid foundation, offering a unique sensory experience and long-lasting wear.

Powder-to-liquid foundations rely on a combination of volatile oils, encapsulated pigments, and water-activated ingredients that change consistency when they come into contact with the skin. The transformation process occurs due to encapsulated liquid technology, where the foundation contains microencapsulated liquid or hydrophilic (water-attracting) ingredients suspended in a dry powder form. When applied, the warmth and natural moisture of the skin break down these encapsulated droplets, releasing the liquid component and creating a smooth, fluid-like finish.

Richard Skiba

Many powder-to-liquid foundations contain volatile silicones or lightweight oils that evaporate upon application, leaving behind a soft, matte finish. This helps the formula spread seamlessly like a liquid foundation while maintaining the airiness of a powder. Additionally, these formulas often include film-forming agents that help the pigment adhere to the skin, ensuring a long-lasting effect. The binding polymers create a breathable, flexible layer that prevents creasing, oxidation, and fading throughout the day.

This foundation technology offers several key benefits. The initial powder form ensures a weightless application, making it comfortable for all-day wear. Unlike traditional powders that may appear chalky or dry, this formulation blends like a liquid and provides buildable coverage. Many powder-to-liquid foundations contain oil-absorbing ingredients like silica, making them ideal for oily and combination skin types. The formula locks onto the skin, reducing the need for touch-ups and maintaining a flawless look. Since it starts as a powder, it is often free of heavy oils and waxes, making it less likely to clog pores compared to traditional liquid foundations.

Several brands have introduced this technology into their product lines, offering unique variations to suit different skin types and preferences. Shiseido Synchro Skin Self-Refreshing Powder Foundation uses ActiveForce™ technology to maintain a fresh, natural look for hours. L'Oréal Paris Infallible Fresh Wear Foundation-in-a-Powder provides a long-wearing matte finish with the comfort of a breathable powder. Catrice One Step Skin Perfector is a hybrid formula that combines skincare benefits with the smooth application of a powder-to-liquid transformation.

As powder-to-liquid foundation technology continues to evolve, consumers can expect even more innovative formulations that offer lightweight, long-lasting, and skin-friendly benefits. This technology represents the future of hybrid makeup, bridging the gap between traditional powders and liquid foundations for a seamless and adaptable beauty experience.

A prime example of long-wear innovation is MAC's Locked Kiss Ink 24HR Lipcolor, which is engineered for ultra-long-lasting colour that resists smudging and fading. This product is particularly appealing to individuals who require their lipstick to remain flawless throughout various activities and environmental conditions [733]. Leading brands like Huda Beauty and Estée Lauder have also introduced 24-hour foundations that adapt to the skin's oil production, effectively preventing creasing and oxidation. These foundations ensure a fresh and natural appearance even after extended wear, addressing the needs of busy professionals and makeup enthusiasts alike [734].

As consumer demand for makeup that aligns with their active lifestyles continues to rise, brands are increasingly prioritizing advanced formulations that balance longevity with comfort. The future of long-wear cosmetics is likely to see further enhancements in lightweight, breathable textures that improve wearability without sacrificing durability. With the growing expectation for high-performance beauty products, brands are poised to innovate continuously, developing even more resilient and skin-friendly formulations that cater to diverse beauty needs [735, 736].

Clean Beauty and Sustainable Makeup

Sustainability has emerged as a pivotal focus within the makeup industry, catalysing innovation towards eco-friendly, biodegradable, and refillable packaging solutions. This shift is largely driven by an increasing consumer consciousness regarding the environmental impacts of beauty products, which has prompted brands to adopt sustainable practices aimed at minimizing waste and reducing plastic consumption. Research indicates that the beauty market is transitioning from a focus on adding ingredients to a paradigm centred on "free from" harmful substances, emphasizing the importance of sourcing raw materials responsibly and implementing sustainable manufacturing processes [737]. This transformation is not merely a trend; it reflects a fundamental change in consumer expectations and behaviours, as evidenced by the projected growth of the sustainable beauty market, which is anticipated to reach $22 billion by 2024 [738].

One of the most significant advancements in sustainable beauty is the introduction of refillable packaging. Brands such as Kjaer Weis, Charlotte Tilbury, and Hourglass have pioneered refillable compacts, lipstick cases, and eyeshadow palettes, allowing consumers to replace only the product while reusing the original container. This innovation not only reduces plastic waste but also enhances the cost-effectiveness and environmental responsibility of luxury makeup [738]. The refillable model aligns with consumer preferences for sustainability, as it encourages the purchase of refills instead of entirely new products, thereby cutting down on excessive packaging and single-use plastic consumption [737, 738]. Furthermore, the integration of sustainable practices into product development and packaging design is increasingly seen as a competitive advantage in the beauty industry, as consumers are more likely to support brands that demonstrate a commitment to environmental stewardship [739].

Another significant shift in sustainable makeup is the replacement of traditional microplastics in glitter and pigments with biodegradable alternatives. Conventional glitter, often composed of microplastics, poses a significant environmental threat, particularly in aquatic ecosystems. In response to these concerns, the beauty industry has begun to adopt biodegradable glitter derived from natural sources such as seaweed, minerals, and cellulose, which decompose naturally and present a safer choice for makeup formulations [737]. This shift not only addresses environmental pollution but also aligns with consumer preferences for products that are both effective and eco-friendly [710].

Microplastics in makeup products present significant environmental and health risks due to their persistence in ecosystems, potential for bioaccumulation, and adverse effects on human health. These tiny plastic particles, often found in products such as glitter, exfoliating scrubs, eyeshadows, and lipsticks, do not easily degrade, leading to their accumulation in aquatic environments and the food chain.

One of the primary concerns regarding microplastics in cosmetics is their contribution to environmental pollution. When these particles are washed off, they enter wastewater systems and eventually reach rivers, lakes, and oceans. Studies indicate that microplastics can accumulate in aquatic environments, posing a threat to marine life. For instance, organisms such as fish and shellfish often mistake microplastics for food, leading to ingestion and subsequent bioaccumulation within the food web [740, 741]. This not only disrupts marine ecosystems but also poses risks to human health when contaminated seafood is consumed [742, 743].

Microplastics can contribute to soil contamination. Improper disposal of makeup products containing microplastics can lead to their breakdown into smaller fragments, which infiltrate the soil and affect plant life. Research has shown that these particles can alter soil composition, reducing its capacity to retain water and nutrients, thereby impacting agricultural productivity [744, 745]. Additionally, microplastics can become airborne through product application, such as aerosol sprays and loose powders, contributing to atmospheric pollution [746].

The potential health risks associated with microplastics in cosmetics are still under investigation, but emerging research highlights several concerning effects. One significant concern is skin penetration. Although microplastics are primarily used for texture enhancement and exfoliation, studies suggest that smaller particles, known as nanoplastics, may penetrate the skin barrier, leading to inflammation and oxidative stress [742]. This could accelerate skin aging and cause irritation, particularly in sensitive individuals [747].

Inhalation and ingestion of microplastics also pose health risks. Products such as loose powders and aerosol formulations can release microplastics into the air, which may be inhaled into the lungs, potentially causing respiratory irritation and inflammation [748]. Furthermore, microplastics in lip products can be ingested over time, accumulating in organs and contributing to long-term health issues, including hormone disruption and gastrointestinal inflammation [749, 750]. The presence of toxic additives in microplastics, such as phthalates and bisphenol A (BPA), raises additional concerns, as these chemicals can leach into the body and interfere with hormonal balance, potentially increasing the risk of metabolic disorders and certain cancers [746, 751].

In response to the environmental and health risks posed by microplastics in cosmetics, regulatory bodies and the cosmetics industry have begun to take action. Several countries, including those in the European Union and Canada, have implemented bans on microbeads in rinse-off cosmetics [742, 752]. However, regulations concerning microplastics in leave-on products, such as makeup, remain limited in many regions [744].

To address these growing concerns, beauty brands are increasingly developing eco-friendly alternatives. Innovations include biodegradable glitter made from plant-based materials and natural exfoliants derived from sources like sugar and crushed fruit seeds [753, 754]. Many companies are reformulating their products to exclude microplastics and are adopting sustainable packaging practices to further reduce their ecological footprint [755].

The movement towards plant-based pigments has gained traction as brands increasingly move away from synthetic dyes and chemical colorants. Natural pigments sourced from ingredients like beetroot, turmeric, and spirulina not only provide vibrant colours but also reduce reliance on petroleum-based ingredients. These plant-based alternatives offer additional skincare benefits, such as antioxidant protection and anti-inflammatory properties, making them particularly appealing for consumers with sensitive skin [710, 737]. The growing demand for such eco-friendly products is indicative of a broader trend towards sustainability in consumer behaviour, where individuals seek products that align with their values regarding health and environmental impact [756].

As sustainability continues to shape the beauty industry, brands are expected to innovate further by developing zero-waste packaging, compostable materials, and multi-use products that promote minimalism in beauty routines. The increasing consumer demand for ethical and environmentally friendly cosmetics signifies that sustainable makeup is no longer a niche trend but rather a fundamental shift in how beauty products are designed, packaged, and consumed [737, 739]. This evolution reflects a broader societal movement towards sustainability, where consumers are not only motivated by personal aesthetics but also by the desire to contribute positively to the environment.

Blue Light Protection and Anti-Pollution Makeup

With the rise of digital lifestyles and urban living, the beauty industry has seen a significant trend towards makeup products that incorporate blue light protection and anti-pollution shields. This shift is largely driven by increasing consumer awareness regarding the detrimental effects of prolonged screen time and environmental aggressors on skin health. Research indicates that blue light, or high-energy visible (HEV) light, emitted by digital devices and artificial lighting, can penetrate the skin more deeply than UV rays, contributing to premature aging, hyperpigmentation, and collagen degradation [705, 757].

Advances in Cosmetology

Consequently, cosmetic brands are responding by developing products that not only enhance beauty but also provide essential skin defence.

To combat the adverse effects of blue light exposure, makeup formulations are increasingly enriched with antioxidants, iron oxides, and botanical extracts. Antioxidants such as vitamin C, niacinamide, and green tea extract are commonly included for their ability to neutralize free radicals generated by blue light, thereby reducing oxidative stress and inflammation [758]. Iron oxides, which serve as natural pigments in foundations and tinted moisturizers, have been shown to effectively block HEV light, making them a critical component in blue light-protective makeup [757]. Studies have demonstrated that these ingredients can mitigate blue light-induced damage, enhancing skin resilience against pigmentation and collagen degradation [705, 757].

In addition to blue light protection, urban living exposes the skin to various pollutants, including particulate matter and toxic gases, which can exacerbate skin aging and inflammation [759, 760]. Makeup products infused with anti-pollution ingredients create a barrier against harmful particles and help neutralize pollutants before they can inflict cellular damage. Ingredients such as hyaluronic acid, algae extracts, and resveratrol not only hydrate the skin but also bolster its natural defences against environmental stressors [759]. Furthermore, detoxifying minerals like zinc and copper are increasingly incorporated into formulations to combat oxidative stress linked to pollution [759, 760].

Leading brands in the beauty industry have embraced this trend by launching innovative products that combine blue light and anti-pollution protection. For instance, Ilia Beauty's Super Serum Skin Tint SPF 40 integrates mineral SPF, plant-based antioxidants, and niacinamide, offering a lightweight foundation that shields the skin from environmental aggressors [759]. Similarly, IT Cosmetics' Your Skin But Better Foundation features hydrating ingredients while protecting against blue light and pollutants [759]. Supergoop's (Re)setting Refreshing Mist SPF 40 exemplifies a setting spray designed to deliver broad-spectrum sun protection alongside blue light defence and pollution resistance throughout the day [759].

As consumer consciousness regarding the impact of blue light and pollution on skin health continues to rise, the demand for multifunctional makeup products is expected to grow. These hybrid beauty solutions not only enhance appearance but also offer long-term skin benefits, reinforcing the trend towards innovative formulations that prioritize both aesthetics and skin health. The future of cosmetics will likely witness further advancements in anti-pollution and blue light-protective technologies, making beauty routines more effective and health-conscious [761].

Colour-Changing and Adaptive Makeup

Colour-changing technology is significantly transforming the cosmetics industry by introducing innovative makeup products that adapt to individual skin chemistry and tones. This advancement is particularly notable in the realm of pH-reactive pigments and undertone-adaptive formulas, which allow for a more customized and universally flattering beauty experience. The integration of such technologies eliminates the guesswork often associated with selecting the right shades, thereby enhancing consumer satisfaction and engagement with beauty products [97, 762].

One prominent application of colour-changing technology is in pH-reactive lip products, such as lipsticks and balms. These formulations utilize dye molecules that respond to the pH level and moisture of the lips, resulting in a unique custom shade for each individual. For instance, products like Dior Addict Lip Glow and Winky Lux's Flower Balm exemplify this technology, shifting from a sheer tint to a deeper hue based on the wearer's body chemistry [97, 762]. The pH-reactive pigments typically belong to a class of dyes such as Red 27 or Red 21, which are initially colourless but develop into vibrant pink, coral, or berry tones upon contact with the skin. The intensity of the colour varies according to factors like lip hydration, pH balance, and temperature, ensuring that no two users experience the same shade [97, 762].

Beyond lip products, adaptive foundation formulas are revolutionizing complexion makeup by adjusting to the skin's undertone upon application. Unlike traditional foundations that require precise shade selection, these innovative formulas employ encapsulated pigments that release colour when blended into the skin. A notable example is the TLM Color-Changing Foundation, which begins as a neutral base and transforms to match the wearer's skin tone upon application [97, 762]. This technology is particularly advantageous for individuals who struggle to find the right foundation shade or experience fluctuations in skin tone due to seasonal changes or tanning [97, 762]. The micro-encapsulated pigments are suspended in lightweight lotions or serums, and when massaged into the skin, they burst to release pigments that blend seamlessly with the natural complexion, creating a personalized match [97, 762].

The appeal of colour-changing makeup lies in its ability to provide convenience, personalization, and innovation in beauty products. Consumers are increasingly drawn to these formulations as they simplify makeup routines and reduce the need for multiple shades, all while offering a more natural and tailored appearance [97, 762]. Furthermore, many of these products incorporate hydrating and nourishing ingredients, enhancing their appeal as hybrids of makeup and skincare [97, 762]. As the beauty industry continues to evolve, it is anticipated that colour-adaptive technology will expand into other categories such as blushes, bronzers, and eyeshadows, thereby providing consumers with smarter, self-adjusting formulas that cater to individual needs [97, 762].

Microencapsulation and Time-Released Pigments

Advancements in microencapsulation technology are significantly transforming the cosmetics industry, particularly in how makeup products deliver skincare benefits alongside colour. Microencapsulation involves encasing active ingredients or pigments within a protective shell, allowing for a controlled and gradual release of these components when activated by external factors such as heat, moisture, or friction. This innovative formulation technique enhances the stability and efficacy of volatile ingredients, thereby improving the overall performance of makeup products [763]. For instance, microencapsulated pigments in foundations and powders can adapt to the skin's oil and moisture levels, ensuring consistent colour payoff while preventing issues like oxidation and fading.

One of the most notable applications of microencapsulation in cosmetics is the provision of time-released hydration. Traditional makeup formulations often lead to dryness or settle into fine lines over time, which can detract from the overall appearance. However, the incorporation of microencapsulated hydrating agents such as hyaluronic acid and vitamin E allows for continuous moisture delivery throughout the day, keeping the skin plump and comfortable even in long-wear formulations. For example, Chanel's Les Beiges Water-Fresh Tint utilizes microfluidic technology to suspend pigment droplets in a lightweight hydrating serum, which burst upon application to release both moisture and colour, resulting in a natural, dewy finish.

Moreover, microencapsulation technology is crucial in developing adaptive colour foundations that resist oxidation and maintain a flawless finish. Long-wear foundations, particularly those designed for oil control, can often darken or change tone due to the skin's natural oils. Microencapsulated pigments help mitigate this effect by adjusting to the skin's oil levels and humidity, ensuring that the foundation remains true to colour without creasing or fading. A prime example is the MAC Studio Fix Tech Cream-To-Powder Foundation, which features microencapsulated pigments that adapt to the skin's oil production, providing a balanced and fresh appearance throughout the day.

Looking ahead, the potential for microencapsulation technology in cosmetics is vast. As consumer demand for multifunctional beauty products increases, we can expect to see this technology expand into other makeup categories such as blushes, bronzers, and setting powders. These advancements promise to offer benefits such as gradual colour release and anti-pollution properties, further revolutionizing the beauty industry by merging the longevity of makeup with the nourishing benefits of skincare.

Customizable and On-Demand Makeup

The rise of personalized beauty and custom-blended makeup systems reflects a significant shift in consumer preferences towards products that cater specifically to individual needs. This trend is driven by the increasing demand for makeup that matches unique skin tones, undertones, and personal preferences, moving away from the limitations of traditional pre-made shades. Custom-blend makeup systems, utilizing advanced technologies such as AI-driven algorithms and skin scanning, allow consumers to create tailored products that meet their specific beauty requirements.

One notable example of this innovation is Lancôme's Le Teint Particulier, an AI-powered foundation-matching system. This system employs a high-precision colorimeter to scan the customer's skin, analysing various factors such as tone and pigmentation. The data collected is processed through AI algorithms, which generate a custom blend of pigments and skincare ingredients, resulting in a foundation that is an exact match for the user's skin [764]. This personalized approach not only addresses the common frustration of finding the right shade but also optimizes hydration and skin benefits tailored to individual needs. Such custom-blended foundations are particularly advantageous for individuals with hard-to-match skin tones, including those with neutral or multi-tonal complexions [765].

In addition to foundations, the emergence of smart beauty devices like L'Oréal Perso is transforming the way consumers create personalized lipsticks and skincare products at home. This device integrates AI-driven shade selection with precise formulation technology, enabling users to mix and dispense their own lip colours and skincare treatments based on real-time data [766]. For instance, the device allows users to blend primary pigments to create custom lipstick shades, while also adjusting skincare formulations according to environmental factors such as humidity and pollution levels [767]. This capability ensures that consumers receive freshly mixed products tailored to their daily needs, making it a revolutionary tool in the realm of adaptive skincare solutions.

Looking towards the future, the landscape of personalized beauty is expected to evolve further with advancements in technology. Innovations may include the incorporation of skin microbiome analysis and real-time shade adaptation, enhancing the precision and effectiveness of custom-blend systems [768]. The shift towards personalized beauty not only enhances customer satisfaction but also contributes to reducing product waste, as consumers are more likely to utilize products that are specifically tailored to their needs [769]. As brands like Lancôme and L'Oréal continue to leverage AI and smart technology, the beauty industry is poised for a transformation that prioritizes individualized

Richard Skiba

experiences over mass-market offerings, marking a significant evolution in how makeup and skincare products are developed and consumed [770].

References

1. Gu, J., et al., *Association of Frontal and Lateral Facial Attractiveness.* Jama Facial Plastic Surgery, 2018. **20**(1): p. 19-23.
2. Przylipiak, M., et al., *Impact of Face Proportions on Face Attractiveness.* Journal of Cosmetic Dermatology, 2018. **17**(6): p. 954-959.
3. Knox, K.N. and M.F. TenEyck, *Beauty Is Only Skin Deep: An Examination of Physical Attractiveness, Attractive Personality, and Personal Grooming on Criminal Justice Outcomes.* Plos One, 2023. **18**(10): p. e0291922.
4. Wong, J.S. and A.M. Penner, *Gender and the Returns to Attractiveness.* Research in Social Stratification and Mobility, 2016. **44**: p. 113-123.
5. Scheibling, C. and M. Lafrance, *Man Up but Stay Smooth: Hybrid Masculinities in Advertising for Men's Grooming Products.* The Journal of Men S Studies, 2019. **27**(2): p. 222-239.
6. Tran, A., R. Rosales, and L. Copes, *Paint a Better Mood? Effects of Makeup Use on YouTube Beauty Influencers' Self-Esteem.* Sage Open, 2020. **10**(2).
7. Richard, A., et al., *Recover Your Smile: Effects of a Beauty Care Intervention on Depressive Symptoms, Quality of Life, and Self-esteem in Patients With Early Breast Cancer.* Psycho-Oncology, 2018. **28**(2): p. 401-407.
8. Kuzu, A., Ş. ErgÖL, and G.P. AslantÜRk, *The Effect of Beauty Services on Women's Stress and Body Image.* Karya Journal of Health Science, 2022. **3**(1): p. 13-17.
9. Pearlman, R.L., et al., *Factors Associated With Likelihood to Undergo Cosmetic Surgical Procedures Among Young Adults in the United States: A Narrative Review.* Clinical Cosmetic and Investigational Dermatology, 2022. **Volume 15**: p. 859-877.
10. Putri, W.L., L.G.S. Putri, and M. Siscawati, *The Beauty Myth, Cosmetics Industry, and Instagram.* 2023: p. 568-580.
11. Hermawan, D., A.M. Ronda, and R.R. Sigit, *Multimodality Discourses of the Miss Universe Beauty Pageant as an Arena of Cultural Production.* International Journal of Environmental Sustainability and Social Science, 2023. **4**(4): p. 1131-1136.

12. Chinski, H., et al., *Rhinoplasty and Its Effects on the Perception of Beauty.* International Archives of Otorhinolaryngology, 2014. **17**(01): p. 047-050.

13. Atiyeh, B.S., et al., *Lip Augmentation With Soft Tissue Fillers: Social Media, Perceptual Adaptation, and Shifting Beauty Trends Beyond Golden Standard Ideals.* Plastic and Reconstructive Surgery Global Open, 2024. **12**(10): p. e6238.

14. Tapsoba, I., et al., *Finding Out Egyptian Gods' Secret Using Analytical Chemistry: Biomedical Properties of Egyptian Black Makeup Revealed by Amperometry at Single Cells.* Analytical Chemistry, 2009. **82**(2): p. 457-460.

15. Metwaly, A.M., et al., *Traditional Ancient Egyptian Medicine: A Review.* Saudi Journal of Biological Sciences, 2021. **28**(10): p. 5823-5832.

16. Agai, J.M., *Resurrection Imageries: A Study of the Motives for Extravagant Burial Rituals in Ancient Egypt.* Verbum Et Ecclesia, 2015. **36**(1).

17. MacNevin, A., *Exercising Options: Holistic Health and Technical Beauty in Gendered Accounts of Bodywork.* Sociological Quarterly, 2003. **44**(2): p. 271-289.

18. Lee, J., et al., *Establishment of Normative Self-Rated Health Status Data and Association Between Ideal Life Expectancy and Social Wellness of General Population in Korea.* Asian Nursing Research, 2019. **13**(2): p. 99-106.

19. Hamp, A., et al., *Gua-sha, Jade Roller, and Facial Massage: Are There Benefits Within Dermatology?* Journal of Cosmetic Dermatology, 2022. **22**(2): p. 700-703.

20. Almaghrabi, Z.A. and H.S. Saati, *Patient Satisfaction on the Holistic Care Approach Rendered by Nurses in the Oncology Ward.* The Egyptian Journal of Hospital Medicine, 2022. **89**(1): p. 6041-6050.

21. Albert, D., *Perception of Ideal Facial Beauty Among Females in South Indian Dravidian PopulationA Questionnaire Survey.* International Journal of Dentistry and Oral Science, 2021: p. 1893-1898.

22. Akhtaruzzaman, M. and A.A. Shafie, *Geometrical Substantiation of Phi, the Golden Ratio and the Baroque of Nature, Architecture, Design and Engineering.* International Journal of Arts, 2012. **1**(1): p. 1-22.

23. Zeina, A.M.A., *The Golden Ratio and Its Impact on Architectural Design.* 202 التصميم الدولية, 2. **12**(2): p. 77-90.

24. Jozsef, C., *The Golden Ratio*. Journal of Modern Physics, 2016. **07**(14): p. 1944-1948.
25. Gjonbalaj, A., et al., *The Golden Ratio and Its Effects on the Perceived Visual Appeal of Photos*. Journal of Student Research, 2021. **10**(1).
26. Bartolo, D.D., et al., *The Golden Ratio as an Ecological Affordance Leading to Aesthetic Attractiveness*. Psych Journal, 2021. **11**(5): p. 729-740.
27. Sakamoto, A., et al., *Golden Ratio Flap Designed Using the Golden Ratio Rectangle*. Plastic and Reconstructive Surgery Global Open, 2024. **12**(1): p. e5508.
28. Liu, R.S.N., *The Golden Ration in the Renaissance Art: A Comparative Study on the Geometrical Layout of the Mona Lisa and the Annunciation*. Communications in Humanities Research, 2023. **3**(1): p. 316-323.
29. Joung, J.Y. and P.G. Badke-Schaub, *The Impact of Aesthetic Preference in Product Design–Golden Ratio and Korean's Preference Proportion*. Archives of Design Research, 2017. **30**(4): p. 5-14.
30. Wang, Y.T., et al., *A Composition-Oriented Aesthetic View Recommendation Network Supervised by the Simplified Golden Ratio Theory*. Expert Systems With Applications, 2022. **195**: p. 116500.
31. Stieger, S. and V. Swami, *Time to Let Go? No Automatic Aesthetic Preference for the Golden Ratio in Art Pictures*. Psychology of Aesthetics Creativity and the Arts, 2015. **9**(1): p. 91-100.
32. Duan, J.S., *Shrinkage Points of Golden Rectangle, Fibonacci Spirals, and Golden Spirals*. Discrete Dynamics in Nature and Society, 2019. **2019**: p. 1-6.
33. Hoppe, A.D., *The Microsociology of Aesthetic Evaluation: Selecting Runway Fashion Models*. Qualitative Sociology, 2021. **45**(1): p. 63-87.
34. Baiz, W.H. and D.S. Khoshnaw, *How toExplore Golden Ratio in Architecture and Designing City*. International Journal of Engineering Research and Applications, 2017. **06**(08): p. 01-07.
35. Bozia, E. and A. Mullen, *Literary Translingualism in the Greek and Roman Worlds*. 2021: p. 45-59.
36. Taher, M.A., et al., *A Brief Analysis of the Ancient Roman Medical System*. International Journal of Unani and Integrative Medicine, 2019. **3**(1): p. 37-40.
37. Kruszewski, A., *From Ancient Patterns of Hand-to-Hand Combat to a Unique Therapy of the Future*. International Journal of Environmental Research and Public Health, 2023. **20**(4): p. 3553.

38. Draycott, J.L., *Approaches to Healing in Roman Egypt.* 2012.

39. Sharma, P. and M.K. Sharma, *Significance of Ayurvedic Cosmetology in Contemporary Context: A Critical Review.* International Research Journal of Ayurveda & Yoga, 2024. **7**(4): p. 55-60.

40. Bhat, D.D.P., D.A.K. Tanwar, and D.R. Jain, *Ayurvedic Dermatology: A Frontier of Skin Care.* 2024: p. 91-102.

41. Sarruf, F.D., et al., *The Scenario of Clays' and Clay Minerals' Use in Cosmetics/Dermocosmetics.* 2023.

42. Amro, B.I., M.N.A. Hajleh, and F. Afifi, *Evidence-based potential of some edible, medicinal and aromatic plants as safe cosmetics and cosmeceuticals.* 2021.

43. Ajayi, S.A., et al., *Sustainable Sourcing of Organic Skincare Ingredients: A Critical Analysis of Ethical Concerns and Environmental Implications.* Asian Journal of Advanced Research and Reports, 2024. **18**(1): p. 65-91.

44. Kumar, V., et al., *Antioxidants for Skin Health.* Recent Advances in Food Nutrition & Agriculture, 2024. **15**.

45. Wood, N.A.R. and T.A. Petrie, *Body Dissatisfaction, Ethnic Identity, and Disordered Eating Among African American Women.* Journal of Counseling Psychology, 2010. **57**(2): p. 141-153.

46. Mills, J.S., A. Shannon, and J. Hogue, *Beauty, Body Image, and the Media.* 2017.

47. Walker, C.E., et al., *Effects of Social Media Use on Desire for Cosmetic Surgery Among Young Women.* Current Psychology, 2019. **40**(7): p. 3355-3364.

48. Toselli, S., N. Rinaldo, and E. Gualdi-Russo, *Body Image Perception of African Immigrants in Europe.* Globalization and Health, 2016. **12**(1).

49. Rajanala, S., M.B.C. Maymone, and N.A. Vashi, *Evolving Beauty— Creating and Transforming Inequalities.* Journal of Cosmetic Dermatology, 2019. **19**(4): p. 913-914.

50. Paramita, N.M.S. and E.M.I. Lestari, *A Discourse of Beauty Standards in Japanese Beauty Product Advertise-Ment (Japanese Women Perspective).* International Journal of Multidisciplinary Applied Business and Education Research, 2023. **4**(10): p. 3470-3480.

51. Jones, G., *Globalization and Beauty: A Historical and Firm Perspective.* 2013.

52. Baines, J., et al., *I Apologize: Body Positivity Love Movements.* English Teaching Practice & Critique, 2024. **23**(2): p. 195-204.

53. Mele, S., V. Cazzato, and C. Urgesi, *The Importance of Perceptual Experience in the Esthetic Appreciation of the Body.* Plos One, 2013. **8**(12): p. e81378.

54. Tanca, J.T., *Resistance Against Beauty Standards Stereotypes and Representation of Women's Beauty Through BLP Beauty Advertisement.* Perspektif, 2024. **13**(1): p. 123-134.

55. Devina, S. and J. Mochtar, *Lim Ju Gyeong's Social Masks in True Beauty.* K Ta Kita, 2022. **10**(3): p. 488-494.

56. Wang, J., et al., *What Is Beautiful Brings Out What Is Good in You: The Effect of Facial Attractiveness on Individuals' Honesty.* International Journal of Psychology, 2015. **52**(3): p. 197-204.

57. Mu, W. and F. Wu, *Blossoming for Whom? Social Approval and Body Image.* 2021.

58. Małolepsza, A., et al., *Assessment of Motivation for Using Aesthetic Medicine Procedures and Post-Treatment Satisfaction.* Journal of Education Health and Sport, 2023. **45**(1): p. 136-143.

59. Redies, C., *Beauty: Neglected, but Alive and Kicking.* British Journal of Psychology, 2014. **105**(4): p. 468-470.

60. Dr. Asma Seemi Malik, N., N. Anam Rafaqat, and M. Zafar, *MARRIAGE PROPOSALS &Amp; SELF-PERCEIVED EXPERIENCES OF FEMALES FOR STANDARD OR IDEAL BEAUTY: AN EXPLORATORY STUDY OF PAKISTAN.* Journal of Arts & Social Sciences, 2023. **10**(1): p. 42-54.

61. Sigdel, S., *Artificial Look: Body Narcissism in the Fashion and Cosmetic Industry.* Tasambo Journal of Language Literature and Culture, 2024. **2**(1): p. 1-11.

62. Tribble, B.L.D., et al., *"No [Right] Way to Be a Black Woman": Exploring Gendered Racial Socialization Among Black Women.* Psychology of Women Quarterly, 2019. **43**(3): p. 381-397.

63. Ingenium Space, *The Role of Innovation in the Beauty Industry: Unleashing Creativity and Transforming the Beauty Landscape.* 2023, Medium.

64. Kenett, Y.N., L.H. Ungar, and A. Chatterjee, *Beauty and Wellness in the Semantic Memory of the Beholder.* Frontiers in Psychology, 2021. **12**.

65. Ntumba, C., S. Aguayo, and K. Maina, *Revolutionizing Retail: A Mini Review of E-Commerce Evolution.* Journal of Digital Marketing and Communication, 2023. **3**(2): p. 100-110.

66. Whang, J.B., et al., *The Effect of Augmented Reality on Purchase Intention of Beauty Products: The Roles of Consumers' Control.* Journal of Business Research, 2021. **133**: p. 275-284.

67. Nugroho, D.D.R., M.Y. Febrianta, and N. None, *The Influence of Augmented Reality on Purchase Intentions Through Consumers of Madame Gie Products*. International Journal of Current Science Research and Review, 2024. **07**(02).
68. Koskinen, V., M. Ylilahti, and T.A. Wilska, *"Healthy to Heaven" — Middle-Agers Looking Ahead in the Context of Wellness Consumption*. Journal of Aging Studies, 2017. **40**: p. 36-43.
69. Ningrum, D.O. and W.D. Ruspitasari, *Beauty Influencer: Homophily Relationship, Product Quality Beauty Product and Purchasing Decision*. International Journal of Science Technology & Management, 2022. **3**(3): p. 641-646.
70. Plemmons, A., *Occupational Licensing's Effects on Firm Location and Employment in the United States*. British Journal of Industrial Relations, 2022. **60**(4): p. 735-760.
71. Choe, M.-H., S.-H. Moon, and J.-S. Lee, *Recognition and Improvement of the Master Craftsman Cosmetology System*. The Korean Society of Beauty and Art, 2020. **21**(3): p. 295-310.
72. Rajegowda, G.M., et al., *An AI-Assisted Skincare Routine Recommendation System in XR*. 2024: p. 381-395.
73. Jadhav, S., *Personalised Skin Care Recommendation Using Machine Learning*. 2023. **11**(1): p. 297-302.
74. Georgievskaya, A., et al., *How Artificial Intelligence Adopts Human Biases: The Case of Cosmetic Skincare Industry*. Ai and Ethics, 2023.
75. Jain, A., et al., *Development and Assessment of an Artificial Intelligence–Based Tool for Skin Condition Diagnosis by Primary Care Physicians and Nurse Practitioners in Teledermatology Practices*. Jama Network Open, 2021. **4**(4): p. e217249.
76. Nelson, C.A., et al., *Patient Perspectives on the Use of Artificial Intelligence for Skin Cancer Screening*. Jama Dermatology, 2020. **156**(5): p. 501.
77. Aamir, A., et al., *Exploring the Current and Prospective Role of Artificial Intelligence in Disease Diagnosis*. Annals of Medicine and Surgery, 2024. **86**(2): p. 943-949.
78. Sangers, T.E., et al., *Towards Successful Implementation of Artificial Intelligence in Skin Cancer Care: A Qualitative Study Exploring the Views of Dermatologists and General Practitioners*. Archives of Dermatological Research, 2022.

79. Li, C., et al., *Diagnostic Capacity of Skin Tumor Artificial Intelligence-Assisted Decision-Making Software in Real-World Clinical Settings.* Chinese Medical Journal, 2020. **133**(17): p. 2020-2026.

80. Escalé-Besa, A., et al., *The Use of Artificial Intelligence for Skin Disease Diagnosis in Primary Care Settings: A Systematic Review.* Healthcare, 2024. **12**(12): p. 1192.

81. Krakowski, I., et al., *Human-Ai Interaction in Skin Cancer Diagnosis: A Systematic Review and Meta-Analysis.* NPJ Digital Medicine, 2024. **7**(1).

82. Mehrabi, J.N., et al., *A Clinical Perspective on the Automated Analysis of Reflectance Confocal Microscopy in Dermatology.* Lasers in Surgery and Medicine, 2021. **53**(8): p. 1011-1019.

83. Kamulegeya, L., et al., *Using Artificial Intelligence on Dermatology Conditions in Uganda: A Case for Diversity in Training Data Sets for Machine Learning.* African Health Sciences, 2023. **23**(2): p. 753-63.

84. Weir, V.R., et al., *A Survey of Skin Tone Assessment in Prospective Research.* NPJ Digital Medicine, 2024. **7**(1).

85. Rokni, G.R., et al., *Artificial Intelligence in Inflammatory Skin Disorders.* Dermatological Reviews, 2024. **5**(3).

86. Jobson, D., V. Mar, and I. Freckelton, *Legal and Ethical Considerations of Artificial Intelligence in Skin Cancer Diagnosis.* Australasian Journal of Dermatology, 2021. **63**(1).

87. Sangers, T.E., et al., *Position Statement of the <scp>EADV</Scp> Artificial Intelligence (<scp>AI</Scp>) Task Force on <scp>AI</Scp>-assisted Smartphone Apps and Web -based Services for Skin Disease.* Journal of the European Academy of Dermatology and Venereology, 2023. **38**(1): p. 22-30.

88. Wang, W., D. Cao, and N. Ameen, *Understanding Customer Satisfaction of Augmented Reality In retail: A Human Value Orientation and Consumption Value Perspective.* Information Technology and People, 2022. **36**(6): p. 2211-2233.

89. An, S., et al., *ARCosmetics: A Real-Time Augmented Reality Cosmetics Try-on System.* Frontiers of Computer Science, 2022. **17**(4).

90. Watson, A., B. Alexander, and L. Salavati, *The Impact of Experiential Augmented Reality Applications on Fashion Purchase Intention.* International Journal of Retail & Distribution Management, 2018. **48**(5): p. 433-451.

91. Smink, A.R., et al., *Try Online Before You Buy: How Does Shopping With Augmented Reality Affect Brand Responses and Personal Data*

Disclosure. Electronic Commerce Research and Applications, 2019. **35**: p. 100854.

92. Ko, E. and H. Wang, *Augmented Reality (AR) App Use in the Beauty Product Industry and Consumer Purchase Intention.* Asia Pacific Journal of Marketing and Logistics, 2021. **34**(1): p. 110-131.

93. Hoffmann, S. and R. Mai, *Consumer Behavior in Augmented Shopping Reality. A Review, Synthesis, and Research Agenda.* Frontiers in Virtual Reality, 2022. **3**.

94. Tan, Y.C., S.R. Chandukala, and S.K. Reddy, *Augmented Reality in Retail and Its Impact on Sales.* Journal of Marketing, 2021. **86**(1): p. 48-66.

95. Nugraha, A.E., et al., *Postural Ergonomic Risk Assesment of Augmented Reality User Interface on Smarthpones in Cosmetic Industry Advertising.* SHS Web of Conferences, 2024. **189**: p. 01051.

96. Caboni, F. and J. Hagberg, *Augmented Reality in Retailing: A Review of Features, Applications and Value.* International Journal of Retail & Distribution Management, 2019. **47**(11): p. 1125-1140.

97. Sihaloho, M.P., K. Kurniawati, and Y. Masnita, *Antecedents and Consequences of Using Artificial Intelligence (Ai) Color Cosmetics.* Journal of Social Research, 2023. **2**(8): p. 2496-2505.

98. Gholizadeh, N., G.R. Rokni, and M. Babaei, *Advantages and Disadvantages of Using AI in Dermatology.* Dermatological Reviews, 2024. **5**(4).

99. Kania, B., K. Montecinos, and D.J. Goldberg, *Artificial Intelligence in Cosmetic Dermatology.* Journal of Cosmetic Dermatology, 2024. **23**(10): p. 3305-3311.

100. Journal, I., *The Future of Organic Cosmetics: AI-Enabled Sustainability.* Interantional Journal of Scientific Research in Engineering and Management, 2024. **08**(02): p. 1-13.

101. Haykal, D., *Leveraging Single Nucleotide Polymorphism Profiling for Precision Skin Care: How SNPs Shape Individual Responses in Cosmetic Dermatology.* Journal of Cosmetic Dermatology, 2024. **24**(1).

102. Xiao, P., et al., *Influence of Platform Satisfaction on the Willingness to Use a New Platform.* Scientific Reports, 2024. **14**(1).

103. Załęcki, P., et al., *Impact of Lifestyle on Differences in Skin Hydration of Selected Body Areas in Young Women.* Cosmetics, 2024. **11**(1): p. 13.

104. Dąbrowska, A., et al., *In Vivo Confirmation of Hydration-Induced Changes in Human-Skin Thickness, Roughness and Interaction With the Environment.* Biointerphases, 2016. **11**(3).

105. Yolanda, M.O., N.K. Jusuf, and I.B. Putra, *Lower Facial Skin Hydration Level Increases Acne Vulgaris Severity Level.* Bali Medical Journal, 2021. **10**(3): p. 1081-1084.

106. Bermudez, Y., et al., *Activation of the PI3K/Akt/mTOR and MAPK Signaling Pathways in Response to Acute Solar-Simulated Light Exposure of Human Skin.* Cancer Prevention Research, 2015. **8**(8): p. 720-728.

107. Kim, S., et al., *Influence of Exposure to Summer Environments on Skin Properties.* Journal of the European Academy of Dermatology and Venereology, 2019. **33**(11): p. 2192-2196.

108. Morin, M., et al., *Skin Hydration Dynamics Investigated by Electrical Impedance Techniques in Vivo and in Vitro.* Scientific Reports, 2020. **10**(1).

109. Hao, Y., W. Song, and L. Qu, *Effects of a Combination of Poria Cocos, Ziziphus Spinose, and Gamma -aminobutyric Acid (GABA) on Sleep Quality and Skin Health: A Randomized Double -blind Placebo -controlled Clinical trial.* Food Science & Nutrition, 2024. **12**(6): p. 3883-3892.

110. Ihemelandu, K. and C. Ihemelandu, *Optimization of a Convolutional Neural Network for the Automated Diagnosis of Melanoma.* Journal of Student Research, 2021. **10**(3).

111. Young, A.E., et al., *Artificial Intelligence in Dermatology: A Primer.* Journal of Investigative Dermatology, 2020. **140**(8): p. 1504-1512.

112. Bandy, A.D., et al., *Intraclass Clustering-Based CNN Approach for Detection of Malignant Melanoma.* Sensors, 2023. **23**(2): p. 926.

113. Yee, J., C. Rosendahl, and L.G. Aoude, *The Role of Artificial Intelligence and Convolutional Neural Networks in the Management of Melanoma: A Clinical, Pathological, and Radiological Perspective.* Melanoma Research, 2023.

114. Díaz-Ramón, J.L., et al., *Melanoma Clinical Decision Support System: An Artificial Intelligence-Based Tool to Diagnose and Predict Disease Outcome in Early-Stage Melanoma Patients.* Cancers, 2023. **15**(7): p. 2174.

115. Helenason, J., et al., *Exploring the Feasibility of an Artificial Intelligence Based Clinical Decision Support System for Cutaneous*

Melanoma Detection in Primary Care – A Mixed Method Study. Scandinavian Journal of Primary Health Care, 2023. **42**(1): p. 51-60.

116. Miller, I., et al., *Performance of Commercial Dermatoscopic Systems That Incorporate Artificial Intelligence for the Identification of Melanoma in General Practice: A Systematic Review.* Cancers, 2024. **16**(7): p. 1443.

117. Jahn, A.S., et al., *Over-Detection of Melanoma-Suspect Lesions by a CE-Certified Smartphone App: Performance in Comparison to Dermatologists, 2D and 3D Convolutional Neural Networks in a Prospective Data Set of 1204 Pigmented Skin Lesions Involving Patients' Perception.* Cancers, 2022. **14**(15): p. 3829.

118. Jutzi, T., et al., *Artificial Intelligence in Skin Cancer Diagnostics: The Patients' Perspective.* Frontiers in Medicine, 2020. **7**.

119. Winkler, J., et al., *Assessment of Diagnostic Performance of Dermatologists Cooperating With a Convolutional Neural Network in a Prospective Clinical Study.* Jama Dermatology, 2023. **159**(6): p. 621.

120. Maron, R.C., et al., *Artificial Intelligence and Its Effect on Dermatologists' Accuracy in Dermoscopic Melanoma Image Classification: Web-Based Survey Study.* Journal of Medical Internet Research, 2020. **22**(9): p. e18091.

121. Marques, L., et al., *Advancing Precision Medicine: A Review of Innovative in Silico Approaches for Drug Development, Clinical Pharmacology and Personalized Healthcare.* Pharmaceutics, 2024. **16**(3): p. 332.

122. Markiewicz, E. and O. Idowu, *Evaluation of Personalized Skincare Through in-Silico Gene Interactive Networks and Cellular Responses to UVR and Oxidative Stress.* Clinical Cosmetic and Investigational Dermatology, 2022. **Volume 15**: p. 2221-2243.

123. Babel, A., et al., *Artificial Intelligence Solutions to Increase Medication Adherence in Patients With Non-Communicable Diseases.* Frontiers in Digital Health, 2021. **3**.

124. Daniel, A., et al., *International Regulatory Requirements for Skin Sensitization Testing.* Regulatory Toxicology and Pharmacology, 2018. **95**: p. 52-65.

125. Li, W., et al., *Motivations, Barriers and Risks of Smart Home Adoption: From Systematic Literature Review to Conceptual Framework.* Energy Research & Social Science, 2021. **80**: p. 102211.

126. Zielonka, A., et al., *Smart Homes: How Much Will They Support Us? A Research on Recent Trends and Advances.* Ieee Access, 2021. **9**: p. 26388-26419.

127. Ali, S.M., T.-B. Nguyen, and W.-Y. Chung, *New Directions for Skincare Monitoring: An NFC-Based Battery-Free Approach Combined With Deep Learning Techniques.* Ieee Access, 2022. **10**: p. 27368-27380.

128. Kim, T.W., et al., *Skincare Device Product Design Based on Factor Analysis of Korean Anthropometric Data.* Cosmetics, 2022. **9**(2): p. 42.

129. Chopra, S., et al., *Factors Significantly Impacting Consumer Acceptance of Entertainment, Domestic, and Housekeeping Smart Home IoT Devices.* 2022.

130. Kolny, B., *Equipping Households With Durable Goods in the Age of the Internet of Things.* Acta Scientiarum Polonorum - Oeconomia, 2022. **20**(3): p. 23-32.

131. Ali, S.M. and W.-Y. Chung, *Monitoring Transepidermal Water Loss and Skin Wettedness Factor With Battery-Free NFC Sensor.* Sensors, 2020. **20**(19): p. 5549.

132. Domb, M., *Smart Home Systems Based on Internet of Things.* 2019.

133. Shouran, Z., A. Ashari, and T.K. Priyambodo, *Internet of Things (IoT) of Smart Home: Privacy and Security.* International Journal of Computer Applications, 2019. **182**(39): p. 3-8.

134. Ayuastina, D. and I.M.B. Suksmadana, *Perancangan Model Machine Learning Untuk Pembuatan Aplikasi Rekomendasi Menggunakan Data Pengenalan Wajah.* Jurnal Nasional Komputasi Dan Teknologi Informasi (Jnkti), 2024. **7**(6): p. 1676-1681.

135. Liu, L., et al., *An Intelligent Diagnostic Model for Melasma Based on Deep Learning and Multimode Image Input.* Dermatology and Therapy, 2022. **13**(2): p. 569-579.

136. du Crest, D., et al., *Skin &Amp; Digital – The 2023 Conversation.* Journal of the European Academy of Dermatology and Venereology, 2023. **38**(3).

137. Kong, F., et al., *Review of Smartphone Mobile Applications for Skin Cancer Detection: What Are the Changes in Availability, Functionality, and Costs to Users Over Time?* International Journal of Dermatology, 2020. **60**(3): p. 289-308.

138. Daneshjou, R., et al., *Lack of Transparency and Potential Bias in Artificial Intelligence Data Sets and Algorithms.* Jama Dermatology, 2021. **157**(11): p. 1362.

139. Wu, D., et al., *A Pilot Study to Assess the Reliability of Digital Image-Based PASI Scores Across Patient Skin Tones and Provider Training Levels.* Dermatology and Therapy, 2022. **12**(7): p. 1685-1695.

140. Fu, H.P., et al., *Evaluation and Adoption Of artificial Intelligence In the retail Industry.* International Journal of Retail & Distribution Management, 2023. **51**(6): p. 773-790.

141. Bhuiyan, M.S., *The Role of AI-Enhanced Personalization in Customer Experiences.* Journal of Computer Science and Technology Studies, 2024. **6**(1): p. 162-169.

142. Chen, J.S., T.-T.-Y. Le, and D. Florence, *Usability and Responsiveness of Artificial Intelligence Chatbot on Online Customer Experience in E-Retailing.* International Journal of Retail & Distribution Management, 2021. **49**(11): p. 1512-1531.

143. Khrais, L.T., *Role of Artificial Intelligence in Shaping Consumer Demand in E-Commerce.* Future Internet, 2020. **12**(12): p. 226.

144. Bhagat, R., V. Chauhan, and P. Bhagat, *Investigating the Impact of Artificial Intelligence on Consumer's Purchase Intention in E-Retailing.* Foresight, 2022. **25**(2): p. 249-263.

145. Sasanuma, K. and G.Y. Yang, *Evaluating the Effectiveness of Recommendation Engines on Customer Experience Across Product Categories.* International Journal of Technology and Human Interaction, 2024. **20**(1): p. 1-22.

146. ElSayad, G. and H. Mamdouh, *Are Young Adult Consumers Ready to Be Intelligent Shoppers? The Importance of Perceived Trust and the Usefulness of AI-powered Retail Platforms in Shaping Purchase Intention.* Young Consumers Insight and Ideas for Responsible Marketers, 2024. **25**(6): p. 969-989.

147. Bonetti, F., et al., *Practice Co-Evolution: Collaboratively Embedding Artificial Intelligence in Retail Practices.* Journal of the Academy of Marketing Science, 2022. **51**(4): p. 867-888.

148. Sujata, J., P. Mukul, and K. Hasandeep, *Role of smart communication technologies for smart retailing.* International Journal of Innovative Technology and Exploring Engineering, 2019. **8**: p. 213-218.

149. Wang, Z., *The Influence of Artificial Intelligence on Retail Marketing.* Advances in Economics Management and Political Sciences, 2024. **71**(1): p. 106-111.

150. Mahmoud, A.B., S. Tehseen, and L. Fuxman, *The Dark Side of Artificial Intelligence in Retail Innovation.* 2020: p. 165-180.

151. Fliorent, R., et al., *Artificial Intelligence in Dermatology: Advancements and Challenges in Skin of Color.* International Journal of Dermatology, 2024. **63**(4): p. 455-461.

152. Du-Harpur, X., et al., *What Is AI? Applications of Artificial Intelligence to Dermatology.* British Journal of Dermatology, 2020. **183**(3): p. 423-430.

153. Andrade, T.A.M.d., et al., *Ex Vivo Model of Human Skin (hOSEC) as Alternative to Animal Use for Cosmetic Tests.* Procedia Engineering, 2015. **110**: p. 67-73.

154. Frade, M.A.C., et al., *Prolonged Viability of Human Organotypic Skin Explant in Culture Method (hOSEC).* Anais Brasileiros De Dermatologia, 2015. **90**(3): p. 347-350.

155. Omiye, J.A., et al., *Principles, Applications, and Future of Artificial Intelligence in Dermatology.* Frontiers in Medicine, 2023. **10**.

156. Haykal, D., H. Cartier, and F. Flament, *A Psychosocial Exploration of Augmented Reality and Virtual Reality Apps in Cosmetic Procedures.* Journal of Cosmetic Dermatology, 2024. **23**(12): p. 3863-3870.

157. Grech, V.S., V. Kefala, and E. Rallis, *Cosmetology in the Era of Artificial Intelligence.* Cosmetics, 2024. **11**(4): p. 135.

158. Kayıran, M.A., et al., *Rates of Skincare Product and Cosmetic Procedure Use in Patients With Acne Vulgaris and the Effective Factors: A Multicenter Study With 1,755 Patients.* Journal of Cosmetic Dermatology, 2021. **21**(6): p. 2566-2576.

159. Schachner, L.A., et al., *Insights Into Acne and the Skin Barrier: Optimizing Treatment Regimens With Ceramide -containing Skincare.* Journal of Cosmetic Dermatology, 2023. **22**(11): p. 2902-2909.

160. Goh, C.L., et al., *Challenges and <scp>real-world</Scp> Solutions for Adoption of Holistic Skincare Routine (Cleansing, Treatment, Moisturization, and Photoprotection) in Acne, Rosacea, Atopic Dermatitis, and Sensitive Skin: An Expert Consensus.* Journal of Cosmetic Dermatology, 2024. **23**(8): p. 2516-2523.

161. Santoro, F. and N. Lachmann, *An Open-Label, Intra-Individual Study to Evaluate a Regimen of Three Cosmetic Products Combined With Medical Treatment of Rosacea: Cutaneous Tolerability and Effect on Hydration.* Dermatology and Therapy, 2019. **9**(4): p. 775-784.

162. Jiang, B., Y. Jia, and C. He, *Promoting New Concepts of Skincare via Skinomics and Systems Biology—From Traditional Skincare and Efficacy-based Skincare to Precision Skincare.* Journal of Cosmetic Dermatology, 2018. **17**(6): p. 968-976.

163. Hashimoto, W. and S. Kaneda, *A Smartphone Application for Personalized Facial Aesthetic Monitoring*. Skin Research and Technology, 2024. **30**(7).

164. Lain, E., et al., *A Practical Algorithm for Integrating Skincare to Improve Patient Outcomes and Satisfaction With Energy-Based Dermatologic Procedures*. Journal of Drugs in Dermatology, 2024. **23**(5): p. 353-359.

165. Schaller, M., et al., *Rosacea Treatment Update: Recommendations From the Global <scp>ROS</Scp> Acea <scp>CO</Scp> Nsensus (<scp>ROSCO</Scp>) Panel*. British Journal of Dermatology, 2017. **176**(2): p. 465-471.

166. Ding, Y., C. Zhang, and L.F. Xiang, *Application of Integrated Skincare in Medical Aesthetics: A Literature Review*. Journal of the European Academy of Dermatology and Venereology, 2023. **38**(S6): p. 5-16.

167. Langeveld, M., et al., *Skin Measurement Devices to Assess Skin Quality: A Systematic Review on Reliability and Validity*. Skin Research and Technology, 2021. **28**(2): p. 212-224.

168. Retzler, J., et al., *Process Utilities for Topical Treatment in Atopic Dermatitis*. Quality of Life Research, 2019. **28**(9): p. 2373-2381.

169. Devaux, S., et al., *Adherence to Topical Treatment in Psoriasis: A Systematic Literature Review*. Journal of the European Academy of Dermatology and Venereology, 2012. **26**(s3): p. 61-67.

170. Alexis, A., et al., *Importance of Treating Acne Sequelae in Skin of Color: 6-month Phase <scp>IV</Scp> Study of Trifarotene With an Appropriate Skincare Routine Including <scp>UV</Scp> Protection in Acne-induced Post-inflammatory Hyperpigmentation*. International Journal of Dermatology, 2024. **63**(6): p. 806-815.

171. Park, B., et al., *3D Wide-field Multispectral Photoacoustic Imaging of Human Melanomas <i>in Vivo</I>: A Pilot Study*. Journal of the European Academy of Dermatology and Venereology, 2020. **35**(3): p. 669-676.

172. Hindelang, B., et al., *Non-invasive Imaging in Dermatology and the Unique Potential of Raster-scan Optoacoustic Mesoscopy*. Journal of the European Academy of Dermatology and Venereology, 2019. **33**(6): p. 1051-1061.

173. Yu, X., et al., *Multiscale Skin Imaging<i>in Vivo</I>using Optical Coherence Tomography*. Laser Physics Letters, 2018. **15**(7): p. 075601.

174. Oshina, I., et al., *Three-Dimensional Representation of Triple Spectral Line Imaging Data as an Option for Noncontact Skin Diagnostics*. Journal of Biomedical Optics, 2022. **27**(09).

175. Marchetti, M.A., et al., *<scp>3D Whole-body</Scp> Skin Imaging for Automated Melanoma Detection*. Journal of the European Academy of Dermatology and Venereology, 2023. **37**(5): p. 945-950.

176. Lee, K., M. Kim, and K. Kim, *3D Skin Surface Reconstruction From a Single Image by Merging Global Curvature and Local Texture Using the Guided Filtering for 3D Haptic Palpation*. Skin Research and Technology, 2018. **24**(4): p. 672-685.

177. Park, H., et al., *Development and Application of Artificial Intelligence-based Facial Skin Image Diagnosis System: Changes in Facial Skin Characteristics With Ageing in Korean Women*. International Journal of Cosmetic Science, 2023. **46**(2): p. 199-208.

178. Liu, Y., et al., *A Deep Learning System for Differential Diagnosis of Skin Diseases*. Nature Medicine, 2020. **26**(6): p. 900-908.

179. Kim, M.A., et al., *Skin Biophysical Properties Including Impaired Skin Barrier Function Determine Ultraviolet Sensitivity*. Journal of Cosmetic Dermatology, 2022. **21**(10): p. 5066-5072.

180. Ong, J.B., A. Ma'aram, and C.H. Tee, *3D Scanner's Accuracy in Different Races of Head and Face Measurement for Ergonomic Design*. Malaysian Journal of Medicine and Health Sciences, 2022: p. 65-70.

181. Markiewicz, E. and O. Idowu, *Personalized Skincare: From Molecular Basis to Clinical and Commercial Applications*. Clinical Cosmetic and Investigational Dermatology, 2018. **Volume 11**: p. 161-171.

182. Zhao, J., et al., *The Application of Skin Care Product in Acne Treatment*. Dermatologic Therapy, 2020. **33**(6).

183. Nakra, T., *Integrating Skincare Into Medical Practice*. International Ophthalmology Clinics, 2024. **64**(3): p. 13-22.

184. Wang, Y., et al., *The Application of Skin Care Product in Melasma Treatment*. Clinical Cosmetic and Investigational Dermatology, 2021. **Volume 14**: p. 1165-1171.

185. Barnes, T.M., et al., *Vehicles for Drug Delivery and Cosmetic Moisturizers: Review and Comparison*. Pharmaceutics, 2021. **13**(12): p. 2012.

186. Wibisono, G., J. Setiawan, and A. Sulaiman, *Skinophile: The Art of Skincare Selection With Haar Wavelet*. International Journal of Science Technology & Management, 2023. **4**(6): p. 1574-1580.

187. Gao, T., et al., *The Role of Probiotics in Skin Health and Related Gut–Skin Axis: A Review*. Nutrients, 2023. **15**(14): p. 3123.

188. Uriasz, J. and Ł. Kikowski, *Application of Systemic Cryotherapy in Cosmetology.* Acta Balneologica, 2023. **65**(3): p. 177-182.

189. Leventhal, L.C., R.C. Bianchi, and S.M.J.V.d. Oliveira, *Ensaio Clínico Comparando Três Modalidades De Crioterapia Em Mulheres Não Grávidas.* Revista Da Escola De Enfermagem Da Usp, 2010. **44**(2): p. 339-345.

190. Kępińska-Szyszkowska, M., et al., *The Application of Repeated Whole-Body Cryotherapy in Atopic Dermatitis and Its Impact on Staphylococcus Aureus Colonization — Pilot Study.* Forum Dermatologicum, 2024.

191. Sadeghzadeh-Bazargan, A., et al., *Evaluation and Comparison of the Efficacy and Safety of Cryotherapy and Electrosurgery in the Treatment of Sebaceous Hyperplasia, Seborrheic Keratosis, Cherry Angioma, and Skin Tag: A Blinded Randomized Clinical Trial Study.* Health Science Reports, 2024. **7**(11).

192. Barara, M., V. Mendiratta, and R. Chander, *Cryotherapy in Treatment of Keloids: Evaluation of Factors Affecting Treatment Outcome.* Journal of Cutaneous and Aesthetic Surgery, 2012. **5**(3): p. 185.

193. Ad, J.M., *Ingenol Mebutate Gel After Cryotherapy of Actinic Keratosis: When Can I Start the Topical Treatment?* Clinical Dermatology Open Access Journal, 2017. **2**(2).

194. Choi, Y.G., et al., *Efficacy and Safety of Precision Cryotherapy to Treat Seborrheic Dermatitis of the Scalp.* Dermatologic Surgery, 2023. **50**(1): p. 47-51.

195. Kwack, M.H., et al., *Effect of a Precision Cryotherapy Device With Temperature Adjustability on Pigmentation.* Indian Journal of Dermatology, 2022. **67**(2): p. 204.

196. Jahromi, B.N., et al., *Formaldehyde 5% in Flexible Collodion Compared to Cryotherapy for Treatment of Female Genital Warts.* Indian Journal of Dermatology, 2022. **67**(4): p. 478.

197. Hassan, S.S., et al., *Efficacy and Safety of Long-Pulse Pulsed Dye Laser Delivered With Compression Versus Cryotherapy for Treatment of Solar Lentigines.* Indian Journal of Dermatology, 2011. **56**(1): p. 48.

198. Ataş, H. and M. Gönül, *Evaluation of the Efficacy of Cryosurgery in Patients With Sebaceous Hyperplasia of the Face.* Journal of Cutaneous Medicine and Surgery, 2016. **21**(3): p. 202-206.

199. Themstrup, L., et al., *Cryosurgery Treatment of Actinic Keratoses Monitored by Optical Coherence Tomography: A Pilot Study.* Dermatology, 2012. **225**(3): p. 242-247.

200. Park, J.W., et al., *Split-face Comparative Trial of 785-nm Picosecond Neodymium:yttrium-aluminum-garnet Laser and Precision Cryotherapy Combination Treatment for Facial Benign Pigmented Lesions.* Dermatologic Therapy, 2021. **35**(2).

201. Kelechi, T.J., et al., *Does Cryotherapy Improve Skin Circulation Compared With Compression and Elevation in Preventing Venous Leg Ulcers?* International Wound Journal, 2016. **14**(4): p. 641-648.

202. Jyoti, S.J. and M. Bagri, *Cryotherapy in Knee Osteoarthritis.* EXECUTIVE EDITOR, 2020. **11**(7): p. 389.

203. Chen, W., et al., *Ultrasound Rejuvenation for Upper Facial Skin: A Randomized Blinded Prospective Study.* Journal of Cosmetic Dermatology, 2024. **23**(12): p. 3942-3949.

204. Friedman, O., et al., *Intense Focused Ultrasound for Neck and Lower Face Skin Tightening a Prospective Study.* Journal of Cosmetic Dermatology, 2020. **19**(4): p. 850-854.

205. Hongcharu, W., K. Boonchoo, and M.H. Gold, *The Efficacy and Safety of the High-intensity Parallel Beam Ultrasound Device at the Depth of 1.5 mm for Skin Tightening.* Journal of Cosmetic Dermatology, 2023. **22**(5): p. 1488-1494.

206. Mazzoni, D., et al., *Review of Non-invasive Body Contouring Devices for Fat Reduction, Skin Tightening and Muscle Definition.* Australasian Journal of Dermatology, 2019. **60**(4): p. 278-283.

207. Ko, E.J., et al., *Efficacy and Safety of Non-invasive Body Tightening With High-intensity Focused Ultrasound (HIFU).* Skin Research and Technology, 2017. **23**(4): p. 558-562.

208. Kim, Y.J., et al., *The Efficacy and Safety of Dual-Frequency Ultrasound for Improving Skin Hydration and Erythema in Patients With Rosacea and Acne.* Journal of Clinical Medicine, 2021. **10**(4): p. 834.

209. Meyer-Rogge, D., et al., *Facial Skin Rejuvenation With High Frequency Ultrasound: Multicentre Study of Dual-Frequency Ultrasound.* Journal of Cosmetics Dermatological Sciences and Applications, 2012. **02**(02): p. 68-73.

210. Malinowska, S. and R.K. Mlosek, *From Sonar to Ultrasound Examination of the Skin - Development and Characterization of the Method.* Aesthetic Cosmetology and Medicine, 2022. **11**(6): p. 203-208.

211. Park, H., et al., *High-Intensity Focused Ultrasound for the Treatment of Wrinkles and Skin Laxity in Seven Different Facial Areas.* Annals of Dermatology, 2015. **27**(6): p. 688.

212. Alam, M., et al., *Ultrasound Tightening of Facial and Neck Skin: A Rater-Blinded Prospective Cohort Study.* Journal of the American Academy of Dermatology, 2010. **62**(2): p. 262-269.

213. Suh, D.H., et al., *Intense Focused Ultrasound Tightening in Asian Skin: Clinical and Pathologic Results.* Dermatologic Surgery, 2011. **37**(11): p. 1595-1602.

214. Hu, S., et al., *Needle-Free Injection of Exosomes Derived From Human Dermal Fibroblast Spheroids Ameliorates Skin Photoaging.* Acs Nano, 2019. **13**(10): p. 11273-11282.

215. Rigotti, G., et al., *Expanded Stem Cells, Stromal-Vascular Fraction, and Platelet-Rich Plasma Enriched Fat: Comparing Results of Different Facial Rejuvenation Approaches in a Clinical Trial.* Aesthetic Surgery Journal, 2016. **36**(3): p. 261-270.

216. Ash, M., et al., *The Innovative and Evolving Landscape of Topical Exosome and Peptide Therapies: A Systematic Review of the Available Literature.* Aesthetic Surgery Journal Open Forum, 2024. **6**.

217. Lee, H.J., et al., *Efficacy of Microneedling Plus Human Stem Cell Conditioned Medium for Skin Rejuvenation: A Randomized, Controlled, Blinded Split-Face Study.* Annals of Dermatology, 2014. **26**(5): p. 584.

218. Kim, S.-N., et al., *The Effects of Human Bone Marrow-Derived Mesenchymal Stem Cell Conditioned Media Produced With Fetal Bovine Serum or Human Platelet Lysate on Skin Rejuvenation Characteristics.* International Journal of Stem Cells, 2021. **14**(1): p. 94-102.

219. Qiang, H., et al., *The Clinical Efficacy of Autologous Platelet-Rich Plasma Combined With Ultra-Pulsed Fractional CO_2 Laser Therapy for Facial Rejuvenation.* Rejuvenation Research, 2017. **20**(1): p. 25-31.

220. Leo, M.S., et al., *Systematic Review of the Use of Platelet-rich Plasma in Aesthetic Dermatology.* Journal of Cosmetic Dermatology, 2015. **14**(4): p. 315-323.

221. Widianingsih, N.P.S., T. Setyaningrum, and C.R.S. Prakoeswa, *The Efficacy and Safety of Fractional Erbium Yag Laser Combined With Topical Amniotic Membrane Stem Cell (AMSC) Metabolite Product for Facial Rejuvenation: A Controlled, Split-Face Study.* Dermatology Reports, 2019.

222. Liang, X., et al., *Efficacy of Microneedling Combined With Local Application of Human Umbilical Cord-Derived Mesenchymal Stem*

Cells Conditioned Media in Skin Brightness and Rejuvenation: A Randomized Controlled Split-Face Study. Frontiers in Medicine, 2022. **9**.

223. Aust, M., et al., *Platelet-Rich Plasma for Skin Rejuvenation and Treatment of Actinic Elastosis in the Lower Eyelid Area.* Cureus, 2018.

224. Gaur, M., M. Dobke, and V.V. Lunyak, *Mesenchymal Stem Cells From Adipose Tissue in Clinical Applications for Dermatological Indications and Skin Aging.* International Journal of Molecular Sciences, 2017. **18**(1): p. 208.

225. Damayanti, R.H., T. Rusdiana, and N. Wathoni, *Mesenchymal Stem Cell Secretome for Dermatology Application: A Review.* Clinical Cosmetic and Investigational Dermatology, 2021. **Volume 14**: p. 1401-1412.

226. Azzam, E.Z., W.M. Elmidany, and A. Zidan, *Micro-Autologous Fat Transplantation (MAFT) for Dorsal Hand Rejuvenation.* The Egyptian Journal of Plastic and Reconstructive Surgery, 2020. **43**(3): p. 517-525.

227. Ablon, G., Z.I. Smith, and G. Munavalli, *Applications of Plasma-Rich Plasma, Exosomes, and Stem Cells in Aesthetics: A Narrative Review.* Dermatological Reviews, 2024. **5**(4).

228. Benar, H. and E.B. Benar, *A New Nonsurgical Combination Approach for Skin Tightening and Remodeling; Endoskin—A Comparative Study.* Journal of Cosmetic Dermatology, 2024. **23**(8): p. 2574-2580.

229. Lee, Y.I., et al., *Randomized Controlled Study for the Anti-aging Effect of Human Adipocyte-derived Mesenchymal Stem Cell Media Combined With Niacinamide After Laser Therapy.* Journal of Cosmetic Dermatology, 2020. **20**(6): p. 1774-1781.

230. Nanić, L., et al., *In Vivo Skin Regeneration and Wound Healing Using Cell Micro-Transplantation.* Pharmaceutics, 2022. **14**(9): p. 1955.

231. Jha, A.K., et al., *Original Article: Platelet-rich Plasma With Microneedling in Androgenetic Alopecia Along With Dermoscopic Pre- and Post-treatment Evaluation.* Journal of Cosmetic Dermatology, 2017. **17**(3): p. 313-318.

232. Butt, G., et al., *Efficacy of Platelet-rich Plasma in Androgenetic Alopecia Patients.* Journal of Cosmetic Dermatology, 2018. **18**(4): p. 996-1001.

233. Du, L., et al., *A Novel and Convenient Method for the Preparation and Activation of PRP Without Any Additives: Temperature Controlled PRP.* Biomed Research International, 2018. **2018**: p. 1-12.

234.   V, M. and S. Murugan P, *Evaluation of the Efficacy of Platelet-Rich Plasma Injections With and Without Microneedling for Managing Atrophic Facial Acne Scars: A Prospective Comparative Study.* Cureus, 2024.

235.   Gupta, M., K.D. Barman, and R. Sarkar, *A Comparative Study of Microneedling Alone Versus Along With Platelet-Rich Plasma in Acne Scars.* Journal of Cutaneous and Aesthetic Surgery, 2021. **14**(1): p. 64.

236.   Ibrahim, Z.A., A.A. El-Ashmawy, and O.A.E. Shora, *Therapeutic Effect of Microneedling and Autologous Platelet-rich Plasma in the Treatment of Atrophic Scars: A Randomized Study.* Journal of Cosmetic Dermatology, 2017. **16**(3): p. 388-399.

237.   Kang, C. and D. Lu, *Combined Effect of Microneedling and Platelet-Rich Plasma for the Treatment of Acne Scars: A Meta-Analysis.* Frontiers in Medicine, 2022. **8**.

238.   Patel, Y., B. Parmar, and D.D. Umrigar, *A Comparative Study of Combined Microneedling With Platelet Rich Plasma Versus Microneedling Alone in Acne Scar.* 2020: p. 63-64.

239.   Singhal, P., et al., *Efficacy of Platelet-Rich Plasma in Treatment of Androgenic Alopecia.* Asian Journal of Transfusion Science, 2015. **9**(2): p. 159.

240.   Rios, M.C.O., *The Role of Platelet-Rich Plasma in Androgenetic Alopecia: A Comprehensive Narrative Review.* 2023: p. 62-63.

241.   Zarei, F. and A. Abbaszadeh, *Stem Cell and Skin Rejuvenation.* Journal of Cosmetic and Laser Therapy, 2018. **20**(3): p. 193-197.

242.   Lee, D.E., N.T. Ayoub, and D.K. Agrawal, *Mesenchymal Stem Cells and Cutaneous Wound Healing: Novel Methods to Increase Cell Delivery and Therapeutic Efficacy.* Stem Cell Research & Therapy, 2016. **7**(1).

243.   Nowacki, M., et al., *Use of Adipose-Derived Stem Cells to Support Topical Skin Adhesive for Wound Closure: A Preliminary Report From Animal in Vivo Study.* Biomed Research International, 2016. **2016**: p. 1-10.

244.   Zavec, A.B., *Extracellular Vesicles for Cosmetic Applications.* 2023.

245.   Silva, W.N., et al., *Macrophage-derived <scp>GPNMB</Scp> Accelerates Skin Healing.* Experimental Dermatology, 2018. **27**(6): p. 630-635.

246.   Kim, H.J., et al., *A Study on Clinical Effectiveness of Cosmetics Containing Human Stem Cell Conditioned Media.* Biomedical Dermatology, 2020. **4**(1).

247. Zappelli, C., et al., *Effective Active Ingredients Obtained Through Biotechnology.* Cosmetics, 2016. **3**(4): p. 39.

248. Herberts, C., M.S.G. Kwa, and H.P.H. Hermsen, *Risk Factors in the Development of Stem Cell Therapy.* Journal of Translational Medicine, 2011. **9**(1).

249. Barker, R.A., et al., *The Challenges of First-in-Human Stem Cell Clinical Trials: What Does This Mean for Ethics and Institutional Review Boards?* Stem Cell Reports, 2018. **10**(5): p. 1429-1431.

250. Bilharinho, V.P., et al., *Therapeutic Use of Mesenchymal Stem Cells May Be a Means of Transmitting Leishmaniasis in Dogs.* 2024.

251. Freeman, M. and M. Fuerst, *Does the FDA Have Regulatory Authority Over Adult Autologous Stem Cell Therapies? 21 CFR 1271 and the Emperor's New Clothes.* Journal of Translational Medicine, 2012. **10**(1).

252. Rinaldi, F. and R.C.R. Perlingeiro, *Stem Cells for Skeletal Muscle Regeneration: Therapeutic Potential and Roadblocks.* Translational Research, 2014. **163**(4): p. 409-417.

253. Mohamed, H., H. Hassan, and S. Ahmed, *Combined Microneedling and Platelet-Rich Plasma in Management of Post-Acne Scars: A Comparative Study.* Minia Journal of Medical Research, 2022. **0**(0): p. 132-134.

254. Yaseen, U., S. Shah, and A. Bashir, *Combination of Platelet Rich Plasma and Microneedling in the Management of Atrophic Acne Scars.* International Journal of Research in Dermatology, 2017. **3**(3): p. 346.

255. Fertig, R., et al., *Microneedling for the Treatment of Hair Loss?* Journal of the European Academy of Dermatology and Venereology, 2017. **32**(4): p. 564-569.

256. Kim, D.H., et al., *Can Platelet-Rich Plasma Be Used for Skin Rejuvenation? Evaluation of Effects of Platelet-Rich Plasma on Human Dermal Fibroblast.* Annals of Dermatology, 2011. **23**(4): p. 424.

257. Meghe, S.R., et al., *Microneedling With PRP for Acne Scars: A New Tool in Dermatologist Arsenal - A Scoping Review.* Journal of Pharmacy and Bioallied Sciences, 2024. **16**(Suppl 2): p. S1417-S1419.

258. Abuaf, Ö.K., et al., *Histologic Evidence of New Collagen Formulation Using Platelet Rich Plasma in Skin Rejuvenation: A Prospective Controlled Clinical Study.* Annals of Dermatology, 2016. **28**(6): p. 718.

259. Shah, K.B., et al., *A Comparative Study of Microneedling With Platelet-Rich Plasma Plus Topical Minoxidil (5%) and Topical Minoxidil (5%)*

Alone in Androgenetic Alopecia. International Journal of Trichology, 2017. **9**(1): p. 14.
260. Robati, R.M., et al., *Efficacy of Microneedling Versus Fractional Er:YAG Laser in Facial Rejuvenation.* Journal of Cosmetic Dermatology, 2020. **19**(6): p. 1333-1340.
261. Kamila, M.Z.-P. and H. Rotsztejn, *The Effectiveness of Ferulic Acid and Microneedling in Reducing Signs of Photoaging: A Split-face Comparative Study.* Dermatologic Therapy, 2020. **33**(6).
262. Sadeghzadeh-Bazargan, A., et al., *Evaluation and Comparison of the Efficacy and Safety of the Combination of Topical Phenytoin and Microneedling With Microneedling Alone in the Treatment of Atrophic Acne Scars: A Controlled Blinded Randomized Clinical Trial.* Skin Research and Technology, 2024. **30**(6).
263. Atiyeh, B.S., O.A. Ghanem, and F. Chahine, *Microneedling: Percutaneous Collagen Induction (PCI) Therapy for Management of Scars and Photoaged Skin—Scientific Evidence and Review of the Literature.* Aesthetic Plastic Surgery, 2020. **45**(1): p. 296-308.
264. Esmat, S., et al., *Automated Microneedling Versus Fractional CO2 Laser in Treatment of Traumatic Scars: A Clinical and Histochemical Study.* Dermatologic Surgery, 2021. **47**(11): p. 1480-1485.
265. Seok, J., et al., *A Potential Relationship Between Skin Hydration and Stamp-type Microneedle Intradermal Hyaluronic Acid Injection in Middle-aged Male Face.* Journal of Cosmetic Dermatology, 2016. **15**(4): p. 578-582.
266. Avcil, M., et al., *Efficacy of Bioactive Peptides Loaded on Hyaluronic Acid Microneedle Patches: A Monocentric Clinical Study.* Journal of Cosmetic Dermatology, 2019. **19**(2): p. 328-337.
267. Sreeharsha, N. and M.A.L. gharsan, *Therapeutics of Microneedling for Skin Repair.* Asian Journal of Research in Pharmaceutical Sciences, 2022: p. 199-204.
268. Tan, M.G., et al., *Radiofrequency Microneedling: A Comprehensive and Critical Review.* Dermatologic Surgery, 2021. **47**(6): p. 755-761.
269. Seo, K.Y., et al., *Skin Rejuvenation by Microneedle Fractional Radiofrequency Treatment in Asian Skin; Clinical and Histological Analysis.* Lasers in Surgery and Medicine, 2012. **44**(8): p. 631-636.
270. Feng, J., J. Qi, and L. Huang, *Histological Damage Characteristics and Quantitive Analysis of Porcine Skin With Non-insulated Microneedle Radiofrequency.* Skin Research and Technology, 2023. **29**(6).

271. Hong, J.Y., et al., *Prospective, Preclinical Comparison of the Performance Between Radiofrequency Microneedling and Microneedling Alone in Reversing Photoaged Skin*. Journal of Cosmetic Dermatology, 2019. **19**(5): p. 1105-1109.

272. Elsaie, M.L., et al., *Nonablative Radiofrequency for Skin Rejuvenation*. Dermatologic Surgery, 2010. **36**(5): p. 577-589.

273. Nilforoushzadeh, M.A., et al., *Biometric Changes of Skin Parameters in Using of Microneedling Fractional Radiofrequency for Skin Tightening and Rejuvenation Facial*. Skin Research and Technology, 2020. **26**(6): p. 859-866.

274. Corrado, C., et al., *Exosomes as Intercellular Signaling Organelles Involved in Health and Disease: Basic Science and Clinical Applications*. International Journal of Molecular Sciences, 2013. **14**(3): p. 5338-5366.

275. Barile, L. and G. Vassalli, *Exosomes: Therapy Delivery Tools and Biomarkers of Diseases*. Pharmacology & Therapeutics, 2017. **174**: p. 63-78.

276. Salah, M. and F.B. Naini, *Exosomes in Craniofacial Tissue Reconstruction*. Maxillofacial Plastic and Reconstructive Surgery, 2022. **44**(1).

277. Gerami, M.H., et al., *Emerging Role of Mesenchymal Stem/Stromal Cells (MSCs) and MSCs-derived Exosomes in Bone- And Joint-Associated Musculoskeletal Disorders: A New Frontier*. European Journal of Medical Research, 2023. **28**(1).

278. Konala, V.B.R., et al., *The Current Landscape of the Mesenchymal Stromal Cell Secretome: A New Paradigm for Cell-Free Regeneration*. Cytotherapy, 2016. **18**(1): p. 13-24.

279. Huang, L., et al., *Exosomes in Mesenchymal Stem Cells, a New Therapeutic Strategy for Cardiovascular Diseases?* International Journal of Biological Sciences, 2015. **11**(2): p. 238-245.

280. Liao, Z., et al., *Exosomes From Mesenchymal Stem Cells Modulate Endoplasmic Reticulum Stress to Protect Against Nucleus Pulposus Cell Death and Ameliorate Intervertebral Disc Degeneration in Vivo*. Theranostics, 2019. **9**(14): p. 4084-4100.

281. Rohde, E., K. Pachler, and M. Gimona, *Manufacturing and Characterization of Extracellular Vesicles From Umbilical Cord–derived Mesenchymal Stromal Cells for Clinical Testing*. Cytotherapy, 2019. **21**(6): p. 581-592.

282. Ha, D.-S., et al., *Mesenchymal Stem/Stromal Cell-Derived Exosomes for Immunomodulatory Therapeutics and Skin Regeneration*. Cells, 2020. **9**(5): p. 1157.

283. Han, C., et al., *Exosomes and Their Therapeutic Potentials of Stem Cells*. Stem Cells International, 2015. **2016**(1).

284. Kim, D.H., et al., *Noninvasive Assessment of Exosome Pharmacokinetics in Vivo: A Review*. Pharmaceutics, 2019. **11**(12): p. 649.

285. Asadpour, A., et al., *Uncovering the Gray Zone: Mapping the Global Landscape of Direct-to-Consumer Businesses Offering Interventions Based on Secretomes, Extracellular Vesicles, and Exosomes*. Stem Cell Research & Therapy, 2023. **14**(1).

286. Lin, W.C., et al., *Haematopoietic Cell‑derived Exosomes in Cancer Development and Therapeutics: From Basic Science to Clinical Practice*. Clinical and Translational Medicine, 2023. **13**(10).

287. Chae, J.B., et al., *The Effects of Hydroporation on Melasma With Anti-aging Cocktail*. Journal of Cosmetic Dermatology, 2017. **16**(4).

288. Sanz, M.T., et al., *Biorevitalizing Effect of a Novel Facial Serum Containing Apple Stem Cell Extract, Pro‑collagen Lipopeptide, Creatine, and Urea on Skin Aging Signs*. Journal of Cosmetic Dermatology, 2015. **15**(1): p. 24-30.

289. Song, I.-B., et al., *Effects of 7-MEGA^{TM}500 on Oxidative Stress, Inflammation, and Skin Regeneration in H_2O_2-Treated Skin Cells*. Toxicological Research, 2018. **34**(2): p. 103-110.

290. Zhou, H., et al., *Anti-Cyclooxygenase, Anti-Glycation, and Anti-Skin Aging Effect of Dendrobium Officinale Flowers' Aqueous Extract and Its Phytochemical Validation in Aging*. Frontiers in Immunology, 2023. **14**.

291. Na, G.H., et al., *Skin Anti-Aging Efficacy of Enzyme-Treated Supercritical Caviar Extract: A Randomized, Double-Blind, Placebo-Controlled Clinical Trial*. Nutrients, 2023. **16**(1): p. 137.

292. Fujinami, K., et al., *Anti-Aging Effects of Polyoxometalates on Skin*. Applied Sciences, 2021. **11**(24): p. 11948.

293. Kim, K.E., et al., *Periorbital Skin Rejuvenation of Asian Skin Using Microneedle Fractional Radiofrequency*. Annals of Dermatology, 2023. **35**(5): p. 360.

294. Gulfan, M.C.B., et al., *Efficacy and Safety of Using Noninsulated Microneedle Radiofrequency Alone Versus in Combination With*

Polynucleotides for the Treatment of Melasma: A Pilot Study. Dermatology and Therapy, 2022. **12**(6): p. 1325-1336.

295. Lee, H.J., et al., *Microneedle Fractional Radiofrequency Increases Epidermal Hyaluronan and Reverses Age-related Epidermal Dysfunction.* Lasers in Surgery and Medicine, 2015. **48**(2): p. 140-149.

296. Zahr, A.S., et al., *An Open-label, Single-site Study to Evaluate the Tolerability, Safety, and Efficacy of Using a Novel Facial Moisturizer for Preparation and Accelerated Healing Pre and Post a Single Full-face Radiofrequency Microneedling Treatment.* Journal of Cosmetic Dermatology, 2018. **18**(1): p. 94-106.

297. Gold, M.H., et al., *Non-insulated Smooth Motion, Micro-needles RF Fractional Treatment for Wrinkle Reduction and Lifting of the Lower Face: International Study.* Lasers in Surgery and Medicine, 2016. **48**(8): p. 727-733.

298. Maloney, M.E., et al., *A Randomized, Single-Center, Double-Blind, Controlled Case Study Evaluating Procedure Pairing of a Neurocosmetic Postprocedure Cream With Radiofrequency Microneedling for Facial Rejuvenation.* Journal of Cosmetic Dermatology, 2024. **23**(12): p. 4077-4084.

299. Wootten, S., et al., *An Evaluation of Electrocoagulation and Thermal Diffusion Following Radiofrequency Microneedling Using an in Vivo Porcine Skin Model.* Journal of Cosmetic Dermatology, 2020. **20**(4): p. 1133-1139.

300. Mamizadeh, M., et al., *Comparison the Effect of Fractional RF Laser With Microneedling on Facial Skin Rejuvenation, Open Pores and Skin Lightening: A Non-Randomized Controlled Clinical Trial.* 2024. **13**(1): p. 16-23.

301. Kim, H.K., et al., *Immediate and Late Effects of Pulse Widths and Cycles on Bipolar, Gated Radiofrequency-Induced Tissue Reactions in in Vivo Rat Skin.* Clinical Cosmetic and Investigational Dermatology, 2023. **Volume 16**: p. 721-729.

302. Cho, S.B., et al., *In Vivo Skin Reactions From Pulsed-type, Bipolar, Alternating Current Radiofrequency Treatment Using Invasive Noninsulated Electrodes.* Skin Research and Technology, 2018. **24**(2): p. 318-325.

303. Choi, M.K., et al., *Successful Treatment of Refractory Melasma Using Invasive Micro-Pulsed Electric Signal Device.* Medical Lasers, 2015. **4**(1): p. 39-44.

304. Dayan, E., et al., *Multimodal Radiofrequency Application for Lower Face and Neck Laxity.* Plastic and Reconstructive Surgery Global Open, 2020. **8**(8): p. e2862.

305. Sasaki, G.H., *The Significance of Trans-Epidermal Water Loss After Microneedling and Microneedling-Radiofrequency Procedures: Histological and IRB-Approved Safety Study.* Aesthetic Surgery Journal Open Forum, 2019. **1**(3).

306. Lee, C. and M.H. Gold, *Updates on Radiofrequency Devices for Skin Tightening and Body Contouring.* Dermatological Reviews, 2020. **1**(3): p. 75-83.

307. Cook, J.L., et al., *Fractional Radiofrequency Microneedling for Skin Rejuvenation.* Dermatological Reviews, 2020. **1**(1): p. 16-19.

308. Saonanon, P., et al., *Skin Tightening by an Insulated Microneedle Radiofrequency Device Combined With Lower Blepharoplasty: A Randomized Fellow Eye Comparison Study.* The Journal of Cosmetic Medicine, 2021. **5**(1): p. 30-35.

309. Chia, C.T., et al., *Radiofrequency-Assisted Liposuction Compared With Aggressive Superficial, Subdermal Liposuction of the Arms.* Plastic and Reconstructive Surgery Global Open, 2015. **3**(7): p. e459.

310. Hendricks, A.J. and S.Z. Farhang, *Dermatologic Facial Applications of Morpheus8 Fractional Radiofrequency Microneedling.* Journal of Cosmetic Dermatology, 2022. **21**(S1).

311. Mehrabi, J.N. and O. Artzi, *Fractional Radiofrequency Based Combinations for Augmented Skin Rejuvenation Results.* Dermatological Reviews, 2020. **1**(1): p. 27-32.

312. Jung, J.W., et al., *A Face-Split Study to Evaluate the Effects of Microneedle Radiofrequency With Q-Switched Nd:YAG Laser for the Treatment of Melasma.* Annals of Dermatology, 2019. **31**(2): p. 133.

313. Gajbhiye, S. and S. Sakharwade, *Silver Nanoparticles in Cosmetics.* Journal of Cosmetics Dermatological Sciences and Applications, 2016. **06**(01): p. 48-53.

314. Salas, M.F., et al., *Nanotechnological Applications in Dermocosmetics.* European Journal of Pharmaceutical Research, 2023. **3**(1): p. 1-7.

315. Aziz, Z.A.A., et al., *Role of Nanotechnology for Design and Development of Cosmeceutical: Application in Makeup and Skin Care.* Frontiers in Chemistry, 2019. **7**.

316. Majerič, P., et al., *Physicochemical Properties of Gold Nanoparticles for Skin Care Creams.* Materials, 2023. **16**(8): p. 3011.

317. Lohani, A., et al., *Nanotechnology-Based Cosmeceuticals*. Isrn Dermatology, 2014. **2014**: p. 1-14.

318. Hidayah, R., W. Soeratri, and N. Rosita, *Nano Carrier as a Cosmetic Delivery System*. Sun International Journal of Engineering and Basic Sciences, 2018. **01**(03): p. 45-48.

319. Bilal, M. and H.M.N. Iqbal, *New Insights on Unique Features and Role of Nanostructured Materials in Cosmetics*. Cosmetics, 2020. **7**(2): p. 24.

320. Raj, S., et al., *Nanotechnology in Cosmetics: Opportunities and Challenges*. Journal of Pharmacy and Bioallied Sciences, 2012. **4**(3): p. 186.

321. Zhang, X.F., et al., *Silver Nanoparticles: Synthesis, Characterization, Properties, Applications, and Therapeutic Approaches*. International Journal of Molecular Sciences, 2016. **17**(9): p. 1534.

322. Mondéjar-López, M., et al., *Biogenic Silver Nanoparticles From Iris Tuberosa as Potential Preservative in Cosmetic Products*. Molecules, 2021. **26**(15): p. 4696.

323. Lu, P.-J., et al., *Analysis of Titanium Dioxide and Zinc Oxide Nanoparticles in Cosmetics*. Journal of Food and Drug Analysis, 2015. **23**(3): p. 587-594.

324. Singh, P. and A. Nanda, *Enhanced Sun Protection of Nano -sized Metal Oxide Particles Over Conventional Metal Oxide Particles: An <i>in Vitro</I> Comparative Study*. International Journal of Cosmetic Science, 2014. **36**(3): p. 273-283.

325. Yoshioka, Y., et al., *Allergic Responses Induced by the Immunomodulatory Effects of Nanomaterials Upon Skin Exposure*. Frontiers in Immunology, 2017. **8**.

326. Pulit-Prociak, J., et al., *Incorporation of Metallic Nanoparticles Into Cosmetic Preparations and Assessment of Their Physicochemical and Utility Properties*. Journal of Surfactants and Detergents, 2018. **21**(4): p. 575-591.

327. Bolzinger, M.A., S. Briançon, and Y. Chevalier, *Nanoparticles Through the Skin: Managing Conflicting Results of Inorganic and Organic Particles in Cosmetics and Pharmaceutics*. Wiley Interdisciplinary Reviews Nanomedicine and Nanobiotechnology, 2011. **3**(5): p. 463-478.

328. Lee, C.C., et al., *Exposure to ZnO/TiO2 Nanoparticles Affects Health Outcomes in Cosmetics Salesclerks*. International Journal of Environmental Research and Public Health, 2020. **17**(17): p. 6088.

329. Shokri, J., *Nanocosmetics: Benefits and Risks*. Bioimpacts, 2017. **7**(4): p. 207-208.

330. Wang, X., et al., *GHK-Cu-liposomes Accelerate Scald Wound Healing in Mice by Promoting Cell Proliferation and Angiogenesis*. Wound Repair and Regeneration, 2017. **25**(2): p. 270-278.

331. Pierre, M.B.R. and I.d.S.M. Costa, *Liposomal Systems as Drug Delivery Vehicles for Dermal and Transdermal Applications*. Archives of Dermatological Research, 2011. **303**(9).

332. Campos, P.M.B.G.M., et al., *Efficacy of Cosmetic Formulations Containing Dispersion of Liposome With Magnesium Ascorbyl Phosphate, Alpha-Lipoic Acid and Kinetin*. Photochemistry and Photobiology, 2012. **88**(3): p. 748-752.

333. Phan, H.T., P.a.H.C.M. City, and V.T.T. Tran, *Preparation and Characterization of Liposomes Encapsulating Calophyllum Inophyllum Oil*. Vietnam Journal of Science Technology and Engineering, 2017. **59**(4): p. 56-60.

334. Srinivas, L. and V.S.V.K. Tenneti, *Drug Delivery Through Liposomes*. 2022.

335. Chen, R., et al., *Advanced Liposome-Loaded Scaffolds for Therapeutic and Tissue Engineering Applications*. Biomaterials, 2020. **232**: p. 119706.

336. Bi, Y., et al., *Liposomal Vitamin D3 as an Anti-Aging Agent for the Skin*. Pharmaceutics, 2019. **11**(7): p. 311.

337. Witting, M., et al., *Interactions of Hyaluronic Acid With the Skin and Implications for the Dermal Delivery of Biomacromolecules*. Molecular Pharmaceutics, 2015. **12**(5): p. 1391-1401.

338. Mostafa, E.S., et al., *A Unique Acylated Flavonol Glycoside From Prunus Persica (L.) Var. Florida Prince: A New Solid Lipid Nanoparticle Cosmeceutical Formulation for Skincare*. Antioxidants, 2021. **10**(3): p. 436.

339. Vishal Tiwari, S.J.N., *Formulation and Evaluation of Solid Lipid Nanoparticles of Naringin to Enhance Its Bioavailability*. 2023. **44**(3): p. 4754-4763.

340. Naseri, N., H. Valizadeh, and P. Zakeri–Milani, *Solid Lipid Nanoparticles and Nanostructured Lipid Carriers: Structure, Preparation and Application*. Advanced Pharmaceutical Bulletin, 2015. **5**(3): p. 305-313.

341. Castellani, S., et al., *Nanoparticle Delivery of Grape Seed-Derived Proanthocyanidins to Airway Epithelial Cells Dampens Oxidative*

Stress and Inflammation. Journal of Translational Medicine, 2018. **16**(1).

342. Sultana, S. and S. Mohammed, *Formulation and In-Vitro Evaluation of Solid Lipid Nanoparticles Containing Nadolol.* International Journal of Pharmaceutical Sciences and Research, 2022. **13**(7).

343. Gaur, P.K., S. Mishra, and S. Purohit, *Solid Lipid Nanoparticles of Guggul Lipid as Drug Carrier for Transdermal Drug Delivery.* Biomed Research International, 2013. **2013**: p. 1-10.

344. Rodríguez-Burneo, N., M.A. Busquets, and J. Estelrich, *Magnetic Nanoemulsions: Comparison Between Nanoemulsions Formed by Ultrasonication and by Spontaneous Emulsification.* Nanomaterials, 2017. **7**(7): p. 190.

345. Alliod, O., et al., *Influence of Viscosity for Oil-in-Water and Water-in-Oil Nanoemulsions Production by SPG Premix Membrane Emulsification.* Chemical Engineering Research and Design, 2019. **142**: p. 87-99.

346. Souto, E.B., et al., *Nanomaterials for Skin Delivery of Cosmeceuticals and Pharmaceuticals.* Applied Sciences, 2020. **10**(5): p. 1594.

347. Ribeiro, R.C.d.A., et al., *Production and Characterization of Cosmetic Nanoemulsions Containing Opuntia Ficus-Indica (L.) Mill Extract as Moisturizing Agent.* Molecules, 2015. **20**(2): p. 2492-2509.

348. Assali, M. and A. Zaid, *Features, Applications, and Sustainability of Lipid Nanoparticles in Cosmeceuticals.* Saudi Pharmaceutical Journal, 2022. **30**(1): p. 53-65.

349. Agnish, S., A.D. Sharma, and I. Kaur, *Nanoemulsions (O/W) Containing Cymbopogon Pendulus Essential Oil: Development, Characterization, Stability Study, and Evaluation of in Vitro Anti-Bacterial, Anti-Inflammatory, Anti-Diabetic Activities.* Bionanoscience, 2022. **12**(2): p. 540-554.

350. Crowley, J.S., A. Liu, and M. Dobke, *Regenerative and Stem Cell-Based Techniques for Facial Rejuvenation.* Experimental Biology and Medicine, 2021. **246**(16): p. 1829-1837.

351. Chang, Y., L. McLandsborough, and D.J. McClements, *Physical Properties and Antimicrobial Efficacy of Thyme Oil Nanoemulsions: Influence of Ripening Inhibitors.* Journal of Agricultural and Food Chemistry, 2012. **60**(48): p. 12056-12063.

352. Rodrigues, E.d.C.R., et al., *Development of a Larvicidal Nanoemulsion With Copaiba (Copaifera Duckei) Oleoresin.* Revista Brasileira De Farmacognosia, 2014. **24**(6): p. 699-705.

353. Elsewedy, H.S., et al., *Enhancement of Anti-Inflammatory Activity of Optimized Niosomal Colchicine Loaded Into Jojoba Oil-Based Emulgel Using Response Surface Methodology.* Gels, 2021. **8**(1): p. 16.

354. Lovelyn, C. and A.A. Attama, *Current State of Nanoemulsions in Drug Delivery.* Journal of Biomaterials and Nanobiotechnology, 2011. **02**(05): p. 626-639.

355. Atrux-Tallau, N., et al., *Skin Cell Targeting With Self-assembled Ligand Addressed Nanoemulsion Droplets.* International Journal of Cosmetic Science, 2013. **35**(3): p. 310-318.

356. Ghule, P.S., *Use of Nanotechnology in Cosmetics and Cosmeceuticals.* International Journal for Research in Applied Science and Engineering Technology, 2024. **12**(10): p. 160-167.

357. Marzuki, N.H.C., R.A. Wahab, and M.A. Hamid, *An Overview of Nanoemulsion: Concepts of Development and Cosmeceutical Applications.* Biotechnology & Biotechnological Equipment, 2019. **33**(1): p. 779-797.

358. Rao, T.R., C. Manikanta, and M. Shashank, *Nanotechnology in Cosmetics: An Overview.* International Journal of Research and Review, 2024. **11**(11): p. 269-289.

359. George, N. and D.G. Devi, *Phytonano Silver for Cosmetic Formulation-Synthesis, Characterization, and Assessment of Antimicrobial and Antityrosinase Potential.* Discover Nano, 2024. **19**(1).

360. Cordeiro, A.C.F., et al., *Allergic Contact Dermatitis After the Use of Cosmetics Containing Parabens: Systematic Review and Meta-Analysis.* Brazilian Archives of Biology and Technology, 2022. **65**.

361. Chow, E. and S. Mahalingaiah, *Cosmetics Use and Age at Menopause: Is There a Connection?* Fertility and Sterility, 2016. **106**(4): p. 978-990.

362. Marie, C., et al., *Changes in Cosmetics Use During Pregnancy and Risk Perception by Women.* International Journal of Environmental Research and Public Health, 2016. **13**(4): p. 383.

363. Bilal, M., S. Mehmood, and H.M.N. Iqbal, *The Beast of Beauty: Environmental and Health Concerns of Toxic Components in Cosmetics.* Cosmetics, 2020. **7**(1): p. 13.

364. Juliano, C.C.A. and G.A. Magrini, *Cosmetic Ingredients as Emerging Pollutants of Environmental and Health Concern. A Mini-Review.* Cosmetics, 2017. **4**(2): p. 11.

365. Chen, X., *The Impact of Hazardous Substances in Cosmetics, and Treatment Measures.* Iop Conference Series Earth and Environmental Science, 2022. **1011**(1): p. 012024.

366. Sharmeen, J.B., et al., *Essential Oils as Natural Sources of Fragrance Compounds for Cosmetics and Cosmeceuticals*. Molecules, 2021. **26**(3): p. 666.

367. Sharma, S., et al., *An Online Survey on Usability, Acceptability, Attitude and Knowledge of Herbal and Synthetic Cosmetic Among Sikkimese Population*. Journal of Drug Delivery and Therapeutics, 2024. **14**(7): p. 129-135.

368. Quoquab, F., A. Jaini, and J. Mohammad, *Does It Matter Who Exhibits More Green Purchase Behavior of Cosmetic Products in Asian Culture? A Multi-Group Analysis Approach*. International Journal of Environmental Research and Public Health, 2020. **17**(14): p. 5258.

369. Liao, C., F. Liu, and K. Kannan, *Occurrence of and Dietary Exposure to Parabens in Foodstuffs From the United States*. Environmental Science & Technology, 2013. **47**(8): p. 3918-3925.

370. Barabasz, W., et al., *Ecotoxicological Aspects of the Use of Parabens in the Production of Cosmetics*. Technical Transactions, 2019(12): p. 99-124.

371. Al-Halaseh, L., et al., *Implication of Parabens in Cosmetics and Cosmeceuticals: Advantages and Limitations*. Journal of Cosmetic Dermatology, 2022. **21**(8): p. 3265-3271.

372. Ngoie Mutunda Jaël, N. and N. Kasamba Ilunga Eric, *Endocrine Disruptors and Additives in Cosmetic Makeup Products: Alert to Users*. Open Access Research Journal of Biology and Pharmacy, 2023. **9**(2): p. 088-095.

373. Fisher, M., et al., *Paraben Concentrations in Maternal Urine and Breast Milk and Its Association With Personal Care Product Use*. Environmental Science & Technology, 2017. **51**(7): p. 4009-4017.

374. Petrić, Z., J. Ružić, and I. Žuntar, *The Controversies of Parabens – An Overview Nowadays*. Acta Pharmaceutica, 2020. **71**(1): p. 17-32.

375. Smith, K., et al., *Urinary Paraben Concentrations and Ovarian Aging Among Women From a Fertility Center*. Environmental Health Perspectives, 2013. **121**(11-12): p. 1299-1305.

376. Malakootian, M., et al., *Concentrations of Urinary Parabens and Reproductive Hormones in Iranian Women: Exposure and Risk Assessment*. Toxicology Reports, 2022. **9**: p. 1894-1900.

377. Campbell, J.L., M. Yoon, and H.J. Clewell, *A Case Study on Quantitative in Vitro to in Vivo Extrapolation for Environmental Esters: Methyl-, Propyl- And Butylparaben*. Toxicology, 2015. **332**: p. 67-76.

378. Shkreli, R., et al., *Selected Essential Oils as Natural Ingredients in Cosmetic Emulsions: Development, Stability Testing and Antimicrobial Activity.* Indian Journal of Pharmaceutical Education and Research, 2023. **57**(1): p. 125-133.

379. Mostafa, A. and H. Shaaban, *GC-MS Determination of Undeclared Phthalate Esters in Commercial Fragrances: Occurrence, Profiles and Assessment of Carcinogenic and Non-Carcinogenic Risk Associated With Their Consumption Among Adult Consumers.* Molecules, 2023. **28**(4): p. 1689.

380. Al-Saleh, I. and R. Elkhatib, *Screening of Phthalate Esters in 47 Branded Perfumes.* Environmental Science and Pollution Research, 2015. **23**(1): p. 455-468.

381. Serrano, S., et al., *Dietary Phthalate Exposure in Pregnant Women and the Impact of Consumer Practices.* International Journal of Environmental Research and Public Health, 2014. **11**(6): p. 6193-6215.

382. Jenkins, R., *Reducing Toxic Phthalate Exposures in Premature Infants.* 2022.

383. Factor-Litvak, P., et al., *Persistent Associations Between Maternal Prenatal Exposure to Phthalates on Child IQ at Age 7 Years.* Plos One, 2014. **9**(12): p. e114003.

384. Hines, C.J., et al., *Development of a Personal Dual-Phase Air Sampling Method for Phthalatediesters.* Journal of Environmental Monitoring, 2010. **12**(2): p. 491-499.

385. Parlett, L.E., A.M. Calafat, and S.H. Swan, *Women's Exposure to Phthalates in Relation to Use of Personal Care Products.* Journal of Exposure Science & Environmental Epidemiology, 2012. **23**(2): p. 197-206.

386. Just, A.C., et al., *Urinary and Air Phthalate Concentrations and Self-Reported Use of Personal Care Products Among Minority Pregnant Women in New York City.* Journal of Exposure Science & Environmental Epidemiology, 2010. **20**(7): p. 625-633.

387. Bornehag, C.G. and E. Nånberg, *Phthalate Exposure and Asthma in Children.* International Journal of Andrology, 2010. **33**(2): p. 333-345.

388. Gevao, B., et al., *Phthalates in Indoor Dust in Kuwait: Implications for Non-Dietary Human Exposure.* Indoor Air, 2012. **23**(2): p. 126-133.

389. Dziobak, M.K., et al., *Demographic Assessment of Mono(2-ethylhexyl) Phthalate (MEHP) and Monoethyl Phthalate (MEP) Concentrations in Common Bottlenose Dolphins (<i>Tursiops Truncatus</i>) From Sarasota Bay, FL, USA.* Geohealth, 2021. **5**(5).

390. Shih, Y.-L., et al., *Sex Differences Between Urinary Phthalate Metabolites and Metabolic Syndrome in Adults: A Cross-Sectional Taiwan Biobank Study.* International Journal of Environmental Research and Public Health, 2022. **19**(16): p. 10458.

391. Laili, R.T.N., O. Pramiastuti, and A. Fahamsya, *Antimicrobial Activity of Mouthwash Ethanol Extract of Curcuma Purpurascens Bl. (Temu Blenyeh) as Affected by Sodium Lauryl Sulfate Concentration Variations.* Jurnal Mandala Pharmacon Indonesia, 2023. **9**(2): p. 396-407.

392. Takagi, Y., et al., *A New Formula for a Mild Body Cleanser: Sodium Laureth Sulphate Supplemented With Sodium Laureth Carboxylate and Lauryl Glucoside.* International Journal of Cosmetic Science, 2014. **36**(4): p. 305-311.

393. Masunaga, A., et al., *Fatty Acid Potassium Improves Human Dermal Fibroblast Viability and Cytotoxicity, Accelerating Human Epidermal Keratinocyte Wound Healing in Vitro and in Human Chronic Wounds.* International Wound Journal, 2021. **18**(4): p. 467-477.

394. Leoty-Okombi, S., et al., *Effect of Sodium Lauryl Sulfate (SLS) Applied as a Patch on Human Skin Physiology and Its Microbiota.* Cosmetics, 2021. **8**(1): p. 6.

395. Yj, S., et al., *Effect of Sodium Lauryl Sulfate on Recurrent Aphthous Stomatitis: A Randomized Controlled Clinical Trial.* Oral Diseases, 2012. **18**(7): p. 655-660.

396. Heetfeld, A., et al., *Challenging a Paradigm: Skin Sensitivity to Sodium Lauryl Sulfate Is Independent of Atopic Diathesis.* British Journal of Dermatology, 2019. **183**(1): p. 139-145.

397. Tabatabaei, M.H., et al., *Cytotoxicity of the Ingredients of Commonly Used Toothpastes and Mouthwashes on Human Gingival Fibroblasts.* Frontiers in Dentistry, 2020.

398. Ziółkowska, D., et al., *Determination of SLES in Personal Care Products by Colloid Titration With Light Reflection Measurements.* Molecules, 2021. **26**(9): p. 2716.

399. Ma, X., et al., *Skin Irritation Potential of Cosmetic Preservatives: An Exposure-relevant Study.* Journal of Cosmetic Dermatology, 2020. **20**(1): p. 195-203.

400. Jairoun, A.A., et al., *An Investigation Into Incidences of Microbial Contamination in Cosmeceuticals in the UAE: Imbalances Between Preservation and Microbial Contamination.* Cosmetics, 2020. **7**(4): p. 92.

401. Halla, N., et al., *Cosmetics Preservation: A Review on Present Strategies.* Molecules, 2018. **23**(7): p. 1571.

402. Hh, Z., et al., *Formaldehyde Health Hazards and Its Precarcinogenic Effects.* Egyptian Journal of Occupational Medicine, 2016. **40**(1): p. 95-108.

403. Xiang, A. and H. Xiang, *Estimating the Carcinogenic Risks of Major Pollutants Released Into the Environment.* 2021.

404. Rovira, J., et al., *Human Health Risks of Formaldehyde Indoor Levels: An Issue of Concern.* Journal of Environmental Science and Health Part A, 2016. **51**(4): p. 357-363.

405. Jackson, E.M., *Formalehyde in Personal Care Products.* Skin Pharmacology and Physiology, 2012. **25**(5): p. 236-240.

406. Jalali, M., et al., *Occupational Exposure to Formaldehyde, Lifetime Cancer Probability, and Hazard Quotient in Pathology Lab Employees in Iran: A Quantitative Risk Assessment.* Environmental Science and Pollution Research, 2020. **28**(2): p. 1878-1888.

407. Zhu, L., et al., *Formaldehyde (HCHO) as a Hazardous Air Pollutant: Mapping Surface Air Concentrations From Satellite and Inferring Cancer Risks in the United States.* Environmental Science & Technology, 2017. **51**(10): p. 5650-5657.

408. Poirier, M., et al., *Mineralogical and Crystal-Chemical Characterization of the Talc Ore Deposit of Minzanzala, Gabon.* Clay Minerals, 2019. **54**(3): p. 245-254.

409. Ajayi, O.M. and S. Amin, *Flow and Performance Effects of Talc Alternatives on Powder Cosmetic Formulations.* International Journal of Cosmetic Science, 2021. **43**(5): p. 588-600.

410. Pi-Puig, T., D.Y. Animas-Torices, and J. Solé, *Mineralogical and Geochemical Characterization of Talc From Two Mexican Ore Deposits (Oaxaca and Puebla) and Nine Talcs Marketed in Mexico: Evaluation of Its Cosmetic Uses.* Minerals, 2020. **10**(5): p. 388.

411. Baba, A.A., J.P. Akinribido, and M.A. Raji, *Upgrading of a Nigerian Vermiculite-Phillipsite Rich Talc Ore by Flotation-Cum-Acid Leaching Routes for Industrial Applications.* Materials Circular Economy, 2021. **3**(1).

412. Kanarek, M.S. and J.C.O.B. Liegel, *Asbestos in Talc and Mesothelioma: Review of the Causality Using Epidemiology.* Medical Research Archives, 2020. **8**(5).

413. Moline, J., et al., *Mesothelioma Associated With the Use of Cosmetic Talc*. Journal of Occupational and Environmental Medicine, 2020. **62**(1): p. 11-17.

414. Bird, T., et al., *A Review of the Talc Industry's Influence on Federal Regulation and Scientific Standards for Asbestos in Talc*. New Solutions a Journal of Environmental and Occupational Health Policy, 2021. **31**(2): p. 152-169.

415. Kradin, R., *Talc and Malignant Mesothelioma*. 2024.

416. Kim, J., et al., *Lung Cancer Probably Related to Talc Exposure: A Case Report*. Industrial Health, 2013. **51**(2): p. 228-231.

417. Sato, E., et al., *Analysis of Particles From Hamster Lungs Following Pulmonary Talc Exposures: Implications for Pathogenicity*. Particle and Fibre Toxicology, 2020. **17**(1).

418. Cho, A., et al., *Pulmonary Talcosis in the Setting of Cosmetic Talcum Powder Use*. Respiratory Medicine Case Reports, 2021. **34**: p. 101489.

419. Chang, C.-J., et al., *Occupational Exposure to Talc Increases the Risk of Lung Cancer: A Meta-Analysis of Occupational Cohort Studies*. Canadian Respiratory Journal, 2017. **2017**: p. 1-12.

420. Kwon, J., *Impact of Naturally Occurring Asbestos on Asbestos Ban: Regulations and Experience of the Republic of Korea*. International Journal of Environmental Research and Public Health, 2022. **19**(2): p. 742.

421. Horie, Y., et al., *Effects of Triclosan on Japanese Medaka (<scp><i>Oryzias Latipes</I></Scp>) During Embryo Development, Early Life Stage and Reproduction*. Journal of Applied Toxicology, 2017. **38**(4): p. 544-551.

422. Weatherly, L.M. and J.A. Gosse, *Triclosan Exposure, Transformation, and Human Health Effects*. Journal of Toxicology and Environmental Health Part B, 2017. **20**(8): p. 447-469.

423. Halden, R.U., et al., *The Florence Statement on Triclosan and Triclocarban*. Environmental Health Perspectives, 2017. **125**(6).

424. Homburg, M., et al., *The Influence of Triclosan on the Thyroid Hormone System in Humans - A Systematic Review*. Frontiers in Endocrinology, 2022. **13**.

425. Ha, N.-Y., D.H. Kim, and J.Y. Ryu, *Relationship Between Triclosan Exposure and Thyroid Hormones: The Second Korean National Environmental Health Survey (2012–2014)*. Annals of Occupational and Environmental Medicine, 2019. **31**(1).

426. Daza-Rodríguez, B., D. Aparicio-Marenco, and J.M. Lázaro, *Association of Triclosan and Human Infertility: A Systematic Review*. Environmental Analysis Health and Toxicology, 2023. **38**(2): p. e2023015.

427. Louis, G.W., et al., *Effects of Chronic Exposure to Triclosan on Reproductive and Thyroid Endpoints in the Adult Wistar Female Rat*. Journal of Toxicology and Environmental Health Part A, 2017. **80**(4): p. 236-249.

428. Anderson, S.E., et al., *Exposure to Triclosan Augments the Allergic Response to Ovalbumin in a Mouse Model of Asthma*. Toxicological Sciences, 2012. **132**(1): p. 96-106.

429. Drury, B., et al., *Triclosan Exposure Increases Triclosan Resistance and Influences Taxonomic Composition of Benthic Bacterial Communities*. Environmental Science & Technology, 2013. **47**(15): p. 8923-8930.

430. Raut, S.A. and R.A. Angus, *Triclosan Has Endocrine-Disrupting Effects in Male Western Mosquitofish, <i>Gambusia Affinis</I>*. Environmental Toxicology and Chemistry, 2010. **29**(6): p. 1287-1291.

431. Fernandes, M., et al., *The Distribution of Triclosan and Methyl-Triclosan in Marine Sediments of Barker Inlet, South Australia*. Journal of Environmental Monitoring, 2011. **13**(4): p. 801.

432. Turan, H., et al., *Potential of Compound-Specific Isotope Analysis (CSIA) to Trace Galaxolide Reactivity and Origin*. Acs Es&t Water, 2025.

433. Dodson, R.E., et al., *Endocrine Disruptors and Asthma-Associated Chemicals in Consumer Products*. Environmental Health Perspectives, 2012. **120**(7): p. 935-943.

434. Ashcroft, S., et al., *Synthetic Endocrine Disruptors in Fragranced Products*. 2024.

435. Audrain, H., et al., *Allergy to Oxidized Limonene and Linalool Is Frequent in the U.K.* British Journal of Dermatology, 2014. **171**(2): p. 292-297.

436. Periyasamy, M.K., S. Sekar, and R. Rai, *Analysis of Hypersensitivity in Fragrance Series by Patch Testing*. Indian Dermatology Online Journal, 2019. **10**(6): p. 657.

437. Lang, M., E. Giménez-Arnau, and J.P. Lepoittevin, *Is It Possible to Assess the Allergenicity of Mixtures Based on <i>in Chemico</I> Methods? Preliminary Results on Common Fragrance Aldehydes*. Flavour and Fragrance Journal, 2016. **32**(1): p. 63-71.

438. Sinisi, A., et al., *Biobased Ketal–Diester Additives Derived From Levulinic Acid: Synthesis and Effect on the Thermal Stability and*

Thermo-Mechanical Properties of Poly(vinyl Chloride). Acs Sustainable Chemistry & Engineering, 2019. **7**(16): p. 13920-13931.

439.   Harley, K.G., et al., *Changes in Latina Women's Exposure to Cleaning Chemicals Associated With Switching From Conventional to "Green" Household Cleaning Products: The LUCIR Intervention Study.* Environmental Health Perspectives, 2021. **129**(9).

440.   Hudspeth, A., et al., *Independent Sun Care Product Screening for Benzene Contamination.* Environmental Health Perspectives, 2022. **130**(3).

441.   Vega, J., et al., *Cyanobacteria and Red Macroalgae as Potential Sources of Antioxidants and UV Radiation-Absorbing Compounds for Cosmeceutical Applications.* Marine Drugs, 2020. **18**(12): p. 659.

442.   Nery, É.M., et al., *A Short Review of Alternative Ingredients and Technologies of Inorganic UV Filters.* Journal of Cosmetic Dermatology, 2020. **20**(4): p. 1061-1065.

443.   Song, Y., et al., *Endocrine-disrupting Chemicals, Risk of Type 2 Diabetes, and Diabetes-related Metabolic Traits: A Systematic Review and Meta-analysis.* Journal of Diabetes, 2015. **8**(4): p. 516-532.

444.   Al-Eitan, L.N., H.A. Aljamal, and R. Alkhatib, *Gas Chromatographic–mass Spectrometric Analysis of Sunscreens and Their Effects on Mice Liver and Kidney Enzyme Function.* Clinical Cosmetic and Investigational Dermatology, 2018. **Volume 12**: p. 11-21.

445.   Wang, S.Q., M.E. Burnett, and H.W. Lim, *Safety of Oxybenzone: Putting Numbers Into Perspective.* Archives of Dermatology, 2011. **147**(7): p. 865.

446.   Fediuk, D.J., et al., *Tissue Deposition of the Insect Repellent DEET and the Sunscreen Oxybenzone From Repeated Topical Skin Applications in Rats.* International Journal of Toxicology, 2010. **29**(6): p. 594-603.

447.   Seirafianpour, F., et al., *Sunscreens Percutaneous Absorption and Ingredients Concentration in Human Plasma and Urine: A Systematic Review.* Dermatology Research, 2022. **4**(1).

448.   Matouskova, K., et al., *Exposure to Low Doses of Oxybenzone During Perinatal Development Alters Mammary Gland Stroma in Female Mice.* Frontiers in Toxicology, 2022. **4**.

449.   Yuan, S., et al., *Environmental Fate and Toxicity of Sunscreen-Derived Inorganic Ultraviolet Filters in Aquatic Environments: A Review.* Nanomaterials, 2022. **12**(4): p. 699.

450. Miller, I.B., et al., *Toxic Effects of UV Filters From Sunscreens on Coral Reefs Revisited: Regulatory Aspects for "Reef Safe" Products.* Environmental Sciences Europe, 2021. **33**(1).

451. Sousa, L.R.D., et al., *Nanoemulsified Essential Oil of Melaleuca Leucadendron Leaves for Topical Application: In Vitro Photoprotective, Antioxidant and Anti-Melanoma Activities.* Pharmaceuticals, 2024. **17**(6): p. 721.

452. Pandika, M., *Looking to Nature for New Sunscreens.* C&en Global Enterprise, 2018. **96**(32): p. 22-25.

453. Vaillant, L., et al., *Combined Effects of Glycerol and Petrolatum in an Emollient Cream: A Randomized, Double-blind, Crossover Study in Healthy Volunteers With Dry Skin.* Journal of Cosmetic Dermatology, 2019. **19**(6): p. 1399-1403.

454. Paepe, K.D., et al., *Silicones as Nonocclusive Topical Agents.* Skin Pharmacology and Physiology, 2014. **27**(3): p. 164-171.

455. Nolan, K. and E.S. Marmur, *Moisturizers: Reality and the Skin Benefits.* Dermatologic Therapy, 2012. **25**(3): p. 229-233.

456. Kang, S.Y., et al., *Moisturizer in Patients With Inflammatory Skin Diseases.* Medicina, 2022. **58**(7): p. 888.

457. Sharifi-Heris, Z., L. Amiri-Farahani, and S.B. Hasanpoor-Azghadi, *A Review Study of Diaper Rash Dermatitis Treatments.* Journal of Client-Centered Nursing Care, 2018.

458. Hon, K.L., et al., *Emollient Treatment of Atopic Dermatitis: Latest Evidence and Clinical Considerations.* Drugs in Context, 2018. **7**: p. 1-14.

459. Wang, S., et al., *Determination of Polycyclic Aromatic Hydrocarbons (PAHs) in Cosmetic Products by Gas Chromatography-Tandem Mass Spectrometry.* Journal of Food and Drug Analysis, 2019. **27**(3): p. 815-824.

460. Jamee, R. and R. Siddique, *Biodegradation of Synthetic Dyes of Textile Effluent by Microorganisms: An Environmentally and Economically Sustainable Approach.* European Journal of Microbiology and Immunology, 2019. **9**(4): p. 114-118.

461. Sharma, H. and P. Shirkot, *Bioremediation of Azo Dyes Using Biogenic Iron Nanoparticles.* Journal of Microbiology & Experimentation, 2019. **7**(1).

462. Floriano, L., et al., *Determination of Six Synthetic Dyes in Sports Drinks by Dispersive Solid-Phase Extraction and HPLC-UV-Vis.* Journal of the Brazilian Chemical Society, 2017.

463. Ramesh, C., et al., *Multifaceted Applications of Microbial Pigments: Current Knowledge, Challenges and Future Directions for Public Health Implications.* Microorganisms, 2019. **7**(7): p. 186.

464. Kobylewski, S. and M.F. Jacobson, *Toxicology of Food Dyes.* International Journal of Occupational and Environmental Health, 2012. **18**(3): p. 220-246.

465. Fikri, E. and Y.W. Firmansyah, *A Short Communication: Contamination and Toxicity Pigment Red 53, Rhodamine B, and Sudan III in Indonesian Cosmetics.* Jurnal Serambi Engineering, 2023. **8**(3).

466. Khade, P., et al., *A Copper Composite Embedded in Graphene Oxide as an Efficient Mordant to Enhance the Properties of Natural Dyes for Cotton Fabric.* Chemistryselect, 2023. **8**(24).

467. Lestari, I., et al., *Pineapple Leaves (Ananas Comosus) Ca-Alginate Immobilized as Adsorbent for Removal of Rhodamine B Dye.* Chemica Jurnal Teknik Kimia, 2023. **10**(1): p. 41.

468. Polak, J., et al., *Toxicity and Dyeing Properties of Dyes Obtained Through Laccase-Mediated Synthesis.* Journal of Cleaner Production, 2016. **112**: p. 4265-4272.

469. Reza, K.M., A.S.W. Kurny, and F. Gulshan, *Photocatalytic Degradation of Methylene Blue by Magnetite+H2O2+UV Process.* International Journal of Environmental Science and Development, 2016. **7**(5): p. 325-329.

470. Wang, Y., et al., *Semirigid Highly Conjugated Zirconium–Organic Framework for the Capture of Micropollutants and Solar-Light Photodegradation.* Inorganic Chemistry, 2023. **62**(23): p. 8863-8873.

471. Rodríguez-Rasero, C., et al., *Use of Zero-Valent Iron Nanoparticles (nZVIs) From Environmentally Friendly Synthesis for the Removal of Dyes From Water—A Review.* Water, 2024. **16**(11): p. 1607.

472. Baliarsingh, S., et al., *Exploring Sustainable Technique on Natural Dye Extraction From Native Plants for Textile: Identification of Colourants, Colourimetric Analysis of Dyed Yarns and Their Antimicrobial Evaluation.* Journal of Cleaner Production, 2012. **37**: p. 257-264.

473. Azman, A.S., C.I. Mawang, and S. AbuBakar, *Bacterial Pigments: The Bioactivities and as an Alternative for Therapeutic Applications.* Natural Product Communications, 2018. **13**(12).

474. Chuberre, B., et al., *Mineral Oils and Waxes in Cosmetics: An Overview Mainly Based on the Current European Regulations and the Safety Profile of These Compounds.* Journal of the European Academy of Dermatology and Venereology, 2019. **33**(S7): p. 5-14.

475. Petry, T., et al., *Review of Data on the Dermal Penetration of Mineral Oils and Waxes Used in Cosmetic Applications.* Toxicology Letters, 2017. **280**: p. 70-78.

476. Pirow, R., et al., *Mineral Oil in Food, Cosmetic Products, and in Products Regulated by Other Legislations.* Critical Reviews in Toxicology, 2019. **49**(9): p. 742-789.

477. Bertoz, V., et al., *A Review on the Occurrence and Analytical Determination of PAHs in Olive Oils.* Foods, 2021. **10**(2): p. 324.

478. Lachenmeier, D.W., et al., *Evaluation of Mineral Oil Saturated Hydrocarbons (MOSH) and Mineral Oil Aromatic Hydrocarbons (MOAH) in Pure Mineral Hydrocarbon-Based Cosmetics and Cosmetic Raw Materials Using 1H NMR Spectroscopy.* F1000research, 2017. **6**: p. 682.

479. Lima, L.L., et al., *Developing Botanical Formulations for Sustainable Cosmetics.* Cosmetics, 2023. **10**(6): p. 159.

480. Zulvera, Z., et al., *Sustainability of Organic Certification in Organic Farming Groups in Padang Pariaman Regency, West Sumatra, Indonesia.* International Journal of Progressive Sciences and Technologies, 2023. **41**(2): p. 697.

481. Ferreira, M.S., et al., *Trends in the Use of Botanicals in Anti-Aging Cosmetics.* Molecules, 2021. **26**(12): p. 3584.

482. Moldes, A.B., et al., *Synthetic and Bio-Derived Surfactants Versus Microbial Biosurfactants in the Cosmetic Industry: An Overview.* International Journal of Molecular Sciences, 2021. **22**(5): p. 2371.

483. De, S., et al., *A Review on Natural Surfactants.* RSC Advances, 2015. **5**(81): p. 65757-65767.

484. Gamage, D.G.N.D., et al., *Assessment of Phytochemical Contents and Total Antioxidant Capacity of Five Medicinal Plants With Cosmetic Potential Under Three Different Drying Methods.* World Journal of Agricultural Research, 2021. **9**(1): p. 24-28.

485. Guzmán, E. and A. Lucía, *Essential Oils and Their Individual Components in Cosmetic Products.* Cosmetics, 2021. **8**(4): p. 114.

486. Sarkic, A. and I. Stappen, *Essential Oils and Their Single Compounds in Cosmetics—A Critical Review.* Cosmetics, 2018. **5**(1): p. 11.

487. Civancik-Uslu, D., et al., *Improving the Production Chain With LCA and Eco-Design: Application to Cosmetic Packaging.* Resources Conservation and Recycling, 2019. **151**: p. 104475.

488. Juliano, C.C.A. and G.A. Magrini, *Radish Root Ferment Filtrate for Cosmetic Preservation: A Study of Efficacy of Kopraphinol©.* 2024.

489. Filipe, G.A., et al., *Development of a Multifunctional and Self-Preserving Cosmetic Formulation Using Sophorolipids and Palmarosa Essential Oil Against Acne-Causing Bacteria.* Journal of Applied Microbiology, 2022. **133**(3): p. 1534-1542.

490. Pérez-Rivero, C. and J.P. López-Gómez, *Unlocking the Potential of Fermentation in Cosmetics: A Review.* Fermentation, 2023. **9**(5): p. 463.

491. Rybczyńska-Tkaczyk, K., et al., *Natural Compounds With Antimicrobial Properties in Cosmetics.* Pathogens, 2023. **12**(2): p. 320.

492. Fonseca-Santos, B., M.A. Corrêa, and M. Chorilli, *Sustainability, Natural and Organic Cosmetics: Consumer, Products, Efficacy, Toxicological and Regulatory Considerations.* Brazilian Journal of Pharmaceutical Sciences, 2015. **51**(1): p. 17-26.

493. Bom, S., H.M. Ribeiro, and J. Marto, *Sustainability Calculator: A Tool to Assess Sustainability in Cosmetic Products.* Sustainability, 2020. **12**(4): p. 1437.

494. Krzyżostan, M., A. Wawrzyńczak, and I. Nowak, *Use of Waste From the Food Industry and Applications of the Fermentation Process to Create Sustainable Cosmetic Products: A Review.* Sustainability, 2024. **16**(7): p. 2757.

495. Cerulli, A., et al., *Licorice (Glycyrrhiza Glabra, G. Uralensis, and G. Inflata) and Their Constituents as Active Cosmeceutical Ingredients.* Cosmetics, 2022. **9**(1): p. 7.

496. Eckelman, M.J., et al., *Applying Green Chemistry to Raw Material Selection and Product Formulation at the Estée Lauder Companies.* Green Chemistry, 2022. **24**(6): p. 2397-2408.

497. Ajayi, O., A. Davies, and S. Amin, *Impact of Processing Conditions on Rheology, Tribology and Wet Lubrication Performance of a Novel Amino Lipid Hair Conditioner.* Cosmetics, 2021. **8**(3): p. 77.

498. Guzmán, E., F. Ortega, and R.G. Rubio, *Chitosan: A Promising Multifunctional Cosmetic Ingredient for Skin and Hair Care.* Cosmetics, 2022. **9**(5): p. 99.

499. Gonçalves, C., et al., *Lipid Nanoparticles Containing Mixtures of Antioxidants to Improve Skin Care and Cancer Prevention.* Pharmaceutics, 2021. **13**(12): p. 2042.

500. Yang, S., et al., *Encapsulating Plant Ingredients for Dermocosmetic Application: An Updated Review of Delivery Systems and Characterization Techniques.* International Journal of Cosmetic Science, 2020. **42**(1): p. 16-28.

501. Ahsan, F.J. and U. Ferdinando, *The Purchase Intention Towards Green Cosmetics Among Female Consumers in Sri Lanka: Role of Health Value as a Mediator.* Colombo Journal of Multi-Disciplinary Research, 2023. **7**(1-2): p. 1-35.

502. Kumar, V., et al., *Understanding the role of artificial intelligence in personalized engagement marketing.* California management review, 2019. **61**(4): p. 135-155.

503. Georgievskaya, A., et al., *How artificial intelligence adopts human biases: The case of cosmetic skincare industry. AI and Ethics.* 2023.

504. Elder, A., et al., *The role of artificial intelligence in cosmetic dermatology—current, upcoming, and future trends.* Journal of Cosmetic Dermatology, 2021. **20**(1): p. 48-52.

505. Jung, S., Y.S. Choi, and J.S. Kim, *Stencil-based 3D facial relief creation from RGBD images for 3D printing.* ETRI Journal, 2020. **42**(2): p. 272-281.

506. Rumestri, A.D.S., R.C. Subagio, and I.E. Kusuma, *Investigating DIY Sneakers for Mass Customization Business Models by using 3D Printing Technology.* Global Journal of Emerging Science, Engineering & Technology, 2023. **1**(2): p. 58-70.

507. Liang, E., et al., *3D Printing Technology Based on Versatile Gelatin-Carrageenan Gel System for Drug Formulations.* Pharmaceutics, 2023. **15**(4): p. 1218.

508. Hay, J.L., et al., *Implementing an Internet-Delivered Skin Cancer Genetic Testing Intervention to Improve Sun Protection Behavior in a Diverse Population: Protocol for a Randomized Controlled Trial.* Jmir Research Protocols, 2017. **6**(4): p. e52.

509. Geisler, A., J. Nguyen, and J. Jagdeo, *Use of Beauty Products Among African American Women: Potential Health Disparities and Clinical Implications.* Journal of Drugs in Dermatology, 2020. **19**(7): p. 772-773.

510. Akbar, S.A., et al., *Personalized Skincare: Correlating Genetics With Skin Phenotypes Through DNA Analysis.* Uhd Journal of Science and Technology, 2024. **8**(1): p. 151-163.

511. Schweitzer, J. and H.I. Maibach, *Pharmacogenomics in Dermatology: Taking Patient Treatment to the Next Level.* Journal of Dermatological Treatment, 2014. **26**(1): p. 94-96.

512. Bu, P., et al., *Development of Home Beauty Devices for Facial Rejuvenation: Establishment of Efficacy Evaluation System.* Clinical Cosmetic and Investigational Dermatology, 2024. **Volume 17**: p. 553-563.

513. Dogyeong Lee, D.L. and J.L. Jaebum Lee, *Utilization of Microcurrent Care Device for Health Intervention and Beauty Care.* J-Institute, 2024. **9**(1): p. 34-45.
514. Hegde, S.S., et al., *A Study on the Use of AI (Artificial Intelligence) in Beauty Industry in India.* International Journal of Research Publication and Reviews, 2023. **4**(4): p. 2936-2941.
515. Garland, E.L., et al., *Mindfulness Broadens Awareness and Builds Eudaimonic Meaning: A Process Model of Mindful Positive Emotion Regulation.* Psychological Inquiry, 2015. **26**(4): p. 293-314.
516. Garland, E.L., et al., *Mindfulness-to-Meaning Theory - Mindfulness Broadens Awareness and Builds Eudaimonic Meaning: A Process Model of Mindful Positive Emotion Regulation.* 2017.
517. Borondo, J.P., N.A. Vila, and J.A.F. Brea, *Comparison of Spa Choice Between Wellness Tourists and Healthcare/Medical Tourists.* Healthcare, 2020. **8**(4): p. 544.
518. Tsartsapakis, I. and A. Zafeiroudi, *Personality Traits and Healthy Eating Habits and Behaviors: a Narrative Review.* Journal of Educational and Social Research, 2024. **14**(2): p. 11.
519. Gohad, P., et al., *Novel Cannabidiol Sunscreen Protects Keratinocytes and Melanocytes Against Ultraviolet B Radiation.* Journal of Cosmetic Dermatology, 2020. **20**(4): p. 1350-1352.
520. Gugliandolo, E., et al., *Effect of Cannabidiol (CBD) on Canine Inflammatory Response: An Ex Vivo Study on LPS Stimulated Whole Blood.* Veterinary Sciences, 2021. **8**(9): p. 185.
521. Joffre, J., et al., *Activation of CB1R Promotes Lipopolysaccharide-Induced IL-10 Secretion by Monocytic Myeloid-Derived Suppressive Cells and Reduces Acute Inflammation and Organ Injury.* The Journal of Immunology, 2020. **204**(12): p. 3339-3350.
522. Sotiropoulou, G., E. Zingkou, and G. Pampalakis, *Redirecting Drug Repositioning to Discover Innovative Cosmeceuticals.* Experimental Dermatology, 2021. **30**(5): p. 628-644.
523. Rashid, J., et al., *Cosmeceuticals: The Bioactive Elements in New-Age Beauty Products.* International Journal of Pharmacy & Integrated Health Sciences, 2023. **4**(2): p. 70-82.
524. Singh, S., V. Singh, and S. Patel, *Cosmeceuticals; The Fusion of Cosmetics and Pharmaceuticals.* Journal of Community Pharmacy Practice, 2024(42): p. 16-27.

525. Badalyan, S.M. and A. Barkhudaryan, *Medicinal Macrofungi as Cosmeceuticals: A Review.* International Journal of Medicinal Mushrooms, 2022. **24**(4): p. 1-13.

526. Jayawardhana, H.H.A.C.K., et al., *Marine Algal Polyphenols as Skin Protective Agents: Current Status and Future Prospectives.* Marine Drugs, 2023. **21**(5): p. 285.

527. Nimisha, N. and A. Singh, *Exploring Marine-Derived Bioactives for Innovative Cosmeceutical Applications: A Review.* Journal of Applied and Natural Science, 2024. **16**(2): p. 478-494.

528. Gutiérrez, C., et al., *Head and Neck Lymphedema: Treatment Response to Single and Multiple Sessions of Advanced Pneumatic Compression Therapy.* Otolaryngology, 2019. **160**(4): p. 622-626.

529. Tepavcevic, B., et al., *The Impact of Facial Lipofilling on Patient-Perceived Improvement in Facial Appearance and Quality of Life.* Facial Plastic Surgery, 2016. **32**(03): p. 296-303.

530. Begum, A.N., et al., *Evaluation of Herbal Hair Lotion Loaded With Rosemary for Possible Hair Growth in C57bl/6 Mice.* Advanced Biomedical Research, 2023. **12**(1).

531. Buscone, S., et al., *A New Path in Defining Light Parameters for Hair Growth: Discovery and Modulation of Photoreceptors in Human Hair Follicle.* Lasers in Surgery and Medicine, 2017. **49**(7): p. 705-718.

532. Tantiyavarong, J., et al., *Red and Green <scp>LED</Scp> Light Therapy: A Comparative Study in Androgenetic Alopecia.* Photodermatology Photoimmunology & Photomedicine, 2024. **40**(6).

533. Kim, H., et al., *Low-Level Light Therapy for Androgenetic Alopecia: A 24-Week, Randomized, Double-Blind, Sham Device–Controlled Multicenter Trial.* Dermatologic Surgery, 2013. **39**(8): p. 1177-1183.

534. Ozgul, A., *The Relationship Between Seborrheic Dermatitis and Body Composition Parameters.* Northern Clinics of Istanbul, 2022.

535. Roy, D. and R. Roy, *Exploring Natural Ways to Maintain Keratin Production in Hair Follicles.* 2024.

536. Shin, D.H., et al., *Ginsenoside Rg3 Up-regulates the Expression of Vascular Endothelial Growth Factor in Human Dermal Papilla Cells and Mouse Hair Follicles.* Phytotherapy Research, 2013. **28**(7): p. 1088-1095.

537. Ding, H., et al., *Analysis of Histological and microRNA Profiles Changes in Rabbit Skin Development.* Scientific Reports, 2020. **10**(1).

538. Oh, G.N. and S.W. Son, *Efficacy of Korean Red Ginseng in the Treatment of Alopecia Areata.* Journal of Ginseng Research, 2012. **36**(4): p. 391-395.

539. Lee, K.-H., et al., *<i>Eclipta Prostrata</I> Promotes the Induction of Anagen, Sustains the Anagen Phase Through Regulation of FGF-7 and FGF-5.* Pharmaceutical Biology, 2019. **57**(1): p. 105-111.

540. Lee, Y., et al., *Panax Ginseng Extract Antagonizes the Effect of DKK-1-induced Catagen-Ike Changes of Hair Follicles.* International Journal of Molecular Medicine, 2017. **40**(4): p. 1194-1200.

541. Alam, F., et al., *Development and Evaluation of Natural Anti-Dandruff Shampoo.* Journal of Natural Remedies, 2023: p. 1125-1134.

542. Bartowska-Trybulec, M., et al., *Effect Of whole Body Cryotherapy on Low Back Pain and Release Of endorphins and Stress Hormones in Patients With Lumbar Spine Osteoarthritis.* Reumatologia/Rheumatology, 2022. **60**(4): p. 247-251.

543. Gizińska, M., et al., *Effects of Whole-Body Cryotherapy in Comparison With Other Physical Modalities Used With Kinesitherapy in Rheumatoid Arthritis.* Biomed Research International, 2015. **2015**: p. 1-7.

544. Draper, D. and B. Roberts, *Cryotherapy: The Dry Benefits.* Moj Sports Medicine, 2018. **2**(1).

545. Ziemann, E., et al., *Whole-Body Cryostimulation as an Effective Method of Reducing Low-Grade Inflammation in Obese Men.* The Journal of Physiological Sciences, 2013. **63**(5): p. 333-343.

546. Ezzo, J., et al., *Manual Lymphatic Drainage for Lymphedema Following Breast Cancer Treatment.* Cochrane Database of Systematic Reviews, 2015. **2015**(5).

547. O'Connor, M., J.V. Wang, and N. Saedi, *Whole- and Partial-body Cryotherapy in Aesthetic Dermatology: Evaluating a Trendy Treatment.* Journal of Cosmetic Dermatology, 2018. **18**(5): p. 1435-1437.

548. Sharma, S., et al., *The Art and Science of Cosmetics: Understanding the Ingredients.* 2023.

549. Nguyen, J., N. Masub, and J. Jagdeo, *Bioactive Ingredients in Korean Cosmeceuticals: Trends and Research Evidence.* Journal of Cosmetic Dermatology, 2020. **19**(7): p. 1555-1569.

550. Bourdier, A., A. Abriat, and T. Jiang, *Impacts of Sensory Multimodality Congruence and Familiarity With Short Use on Cosmetic Product Evaluation.* International Journal of Cosmetic Science, 2023. **45**(5): p. 592-603.

551. Brianza, G., et al., *<i>QuintEssence:</I>A Probe Study to Explore the Power of Smell on Emotions, Memories, and Body Image in Daily Life.* Acm Transactions on Computer-Human Interaction, 2022. **29**(6): p. 1-33.

552. Dini, I. and S. Laneri, *The New Challenge of Green Cosmetics: Natural Food Ingredients for Cosmetic Formulations.* Molecules, 2021. **26**(13): p. 3921.

553. Spence, C. and T. Zhang, *Multisensory Contributions to Skin -cosmetic Product Interactions.* International Journal of Cosmetic Science, 2024. **46**(6): p. 833-849.

554. Rizzi, V., et al., *Neurocosmetics in Skincare—The Fascinating World of Skin–Brain Connection: A Review to Explore Ingredients, Commercial Products for Skin Aging, and Cosmetic Regulation.* Cosmetics, 2021. **8**(3): p. 66.

555. Bouhout, S., et al., *Physiological Benefits Associated With Facial Skincare: Well-being From Emotional Perception to Neuromodulation.* International Journal of Cosmetic Science, 2023. **45**(4): p. 458-469.

556. Ndao, D.H., et al., *Inhalation Aromatherapy in Children and Adolescents Undergoing Stem Cell Infusion: Results of a Placebo -controlled Double -blind Trial.* Psycho-Oncology, 2010. **21**(3): p. 247-254.

557. Esparham, A., et al., *Pediatric Headache Clinic Model: Implementation of Integrative Therapies in Practice.* Children, 2018. **5**(6): p. 74.

558. Parvizi, M.M., et al., *Complementary and Integrative Remedies in the Treatment of Chronic Pruritus: A Review of Clinical Trials.* Journal of Cosmetic Dermatology, 2022. **21**(11): p. 5360-5369.

559. Nathenson, P. and S.L. Nathenson, *Complementary and Alternative Health Practices in the Rehabilitation Nursing.* Rehabilitation Nursing, 2017. **42**(1): p. 5-13.

560. Rajahthurai, S.D., et al., *Use of Complementary and Alternative Medicine and Adherence to Medication Therapy Among Stroke Patients: A Meta-Analysis and Systematic Review.* Frontiers in Pharmacology, 2022. **13**.

561. Bilgili, S.G., et al., *The Use of Complementary and Alternative Medicine Among Dermatology Outpatients in Eastern Turkey.* Human & Experimental Toxicology, 2013. **33**(2): p. 214-221.

562. Datta, H.S. and R. Paramesh, *Trends in Aging and Skin Care: Ayurvedic Concepts.* Journal of Ayurveda and Integrative Medicine, 2010. **1**(2): p. 110.

563. Hirudkar, V.N. and V. Shivhare, *A Review on Ayurvedic Cosmeceuticals and Their Mode of Actions.* Journal of Drug Delivery and Therapeutics, 2022. **12**(6): p. 204-206.

564. Choe, S.J., et al., *Psychological Stress Deteriorates Skin Barrier Function by Activating 11β-Hydroxysteroid Dehydrogenase 1 and the HPA Axis.* Scientific Reports, 2018. **8**(1).

565. Balieva, F., et al., *Perceived Stress in Patients With Inflammatory and Non-Inflammatory Skin Conditions. An Observational Controlled Study Among 255 Norwegian Dermatological Outpatients.* Skin Health and Disease, 2022. **2**(4).

566. Birdi, G., M. Larkin, and R. Knibb, *Prospective Analysis of the Temporal Relationship Between Psychological Distress and Atopic Dermatitis in Female Adults: A Preliminary Study.* Healthcare, 2022. **10**(10): p. 1913.

567. Romana-Souza, B., W. Silva-Xavier, and A. Monte-Alto-Costa, *Topical Retinol Attenuates Stress-induced Ageing Signs in Human Skin Ex Vivo, Through<scp>EGFR</Scp> Activation Via<scp>EGF</Scp>, but Not<scp>ERK</Scp> And<scp>AP</Scp>-1 Activation.* Experimental Dermatology, 2018. **28**(8): p. 906-913.

568. Bertino, L., et al., *Oxidative Stress and Atopic Dermatitis.* Antioxidants, 2020. **9**(3): p. 196.

569. Schut, C., et al., *Psychological Stress and Skin Symptoms in College Students: Results of a Cross-Sectional Web-Based Questionnaire Study.* Acta Dermato Venereologica, 2016. **96**(4): p. 550-551.

570. Jia, Y., et al., *Hydrogel Dressing Integrating FAK Inhibition and ROS Scavenging for Mechano-Chemical Treatment of Atopic Dermatitis.* Nature Communications, 2023. **14**(1).

571. Crego, A.L.F., A. Therianou, and P. Hashemi, *A Catena Between Psychiatric Disorders and Non-Scarring Alopecias—A Systematic Review.* Skin Health and Disease, 2022. **3**(3).

572. Rosenkranz, M.A., et al., *A Comparison of Mindfulness-Based Stress Reduction and an Active Control in Modulation of Neurogenic Inflammation.* Brain Behavior and Immunity, 2013. **27**: p. 174-184.

573. Monaheng Sefotho, M., et al., *The Psychosomatic Interface of Stress and Skin Disorders: Patient Experiences and Perceptions.* 2023. **2**(2): p. 26-33.

574. Rosenkranz, M.A., et al., *Reduced Stress and Inflammatory Responsiveness in Experienced Meditators Compared to a Matched Healthy Control Group*. Psychoneuroendocrinology, 2016. **68**: p. 117-125.

575. Guéniche, A., et al., *A Dermocosmetic Formulation Containing Vichy Volcanic Mineralizing Water,<i>Vitreoscilla Filiformis</I>extract, Niacinamide, Hyaluronic Acid, and Vitamin E Regenerates and Repairs Acutely Stressed Skin*. Journal of the European Academy of Dermatology and Venereology, 2022. **36**(S2): p. 26-34.

576. Kolankowska-Trzcińska, M., *Psychocosmetology - The Opportunity to Reduce Stress in a Beauty Salon With the Use of Music Therapy, Massage, Yoga and Meditation*. Aesthetic Cosmetology and Medicine, 2022. **11**(4): p. 123-130.

577. Sevinc, G., et al., *Common and Dissociable Neural Activity After Mindfulness-Based Stress Reduction and Relaxation Response Programs*. Psychosomatic Medicine, 2018. **80**(5): p. 439-451.

578. William Yoo, N., *The Impact of Artificial Intelligence on Marketing Strategies*. International Journal of Science and Research Archive, 2024. **13**(1): p. 3211-3223.

579. Alvi, A. and O.C. Mupona, *Exploring the Ethical Challenges of Ai in Personalised Marketing in Context of Beauty and Wellness*. International Journal of All Research Education & Scientific Methods, 2023. **12**(02): p. 12-02.

580. Yupelmi, M., et al., *A Comprehensive Exploration of Entrepreneurial Strategies in the Makeup and Beauty Industry: The Role of Social Media Marketing*. Indonesian Journal of Computer Science, 2023. **12**(5).

581. Lei, W. and J.H. Lee, *The Impact of K-Beauty Social Media Influencers, Sponsorship, and Product Exposure on Consumer Acceptance of New Products*. Fashion and Textiles, 2021. **8**(1).

582. Yang, X., *Comparing Marketing Strategies for Cosmetics Between China and the U.S.* 2024. **2**(1): p. 32-45.

583. Thamrin, T., et al., *Investigating the Online Shopping Pattern for Beauty Brands Most Liked by Indonesian Women*. Frontiers in Business and Economics, 2022. **1**(1): p. 24-34.

584. Lee, J.-K. and K.H. Kwon, *Why Is Generation MZ Passionate About Good Consumption of K-cosmetics Amid the COVID-19 Pandemic?* Journal of Cosmetic Dermatology, 2022. **21**(8): p. 3208-3218.

585. Rajab, M.A., *Relationship of E-Commerce, Influencer Marketing and Social Media to Digital Marketing (Marketing Management Literature Review).* Dinasti International Journal of Economics Finance & Accounting, 2021. **2**(4): p. 443-455.
586. Wibisono, N., et al., *E-WoM engagement and purchase intention on social commerce specialized in beauty products: a perspective from young female consumers.* International Journal of Applied Business Research, 2023: p. 26-46.
587. Riwayat, A.A.P., A.D. Susilawati, and Z. Naqiah, *Purchasing Patterns Analysis in E-Commerce: A Big Data-Driven Approach and Methodological.* International Journal Software Engineering and Computer Science (Ijsecs), 2024. **4**(1): p. 148-164.
588. Lee, J.-G., A. Sadachar, and S. Manchiraju, *What's in the Box? Investigation of Beauty Subscription Box Retail Services.* Family and Consumer Sciences Research Journal, 2019. **48**(1): p. 85-102.
589. Krichen, M., et al., *Blockchain for Modern Applications: A Survey.* Sensors, 2022. **22**(14): p. 5274.
590. Udokwu, C., et al., *Exerting Qualitative Analytics and Blockchain Requirement-Engineering in Designing and Implementing a Luxury Products Authentication System.* Inventions, 2023. **8**(1): p. 49.
591. V., S.H.V., et al., *Mitigating Counterfeiting Using Blockchain Enabled Product Authentication.* International Journal for Research in Applied Science and Engineering Technology, 2023. **11**(4): p. 583-589.
592. Pindado--Ortega, C., et al., *Prescribing Habits for Androgenic Alopecia Among Dermatologists in Spain in 2019–2020: A Cross-Sectional Study.* Skin Appendage Disorders, 2020. **6**(5): p. 283-286.
593. Melo, D.F., et al., *Hair-to-Hair Trichoscopy: An Objective Method to Assess Effectiveness of Botulinum Toxin in a Clinical Trial for Androgenetic Alopecia.* Skin Appendage Disorders, 2023. **10**(1): p. 41-45.
594. Salyenkova, O., *Immunomorphological Features of Female Patient's Skin With Androgenetic Alopecia in the Treatment of Platelet-Rich Plasma in Combination With Topical Minoxidil 2 % Lotion.* Technology Transfer Innovative Solutions in Medicine, 2021: p. 22-25.
595. Meyer-Gonzalez, T., et al., *Current Controversies in Trichology: A European Expert Consensus Statement.* Journal of the European Academy of Dermatology and Venereology, 2021. **35**(S2): p. 3-11.
596. Malakar, S., et al., *Trichoscopy.* 2021: p. 295-322.

597. Bortone, G., et al., *A New Method for the Follow-Up of Patients With Alopecia Areata.* Journal of Clinical Medicine, 2024. **13**(13): p. 3901.

598. Sharma, A. and M. Mhatre, *Cosmetic Trichology: Hair Cosmetics, Styling, and Their Effect on the Hair Fiber!* Indian Dermatology Online Journal, 2020. **11**(4): p. 598.

599. Hussain, F. and F. Dubash, *BC07 Hair Oiling: A Paradigm Shift in the Deep-Rooted Ritual From East to West.* British Journal of Dermatology, 2024. **191**(Supplement_1): p. i72-i73.

600. Trüeb, R.M., et al., *The Problem With Capitalism in the Trichological Sciences.* International Journal of Trichology, 2023. **15**(3): p. 79-84.

601. Trüeb, R.M., H. Dutra, and M.F.R.G. Dias, *Autistic-Undisciplined Thinking in the Practice of Medical Trichology.* International Journal of Trichology, 2019. **11**(1): p. 1.

602. Musbah, F., *Primary Cicatricial Alopecia Among Lybian Patients: A Clinicopathological and Epidemiological Study.* Iberoamerican Journal of Medicine, 2020. **2**(4): p. 275-278.

603. Yoon, J.-H. and J.W. Choi, *Primary Cicatricial Alopecia in a Single-race Asian Population: A 10-year Nationwide Population-based Study in South Korea.* The Journal of Dermatology, 2018. **45**(11): p. 1306-1311.

604. Thunga, S., et al., *<scp>AI</Scp> in Aesthetic/Cosmetic Dermatology: Current and Future.* Journal of Cosmetic Dermatology, 2024. **24**(1).

605. Wood, L. *Global $27.9 Billion Hair Transplant Market Forecast to 2027.* 2021 [cited 2024 30/1/2024]; Available from: https://www.globenewswire.com/news-release/2021/06/18/2249450/28124/en/Global-27-9-Billion-Hair-Transplant-Market-Forecast-to-2027.html?utm_source=chatgpt.com.

606. Market Data Forecast. *Global Hair Loss Treatment Products Market Size, Share, Trends & Forecast Report – Segmented By Disease Type (Alopecia Areata, Cicatricial Alopecia, Traction Alopecia, Alopecia Totalis, Alopecia Universalis, Androgenetic Alopecia and Others), End-Use (Homecare Settings and Dermatology Clinics), Sales Channel (OTC and Prescription), and Region (North America, Europe, Asia Pacific, Latin America, Middle east and Africa) – Industry Analysis from 2024 to 2032.* 2024 [cited 2024 30/1/2024]; Available from: https://www.marketdataforecast.com/market-reports/hair-loss-treatment-products-market.

607. Fortune Business Insights. *Alopecia Treatment Market Size, Share & Industry Analysis, By Route of Administration (Topical, Injectable, Oral), By Gender Type (Male, Female), By Age Group (Below 18 years,*

18 - 34 Years, 35 - 49 Years, Above 50 Years), By End User and Regional Forecast, 2020-2032. 2025 [cited 2025 30/1/2025]; Available from: https://www.fortunebusinessinsights.com/alopecia-treatment-market-102822.

608. Su, J., et al., *An Intelligent Scalp Inspection and Diagnosis System for Caring Hairy Scalp Health.* 2018.

609. Ha, C., T. Go, and W. Choi, *Intelligent Healthcare Platform for Diagnosis of Scalp and Hair Disorders.* Applied Sciences, 2024. **14**(5): p. 1734.

610. Kim, S., et al., *Smartphone-Based Multispectral Imaging and Machine-Learning Based Analysis for Discrimination Between Seborrheic Dermatitis and Psoriasis on the Scalp.* Biomedical Optics Express, 2019. **10**(2): p. 879.

611. Chang, W.-J., et al., *ScalpEye: A Deep Learning-Based Scalp Hair Inspection and Diagnosis System for Scalp Health.* Ieee Access, 2020. **8**: p. 134826-134837.

612. Kageyama, T., et al., *Reprogramming of Three-Dimensional Microenvironments for <i>in Vitro</i> Hair Follicle Induction.* 2022.

613. Owczarczyk-Saczonek, A., et al., *Therapeutic Potential of Stem Cells in Follicle Regeneration.* Stem Cells International, 2018. **2018**: p. 1-16.

614. Paik, S.H., et al., *Skin Equivalent Assay: An Optimized Method for Testing for Hair Growth Reconstitution Capacity of Epidermal and Dermal Cells.* Experimental Dermatology, 2019. **28**(4): p. 367-373.

615. Lin, X., Z. Liang, and J. He, *Morphogenesis, Growth Cycle and Molecular Regulation of Hair Follicles.* Frontiers in Cell and Developmental Biology, 2022. **10**.

616. Wang, X., et al., *Hair Follicle and Sebaceous Gland De Novo Regeneration With Cultured Epidermal Stem Cells and Skin-Derived Precursors.* Stem Cells Translational Medicine, 2016. **5**(12): p. 1695-1706.

617. Son, M.J., et al., *A Novel and Safe Small Molecule Enhances Hair Follicle Regeneration by Facilitating Metabolic Reprogramming.* Experimental & Molecular Medicine, 2018. **50**(12): p. 1-15.

618. Xiao, S., et al., *As a Carrier–transporter for Hair Follicle Reconstitution, Platelet-Rich Plasma Promotes Proliferation and Induction of Mouse Dermal Papilla Cells.* Scientific Reports, 2017. **7**(1).

619. Kost, Y., et al., *Exosome Therapy in Hair Regeneration: A Literature Review of the Evidence, Challenges, and Future Opportunities.* Journal of Cosmetic Dermatology, 2022. **21**(8): p. 3226-3231.

620. Rajendran, R.L., et al., *Extracellular Vesicles Derived From MSCs Activates Dermal Papilla Cell in Vitro and Promotes Hair Follicle Conversion From Telogen to Anagen in Mice.* Scientific Reports, 2017. **7**(1).

621. Stevens, J. and S. Khetarpal, *Platelet-Rich Plasma for Androgenetic Alopecia: A Review of the Literature and Proposed Treatment Protocol.* International Journal of Women's Dermatology, 2019. **5**(1): p. 46-51.

622. Lee, E., et al., *The Efficacy of Adipose Stem Cell-derived Exosomes in Hair Regeneration Based on a Preclinical and Clinical Study.* International Journal of Dermatology, 2024. **63**(9): p. 1212-1220.

623. Krane, N.A., E.A. Christofides, and Y. Halaas, *Advances in Hair Restoration.* Current Otorhinolaryngology Reports, 2021. **9**(4): p. 436-441.

624. Veraitch, O., et al., *Human Induced Pluripotent Stem Cell–Derived Ectodermal Precursor Cells Contribute to Hair Follicle Morphogenesis in Vivo.* Journal of Investigative Dermatology, 2013. **133**(6): p. 1479-1488.

625. Morgan, B., *The Dermal Papilla: An Instructive Niche for Epithelial Stem and Progenitor Cells in Development and Regeneration of the Hair Follicle.* Cold Spring Harbor Perspectives in Medicine, 2014. **4**(7): p. a015180-a015180.

626. Hagenaars, S., et al., *Genetic Prediction of Male Pattern Baldness.* 2016.

627. Thor, D., et al., *A Novel Hair Restoration Technology Counteracts Androgenic Hair Loss and Promotes Hair Growth in a Blinded Clinical Trial.* Journal of Clinical Medicine, 2023. **12**(2): p. 470.

628. Yin, C.-S., et al., *Efficacy of Probiotics in Hair Growth and Dandruff Control: A Systematic Review and Meta-Analysis.* Heliyon, 2024. **10**(9): p. e29539.

629. Hu, P., et al., *Scalp Microbiome Composition Changes and Pathway Evaluations Due to Effective Treatment With Piroctone Olamine Shampoo.* International Journal of Cosmetic Science, 2024. **46**(3): p. 333-347.

630. Rasheedkhan Regina, V., et al., *Decoding Scalp Health and Microbiome Dysbiosis in Dandruff.* 2024.

631. Domenico, E.G.D., et al., *Probiotic-Enriched Oily Suspension in Modulating Skin Microbiome and Treating Seborrheic Dermatitis.* 2023.

632. Reygagne, P., et al., *The Positive Benefit of Lactobacillus Paracasei NCC2461 ST11 in Healthy Volunteers With Moderate to Severe Dandruff.* Beneficial Microbes, 2017. **8**(5): p. 671-680.

633. Tsai, W.-H., et al., *Heat-Killed Lacticaseibacillus Paracasei GMNL-653 Ameliorates Human Scalp Health by Regulating Scalp Microbiome.* BMC Microbiology, 2023. **23**(1).

634. Wang, Y., et al., *Effects of a Postbiotic Saccharomyces and Lactobacillus Ferment Complex on the Scalp Microbiome of Chinese Women With Sensitive Scalp Syndrome.* Clinical Cosmetic and Investigational Dermatology, 2023. **Volume 16**: p. 2623-2635.

635. Bae, W.Y., et al., *Heat-treated <i>Limosilactobacillus Fermentum</I><scp>LM1020</Scp> With Menthol, Salicylic Acid, and Panthenol Promotes Hair Growth and Regulates Hair Scalp Microbiome Balance in Androgenetic Alopecia: A Double-blind, Randomized and Placebo-controlled Clinical Trial.* Journal of Cosmetic Dermatology, 2024. **23**(9): p. 2943-2955.

636. Mayer, W.J., et al., *Biomolecules of Fermented Tropical Fruits and Fermenting Microbes as Regulators of Human Hair Loss, Hair Quality, and Scalp Microbiota.* Biomolecules, 2023. **13**(4): p. 699.

637. Li, Z., et al., *Gut Microbiota, Skin Microbiota, and Alopecia Areata: A Mendelian Randomization Study.* Skin Research and Technology, 2024. **30**(7).

638. Dréno, B., et al., *Microbiome in Healthy Skin, Update for Dermatologists.* Journal of the European Academy of Dermatology and Venereology, 2016. **30**(12): p. 2038-2047.

639. Darwin, E., et al., *Low-Level Laser Therapy for the Treatment of Androgenic Alopecia: A Review.* Lasers in Medical Science, 2017. **33**(2): p. 425-434.

640. Avci, P., et al., *Low-level Laser (Light) Therapy (LLLT) for Treatment of Hair Loss.* Lasers in Surgery and Medicine, 2013. **46**(2): p. 144-151.

641. Yang, K., et al., *Hair Growth Promoting Effects of 650 Nm Red Light Stimulation on Human Hair Follicles and Study of Its Mechanisms via RNA Sequencing Transcriptome Analysis.* Annals of Dermatology, 2021. **33**(6): p. 553.

642. Jiménez, J.J., et al., *Efficacy and Safety of a Low-Level Laser Device in the Treatment of Male and Female Pattern Hair Loss: A Multicenter, Randomized, Sham Device-Controlled, Double-Blind Study.* American Journal of Clinical Dermatology, 2014. **15**(2): p. 115-127.

643. Krefft-Trzciniecka, K., et al., *Human Stem Cell Use in Androgenetic Alopecia: A Systematic Review.* Cells, 2023. **12**(6): p. 951.

644. Da Silva, L.F. and A. Baptista, *The Use of Phototherapy With Different Wavelengths in the Treatment of Androgenetic Alopecia.* 2024. **1**(1): p. bjhh10.

645. Torres, A.E. and H.W. Lim, *Photobiomodulation for the Management of Hair Loss.* Photodermatology Photoimmunology & Photomedicine, 2021. **37**(2): p. 91-98.

646. Akomeah, F.K., *Topical Dermatological Drug Delivery: Quo Vadis?* Current Drug Delivery, 2010. **7**(4): p. 283-296.

647. Zheng, L., et al., *Ginsenosides Rb₁ and Rd Regulate Proliferation of Mature Keratinocytes Through Induction of P63 Expression in Hair Follicles.* Phytotherapy Research, 2012. **27**(7): p. 1095-1101.

648. Gupta, A.K. and S. Polla Ravi, *Concepts, Terminology, and Innovations in Follicular Unit Excision Hair Restoration Surgery.* Facial Plastic Surgery, 2023. **40**(02): p. 146-157.

649. Lin, X., et al., *Robotic Hair Harvesting System: A New Proposal.* 2011: p. 113-120.

650. Orăsan, M.S., et al., *Topical Products for Human Hair Regeneration: A Comparative Study on an Animal Model.* Annals of Dermatology, 2016. **28**(1): p. 65.

651. Hu, S., et al., *Dermal Exosomes Containing miR-218-5p Promote Hair Regeneration by Regulating B-Catenin Signaling.* Science Advances, 2020. **6**(30).

652. Hwang, S.B., H.J. Park, and B.H. Lee, *Hair-Growth-Promoting Effects of the Fish Collagen Peptide in Human Dermal Papilla Cells and C57bl/6 Mice Modulating WNT/B-Catenin and BMP Signaling Pathways.* International Journal of Molecular Sciences, 2022. **23**(19): p. 11904.

653. Al-Busairi, O.K., et al., *Androgenetic Alopecia in Al-Qalyubia Governorate: A Comprehensive Review.* The Egyptian Journal of Hospital Medicine (April 2024). **95**: p. 2056-2058.

654. Grand View Research, *Nail Salon Market Size, Share & Trends Analysis Report By Service (Manicure, Pedicure), By End-user (Men, Women), By Age Group (Below 18, 19 to 40), By Region (Asia Pacific, North America), And Segment Forecasts, 2023 - 2030.* 2023.

655. Jia, T., et al., *Assessing the Risk of Organophosphate Esters From Nail Polish: Indoor Emissions, Fate Modeling, and Health Risk Assessment.* 2024. **1**(7): p. 704-713.

656. Zembala, P., et al., *Emerging Trends in Gel Nail Allergies: Prevalence, Symptoms, and Occupational Hazards Associated With Acrylate Sensitization.* Journal of Education Health and Sport, 2023. **45**(1): p. 57-75.
657. Nguyễn, L.V., et al., *Occupational Exposure of Canadian Nail Salon Workers to Plasticizers Including Phthalates and Organophosphate Esters.* Environmental Science & Technology, 2022. **56**(5): p. 3193-3203.
658. Woolridge, K. and D. Hooper, *Complications of Gel Manicures.* Our Dermatology Online, 2021. **12**(e): p. e75-e75.
659. Batory, M., E. Wołowiec-Korecka, and H. Rotsztejn, *The Effect of Various Primers Improving Adhesiveness of Gel Polish Hybrids on pH, TOWL and Overall Nail Plates Condition.* Journal of Cosmetic Dermatology, 2019. **18**(5): p. 1529-1538.
660. Gupta, A.K., et al., *<i>In Vitro</I> Efficacy of Tavaborole Topical Solution, 5% After Penetration Through Nail Polish on <i>ex Vivo</I> Human Fingernails.* Journal of Dermatological Treatment, 2018. **29**(6): p. 633-636.
661. Філіпцова, О.B., et al., *Study of Behavior of Females Consumers of Gel Nail Polish in Ukraine.* 2021.
662. Güder, H. and Z.G. Özünal, *Follow-Up of Favipiravir-Induced Nail Fluorescence: Implications for Nail and Drugs.* Dermatology Practical & Conceptual, 2023: p. e2023011.
663. Özçelik, S. and F.A. Kılıç, *Effects of Isotretinoin on the Growth Rate and Thickness of the Nail Plate.* International Journal of Dermatology, 2021. **60**(10): p. 1258-1262.
664. Morrison, A., et al., *A Randomised Controlled Trial of Interventions for Taxane-Induced Nail Toxicity in Women With Early Breast Cancer.* 2021.
665. Khaja, M., et al., *Nail Polish Remover Induced Methemoglobinemia: An Uncommon Occurrence.* Cureus, 2022.
666. Strømme, M., et al., *Calcium and Silicon Delivery to Artificial and Human Nails From Nail Polish Formulations.* Cosmetics, 2020. **7**(1): p. 15.
667. Sudduth, J.D., et al., *Surgical Management of Pachyonychia Congenita in a 3-Year-Old.* Archives of Plastic Surgery, 2023. **50**(06): p. 573-577.
668. Hossain, M.S., et al., *Effect of Red Nail Polish on Pulse Oximetry Reading.* Kyamc Journal, 2021. **11**(4): p. 181-183.

Richard Skiba

669. Savitha, S., R. Nagalakshmi, and S.S. Mariam, *Retronychia: A Misdiagnosed Cause of Paronychia.* Journal of Cutaneous and Aesthetic Surgery, 2023. **16**(4): p. 343-345.
670. Munprom, K., et al., *Ex Vivo Fungal Nail Penetration Study: Effects of Causative Organisms, Nail Polish and Age.* Mycoses, 2025. **68**(1).
671. Haneke, E., et al., *Chronic Retronychia: Nonsurgical Treatment.* Skin Appendage Disorders, 2022. **8**(4): p. 291-294.
672. Monti, D., et al., *Ciclopirox Hydroxypropyl Chitosan (CPX-HPCH) Nail Lacquer and Breathable Cosmetic Nail Polish: In Vitro Evaluation of Drug Transungual Permeation Following the Combined Application.* Life, 2022. **12**(6): p. 801.
673. Quang, N.M., et al., *A New Environmentally Friendly Chemical Mechanical Polishing Method Applied for Surface Finishing Ti-6Al-4v Alloy.* Journal of Machine Engineering, 2023.
674. Young, A.S., et al., *Phthalate and Organophosphate Plasticizers in Nail Polish: Evaluation of Labels and Ingredients.* Environmental Science & Technology, 2018. **52**(21): p. 12841-12850.
675. Albucker, S.J., et al., *Risk Factors and Treatment Trends for Onychomycosis: A Case–Control Study of Onychomycosis Patients in the All of Us Research Program.* Journal of Fungi, 2023. **9**(7): p. 712.
676. Heaton, T., et al., *Laboratory Estimation of Occupational Exposures to Volatile Organic Compounds During Nail Polish Application.* Workplace Health & Safety, 2019. **67**(6): p. 288-293.
677. Kovalenko, V. and V. Kotok, *Determination of the Applicability of Zn-Al Layered Double Hydroxide, Intercalated by Food Dye Orange Yellow S, as a Cosmetic Pigment.* Eastern-European Journal of Enterprise Technologies, 2020. **5**(12 (107)): p. 81-89.
678. Canavan, T., et al., *Single-Center, Prospective, Blinded Study Comparing the Efficacy and Compatibility of Efinaconazole 10% Solution in Treating Onychomycosis With and Without Concurrent Nail Polish Use.* Skin Appendage Disorders, 2018. **5**(1): p. 9-12.
679. Anderson, S., et al., *The Impact of Gel Fingernail Polish Application on the Reduction of Bacterial Viability Following a Surgical Hand Scrub.* Veterinary Surgery, 2021. **50**(7): p. 1525-1532.
680. Banerjee, P., et al., *Emerging Technologies in Hair and Nail Diagnosis and Treatment.* Dermatological Reviews, 2024. **5**(4).
681. Jones, L.A., *Artificial Intelligence and Robotics in the Nail Care Industry.* 2024: p. 274-295.

682. Cohen, P.R., *Genital Rejuvenation: The Next Frontier in Medical and Cosmetic Dermatology.* Dermatology Online Journal, 2018. **24**(9).

683. Reyhan, F.A. and E. DaĞLi, *Kadınların Kozmetik Jinekoloji Konusundaki Görüş Ve Tutumları Üzerine Nitel Bir Araştırma.* Ankara Sağlık Bilimleri Dergisi, 2022. **11**(2): p. 188-197.

684. Ahluwalia, J., M.M. Avram, and A. Ortiz, *Lasers and Energy-based Devices Marketed for Vaginal Rejuvenation: A Cross-sectional Analysis of the MAUDE Database.* Lasers in Surgery and Medicine, 2019. **51**(8): p. 671-677.

685. Salvatore, S., et al., *Early Regenerative Modifications of Human Postmenopausal Atrophic Vaginal Mucosa Following Fractional CO2 Laser Treatment.* Open Access Macedonian Journal of Medical Sciences, 2018. **6**(1): p. 6-14.

686. Cheng, C., et al., *The Strategy for Vaginal Rejuvenation: CO2 Laser or Vaginoplasty?* Annals of Translational Medicine, 2021. **9**(7): p. 604-604.

687. Perino, A., et al., *Vulvo-Vaginal Atrophy: A New Treatment Modality Using Thermo-Ablative Fractional CO2 Laser.* Maturitas, 2015. **80**(3): p. 296-301.

688. Ergül, A., et al., *Using Google Trends for Evaluation of Public Interest in Female Genital Aesthetic Procedures.* Dermatologic Surgery, 2023. **49**(8): p. 762-765.

689. Photiou, L., et al., *Review of Non-invasive Vulvovaginal Rejuvenation.* Journal of the European Academy of Dermatology and Venereology, 2019. **34**(4): p. 716-726.

690. Mirastschijski, U., D. Jiang, and Y. Rinkevich, *Genital Wound Repair and Scarring.* Medical Sciences, 2022. **10**(2): p. 23.

691. Peters, B.R., et al., *Optimizing Aesthetics in Gender-Affirming Vaginoplasty and Vulvoplasty: A Narrative Review and Discussion Based on Over 600 Cases of Transfeminine Vulvar Construction.* Translational Andrology and Urology, 2024. **13**(2): p. 274-292.

692. Alrashed, H., et al., *Women's Knowledge, Attitudes, and Practice About Female Genital Cosmetic Surgery: A Cross-Sectional Study in Saudi Arabia.* Cureus, 2023.

693. Kirkman, M., et al., *Health Professionals' Perspectives on Female Genital Cosmetic Surgery: An Interview Study.* 2023.

694. Koehler, A., et al., *(De-)Centralized Health Care Delivery, Surgical Outcome, and Psychosocial Health of Transgender and Gender-Diverse People Undergoing Vaginoplasty: Results of a Retrospective,*

Single-Center Study. World Journal of Urology, 2023. **41**(7): p. 1775-1783.

695.   Barbara, G., et al., *Vaginal rejuvenation: current perspectives.* International journal of women's health, 2017: p. 513-519.

696.   Davies, O., S. Williams, and K. Goldie, *The therapeutic and commercial landscape of stem cell vesicles in regenerative dermatology.* Journal of Controlled Release, 2023. **353**: p. 1096-1106.

697.   Ku, Y.C., et al., *The potential role of exosomes in aesthetic plastic surgery: a review of current literature.* Plastic and Reconstructive Surgery–Global Open, 2023. **11**(6): p. e5051.

698.   Hoang, D.M., et al., *Stem cell-based therapy for human diseases.* Signal transduction and targeted therapy, 2022. **7**(1): p. 1-41.

699.   Mousaei Ghasroldasht, M., et al., *Stem cell therapy: from idea to clinical practice.* International journal of molecular sciences, 2022. **23**(5): p. 2850.

700.   Shah, M., et al., *Exosomes for Aesthetic Dermatology: A Comprehensive Literature Review and Update.* Journal of Cosmetic Dermatology, 2025. **24**(1): p. e16766.

701.   Nautiyal, A. and S. Wairkar, *Management of Hyperpigmentation: Current Treatments and Emerging Therapies.* Pigment Cell & Melanoma Research, 2021. **34**(6): p. 1000-1014.

702.   Mathpati, S., et al., *Efficacy and Safety of Topical Trihydroxybenzoic Acid Glucoside and Alpha-Arbutin Containing Formulation Along With a Sunscreen in Facial Hyperpigmentation.* International Journal of Research in Dermatology, 2022. **8**(5): p. 466.

703.   Goberdhan, L., et al., *Efficacy and Safety of Novel Topical Pigment-correcting Regimen With Biweekly Diamond Tip Microdermabrasion Procedures on Facial Hyperpigmentation.* Journal of Cosmetic Dermatology, 2024. **23**(5): p. 1726-1733.

704.   Yoo, J., *Differential Diagnosis and Management of Hyperpigmentation.* Clinical and Experimental Dermatology, 2021. **47**(2): p. 251-258.

705.   Campiche, R., et al., *Pigmentation Effects of Blue Light Irradiation on Skin and How to Protect Against Them.* International Journal of Cosmetic Science, 2020. **42**(4): p. 399-406.

706.   Zasada, M., et al., *Efficacy of Tri-Active Brightening and Anti-Aging Complex in Treatment of Facial Skin Hyperpigmentation.* Journal of Pharmacy and Pharmacology, 2016. **4**(10).

707.   Cohen, P.R., *Scrotal Rejuvenation.* Cureus, 2018.

708. Vanaman, M., et al., *Emerging Trends in Nonsurgical Female Genital Rejuvenation.* Dermatologic Surgery, 2016. **42**(9): p. 1019-1029.

709. Desai, S., G. Kroumpouzos, and N.S. Sadick, *Vaginal Rejuvenation: From Scalpel to Wands.* International Journal of Women's Dermatology, 2019. **5**(2): p. 79-84.

710. Ikhsan, R.B., et al., *The Impact of Pro-Environment Belief and Personal Norm Toward the Beauty Purchase Behavior.* Mix Jurnal Ilmiah Manajemen, 2023. **13**(2): p. 268.

711. Wu, C., J. Yang, and Z. Ma, *How Online Celebrity Live Streaming Promotes Consumption? --- A Theoretical and Empirical Test Based on the Howard-Sheth Model.* 2023.

712. Grand View Research, *Cosmetics Market Size, Share & Trends Analysis Report By Product (Skin Care, Hair Care), By End-user (Men, Women), By Distribution Channel (Offline, Online), By Region (North America, Europe), And Segment Forecasts, 2024 - 2030.* 2023.

713. Bouslimani, A., et al., *The Impact of Skin Care Products on Skin Chemistry and Microbiome Dynamics.* BMC Biology, 2019. **17**(1).

714. Gladenkova, T.A., *Beauty and Personal Care Transnationalization: Main Changes in Its Spatial Structure.* Geography Environment Sustainability, 2020. **13**(1): p. 244-250.

715. Kurniawati, A., J. Lubis, and M.A. Al-Ihsan, *The Effect of Digital Marketing and Personal Selling on Consumer Purchase Decisions in Beauty Products.* Almana Jurnal Manajemen Dan Bisnis, 2023. **7**(1): p. 106-114.

716. Adiningtyas, Y. and E. Yunus, *The Influence of Consumer Knowledge of Halal Supply Chain Practices on Purchase Intention in Halal Personal Care &Amp; Beauty Products.* Jurnal Aplikasi Bisnis Dan Manajemen, 2024.

717. Kim, J., *Comparative Analysis of Beauty Application Technologies in the 4th Industrial Revolution.* Journal of the Korean Society of Cosmetology, 2023. **29**(1): p. 239-246.

718. Pambudi, Y.J. and J.P.W. Dwinata, *Customer intention to use AI technology on beauty industry.* The Asian Journal of Technology Management, 2023. **16**(2): p. 136-151.

719. Gasenko, K., *Revolutionizing Beauty: How Artificial Intelligence Is Transforming the Beauty Industry in the Usa.* Věda a Perspektivy, 2024(7(38)).

720. Dutta, S.S., *Revolutionizing Retail: An Empirical Study on the Impact of Generative AI in Omnichannel Strategies*. International Journal for Multidisciplinary Research, 2024. **6**(5).
721. Sengupta, A. and L. Cao, *Augmented Reality's Perceived Immersion Effect on the Customer Shopping Process: Decision-Making Quality and Privacy Concerns*. International Journal of Retail & Distribution Management, 2022. **50**(8/9): p. 1039-1061.
722. Windasari, N.A. and H.B. Santoso, *Augmented Reality Experiential Marketing in Beauty Product: Does It Differ From Other Service Touchpoints*. Jurnal Sistem Informasi, 2022. **18**(2): p. 50-67.
723. Lele, A., *Factors Influencing Consumer Loyalty in Augmented Reality Beauty Apps: Sephora Virtual Artist Empirical Study*. 2023.
724. Ratajczak, P., et al., *The Growing Market for Natural Cosmetics in Poland: Consumer Preferences and Industry Trends*. Clinical Cosmetic and Investigational Dermatology, 2023. **Volume 16**: p. 1877-1892.
725. Draelos, Z.D., et al., *International Consensus on Anti-Aging Dermocosmetics and Skin Care for Clinical Practice Using the RAND/UCLA Appropriateness Method*. Journal of Drugs in Dermatology, 2023. **23**(1): p. 1337-1343.
726. Boyer, F., et al., *Broad-spectrum Sunscreens Containing the <scp>TriAsorB™</Scp> Filter: In Vitro Photoprotection and Clinical Evaluation of Blue Light-induced Skin Pigmentation*. Journal of the European Academy of Dermatology and Venereology, 2023. **37**(S6): p. 12-21.
727. Dumbuya, H., et al., *Impact of Iron-Oxide Containing Formulations Against Visible Light-Induced Skin Pigmentation in Skin of Color Individuals*. Journal of Drugs in Dermatology, 2020. **19**(7): p. 712-717.
728. Zhou, C., et al., *Guide to Tinted Sunscreens in Skin of Color*. International Journal of Dermatology, 2023.
729. Senthilkumar, K. and A. Vijayalakshmi, *Review: Advances in Self-Preservation Techniques in Cosmetics Using Hurdle Technology*. South Eastern European Journal of Public Health, 2024: p. 1061-1072.
730. Sasounian, R., et al., *Innovative Approaches to an Eco-Friendly Cosmetic Industry: A Review of Sustainable Ingredients*. Clean Technologies, 2024. **6**(1): p. 176-198.
731. Du, X.-N., et al., *Decoding Cosmetic Complexities: A Comprehensive Guide to Matrix Composition and Pretreatment Technology*. Molecules, 2024. **29**(2): p. 411.

732. Gupta, V., et al., *Nanotechnology in Cosmetics and Cosmeceuticals— A Review of Latest Advancements.* Gels, 2022. **8**(3): p. 173.

733. Mitterer-Daltoé, M.L., et al., *Use of Cosmetic Creams and Perception of Natural and Eco-Friendly Products by Women: The Role of Sociodemographic Factors.* Cosmetics, 2023. **10**(3): p. 78.

734. Kaul, S., et al., *Role of Nanotechnology in Cosmeceuticals: A Review of Recent Advances.* Journal of Pharmaceutics, 2018. **2018**: p. 1-19.

735. Vogel, E.M., et al., *Challenges of Nanotechnology in Cosmetic Permeation With Caffeine.* Brazilian Journal of Biology, 2022. **82**.

736. Gwanya, H.Y., et al., *Harnessing the Potential of Helinus Integrifolius in Cosmeceutical Research: Toward Sustainable Natural Cosmetics.* Cosmetics, 2024. **11**(4): p. 126.

737. Lee, J.-K. and K.H. Kwon, *Sustainable Changes in Beauty Market Trends Focused on the Perspective of Safety in the Post-coronavirus Disease-19 Period.* Journal of Cosmetic Dermatology, 2022. **21**(7): p. 2700-2707.

738. Rathore, S., B. Schuler, and J. Park, *Life Cycle Assessment of Multiple Dispensing Systems Used for Cosmetic Product Packaging.* Packaging Technology and Science, 2023. **36**(7): p. 533-547.

739. Yang, J. and M.B.B. Hamid, *Sustainable Beauty: A Conceptual Paper of How Sustainable Marketing Impact Consumer Behaviour in the Cosmetic Industry.* Advances in Economics Management and Political Sciences, 2024. **93**(1): p. 54-59.

740. Napper, I.E., et al., *Characterisation, Quantity and Sorptive Properties of Microplastics Extracted From Cosmetics.* Marine Pollution Bulletin, 2015. **99**(1-2): p. 178-185.

741. Wu, X., et al., *Assessment on the Pollution Level and Risk of Microplastics on Bathing Beaches: A Case Study of Liandao, China.* Environmental Monitoring and Assessment, 2023. **195**(3).

742. Sun, A. and W.X. Wang, *Human Exposure to Microplastics and Its Associated Health Risks.* Environment & Health, 2023. **1**(3): p. 139-149.

743. Zhao, S., *A Summary of the Transporting Mechanism of Microplastics in Marine Food Chain and Its Effects to Humans.* Iop Conference Series Earth and Environmental Science, 2022. **1011**(1): p. 012051.

744. Yang, Y., et al., *Microplastics Provide New Microbial Niches in Aquatic Environments.* Applied Microbiology and Biotechnology, 2020. **104**(15): p. 6501-6511.

745. Bansal, O.P. and A.K. Singh, *A Review on Microplastic in the Soils and Their Impact on Soil Microbes, Crops and Humans*. International Journal of Research -Granthaalayah, 2022. **10**(9): p. 245-273.

746. Prata, J.C., et al., *Environmental Exposure to Microplastics: An Overview on Possible Human Health Effects*. The Science of the Total Environment, 2020. **702**: p. 134455.

747. Chowdhury, O.S., et al., *Advancing Evaluation of Microplastics Thresholds to Inform Water Treatment Needs and Risks*. Environment & Health, 2024. **2**(7): p. 441-452.

748. Nguyen, N.T., L.T.K. Oanh, and N.D.T. Chi, *The Presence of Microplastics in Personal Care and Cosmetic Products (PCCPs) Commonly Used in Ho Chi Minh City*. Iop Conference Series Earth and Environmental Science, 2024. **1349**(1): p. 012012.

749. Kour, J., P. Bhatt, and S. Basnet, *Overall Migration of Microplastics in Mineral Water and Non-Alcoholic Beverages*. Bibechana, 2023. **20**(1): p. 21-26.

750. Li, W., et al., *Desorption of Bisphenol a From Microplastics Under Simulated Gastrointestinal Conditions*. Frontiers in Marine Science, 2023. **10**.

751. Bansal, O.P., *Microplastic in the Aquatic Environment and Their Impact on Aquatic Organisms and Humans: A Review*. Acta Scientific Pharmaceutical Sciences, 2023. **7**(10): p. 34-55.

752. Bashir, S.M., et al., *Personal Care and Cosmetic Products as a Potential Source of Environmental Contamination by Microplastics in a Densely Populated Asian City*. Frontiers in Marine Science, 2021. **8**.

753. Napper, I.E. and R.C. Thompson, *Release of Synthetic Microplastic Plastic Fibres From Domestic Washing Machines: Effects of Fabric Type and Washing Conditions*. Marine Pollution Bulletin, 2016. **112**(1-2): p. 39-45.

754. Koelmans, A.A., E. Besseling, and W.J. Shim, *Nanoplastics in the Aquatic Environment. Critical Review*. 2015: p. 325-340.

755. Lee, S. and T.G. Lee, *A Novel Method for Extraction, Quantification, and Identification of Microplastics in CreamType of Cosmetic Products*. Scientific Reports, 2021. **11**(1).

756. Jaini, A., et al., *Antecedents of Green Purchase Behavior of Cosmetics Products*. International Journal of Ethics and Systems, 2019. **36**(2): p. 185-203.

757. Coats, J.G., et al., *Blue Light Protection, Part II—Ingredients and Performance Testing Methods.* Journal of Cosmetic Dermatology, 2020. **20**(3): p. 718-723.

758. François-Newton, V., et al., *Antioxidant and Anti-Aging Potential of Indian Sandalwood Oil Against Environmental Stressors in Vitro and Ex Vivo.* Cosmetics, 2021. **8**(2): p. 53.

759. Velasco, M.V.R., et al., *Active Ingredients, Mechanisms of Action and Efficacy Tests of Antipollution Cosmetic and Personal Care Products.* Brazilian Journal of Pharmaceutical Sciences, 2018. **54**(spe).

760. Rembiesa, J., et al., *The Impact of Pollution on Skin and Proper Efficacy Testing for Anti-Pollution Claims.* Cosmetics, 2018. **5**(1): p. 4.

761. Charitakis, A., et al., *Overcoming Skin Damage From Pollution via Novel Skincare Strategies.* Current Pharmaceutical Design, 2022. **28**(15): p. 1250-1257.

762. Simay, A.E., et al., *The E-Wom Intention of Artificial Intelligence (AI) Color Cosmetics Among Chinese Social Media Influencers.* Asia Pacific Journal of Marketing and Logistics, 2022. **35**(7): p. 1569-1598.

763. Green, L.J., et al., *Silica-Based Microencapsulation Used in Topical Dermatologic Applications.* Archives of Dermatological Research, 2023. **315**(10): p. 2787-2793.

764. Culiberg, B., et al., *The Role of Moral Foundations, Anticipated Guilt and Personal Responsibility in Predicting Anti-Consumption for Environmental Reasons.* Journal of Business Ethics, 2022. **182**(2): p. 465-481.

765. Issa, F.M., *The Influence of Relationship Quality on Electronic Word of Mouth for Mobile Review Site Users in Saudi Arabia Market.* Ibusiness, 2021. **13**(04): p. 155-178.

766. Cavallo, A., A. Ghezzi, and B.V.R. Guzmán, *Driving Internationalization Through Business Model Innovation.* Multinational Business Review, 2019. **28**(2): p. 201-220.

767. Dumont, I., *Étude Exploratoire Sur L'expérience De Familles Dont Un Membre Est Décédé en Contexte D'aide Médicale À Mourir Au Québec.* Intervention, 2023(156): p. 23-37.

768. Batmetan, J.R., et al., *Aspects of Leadership in the Implementation of IT Infrastructure Library Domain Service Strategy at University.* 2023. **2**(2): p. 119-137.

769. Dong, Z. and P. Dai, *Dynamic Mechanism of Digital Transformation in Equipment Manufacturing Enterprises Based on Evolutionary Game Theory: Evidence From China.* Systems, 2023. **11**(10): p. 493.

770.   Apichottanakul, A., et al., *Customer Behaviour Analysis Based on Buying-Data Sparsity for Multi-Category Products in Pork Industry: A Hybrid Approach.* Cogent Engineering, 2021. **8**(1).

Index

A

Acupuncture, 5, 28, 252, 259, 260, 261, 262, 263, 266, 268, 282, 283, 284, 285, 286, 287, 290

Adaptive, 7, 420, 421, 422, 423, 424

AI and beauty, 404

AI in skin analysis, 31

AI in trichology, 317

AI-driven diagnostics, 297

AI-powered nail scanners, 364, 366, 367, 368, 369, 370

Anti-aging, 83, 85, 93, 99, 115, 119, 120, 127, 129, 136, 138, 139, 140, 149, 153, 157, 161, 162, 164, 165, 167, 169, 170, 172, 173, 174, 175, 177, 178, 179, 180, 181, 182, 185, 215, 219, 221, 226, 256, 268, 278, 284, 289, 394, 407

Anti-aging solutions, 99, 153, 226, 394

Anti-pollution, 419, 420, 423

Aromatherapy, 5, 28, 252, 278, 282, 283, 284, 285, 286, 287, 289, 290, 291, 478

At-home beauty devices, 249

At-home nail care, 358

Ayurveda, 5, 12, 270, 282, 283, 285, 286, 429, 479

Ayurveda in beauty therapy, 282, 286

B

Beauty, 1, 3, 4, 5, 7, 1, 3, 4, 5, 6, 7, 8, 9, 10, 11, 12, 13, 14, 15, 16, 17, 18, 19, 20, 21, 23, 24, 25, 28, 29, 30, 31, 33, 34, 39, 42, 43, 44, 47, 48, 49, 52, 53, 54, 55, 56, 57, 59, 60, 61, 69, 80, 90, 95, 100, 102, 163, 175, 184, 194, 197, 213, 214, 215, 216, 220, 221, 222, 223, 227, 228, 229, 230, 233, 234, 235, 236, 237, 238, 239, 240, 241, 242, 243, 244, 245, 246, 247, 248, 249, 250, 251, 252, 253, 254, 259, 262, 263, 266, 269, 274, 275, 276, 278, 279, 280, 281, 282, 283, 284, 285, 286, 287, 291, 292, 293, 294, 295, 296, 297, 298, 299, 301, 302, 303, 304, 305, 306, 307, 308, 309, 310, 311, 355, 357, 359, 360, 364, 366, 367, 393, 394, 395, 396, 397, 398, 399, 400, 401, 402, 403, 404, 405, 406, 407, 408, 409, 410, 411, 412, 414, 415, 416, 417, 418, 420, 421, 423, 424, 426, 427, 428, 430, 431, 432, 434, 461, 474, 475, 480, 481, 482, 493, 494, 495, 496

Beauty apps, 295, 296, 405

Beauty certifications, 228, 229

Beauty customization, 309, 310

Beauty e-commerce, 302

Beauty influencers, 395

Beauty innovation, 359, 398, 399

Beauty marketing, 298

Biodegradable, 4, 19, 28, 161, 163, 164, 177, 187, 215, 216, 217, 218, 219, 220, 223, 224, 225, 226, 227, 228, 235, 310, 360, 363, 364, 389, 395, 399, 400, 415, 416, 417

Biodegradable ingredients, 19, 217, 228, 395

Bioengineered, 6, 225, 255, 257, 279, 322, 323, 348, 349, 352, 353

Bioengineered hair growth, 348, 349, 352

T

V

www.ingramcontent.com/pod-product-compliance
Lightning Source LLC
Chambersburg PA
CBHW050556270326
41926CB00012B/2076